The Struggle
for Development

The Struggle for Development

National Strategies in an International Context

Edited by

MANFRED BIENEFELD and MARTIN GODFREY

Institute of Development Studies, University of Sussex

JOHN WILEY & SONS LIMITED

Chichester · New York · Brisbane · Toronto · Singapore

Library of Congress Cataloging in Publication Data:
Main entry under title:
The Struggle for development.

   Includes indexes.
   1. Underdeveloped areas—Economic policy.
2. International economic relations. I. Bienefeld, M. A. II. Godfrey, Martin.
HC59.7.S874   338.9'009172'4   81-19821

ISBN 0 471 10152 4   AACR2

British Library Cataloguing in Publication Data:
The Struggle for development.
   1. Underdeveloped areas—Economic
   conditions.
   I. Bienefeld, M.   II. Godfrey, M.
   330.9172'4   HC59.7

   ISBN 0 471 10152 4

Typeset by Activity, Salisbury, Wilts
and printed in The United States of America

Contents

List of Contributors

Manfred Bienefeld is a Fellow of the Institute of Development Studies at the University of Sussex and was Co-director of the M.Phil. (Development Studies) in 1977–79 and 1980–82.

J. K. J. Thomson is a Lecturer in History in the School of European Studies at the University of Sussex.

Martin Bronfenbrenner is Professor of Economics at Duke University, North Carolina, and was a Visiting Fellow of the Institute of Development Studies in 1978–79.

Gordon White is a Fellow of the Institute of Development Studies and was Co-director of the M.Phil. (Development Studies) in 1979–81 and 1981–83.

Terry Byres is a Lecturer in the Department of Economics at the School of Oriental and African Studies, University of London.

Regis de Castro Andrade, is a member of staff of the Centro de Estudos de Cultura Contemporanea, São Paulo, Brazil.

Tony Michell is a Lecturer in Economic and Social History at the University of Hull. From 1978 to 1980 he worked at the Economic Planning Board and the Regional Development Research Institute in South Korea.

Ennio Rodríguez is a Lecturer in Economics at the University of Costa Rica and was a member of the 1977–79 M.Phil. (Development Studies) course.

Anthony Coughlan is a Senior Lecturer in Social Administration and Policy in the Department of Social Studies, Trinity College, University of Dublin.

Martin Godfrey is a Fellow of the Institute of Development Studies and was Co-director of the M.Phil. (Development Studies) course in 1977–79.

Introduction

MANFRED BIENEFELD and MARTIN GODFREY

The central question addressed by this volume is: 'What are the prospects of development in the currently less developed economies and to what extent do these prospects depend on the effective implementation of national development strategies which take cognizance of the dominant trends in the international economy?' More specifically we are interested in the circumstances under which these economies could achieve a full-fledged industrialization, or other form of development, which would allow them to: develop their forces of production progressively; eventually mount a genuine competitive challenge to existing producers in various areas of production; and gradually spread the benefits of this development to the broad mass of their population.

In discussing the determination of the limits on this process for such economies the emphasis of this volume is on the relative weight to be given to external and internal variables, on the identification of possibly significant differences between nationally and internationally 'rational' choices, and on the interaction between these various spheres. Differences in opinion about the relative importance to be attached to each of these derive in part from different analytical perceptions of how variables are connected within a social system, and in part from differences in the concrete cases which are used as the basis for judgements. This volume does not attempt to develop a particular perspective but rather attempts to sharpen our understanding of these differences by bringing a variety of analytical perspectives to bear upon these issues with reference to selected country cases, in order to document the interaction between analytical perception and material circumstance and in order to improve our understanding of just how and why different theoretical approaches diverge on these issues. The basic premise of our approach is that the various theoretical approaches which do exist are not mutually exclusive, totally distinct spheres, but are rather deeply intertwined and have many

1

common points of reference. That does not, of course, imply that their conclusions may not be utterly incompatible or different in terms of the interests they serve in the first instance. But unfortunately the nature, or fervour, of any set of conclusions does not validate an analysis, as is all too evident when one looks at the range of strategic choices which can be espoused from a Marxist or neo-classical perspective, each claiming to represent the interests of the population as a whole.

Analytical Perceptions

As far as analytical perceptions are concerned, the possibility of a conflicting rationality between the national and the international spheres was denied by the longstanding view, largely derived from classical and neo-classical trade theory, that integration into the international capitalist system is always beneficial for any national economy, developed or less developed. This view was first challenged by economists like List and Carey, looking at the world from the point of view of nation states like Germany and the United States seeking to industrialize in a world where British producers dominated the markets for manufactures. The post-Second World War challenge came initially from the development economists of the 1950s. Singer, Prebisch, Lewis, Mandelbaum, Rosenstein-Rodan and Nurkse, among others, were important in this respect in their prescription of disengagement from the international capitalist system—at least to the extent of planned, capitalist, import-substituting industrialization behind a tariff or quota wall. The crux of their argument was that the developing countries had a set of characteristics which in the modern world would not allow them to achieve full employment in the context of an open market. Once that was admitted one had established the case for a new discipline called 'development economies'. This discipline concerned itself with the ways and means by which the resources thus left idle could be mobilized.

Parts of their theories survive more or less intact among more recent dependency and underdevelopment theorists. For instance, the Emmanuel—Amin theory of unequal exchange could be regarded as a restatement in Marxist language of the Prebisch–Singer–Lewis analysis of the differing effects of productivity increases at centre and periphery arising from the differing degrees of competition in their product and labour markets. But, unlike the later dependency school, most development economists operated with a Harrod—Domar type of growth model and looked favourably on foreign investment and aid as a means of easing the capital constraint, since it would increase capital goods imports, improve the balance of payments, reduce inflationary pressures and transfer technology. In effect capital was understood as physical machinery, or even as finance, but not as a social relation embodying certain central and certain internationally defined objectives.

Nurkse anticipated some ambiguities from the use of foreign capital, although he did not raise these to the level of elaborating conflicting objectives. Nevertheless he was one of the few early development economists to anticipate the dependency emphasis on problems arising from non-trade contracts between central and peripheral countries. He pointed to the international demonstration effect arising from the spread of knowledge in underdeveloped countries of the consumption standards of rich countries. Drawing a parallel with Duesenberry's work on the interdependence of individual consumption functions, Nurkse suggested that 'the presence or the mere knowledge of new goods and new methods of consumption tends to raise the general propensity to consume' and that 'the temptation to copy American consumption patterns tends to limit the supply of investible funds by inhibiting the willingness to save'. There is an obvious affinity here with the later emphasis on consumption patterns of, say Sunkel or Furtado, but there *is* a difference. Nurkse was still operating within a Harrod–Domar framework and thus emphasizing the demonstration effect only on the rate of saving and hence on the rate of growth. He recognised that disengagement from the international economy was logically implied by his analysis but regarded this as a 'defeatist solution', preferring to try to raise the rate of saving by a compulsory savings scheme, backed up by foreign investment and aid.

It is not, perhaps, surprising that the development economists who seem to get closest to the dependency position and who lay the foundations for defining a specific, and separate, national rationality for capital are those who question the Harrod–Domar emphasis on capital as the sole constraint and emphasize rather the inadequacy of the inducement to invest. For example, Myrdal (whose 'circular-causation' challenge to equilibrium economics is an unacknowledged influence on dependency and 'uneven development' theory) drew attention to the fact that the need for capital in underdeveloped countries

> does not represent an effective demand in the capital market. Rather, if there were no exchange controls and if, at the same time, there were no elements in their national development policies securing high profits for capital—i.e. if the forces in the capital market were given unhampered play—capitalists in underdeveloped countries would be exporting capital. (Myrdal, 1957:53)

If the problem is seen to be on the side of the inducement to invest rather than of the supply of capital, then the logic of inviting an inflow of *foreign* capital is called into question, because capital is no longer a homogeneous concept responding to an undifferentiated global logic. Hirschman (1971:227) posed this question more explicitly: 'Could the inflow of foreign capital stunt what might otherwise be vigorous local development of the so-called missing or scarce factors of production?' His view was that it could—sometimes in an absolute sense, for instance through the foreign takeover of local banks or businesses, more often in relation to what might have happened in the absence of the foreign investment. His evidence for this was the fact that during wars, depressions, national expropriations and international sanctions, the domestic supply of entrepreneurs, managers, technology and saving seems to be 'far more elastic than is ever suspected under business-as-usual conditions'. His conclusion that 'a policy of selective liquidation and withdrawal of foreign private investment' would be in the best interests of Latin America would be endorsed by most dependency authors.

Where members of the dependency school part company from 'global law of value' Marxism and from development economists (often their earlier selves) is in their rejection of an undifferentiated conception of the 'historically progressive' role of capitalism, or of modernization theory and in their emphasis on the nation state, but not in isolation, rather set in the context of the global evolution of capitalism. From the development economists they differed further because of their incorporation of a strong historical dimension into their analysis; their endogenization of the state as 'the crucial battleground between the different social groups' (Sunkel, 1979:29); and their use of a dialectical rather than an equilibrium mode of analysis. This difference in approach is reflected in the different set of questions addressed by them. The most important of these questions, assumed away by 'modernization' development economists and by many orthodox Marxists, is one of those raised by this volume: 'What are the special obstacles which peripheral status, or relative technological backwardness, places in the way of the generation of a cumulative' dynamic nationally focused process of capitalist accumulation?*

The typical dependency answer to this question is, as already indicated, a gloomy one. None is more gloomy than Gunder Frank, perhaps unfortunately the author who has come to symbolize the dependency approach for readers outside Latin America. As Booth has pointed out (Oxaal *et al*, 1975) Frank's analysis is less mechanistic and metropole-oriented than is usually supposed, emphasizing 'the impregnation of the satellite's domestic economy with the same capitalist structure and its fundamental contradictions' as more important than 'the drain of economic surplus' from satellite to metropolis with which he is usually associated (Frank, 1967:10). However, he remains strongly insistent on the impossibility of capitalist development at the periphery:

> the economic basis of a developmentalist national bourgeois class ... has been entirely eliminated or prevented from forming at all, thus precluding further or future development under capitalism ... short of socialist revolution, (Frank, 1978:10)

While critical of Frank, most of the more radical dependency authors share his scepticism about the prospects for capitalist development at the periphery. For

---

*The question was never perhaps directly addressed at this level of generality by the *dependentistas*. Much of their work was geographically localized and historically circumscribed, but this is the general question implicit in that work.

example, Dos Santos (1973) would put more emphasis than does Frank on the elements within a nation which determine the effects of international situations upon national reality and on the assimilation of the national bourgeoisie by foreign capital in the role of 'dominated dominators' and less on the surplus drain. He also emphasizes the inability of peripheral societies to develop a capital goods sector as a defining characteristic. However, he would agree that capitalist development or at least '*autonomous*' capitalist development is not possible and that a socialist path offers the only escape for peripheral societies.

Similar conclusions are reached via a different route by those who analyse the plight of the periphery largely in terms of 'unequal exchange'. Thus Amin (1978) describes his 'peripheral model', based on low-wage exports and (in the consequent absence of an internal mass market) on the production of luxury goods for internal demand, with 'new' mechanisms of domination by transnational corporations superimposed; and regards it as a 'dead end' with no possibility of transition to a 'self-centred' system based on production of mass-consumption and capital goods. He sees self-reliance, therefore, as a necessary strategy for transition to socialism. Marini (1972:14) extends a similar analysis to 'subimperialism' ('the form which dependent capitalism assumes upon reaching the stage of monopolies and finance capital') in Brazil. In this case the low-wage exports are of manufactured goods and the state takes an increasingly important role (in conjunction with foreign capital), but the whole system is crucially dependent on the superexploitation of labour. The successful pursuit of wage demands by urban and rural workers would 'close all exits for capitalist develoment in Brazil'.

Perhaps the gloomiest vision belongs to the 'marginality' writers within the dependency school, such as Quijano (1974) and Nun (1969). In their view, the new 'hegemonic' monopolistic sectors are grafted on to, but not integrated with, the Latin American production matrix, bringing it permanently to the verge of breakdown. They suggest that competitive and monopoly capitalism are crucially different from each other, as far as labour absorption possibilities are concerned. Under competitive capitalism, technical change causes a fall in product price, which leads to a rise in demand for the product, which leads in turn to a rise in the demand for labour. Under monopoly capitalism, on the other hand, technical change does not result in a fall in price but partly in an increase in profits, partly an increase in wages, which encourages stagnation in the demand for labour. Moreover, the fact that the labour force in the hegemonic sector is a non-competing group breaks the link with wage determination. So surplus population, on this analysis, is not a reserve but an excluded (and permanently excluded) labour force. This 'marginalized' labour force or 'marginal mass' is a *non-functional* surplus population—over and above what is necessary to perform a Marxian industrial-reserve-army role. This is a profoundly pessimistic, even catastrophic, vision, not only questioning the employment-generating performance of peripheral capitalism, but also denying its capacity to create a socially and politically viable mode of production.

The Caribbean dependency school is on the whole less pessimistic about the possibilities of capitalist development, as long as the plantation economy model is replaced by a localized or 'people's' capitalism which is able to improve a national focus on accumulation. A notable exception is Thomas (1974) who points to the divergence in the economic rationality of the colonial power and that of the colony so that colonialism led to a separation of the pattern and growth of domestic resource use from the pattern and growth of domestic demand; and to divergence between domestic demand and the needs of the broad mass of the population. Even in the case of the most successful small capitalist econmies at the periphery, he sees no real possibility of development 'beyond misleading rises in per capita income or indeed of even sustaining such advances on a long-term basis... unless a comprehensive socialist strategy is developed' (Thomas, 1974:106). He recognizes, however, in 'some of the larger economies' the possibility of a national capitalist development of productive forces as a genuine alternative to socialism.

Perhaps the most complex member of the dependency school, so critical in his more recent writing of most of its conclusions as almost to place himself outside it, is Cardoso. Like other *dependentistas*, he emphasizes the absence of capital goods and national financial sectors, the partial and slow import of technology and penetration by foreign enterprises as characteristics of dependency, which he defines as the situation 'when the accumulation and expansion of capital cannot find its essential dynamic component within the systems' (Cardoso and Faletto, 1979:xx). However, he sees the relationship between national and international forces as forming a

> complex whole whose structural links are not based on mere external forms of exploitation and coercion, but are rooted in coincidences of interests between local dominant classes and international ones and, on the other side, are challenged by local dominated groups and classes. (Cardoso and Faletto, 1979:xvi)

Most important in the context of this volume, he therefore refuses to place theoretical limits on national capitalist development at the periphery. He sees dependent capitalism as capable of growth and of transforming social relations of production, although not of resolving the employment and poverty problems of the majority of the population. He insists, however, on the need to analyse particular situations rather than to develop general theories:

> We do not try to place theoretical limits on the probable course of future events. These will depend, not on academic predictions, but on collective action guided by political wills that make work what is structurally barely possible. (Cardoso and Faletto:175)

Sharing some of Cardoso's views but not his aversion to grand theory is the most influential 'Marxist' critic of the dependency approach, Bill Warren. Warren turns Frankism on its head and suggests on the basis of 'empirical observations' that

> the prospects for successful capitalist development implying industrialization, of a significant number of major underdeveloped countries are quite good; that substantial progress in capitalist industrialisation has already been achieved; that the period since the Second World War has been marked by a major upsurge in capitalist social relations and productive forces (especially industrialization) in the Third World; that in so far as there are obstacles to this development, they originate not in current imperialist-Third World relationships, but almost entirely from the internal contradictions of the Third World itself; that the imperialist countries' policies and their overall impact on the Third World actually favour its industrialisation; and that the ties of dependence binding the Third World to the imperialist countries have been, and are being, markedly loosened, with the consequence that the distribution of power within the capitalist world is becoming less uneven. (Warren, 1973:3)

Among the 'internal contradictions' of underdeveloped countries which cause 'serious problems' for their capitalist industrialization, Warren emphasizes, along with agricultural stagnation, excessive urbanization and growing unemployment, the ' "premature" spread of socialism prior to the development of industrial capitalism' (Warren, 1973:42).

Meanwhile a neo-classical backlash against the interventionist–protectionist approach to development and industrialization has denied any validity to the 'special subject' of development economics. The new conventional wisdom, found first in its purest form in Little, Scitovsky and Scott (1970) and underlying most recent IMF and World Bank diagnoses of 'what is wrong with country X', asserts the applicability of equilibrium economics and centres on the evils of protectionism, which violates the principle of comparative advantage and gives rise to distortions in domestic factor and product markets. 'Getting factor prices right' is the central policy prescription of this school, which usually means reducing the price of labour, raising that of capital and reducing the price of domestic currency in terms of foreign currencies, along with a reduction in tariff rates to a low and uniform level and a removal of quantitative import restrictions. In its more sophisticated version, that of McKinnon (1973), an increase in the price of capital, as part of a package of monetary, fiscal and trade liberalization policies, is seen as opening up investment opportunities in 'fragmented economies', previously hidden by indivisibilities in the pre-capitalist sector.

These are the debates which provide the context for this book's discussion—a discussion which does not set out to establish or to defend a particular argument, or to justify a particular strategy. It sets out to illustrate how different theoretical approaches dealing with different concrete situations confront the problem of reconciling the internal and the external, the national and the international as well as the economic and the political spheres of reality.

The unifying theme of the book is the focus on these questions, rather than on the development of a common approach to them. The various theoretical approaches to development must ultimately confront a common and a concrete problem, namely that of accelerating the development of the material forces of production in today's developing countries in a manner which is socially and politically beneficial to their populations, and especially to the poorest 60 per cent.

The only purpose in studying these processes of social change is to allow them to be influenced and shaped by people as social and political beings. Furthermore it is because political intervention in the social process continues to be primarily determined at a national level, that this must occupy a central position in our analysis. At the same time the global system of material production and reproduction has now reached such a degree of international complexity through ownership, commodity trade and technological and financial links, that in so far as these political processes are determined, influenced or constrained by the form of the material process of production, the possibility of formulating or implementing a nationally defined set of policies is effectively constrained. The task of development studies is to define the extent and the significance of such constraints arising from different types and degrees of economic links with the external world.

If the discussions which follow convey a message it is that an answer to such a question can be given only in the particular since it depends crucially on three sets of conditions: the physical and material circumstances of the country, including the size, resources, location and climate; the social and political situation, including the way in which productive ends are served and controlled, incomes are distributed and non-consumed resources are allocated, and the form of state, the political process, and the ideological perceptions of its population; and finally the nature of international economic and political circumstances and their changes over time.

The case studies which follow are selected to cover a wide range of illustrative cases, including some where the conflict between a national or an international rationality has been virtually negligible over much of the 1970s (Ireland, Costa Rica); to others where capitalist development, with extensive state involvement, has created the strongest basis for an effective national bourgeois strategy (Japan, South Korea, Brazil); to yet others where a similar market-oriented strategy led by a much weaker state, holds out little promise of creating such a possibility in the foreseeable future (Kenya, India). At the other end of the spectrum there are cases which have chosen to pursue a broadly socialist strategy, providing for less room for the private ownership of productive assets. Their degree of material success has varied largely with their capacity to mobilize their people politically, and thence economically. They too have had to take continuing risks in deciding first what levels and degrees of involvement with the international economy they could accept or forgo, and to pay a price for misjudging their capacity to sustain any particular set of links without compromising the fundamental elements of their national policies.

But the issue which provides the critical background to these discussions concerns the trends at the interntional level in the availability of finance and markets to different types of economies. In this repect it may well be the case that the experience of the 1970s will be a bad guide to the 1980s because these conditions may well change significantly. Already many developing countries have suffered major reverses in their real levels of consumption per head; in many real wages have fallen dramatically and GDP growth has simply come to mean increasing production for export in a desperate and often futile bid to close a widening trade gap.

In the coming decade the question of whether or not a nation has built a substantial nationally based economic and political structure may come to be of the greatest significance, because the choice will often polarize into one where a shrinking minority may try to defend its old standards of living by an increasingly repressive exploitation of the few internationally saleable commodities over which they have control, or in which they may be moved to a more 'self-reliant' and nationally-oriented strategy by the realities of the international market but at the cost of a significant reduction in the living standards of those in the modern sector.

In short, whatever lessons one may draw from the experience analysed in the following chapters, it must be recognized that these reflect the 1970s and not the 1980s. These are likely to provide a much harsher environment where the need for national strategies will increase dramatically as far as the poorest 60 per cent are concerned, but where at the same time the possibility of such national strategies is likely to decline—if necessary through armed intervention if recent signals are to be believed.

It seems to us as a result at least unwise and probably disastrous to extrapolate certain excessively optimistic interpretations of the experience of certain developing countries in the 1970s into the 1980s, and to put central emphasis on export promotion drives. Even though a very few might still have this option, their numbers are currently shrinking, and some who think they have already succeeded via this role may well face a rude awakening in the coming decade. In the final analysis capitalism's ability to disperse material benefits to the spatial and social fringes of society is centrally related to its capacity to create conditions of full employment, and it is just that capacity which has been called into question in the 1970s and which is most unlikely to be restored in the 1980s, Japan, South Korea and Singapore serving merely as the exceptions which prove the rule.

Under these circumstances an effective national policy is one which is able to integrate the internationally competitive part of its economy into the international market in a manner which does not impede politically or economically its capacity simultaneously to create a national economic context which allows the full mobilization of all remaining productive resources according to the principles of comparative advantage, as nationally applied. Since such a process will have an impact on the pattern of imports it must be combined with a degree of trade management which effectively recognizes the current and prospective impossibility of achieving full employment on the theoretically optimal basis of achieving international competitive states for all available resources. Under these circumstances the importance of effective and strong state control over central parts of the material base of the economy, including finance and industry, emerges as a critical requirement for the formulation of such policies. The only exceptions are a few, very small economies which can exploit locational and other advantages to a sufficient degree. Such a strategy is necessarily precarious and extremely 'dependent'; it may nevertheless objectively be the best available option.

Of course such national and state control may be a necessary but not a sufficient condition for the pursuit of a policy to serve the long-term interests of its population. That will finally depend on the political situation and on the extent to which choices made at the political level can be effectively implemented at the material base of the society.

Country Cases

In effect, the relevance of this book's chapters to these debates rests not in any appeal to ideological first principles, nor in an exploration of the inner logic of the competing theories, nor in the marshalling of cross-sectional data from a wide range of countries. The attempt, rather, is to learn from the historical experience of political economies of various types at different stages in their industrialization process, against the background of the evolving international context. To try to derive generalizable conclusions from such case studies is, we recognize, to cross a methodological minefield, but to reach such conclusions without an analysis of country experience and prospects is even more dangerous.

Before considering the recent experiences of different types of developing countries, the chapters which follow give some thought to the way in which these issues presented themselves in an earlier and essentially different historical context. Hence the chapter on *Britain's* early industrialization provides an introduction to and summary of the extensive and often heated debate about the relative importance of foreign trade in Britain's rapid growth from the mid-eighteenth century. It illustrates rightly the importance both of Britain's access to global markets, as a means of releasing bottlenecks, and of freeing the rhythm of expansion from its otherwise inexorable links with agricultural growth, as the physiocrats so eloquently demonstrated. It also provided a stimulus for investment and for a relatively greater degree of specialization than would otherwise have been possible.

At the same time it places these things firmly in perspective by emphasizing that for Britain these things were factors which ecouraged and stimulated a nationally based process of growth and investment. The state, having established a unified market and a liberal domestic investment climate, having provided an infrastructure in transport and finance, and having established various central industries, especially in textiles, through extremely nationalistic and protectionist measures, soon found itself in a position where its technological capabilities no longer required such assistance, a point of which it was finally convinced when the industrialization of the newly independent United States, made possible by its new and widely used freedom to protect its industries, created a boom in Great Britain, and not the disaster so widely feared and predicted.

The implication which arises from this should warn against the common pedantic discussions of whether the industrialization of Britain was caused by its access to external markets, or in a slightly amended version whether Britain's imperial dominance consisted of access to markets, or capital export as some other specific objective. But such questions are aimed at unreasonable straw men for the real issue is to consider the extent to which the external environment provided a complement and a stimulus to the internal process of accumulation, so that imperialism refers to an unequal relationship in which a dominant power can manipulate (to a degree) the terms of a relationship to suit its ever-changing and politically defined requirements. In this sense Britain's ability to gain access to raw material imports, to markets and to finance by virtue of its growing maritime dominance emerges clearly enough.

But Thomson's chapter also points to the undeniable fact that these advantages are seized by a process which is nationally based and which is in turn transformed by this connection. It also emphasizes the limits imposed on Britain's use of that advantage, and suggests that in this sense 'the nature of Britain's industrialisation... was unique and thus provides little basis for direct comparison's for currently industrializing countries because Britain's problem in its relationship with the external world at that time was the exact opposite of that facing underdeveloped countries today. If theirs derives from the extent to which they lag *behind* already industrialized nations, Britain's lay in the extent to which it was *ahead* of other economies, so that the limited extent of external technological development eventually constrained the growth of the British economy. In sharp contrast later industrializers are faced with a bewildering array of technologies the relative capital intensity of which fosters the generation of surplus labour, which is less readily eased by the possibility of massive permanent emigration like that from Britain and Europe in the nineteenth century although international labour flows have increased in the past decade. The really crucial difference however, is rightly emphasized by Thomson, which is that Britain's problem in overseas trade lay in the high price and limited availability of *imports*, whereas underdeveloped countries today face enormous difficulty in developing internationally competitive *exports*, which would provide them access to the technology they need to attain that competitiveness. Thus Britain's industrialization was unique for two reasons: 'the fact that the means for achieving economic growth were so restricted—this was the basic cause of Britain's industrialisation being gradual and widely-based; and the fact that Britain's advance was so solitary'.

Perhaps more often than Britain and other early industrializers *Japan* is taken as a point of reference by those concerned with underdeveloped countries today. Not unnaturally they raise the question of whether others can emulate Japan because, as Bronfenbrenner puts it at the beginning of Chapter 3, 'Japan remains the outstanding if not the only case of sustained economic growth under capitalism by a non-European country without European colonization, and without unhealthy or paralytic dependence on the West'.

Bronfenbrenner is sceptical about the relevance of Japan's early industrialization experience for Third World development strategists today. He bases this scepticism *not* on arguments that 'the Japanese are different' but on four main differences in circumstances: (i) the advantage of domestically-maintained peace and tranquillity, enjoyed by Meiji Japan, is not shared by today's developing countries; (ii) Japan, he suggests had freer access to the most important Northern and Western markets; (iii) Japan did not suffer from the 'revolution of rising expectations' which leads to a refusal to accept increasing inequality in internal income distribution as the price of growth, and finally (iv) the influence of various development theories has not yet led ruling groups in the Third World to blame their countries' plight on imperialism and colonialism and to seek 'quasi-reparations' in the form of aid and concessionary loans from the West to finance levels of wages, technologies and social welfare institutions in advance of levels of develoment.

One could, of course, interpret these same points in a somewhat different manner. First, one might say that most of these conditions seem to have been reproduced in South Korea. Second one might stress that the validity of the belief in trickle down and hence the value of a willingness to forgo 'rising expectations', and the likelihood that 'peace and tranquillity' can be maintained depends on whether or not an effective, national process of accumulation and growth is set in motion as a result. Finally, while it may be true that the early Japanese leaders did not entertain foolish hopes with respect to the benefits they might obtain from Western charity, they were inordinately and acutely aware of the damage which they thought that imperialism and colonialism had done to other, neighbouring states which led them to formulate policies from such a singularly single-minded and coherent national perspective. Indeed this emerges clearly in the rest of Bronfenbrenner's discussion of the particular features of Japanese policy. One might add that many of these features have survived to the present day, so that even today Japan is characterized by a marked nationalism in its financial structure, its trade patterns, its investment policies and its treatment of direct foreign investment.

Bronfenbrenner's scepticism about the value of the Japanese experience as a model seems to us to be overdone. The 'six basic decisions' that he identifies as a necessary condition of Japan's success are at least of interest to later industrializers. These are the decisions: (i) to centralize the Japanese government and economy; (ii) to transform the *samurai* into a class of businessmen and financiers to act as managers and entrepreneurs in conjunction with an activist state; which (iii) pursued a single-minded and effective programme of acquiring existing foreign technologies by, among other things, setting up pilot plants; and (iv) financing investment in industrial enterprises; (v) to build up an extensive national education system, including a network of technical schools and colleges; and (vi) the postponement of military adventures, though it must be said that developments after the turn of the century would suggest that this may have been purely an acceptance of relative weakness.

Particularly interesting in the context of our preoccupation with the interaction between the national and the international is Bronfenbrenner's stress on the care with which the Japanese state made use of inputs from abroad. Thus, the Meiji state

> selected and hired foreign experts on short-term bases and always subordinate to native Japanese executives. They selected ... Japanese students for foreign training, and financed this training themselves. They imported capital equipment, either to be used as imported for production or as models for modification.

This, combined with its hostility to Western imperialism and its minimal use of foreign loans, also emphasized by Bronfenbrenner, suggests that the answer to his final rhetorical question may not be as straightforward as he implies. Certainly, the fact that Japan was not extensively colonized would have prevented Meiji statesmen claiming that 'they are rich *because* we are poor' but their actions indicate absolutely clearly that they believed Japan would remain poor and weak if it allowed its pattern of development to be determined by 'them'. This does not, of course, make Japan a 'model' for mechanical application, but it illustrates the importance which was, and is, attached by Japan to the establishment of political and economic conditions which would allow the formulation and implementation of a national development strategy. That lesson seems to retain considerable relevance, though the possibilities of heeding it vary widely over time and space, and the desirability of heeding it in its Japanese political form must be judged not merely in terms of the material wealth it produced, but also in terms of its potential for conflict.

The very different experience of *China* before 1949 is useful for putting the 'lessons of Japanese experience' in perspective. White argues in Chapter 4 that the Kuomintang state (in contrast to that of Meiji Japan) was too weak—'politically divided, administratively incompetent and socio-economically regressive'—to enable China to follow the Japanese path to capitalist development. Given this weakness, exacerbated by international intervention, his view is that capitalist development in China would have taken a dependent and distorted form, with foreign dominance of key sectors, an uneasy coexistence of an urban bourgeoisie and a conservative landed class, an enclave pattern of unevenly distributed industrialization resulting in massive migration, rural stagnation and urban overcrowding, massive inequality and exploitation, and pervasive corruption.

Underlying this conclusion is the fact that White, like the Meiji rulers of Japan, attaches great importance to external factors as a constraint on earlier Chinese development. He points out that after a hundred years of foreign economic penetration China had little of the substance of economic development; that such pockets of economic progress as did exist were dominated by foreign economic concerns and directed towards foreign interests; and that the *political* impact of foreign domination has been particularly debilitating. The only 'positive' contribution of imperialism was a dialectical one—

> to start a process in China which culminated in its own destruction—it changed the constellation of social, economic and political forces within the country and instilled the faith among Chinese across a wide political spectrum that the only way to achieve national regeneration was to create a counter-state capable of destroying foreign dominance.

White's counterfactual picture of what Chinese capitalism would have looked like in the absence of the 1949 revolution finds echoes in Byres' description of actual capitalist development in *India*, whose 'crisis of accumulation' he relates more to its historical roots and to the internal processes of class formation, in town and country, than to current external pressures. Nevertheless he echoes Bronfenbrenner when he suggests that the crisis is exacerbated by aid, which takes pressure off the state to mobilize resources domestically, and by private foreign investment, which has contributed to an upsurge of growth in luxury industries—presumably to meet the 'rising expectations' of certain classes at least—and in the process has imparted an excessive degree of capital-intensity to industry, thus reducing employment creation and intensifying the 'structural stasis' of the Indian economy.

Some readers may question the use of terms such as 'crisis' and 'stasis' to describe an industrial sector which has grown at an annual average rate of around 6 per cent since 1947 and which contains a wide range of basic and capital goods industries, sophisticated by most Third World standards. Byres' case rests on the slowing down in the rate of industrial growth since 1965 (to around 4 per cent per year) and on the 'inadequate development' of the capital-goods (particularly machine tools) and oil industries. Comparing India unfavourably with China, he suggests that she 'continues to labour under the constraint upon her industrial growth imposed by her inability to manufacture her own machinery and equipment' and quotes Dasgupta's verdict that the oil 'exploration programme has always been half-hearted, unimaginative and lopsided'. He points out also that India's industrial growth has had no impact on the structure of the working population and that the proportion of the male labour force in agriculture was the same in 1971 as it had been in 1881.

With regard to internal processes of class formation Byres suggests an ascendancy of the commercial over the manufacturing bourgeoisie and of a domination of medium/smaller scale capital by a monopoly capital which veers towards financial manipulation rather than productive performance. In this context, he argues, the state has not been successful in playing the catalytic role in industrialization assigned to it by an urban bourgeoisie conscious of its own weakness and suggests that it is its failure to generate rapid accumulation by major investments in capital goods industries which is of greater significance ✓ than the existing narrowness of the home market.

The experience and trajectory of the *Brazilian* economy is of particular interest for our discussion because in this case a large economy which had built a substantial industrial base through a nationalist import substitution strategy, shifted sharply towards a more internationally oriented strategy, though with continuing extensive state participation in the economy. In Chapter 6 Andrade analyses this process of internationalization of the economy which was accompanied by rapid growth. He finds it difficult to give an unambiguous answer to the crucial question of the medium-term viability of this process. He lists the pressures building up in the Brazilian economy—monopolization, the absence of research and development, foreign indebtedness, income concentration, maintenance of traditional structures in rural areas, mushrooming cities etc.—and recognizes them as 'liabilities'. He also realizes clearly that for the poorest 50 per cent of the population the rapid growth which was achieved produced few if any benefits. But at the same time he points out that, from the point of view of capital accumulation,

> these liabilities can be turned into assets. Deep internationalization can mean that returns to foreign capital become more and more dependent upon the expansion of the internal market. Heavy unemployment or semi-employment can keep wages low and unions weak. Traditional agriculture can be a source of cheap food. Income concentration can soothe the middle classes. Heavy external indebtedness can trigger off big new investment projects which otherwise would not be considered, and so on.

As for the future, Andrade foresees a five-pronged survival strategy for Brazil's 'savage capitalism': the capitalization of the primary sector, both in agriculture and mining, with the heavy participation of MNCs; the development of energy, armaments, roads and communications programmes; the consolidation of the motor-vehicle industry; the substitution of alcohol for oil as a source of fuel; and an expansion of commercial relations with other Latin American, African and socialist countries. He concludes by suggesting that Brazil may be entering a new phase in which external factors become relatively more important, owing to foreign control of oil and technology and to the growing importance of investment decisions related to multinational strategies rather than to the internal market. He points to growing social and political strains which suggest that, while capitalist expansion may continue, it will be accompanied by continued political and economic instability.

In the context of our general discussion, Brazil illustrates the extent to which an internationally oriented capitalism can under certain national and international circumstances produce extremely rapid growth while yielding few if any benefits to the poorest half of the population and while having a most ambiguous effect on the economic and the political bases required to formulate and implement those strategies required to establish the longer term strength and competitiveness of the country. It is not hard to show that the policies of the past fifteen years have not served the interests of the poorest half of the population. Whether they will serve their interests in future, as trickle-down theories would suggest, must be deemed highly uncertain in view both of internal and of international developments.

If our underlying question is posed in terms of emulating Japan, many would choose *South Korea* as the capitalist peripheral economy with the best chance of success in this respect. In Chapter 7 Michell asks whether, indeed, Korea can be regarded as a vision of the future for labour surplus economies. He questions the conventional view of the overwhelming importance of manufactured exports to Korea's success, allied with a responsive government strongly committed to growth, a highly educated and well-motivated labour force—and little else. Certainly the Korean experience shows how a densely populated country, with little agricultural potential, few natural resources except its well-disciplined population and a close relationship with Japan and the US, more than tripled its income per head in seventeen years, to $776 in 1978, growing rapidly in the easy circumstances of the international economy before 1973 and continuing to do so in the less easy circumstances thereafter, at least until 1979.

However, Michell suggests that anyone seeking to use the Korean experience as an easily applicable general model should consider the following questions.

Would a government be prepared to risk a high rate of inflation through the type of financial policies used in Korea? Indeed, was the controllability of this inflation dependent on the underlying stability of international raw material prices during the 1960s? Could a country with a banking system in private hands achieve the sort of investment required in Korea? How could a docile labour force evolve in a society without neo-confucian traditions? Would the labour force accept a generation of sacrifice in order to achieve growth? Given that Koreans only adopted the export of manufactures *faute de mieux* could other countries be persuaded to adapt to the realities of export-led growth? Is not the Korean achievement to have walked the line precisely between the Scylla of autarchy and the Charybdis of multinational domination?

Moreover, for all its success so far, Michell emphasizes the difficult transition faced by Korea in the 1980s—from cheap-labour-based to technology-based industrialization. He points to the danger, for an economy as large as Korea, of a 'medium-level equilibrium trap'. When citizens demand better houses, their cars require better roads and everyone needs better education, can a country such as Korea sustain the levels of investment needed to satisfy all these areas when ICORs in industry also need to rise fast? As he says, confrontation with this question will ensure continued interest in Korea's experience during the 1980s.

In general it is the cohesiveness, the pervasiveness, the effectiveness and the deep-rooted nationalism of the Korean state's economic involvement, as expressed in its policies on direct foreign investment, technology or investment which is evocative of the Japanese experience. It is further its capacity to push this process of state capitalist accumulation to the point of labour scarcity and the consequent diffusion of material benefits throughout most of the society which made it analytically and politically so important. For South Korea the question is whether under changing international conditions and with rising real wages it can sustain that dynamism. If it can then the social and political benefits which a full employment capitalism can deliver will be feasible. If it cannot, it may well generate dangerous and explosive social and political conflict.

At this point the discussion turns to the very small economies' attempts to find a small niche in the international economy. Rodriguez argues in Chapter 8 that *Costa Rica*, given its particular circumstances, has not done badly out of its dependent integration as a tiny primary producer into the international capitalist system. He argues that this was probably the most progressive option available in that an attempt at socialist transformation would have entailed higher costs for labour, given the smallholder production of export crops, the liberal/democratic nature of the state, the relative absence of repression as a means of political control, and the degree of external opposition which any socialist struggle would have confronted. However, he recognizes that Costa Rica is at a crossroads. The current recession is emphasizing the vulnerability of a small economy dependent on a few primary products for its foreign exchange, while the investment opportunities arising from the easy stage of import substitution are exhausted. Under these circumstances he identifies three political options, broadly corresponding to some of the competing theories discussed above. Costa Rican 'liberals' are promoting the neo-classical prescription of 'getting factor prices right'; the radicals argue that disengagement from the international capitalist system is a necessary basis for a transition to socialism; while the social democrats, in the spirit of the old development economists, emphasize the need to increase state intervention to maintain accumulation and to generate employment. If the 1980s really do turn out to be a period of greater conflict and uncertainty the integrationist alternative is likely to be more problematic and more risky, and the effective democratic social control of the country's resources is likely to be more desirable than ever. The trouble is that what is desirable may not be attainable, but the answer to what is attainable is not a matter for academic analysis, but for political struggle by those directly concerned.

Ireland may seem to be in a rather different category from the other peripheral economies considered in this book, because of its membership of the EEC, its social characteristics and its level of income per head. However, as Coughlan's Chapter 9 makes clear, it faces problems which are similar to those faced by other peripheral economies relying on foreign capital and manufactured exports as the motor for economic growth. In Ireland, too, these outward-looking policies have produced growth and a substantial industrial base, and although it is questionable whether Ireland could have done better with any alternative, and feasible, strategy, it is equally true that future uncertainty is increased by its consequent crucial dependence on continuing capital injections by foreign-owned firms; on the state's capacity to carry the debts it has assumed in implementing its present policies; and on its ability to make the transition from an industrialization strategy based largely on relatively cheap labour to one based on higher technology and skills. In its favour are its political stability, its widely respected and efficient Industrial Development Authority and its location within the EEC. Against it are its relatively feeble efforts at establishing a stronger technical base in key sectors, the world recession and intensified competition in the markets for manufactured exports, the enlargement of the EEC to include Greece, Spain and Portugal, and the relatively limited impact of the very rapid export-led growth of the 1960s and 1970s on Irish employment and income per head.

In the final analysis the external dependence of an economy like Ireland's is unavoidable, but the form and the degree of it is nevertheless of great importance if only because it largely determines the way in which the country is able to respond to future economic changes, even though there is no way it could avoid being strongly affected by these.

In Chapter 10 Godfrey explores the controversy about the role of the national bourgeoisie in *Kenya*. Is that bourgeoisie, with its roots in the pre-colonial past, moving increasingly into manufacturing, as some claim, and defining a nationally oriented strategy separate from that of international capital? Or is it a class essentially in alliance with foreign capital and no serious threat to it? While it is true that the number of Kenyan capitalists is increasing and that they are continually moving into new sectors of activity, it is unlikely that this group represents a 'national bourgeoisie' with a 'progressive' role.

Hence, the real political question for Kenya's people in the 1980s is: 'Is an alternative pattern historically possible which would expand Kenyan productive forces faster, with lesser costs in terms of the current living standards of the masses?' This question in turn reduces to one, partly of the prospects for Kenyan capitalism and partly of the nature of the alternative. Prospects, crucially dependent on the 'success of the new strategy of export-led manufacturing growth (Kenya, unlike Costa Rica, is no longer at a crossroads), are judged to be poor. 'Costs in terms of the current living standards of the masses' of the existing pattern of Kenyan development are not regarded as negligible. And Leys' suggestion that the likely alternative is a strategy '*labelled* socialist, put forward by the petty bourgeoisie, involving 'state socialism' in industry and trade along lines already broadly charted in Ghana, Uganda and Tanzania' is judged to be neither as self-evident as Leys assumes nor as self-evidently less preferable. The populism of the current Kenyan government is seen as having its limits, but the crucial question of whether it represents the limit of what is 'historically possible' as an alternative to the existing pattern has hardly been touched on in the Kenyan development debate so far.

In some sense the *Tanzanian* case raises a similar question to that of Kenya. Is there a realistic alternative to the current policy, or alternatively can the present state sustain a process of accumulation sufficiently dynamic to combine growth with equity, while coping with the massive current fluctuations in the international economy?

The chapter on Tanzania shows that country's mass-based ruling Party moving towards a self-reliance strategy, in response to the contradictions and limits of an initial market-oriented strategy. This response was designed to increase its effective control over the nation's material and political affairs, and it was consolidated by blocking the various avenues by which private capital sought to exercise direct and indirect political influence. However, the attempt to stimulate a more dynamic and coherent resource mobilization under difficult political and economic circumstances bureaucratized the Party and eroded its political base in a dangerous manner.

Even though the general performance of the economy has been far from disastrous, a major foreign exchange crisis has, from the mid-1970s, deepened the system's political and economic contradictions. Hence in spite of the fact that in some respects the leadership has demonstrated considerable flexibility and responsibility in its response to these developments, the combined drought, war, and administrative and political weakness have produced a very deep crisis in 1980/81. Even so the chapter concludes that the problems and shortcomings of Tanzania's efforts at greater self-reliance are neither such that they totally invalidate the strategy, nor can they be ignored by believers in such alternatives by the simple expedient of denying the existence of such a strategy in Tanzania. Rather, a sympathetic evaluation of the experience must accept that in many respects the problems experienced represent central contradictions associated with such strategies, though naturally to varying degrees. This still permits the conclusion that a more self-reliant strategy has much to recommend it for countries like Tanzania, and indeed that it may be the best realistically available alternative for most Tanzanians, particularly in the international circumstances most likely to prevail in the coming decade. Unfortunately the difficulties encountered over the past six years may by now have created political conditions which may have undermined the political foundations of the policy to such a degree that it has itself ceased to be a feasible alternative. In that event, whatever some leftists may dream of, the forces that will exert power will be those that effectively represent international capital's interests.

Finally the book turns to North Korea, the case with the most comprehensive and nationalist state involvement in its economy. Elsewhere Foster–Carter has elaborated the point made by White in Chapter 12 that North Korean *Juche* corresponds closely to the strategy proposed for the transition to socialism by the radical Caribbean dependency economist, Clive Thomas (1974), which aims at 'converging resource use and demand' and 'converging needs with demand'. White judges that the North Koreans have done a 'creditable job' in combining rapid development with a high degree of autonomy, while avoiding being tied to the international political economies of socialism or capitalism but trying to use the opportunities offered by each. As he says, 'these are remarkable achievements for a small country confronted by a hostile or suspicious West and a divided East'. At the same time he emphasizes the problems and costs of that process: the negative side of the intense political mobilization; and, in the economy, the planning rigidities, microeconomic inefficiences and waste, and problems with quality, incentives and meeting consumer demands. The difficulties involved in attempting to expand links with the capitalist world market, which was deemed necessary towards the end of the 1970s, are also underlined.

Once again this case draws attention to the importance of a strong state and a united nation; to the importance of emphasizing domestic demand and *dynamic* comparative advantage as the bases of economic strategy, and to the need for the careful and skilful use of external resources to boost self-reliant development, without undermining the coherence of national policy. There are clear parallels here with the points that he makes about post-revolution China in Chapter 4, parallels which extend to the fact that in both the North Korean and Chinese cases the early very high degrees of national self-reliance have emerged as temporary phases leading to a reopening of contacts with the international economy at later stages, but from positions of greater relative strength from which to control the forms and the consequences of that interaction.

By Way of a Conclusion

To policy-makers and to those responsible for making effective decisions about the allocation of material resources it may seem banal and obvious to conclude such a discussion by stressing the absence of general solutions, and their specificity as to time, place and class or social group. But this does not mean that each case is unique, or that simple commonsense at the project level is a sufficient basis for decisions. Indeed there is nothing more subject to universalistic fashions than the prevailing commonsense about some current problem, and in any case an advance in our understanding does not lie in asserting one level of reality over another, or one level of abstraction over another, but rather in uniting these in a fruitful and effective manner. Indeed as social and economic structures become more complex and more independent the need to understand any particular concrete case within its broader social, economic and political context become ever greater. Hence the problem of changing any specific concrete reality must be addressed at many levels simultaneously and frequently appropriate choices at every level will be a necessary condition for success, even though no one of them will be sufficient for success.

In focusing on the national/international connection we have not therefore asserted it above all others in importance. We do suggest that it is an increasingly important issue as the complexity of the international economy grows and thereby calls into question the modern nation state as the effective political sphere within which the terms and conditions of social and economic relationships are primarily defined. It is our contention that the extent to which that change proceeds is itself a willing or unwilling result of the choices made within particular nation states by various actors, and that the future economic and political consequences of these choices are of the greatest importance because they will fundamentally affect the degree of effective social and political control which can in future be exerted over the material process of production by those in control of a particular state. Unfortunately the choice is as complex as it is important.

Given the inevitable uncertainty of the future, the basic objective of any national policy aiming at the long-term standard of living of the mass of the population must be to increase its productive capacity and its flexibility by raising levels of skills and by strengthening the society's technological base. At the same time it must create the material and the political conditions which allow such policies to continue to be formulated and implemented.

The dilemma lies in the difficulty of reconciling the acquisition and use of external finance and technology with these objectives and here the net balance swings one way or the other in accordance with changes in a number of critical factors. The importance of a specific nationalist policy changes with: the size of the economy and hence the extent of the external and dynamic economies to be attained; the coherence and administrative capacity of the state, which will determine the likelihood that any such potential will actually be realized; the degree of external hostility with which such efforts are met; and finally, the intensity of competitive pressure existing in the international markets for technology and machinery, and hence the volume and terms of the availability of international finance.

The effective pursuit of such a national policy should eventually actually increase rather than decrease the rate at which external technologies and finance are effectively acquired, while complementing and accelerating the domestic development of such capabilities.

Such nationalist policies can be combined with different forms of ownership of the means of production but they do necessarily require an inhibition of the freedom of individuals to use their resources as they wish in the international sphere so that attempts to pursue such strategies in the context of the extensive private ownership of resources must include some effective controls over international capital flows (and the political basis for sustaining these against the potential opposition of private capitalists). In addition the state must either have the capacity directly to implement major strategic long-term infrastructural industrial and technological/educational projects and have a degree of control over 'private capitalists' to induce them to act in the spirit of such a nationalist policy or, to put it differently, to induce them to define their own long-term interests as national capitalists, even if their actual activities should extend beyond the nation's borders.

In this sense the case studies reflect the degree to which the objective material benefits to be derived from 'nationalist' policies will vary over space and time. Beyond this, political correlates of these choices are more complex than is often supposed. Hence a state controlled effectively by private capitalist interests may under highly restricted circumstances (strategic importance in terms of raw materials or labour or both, strategic, favourable international circumstances) generate a pattern and a pace of accumulation which generates effective labour scarcity and leads to a diffusion of material benefits and may even allow for some liberalization of the political process because it does represent the material interests of the mass of the population to a significant and possibly in the short term even to the best possible extent. In very small economies this may happen even if this private capital operates effectively from an international perspective. In larger economies it requires a strong state capable of imposing a national focus on this process of accumulation.

It would also appear, however, that the conditions which allow such a reconciliation of the material interests of capital and labour are unstable and impermanent. As the conditions for sustaining full employment are eroded social polarization, political repression and international conflicts emerge which will normally combine to transform that mutuality of interests into a fundamental antagonism. In the relatively stronger economies this may actually reinforce the nationalism of capital, although in the absence of full employment it is more likely to be associated with fascism. In the weaker economies it is more likely to lead to 'save himself who can', involving the abandonment of all effective efforts to build a national base of accumulation and the escape of individual capitals into closer co-operation with, or subservience to, various dominant international capitals.

In any event most such forms of development, even under favourable conditions, produce a type of growth which is not in the material interests of the mass of the population, though clearly in the interests of certain dominant classes or groups, which often include some sections of skilled labour. Furthermore, in most of these the promise that trickle down will eventually justify the suffering involved for the bottom 60 per cent is as empty as it is cynical.

Unfortunately, when a state comes to free itself from the domination of private capitalist interest as exercised through control of the ideological or the political spheres and backed up by control of the material means of production, there is no guarantee that such a state will represent the interest of its population as a whole. There is unfortunately no self-evident set of practices which serve some homogeneous interest of 'workers and peasants', quite apart from the issue of a separate bureaucratic interest which may or may not come to dominate in such a situation.

In such a context the questions of what risks should be taken with respect to foreign involvement, or urban/rural relations, of the commensuration of effort and reward, of sustaining a common commitment while also eliciting individual effort and initiative, of achieving a level of current restraint in consumption which permits a rapid rate of accumulation without thereby undermining the political foundations of the policy, provide plenty of scope for conflict and even for failure.

For all that, the record of such strategies in the developing world is such that for the poorest 60 per cent the struggle for control of the state must still be a priority. The hope that global full employment will diffuse material benefits to them automatically is more forlorn now than it has been for some time. On the other hand the idea that gaining political control of the state is to open the door to unambiguous policies emerging from some permanent consensus emanating from the total political involvement of the masses in a sort of perpetual cultural revolution is an unrealistic picture produced by the hyperactive imaginations of people who have not had a great deal of responsibility for co-ordinating complex processes of production, requiring a vital concrete and measurable output at a time when it is needed for further reproduction. Such systems must work with a degree of hierarchy, a degree of direction, a degree of compulsion even. These are things to be traded off against a different set of costs and benefits, differently distributed among social classes under different forms of social and economic organization. It is for people to make such choices. It is for analysis to provide as clear an idea as is possible concerning their most likely implications and consequences. We hope this volume contributes to that task.

References

Amin, S. (1978). *Unequal Development* (Harvester, Hassocks).

Cardoso, F. H. with Faletto, E., (1979). *Dependency and Development in Latin America* (University of California Press, Berkeley, Los Angeles and London).

Dos Santos, T. (1973). 'The crisis of development theory and the problems of dependence in Latin America', in E. Bernstein (ed.), *Underdevelopment and Development* (Penguin, Harmondsworth).

Frank, A. G. (1967). *Capitalism and Underdevelopment in Latin America: Historical Studies of Chile and Brazil* (Monthly Review Press, New York and London).

—— (1978). *Dependent Accumulation and Underdevelopment* (Macmillan, London).

Hirschman, A. (1971). *A Bias for Hope* (Yale University Press, New Haven).

Little, I., Scitovsky, T. and Scott, M., (1970). *Industry and Trade in Some Developing Countries: a comparative study* (Oxford University Press, London).

McKinnon, Ronald I. (1973). *Money and Capital in Economic Development* (Brookings Institution, Washington DC).

Marini, R. M. (1972). 'Brazilian sub-imperialism', *Monthly Review*, no. 9, February.

Myrdal, G. (1957). *Economic Theory and Underdeveloped Regions* (Methuen, London).

Nun, J. (1969). 'Superpoblación relativa, ejército industrial de reserva y masa marginal', *Revista Latinoamericana*, 5, no. 2.

Oxaal, I., Barnett, T. and Booth, D. (eds) (1975). *Beyond the Sociology of Development* (Routledge and Kegan Paul, London).

Quijano, A. (1974). 'The marginal pole of the economy and the marginalised labour force', *Economy and Society*, 3, no. 4.

Sunkel, O. (1979). 'The development of development thinking', Chapter 1 in J. J. Villamil (ed.), *Transnational Capitalism and National Development* (Harvester, Hassocks).

Thomas, C. Y., (1974). *Dependence and Transformation* (Monthly Review Press, New York and London).

Warren, B. (1973). 'Imperialism and capitalist industrialisation', *New Left Review*, 81, September/October, 3–44.

The Struggle for Development:
National Strategies in an International Context
Edited by M. Bienefeld and M. Godfrey
© 1982 John Wiley & Sons Ltd.

Chapter 1

The International Context for National Development Strategies: Constraints and Opportunities in a Changing World

Manfred Bienefeld

The struggle for national development inevitably takes place in an international context, the changing circumstances of which define both constraints and opportunities for the various protagonists. This chapter provides one view of that context which emphasizes the importance of the changes it has undergone since 1945, and suggests that each individual country's experience can be analysed and understood only in relation to those changes.

Because of the inadequacy of any view which conceives of these international developments as exogenously given facts which impinge equally on all countries, so long as one allows for differential resource endowments, it is essential to analyse the links which transmit signals and pressures between the international and the various national spheres, thereby attaching relative significance to the nation state because it has the capacity, albeit a variable and limited one, to define those links.

The discussion which follows focuses on competitive economic relations as particularly powerful, though highly ambiguous, transmitters of pressure, inducing national adjustment to international change. It suggests that the benign circle of causation which free trade theory associates with such competitive relations was experienced in the 1950s and 1960s by the (OECD) industrialized countries, but argues that the 1970s, and the experience of most developing countries since 1945, indicate that this result depended on a number of conditions which have been eroded since the late 1960s.

The chapter concludes by considering the implications of this interpretation of the international context for development strategy. It suggests that while fuller integration into the international economy is generally desirable it can easily undermine the state's effective ability to set limits to the social and material conditions ultimately reflected in, and judged by, the competitive economic process, or to direct the process of economic (material) growth towards some specified and defensible social objectives.

Ascribing such central significance to the economic links between a nation and the international system does not imply the dominance of economic factors, nor does the fact that those links are treated as variable imply that any nation can hope to insulate itself totally from the external world, even if that could be shown to be desirable in a particular circumstance. Indeed, the argument which follows stresses the derivative status of economic factors, and emphasizes the potential benefits of trade, by stressing the importance of the domestic political task of perpetually redefining the appropriate (to its social objectives) economic links a nation should maintain with the outside world. Moreover, not only must such 'appropriate links' be defined in relation to particular national circumstances, they must also be based on an assessment of international developments, whose analysis therefore constitutes an essential input into the formulation of national development strategies.

While in this context it is not possible adequately to survey the different ways in which the international sphere is conceived, either explicitly or implicitly, in the development literature, it is worth noting that the interpretation of this chapter differs in some important respects from most prevailing alternatives, although it inevitably shares common ground with many of these.

It does not share the optimism of the now strongly reasserted free trade orthodoxy,[1] which has recently gone so far as to assert that if, under present circumstances, market signals were allowed total freedom to assert themselves, the costs of adjustment would be 'negligible' (OECD, 1979a). It also disagrees with the argument that the recent dramatic growth of the NICs (Newly Industrializing Countries) was primarily the result of the internal economic and trade policies adopted by those countries (Bhagwati, 1978; Krueger, 1978), or that this growth can be extrapolated and generalized on the basis of Vernon's product cycle thesis (Vernon, 1966), or of some related notion of a progressive and sequential movement up a technological ladder (Keesing, 1979; Balassa, 1980).

On the other side of the debate it stands opposed to various Marxist formulations: which share the basic principle of the product cycle as a central feature of the operation of international capital and consider it likely to lead to a renewal of existing international hierarchies based on a new pattern of technologically based specialization (Palloix, 1971); which see in the developing countries generally a growth of national bourgeois states taking their place in an (economically conceived) international market (Warren, 1980); which see the international logic of capital as essentially definable without reference to the national political basis of capital and as unfolding largely in accordance with the law of value, under the aegis of the multinational firm (Murray, 1972);

which place key emphasis on the distinctions between merchant and industrial capital, and discuss the international operation of industrial capital largely without reference to its nationality (Kay, 1975); which place primary emphasis on the idea of *unequal exchange* or the imperialism of trade (Emmanuel, 1972; Amin, 1973; Braun, 1973—see the recent excellent critical survey by Evans, 1981b); or which derive the crisis essentially from the third world's political reactions in the context of international class struggle (Amin, 1974). Finally it does not share the premises of those arguments which derive current international contradictions primarily from shortages of oil, or of liquidity (OECD, 1977; Brandt, 1980).

While indebted to the foregoing analyses for many theoretical and empirical insights, the argument which follows represents an attempt at a synthesis which considers the international situation to be dominated by four long-term trends which have gradually widened certain critical economic imbalances to the point of creating a dangerous political crisis. These trends are made manifest in: the secularly declining profit rates of the OECD economies (OECD, 1979b); the major divergence in productivity growth between the US and the UK on the one hand, and Japan, West Germany and France on the other; the increasingly critical balance with respect to the supply of and demand for certain important raw materials; and finally, the extreme difficulties experienced by the developing countries in combining equilibrium in their balance of payments with a type of growth which is socially and politically sustainable without the threat of instability, or the need for extensive political repression.

It is argued that in considering the interaction of the national and international interests, and of the interests of capital and labour within such a context, it becomes possible to see more clearly the nature of the relationship between the economic and the social and political spheres. Indeed this issue is at the centre of the following section, which considers the implications of the global reach of the principle of competitive economic relations.

The Competitive principle and Political Interdependence

Production is above all a social process. It requires the organization and co-ordination of labour working towards specified objectives and under mutually acceptable conditions as regards effort and reward. Under guild manufacture, or in a socialist economy, the fact that this is first and foremost a social and political process is clear. However, when the exchange of products begins to take place under competitive conditions, attendant changes in the organization of production may obscure this fact by creating the illusion that the process of production can now be adequately understood in economic terms. This is not the case, although it is true that the introduction of the competitive principle inevitably has a profound impact on the process of production and exchange. This effect, and its implication for international relations, is our first concern.

For present purposes the competitive principle is said to apply whenever products are sold in markets alongside other comparable products, with no restriction on, or reference to, the social conditions under which they were produced. Hence there could be markets where many producers sell similar products, but where the principle does not apply because all have their production process carefully controlled by some particular guild (Bienefeld, 1979). However, as soon as uncontrolled producers from the surrounding countryside enter such markets, the competitive principle begins to exert its influence, as the recent historical literature on proto-industrialization makes marvellously clear in its emphasis on the importance of 'arms length' markets (Mendels, 1972; Deyon, 1980).

The great importance of this change lies in the fact that all producers linked through such markets are drawn into an interdependence which implies, for each participant, that henceforth the viability of its socially and politically determined organization of production, or the adequacy of its productivity performance, can only be etablished in relation to that achieved in other 'linked' units. When the social units thus linked are specialized producers the effects are most unambiguous. Under the slogan 'Compete or perish (economically)!' such producers cannot avoid adjusting their prices to those of their most efficient competitors (so long as that efficiency can be reproduced by others and is not a rent for some scarce input), and in the process they must either lower their level of consumption, improve or intensify their process of production, or lower the prices of their material inputs. This fundamental consequence of the operation of the competitive principle remains unchanged even when the social units thus linked are larger, more diverse units of production, such as nation states, although in such cases the impact is less direct and the range of possible responses much wider. In order to clarify this point it is worth considering this competitive adjustment process in greater detail.

Without doubt the most deeply contradictory element of the competitive economy is that which makes the maximization of consumption its *raison d'être*, while at the same time transforming it into a cost of production, which the logic of the system forces each producer to minimize. In this sense the competitive system comes close to incorporating that apparent 'absurdity' of mercantilist thought which saw the prosperity of the nation achieved through the poverty of its inhabitants. Today it is within the many-faceted concept of efficiency that this contradiction is embedded. Efficiency (relative to other producers) is achieved on three battlefronts: favoured access (through ownership—an eminently political fact) to the materials required for production; possession of superior knowledge—i.e. technological or organizational; or lesser consumption/greater effort on the part of the producers. As a result, wherever and whenever resource access is 'given', and technology differentials are small, success, or rather survival, in the competitive process depends on the capacity of producers to restrict their own consumption per unit of effort expended.[2] As one might expect, under such circumstances the highest levels of 'efficiency' are attained in situations where the mass of producers are separated from those who exercise authoritarian control over production and who are willing to accept a relatively higher degree of self-denial 'on behalf' of the producers before losing their belief in the longer term virtues of the system. These might be Prussian junkers, Virginia slave-owners, Argentine *latifundistas* or Manchester capitalists—all are in principle compatible with the competitive system. Furthermore, all of these necessarily respond to the pressure exerted by that system (Brenner, 1977), and each has a material incentive to improve the efficiency of production—i.e. to lower the costs of production.

However, unlike capitalist entrepreneurs, non-capitalist masters did not 'respond' under the constant threat of economic destruction. If their production lagged behind in productivity, general incomes would fall, even the master's personal consumption might be affected but the survival of the enterprise was not usually at stake. By contrast, if the individual capitalist's enterprise lagged behind the likely consequence was bankruptcy. Hence, while the profit motive was common to all, it was the survival motive which distinguished the capitalist master, and left him to obey only one law and one commandment, 'Accumulate! Accumulate!'. For the capitalist the lesson of the fable of the tortoise and the hare could never be that 'slow and steady wins the race', it had to be that 'no matter how big your lead in the race may appear, you can never let up and never stop looking over your shoulder'.

Furthermore, the capitalist producer's stronger inducement to seek continuously greater efficiency was combined under capitalism with a greater flexibility due to the decentralized ownership and control of the investible surplus and the creation of 'free' wage labour. Historically, it is possible to assert that this combination established its superiority, not as a logically necessary consequence of the operation of competitive markets, but because during the early phase of the development of the global economy (Wallerstein, 1979) it proved generally most 'efficient', but it is important to specify the forms of capitalism which did in fact emerge triumphant in this sense, to understand the reasons for that success, to consider the possibility that the most recent experience of the world economy suggests a change in this 'optimal' (i.e. competitively most successful) form of the social organization of production, and to bring that conclusion to bear on the efforts of technologically relatively backward economies to develop within the present global context. The first two of these tasks will be very briefly discussed in the next section; the third task will occupy the rest of this chapter, while the fourth and last will be primarily addressed in the country studies which make up the remainder of this volume.

Competitive Forms of Production: Natural Selection in a Competitive Context

At one level the history of capitalism can be seen as an amazingly successful resolution of that potential conflict between the need simultaneously to increase consumption and to reduce the costs of production. The magic wands which resolved this apparent paradox were technology, time and the modern nation state: technology, because it allowed costs of production to be lowered and competitiveness to be maintained even as the consumption levels of labour rose; time, because the dynamic nature of the process allowed it to avoid a perpetuation of that situation where the equilization of technological capacities necessarily focuses the competitive process on the cheapening of the labour input through wage reductions or the intensification of labour; and the nation state, because it allowed the competitive process to be regulated and helped to concentrate the process of accumulation spatially, so that full employment became a real, though always problematic, possibility in particular countries.

Since these achievements were not realized without the exploitation of many groups and regions, or without periodic and global conflict, the simple extrapolation into the future of this historically progressive aspect of capitalism is not defensible. Furthermore, striking though its material success has been in the industrialized world, where real wages increased steadily and by more than 500 per cent between 1860 and 1960 (Phelps Brown and Browne, 1968), this does not alter the fact that the fundamental logic of competitive capitalism continues to imply that under conditions of excess labour supply, the wage will tend to be reduced progressively until full employment is achieved, *irrespective of the prevailing level of technical sophistication and hence of average productivity*. Furthermore, *in principle* this downward pressure respects no social or humanitarian boundaries, unless the competitive principle can be set aside by some limits being effectively imposed on all competing producers. Otherwise this process would not even halt at some 'cost of reproduction of labour', except in a tautological, long-run sense.[3] Indeed, from within the confines of the competitive process it was perfectly logical and technically correct for Nassau Senior to state, at the height of the Irish famine in 1848, when Irish food exports were running at a high level while millions in Ireland were starving, that he *feared the famine of 1848 in Ireland would not kill more than a million people, and that would scarcely be enough to do much good*, (Woodham–Smith, 1968).

This is not meant to suggest the imminent collapse of real wage levels in the industrial countries, but rather to draw attention to the need to view the real wage experience of the industrialized countries not as the natural consequence of the productivity increases achieved under competitive conditions, but rather as the result of a combination of economic and political circumstances which led to nationally concentrated processes of accumulation able to approach full employment, and able to maintain their competitiveness, in spite of the resulting real wage increases, by means of a sustained technological dynamism and the direct use of economic, political and military power whenever necessary—and possible.

This process was politically formalized and institutionalized through the emergence of economistic trade unions within these economies, which often pushed real wage increases to the limits of what was internationally sustainable by such technical/economic or political/military means. At the same time these organizations reproduced aspects of this international pattern within the industrial economies, by ensuring full employment and rising real wages for various categories of labour even when there was little prospect of general full employment. Possibly the most striking consequence of this development is the fact that in many industrial countries, the periods of high and protracted unemployment—i.e. the 1870s, 1930s and 1970s—were often accompanied by real wage increases for those who remained in employment, which equalled or exceeded their respective long-term trend increases (Phelps Brown and Browne, 1968, Figure 1B, p. 31).

In other words, capitalism's relative success in achieving a considerable (though still deeply problematic) reconciliation of economic and social objectives, for the majority of the population in the industrialized countries, has been significantly based on processes of exclusion and concentration, effectively shaped by the actions of nation states, firms and trade unions which established the limits within which the competitive principle has operated.

Hence it was not simply 'capitalist production' which historically demonstrated its relative superiority in the competitive struggle, it was 'capitalism, as organized in an effective, modern nation state', which must claim this distinction. The qualification is most important. There is no major capitalist industrial country which achieved its rapid economic advance under capitalism without a strong state: capable of unifying domestic markets; able to exercise effective control over its competitive links with the outside world; successful in creating favourable conditions for concentrated domestic investment; able to defend the nation's external interests by force when necessary; and able to establish a 'free' labour force in the context of some minimal socially defined limits within which the competitive process operated domestically. The histories of nineteenth-century Germany, Italy, France, Japan, Russia and the United States all exemplify this proposition, though they also illustrate the variety of ways in which states could fulfil these conditions. Even Great Britain's experience leaves no doubt about the importance of the British state's role: in establishing a unified national market at an early date; in establishing its control over international trade routes; and in obtaining favoured access to various markets and sources of raw material.

In considering the reasons why such a national form of capitalism should have proved most successful, a number of factors deserve consideration. First is the obvious fact that capital is a social relation and that, as such, it can exist only within the context of some political entity which creates the social and material conditions necessary for its existence. Second is the importance of creating a sphere of relative social homogeneity and stability, within which the competitive process can unfold relatively smoothly, and which can be protected from potentially disruptive contacts with competitors outside of this sphere. Third is the fact that the incentive for technical innovation (which allows competitiveness to be reconciled with improved social conditions) is increased, and the conditions for it are improved, in so far as national policies induce capital accumulation to take an intensive (concentrated), rather than an extensive (dispersed) form. Fourth is the related fact that both the control of labour and the development of its skill are likely to be facilitated by increasing real (social) wages, so that these also contribute to efficiency. Fifth is the need to possess some means of physical force which can, at least, guard against the danger that others might seek to gain some unfair advantage by blocking a nation's access to markets or raw materials, or at best, obtain such advantages for the economy in question. If these factors were of central importance in accounting for the success of capitalism in this particular form, it was that success which, through the natural selection based on a survival of the fittest, led to the continuing efforts to replicate the modern national state.

When nation states are linked through competitive relations the effect, as before, is to create a powerful interdependence. Indeed, so long as the competitive principle is allowed to apply, any divergence in the evolution of national social processes of production which alters their relative competitiveness, and hence eventually their balance of payments (as the summary of the nation's external econmic transactions), will generate an irresistible pressure for adjustment which overrides social or political opposition. In this sense one can say that economics dominates politics and, for this reason, also, international economic balances deserve special attention in a world where the competitive principle applies widely.

This should not, however, lead to the economistic fallacy that therefore this need for adjustment can be understood in purely economic terms, or that the policies required to bring it about can be derived from within the confines of economics. Both the original divergence and the changes needed to bring the economic indicators back into balance reflect social and political factors which cannot be treated as mere 'dependent' variables that either will, or should, necessarily adjust in accordance with some particular set of economic signals. The great importance of such economic signals lies in their role as transmitters of information, as means of making certain comparisons between different social situations, but the adjustments which they 'demand' must always be analysed and evaluated in terms of their social and political substance. This is a central issue because when one is dealing with nation states there is always some possibility of political intervention to modify the manner in which, and the extent to which, such international competitive pressures can induce adjustment in the domestic organization of production, and in this ultimate sense the political sphere dominates the economic.

To be sure, such intervention is frequently a mistake, and in any case no amount of political intervention can allow a nation to avoid balancing its external accounts in the longer run, or to avoid the necessity of adjustment if it assumes foreign exchange liabilities exceeding its capacity to earn hard currencies given the social conditions of production it has chosen to maintain. Such intervention does, however, create circumstances in which the assumption of foreign exchange liabilities can become a matter of conscious choice to be reconciled with other aspects of social and economic policy.

Although the conditions for such intervention cannot be extensively explored here, there is no doubt that such conditions do exist. They arise whenever the divergence between national and international levels of efficiency is such that an unqualified application of the competitive principle would demand a degree of social or political change which was either unattainable or undesirable for social or political reasons, or simply because it impaired the economy's long-term competitiveness. Furthermore, such conditions are more likely to apply: when the efficiency differential to be bridged is very wide; when the technological level of the weaker economies is such that they must seek to attain competitiveness primarily by means of lowering labour costs; when the global economy is far removed from full employment and especially when this is also true within the leading economies; when the transfer of technology between different types of economies is relatively inhibited; and when there are significant dynamic economies to be derived within particular nations by an intensive, nationally coherent and forward-looking allocation of investable resources.

While most of these factors emphasize the importance for the lagging economies of the careful regulation of their links with external competitive markets (List, 1904; Senghaas, 1979; Diaz-Alejandro, 1978), the issue is also of great potential importance for the leading economies. If over an extended period the relatively advanced nations are able, on the basis of their technological, social and related political/military strength, to maintain their competitiveness even while constantly increasing the differential between their social conditions of production (i.e. the social wage and the intensity of labour demanded) and those prevailing in the less developed countries, that widening gap creates a growing danger of the emergence of competitive pressures, whose social and political implications could not be readily absorbed. Should the relative technological lead of the advanced economies be eroded, as for example by an increased global mobility of technology (Soete, 1981; Froebel *et al.*, 1980), or should the political and institutional market power which may have sustained these divergent trends decline, then in the context of vast global labour reserves the competitive process would come to focus primarily on the wage cost differential[4] with potentially explosive consequences if absolute disparities in social conditions of production were very wide.

Certainly the tendency of nations to regulate their exposure to international competitive pressures in accordance with their relative economic circumstances is an all but universal feature of the history of capitalism. It is illustrated by the early protectionism of today's industrial powers,[5] common responses to the conditions of the 1930s, and their post-Second-World-War policies, which combined high subsidies for domestic food production with cascading tariffs on manufactured exports from less developed countries (escalating with increased degrees of fabrication). One may, of course, accept these facts but argue that they do not indicate the necessity of the national regulation of external economic links, but rather the inevitability of economically irrational political intervention in the competitive process so that all protectionist demands are treated *by definition* as macroeconomically irrational political pressures arising because specific interest groups press short-term sectional advantages against the 'general interest'. Furthermore, it can be argued that since the liberalization of trade has historically been loosely associated with rapid economic growth, especially in the 1950s and 1960s, the freeing of trade is a cause of such growth (Balassa, 1966). In fact, however, it is necessary to consider the possibility that the liberalization of trade is itself facilitated by the circumstances conducive to rapid economic growth, and even though under such conditions it undoubtedly helps to reinforce that growth, this beneficial consequence of freer trade cannot be considered universal. Indeed, when the conditions for rapid economic growth are no longer given, the social and political consequences of entering further liberalization could even become dangerously divisive and destabilizing.

What follows is an interpretation of the period since 1945, which suggests that by the end of the 1970s such a situation may again have arisen.

Post-war Developments Summarized

The post-war period has been characterized by a range of striking political and economic developments. Of greatest concern to this chapter's discussion are: a historically unprecedented growth of output and consumption; the multiplication of independent nation states, together with very large increases in the absolute differences between income and consumption per head in the richest and the poorest nations, and also between the OECD countries and the rest; an increase in cultural interdependence, based on an explosive growth in travel and communications; a deepening of economic interdependence as a result of capital and trade flows, with labour flows playing a lesser role; an increase in the concentration of international production, when considered by firm, though a decrease when considered by nation; an increase in the importance of supranational organizations and a strengthening of international economic and political institutions; the emergence of important bottlenecks in the supply of certain material inputs, together with the threat of major ecological problems following from accelerating levels of material consumption; high levels of population growth, together with disappointing growth in food production in most parts of the world; a political transition from a primarily bipolar East–West divide, with one power clearly dominant in each 'camp', to a multipolar situation by the 1970s; a rapid expansion of international financial instititutions with a sharp structural shift towards private international financial flows after the mid 1960s; a 'miraculous' period of growth in a number of semi-industrialized countries (the NICs: especially Brazil, South Korea, Taiwan, Singapore) which began largely in the latter half of the 1960s; and finally the re-emergence in the 1970s of deep problems within the international economy, which have created a more and more polarized and volatile international situation both economically and politically.

Undoubtedly, even this long list has missed out important areas. Its purpose is merely to indicate the main issues which the following acount will attempt to relate to each other in the context of the four long-term trends identified earlier.

The following discussion will consider in turn the separate post-war experiences of the North-west (the OECD countries) and the South, followed by a conclusion which will briefly consider the experience of the socialist countries (the 'North-east') in relation to the trends identified in the capitalist world.

The Industrial West's Golden Age: The Growth of Output, Free Trade and Contradictions

Between 1945 and 1973 the industrial countries underwent a process of rapid growth and accelerating mutual integration, which was stimulated by Marshall Aid and facilitated by the stability and liquidity provided by the Bretton Woods arrangements, especially by the convertibility of the gold-based dollar, the relative stability of exchang rates and the IMF's ability to smooth out minor disequilibria in external payments. Under conditions of generalized full employment and relative price stability, the growth of commodity and capital flows between the OECD economies outstripped the growth of output by a substantial margin. When trade barriers between these countries were gradually lowered in the 1960s, this extension of the competitive principle was associated with broadly favourable social and economic developments because, apart from Japan, the social and cultural homogeneity of the countries concerned was considerable. Initial intercountry real wage differentials, though significant, were small by international standards and tended to be associated with productivity differentials which reduced the competitive advantages they might have conferred. As a result the pressures for adjustment conveyed by the extension of the competitive principle were modest in scale and could be readily accommodated.

Even such gradual pressure could easily have led to resistance and conflict, if growth had not been rapid and if the US, which was slowly losing an enormous economic lead, had not decided at the end of the war that West European and Japanese economic expansion were the best safeguards against communism in France and Italy, and against instability or revanchism in the volatile political situations of Japan and Germany. This was a magnanimous and an important decision which reflected the lessons learned at the end of the First World War. It was made somewhat easier because European reconstruction was in the short run economically highly complementary to US requirements by providing demand for its war-inflated capital goods industry, and because fears about future competition were muted by the extent of the US's economic dominance.

To most observers the process appeared remarkably reassuring. They saw convergence between the industrial countries, and expected convergences with the socialist bloc, the end of ideology, and even the waning of the nation state. There were some voices in the academic wilderness pointing to emerging problems, (Triffen, 1960; Melman, 1965; Mandel, 1964), but such 'Cassandras' were easily ignored in the midst of such euphoria. Of course, there was de Gaulle, and the Japanese, who both in their different ways seems stubbornly wedded to an apparently irrelevant nationalism, but it was possible to think that the EEC might take care of the former, and the proximity of China and the Soviet Union of the latter. There was also the developing world which was rife with nationalist talk about balanced growth, import substitution and the like, but it seemed possible to believe that global economic growth could generate enough resources to provide the capital required to allow even them to resolve their special problem.

In short, because the adjustments required to accommodate the economic signals transmitted through the competitive links between the OECD economies were relatively modest, and because the US was content initially to see its economic lead eroded, a general political 'atmosphere' prevailed which fostered trade liberalization, detente, decolonization and developmentalism. From this perspective it was easy to feel that the problems of the pre-war world had been banished to the pages of history as deplorable monuments to an earlier age of economic and political ignorance (Tinbergen, 1962).

In retrospect, however, it is possible to see that the harmony and calm which prevailed in the OECD world during this period were superficial and deceptive. In actual fact the underlying long-term trends in national economic performance differed so markedly that major adjustments had become necessary by the late 1960s. At this point the world again entered a phase in which the social and political arrangements in all countries, including the industrial countries, would be subject to powerful, open-ended and relatively unpredictable pressures transmitted through their links with the international economy. These pressures continue to increase today, and no 'new order', able to recapture the harmony of the preceding period, is on the horizon.

Two trends at work within the OECD bloc undermined the apparent harmony most fundamentally and must be the starting point for an analysis of broader international developments. The first was the substantial, long-term differential in rates of industrial productivity growth in different OECD countries. The second was the emergence of structural economic problems common to the OECD as a whole and manifesting themselves in a general long-term decline in rates of profit.

The first trend primarily reflected the long-term deterioration in the competitiveness of the US and the UK economies because of lagging productivity growth (*AER*, 1980; Meier, 1977; US BLS, 1977). This trend began early in the post-war period but caused little concern for a long time, for a number of reasons.

First, it represented initially a process of convergence which narrowed intercountry differences in the social conditions of production because it resulted in a progressive reduction of the gap between the US (and Canada) and other OECD countries, especially as regards the price of labour ('the social wage') and the ability to apply technical advances to production (innovative capacity). This further ensured that the pressures for adjustment transmitted through international competitive links would not be disruptive, which encouraged trade liberalization, made demand patterns more similar across countries, increased trade and encouraged intra industrial specialization (Grubel and Lloyd, 1975).

Secondly, in so far as it was understood as a process of convergence, it was naturally regarded as temporary, merely reflecting a process of reconstruction in Europe, and of 'catching up' and reconstruction in Japan. This meant that once the gap had been narrowed, the differentials in economic performance were expected to decline.

Thirdly, its consequences were obscured by the dollar's reserve currency status, as a result of which the US could persistently combine trade surpluses with balance of payments deficits based on capital exports to other OECD members, the former reflecting the basic strength of the US economy in the production of goods and knowledge, the latter reflecting the expansion of US multinationals into European production, and incidentally providing the liquidity necessary for the growing international economy. Under these circumstances some decline in the US trade surplus did not call for urgent adjustment in the short or medium term.

Fourthly, large US capital flows to the other OECD economies (excepting Japan) allowed the US economy to share in their relative economic success, and the presence which US capital established in these economies was so significant that it was bound to allay fears concerning the possibility of an eventual competitive challenge from these economies.

Fifthly, faith in the ideology of free trade weakened such concerns, since no-one armed with a belief that there can be no insufficiency of aggregate demand and that the market always tends towards full employment equilibrium, will be concerned about the growth of competitors. The fact that, within the OECD, the rapid growth of intraindustrial specialization accompanied continued full employment confirmed the view that the potentially disruptive competitive displacement of major industrial sectors was most unlikely. Indeed, so long as OECD employment levels remained high, the optimists would continue to be proved right by history.

Finally, the fact that the US needed strong allies in both the Atlantic and the Pacific to safeguard the system on which its power and prosperity rested gave it a continuing self-interst in European and Japanese prosperity. Given the emerging strength of the Soviet bloc, the problems of the developing world, and the political uncertainties in some major European countries, these concerns were of major importance in providing Marshall Aid and other forms of assistance in those areas considered most sensitive. The contrasting tough stance adopted on war debts and post-war assistance to Britain, which was regarded as politically safe and a potential competitor, indicates the dominance of pragmatic considerations of political economy, rather than some boundless faith in the universal benefits of unilateral pump-priming.

By the second half of the 1960s the continuing disparities in economic performance began to cast doubt on the convergence thesis. Although the gap had by now narrowed dramatically, the respective productivity trends remained as far apart as ever, and the results began to threaten the economic, the political and the institutional bases of the post-war boom (MacEwan, 1975; Meier, 1977). The US trade surplus dwindled away (recording its first deficit this century in 1971), and with the increasing capital outflows associated with the invasion of Vietnam, the US balance of payments deteriorated sharply.

Now, as foreign dollar claims agains the US increased, reaching $63 billion by November 1971, confidence in the dollar as a safe reserve currency collapsed. More and more creditors preferred gold, and by 1971 US gold reserves had fallen to $10.1 billion, from $24.6 billion in 1949 (Perlo, 1973:183). Furthermore, this was not merely the signal for a technical adjustment in the exchange rate. It reflected a growing disjunction between US economic strength and its global political role. The fact that the Vietnam War was the haystack that broke the camel's back served to emphasize the point.

By this time the devaluation of the dollar had become unavoidable, although this had far-reaching consequences because the dollar was the 'stable value' underpinning the international trading system established at Bretton Woods. Those negotiations had opted for a gold-based dollar and relatively fixed exchange rates, because with the 1930s on their minds they feared the trade-inhibiting and potentially destabilizing effects of flexible rates, at times of high unemployment (Gardner, 1956; Brett, 1981). Now, just when unemployment levels in the OECD were about to rise once again, economic pressures swept aside these defences. On 14 August 1971 President Nixon announced the end of the gold-based dollar, and the effective end of the Bretton Woods system in what he termed modestly 'one of the most important decisions in the history of the world' (*The Times*, 15.8.1971).

The value of the dollar fell but the US balance of payments continued to deteriorate, still weighed down by the Vietnam war and suffering from relatively low productivity growth in the US. By 1973 the US balance of payments was more deeply in the red than ever and the government prepared for tough trade negotiations with the Europeans. As reported in July 1973 by an aide to the Secretary of State for Trade, they were 'refining a controversial strategy for international trade negotiations ... the aim [of which] is to strengthen the U.S. hand in the trade talks in the hope ... easing the U.S. balance-of-payments deficit. The linkage strategy recognises the weakness in the U.S. bargaining position on trade, and seeks to offset it by tying the talks to other issues, where U.S. negotiating leverage is better ...' (Ffowlkes, 1973). The areas of greater leverage were 'defense, monetary and energy issues'. On energy the strategy was particularly blunt and explicit, setting out clearly that a large increase in oil prices would affect the US's main industrial competitors much more severely than the US, and going on to suggest that the consequent accumulation of funds in the Middle East would be a lesser problem for the US because 'it has the largest capital market in the world ... which would serve as a magnet for Arab investment. It concluded by noting that 'all but a few of the major integrated oil companies are U.S. owned, and other countries *might reasonably expect* these companies to favor the U.S. market were the energy problem to reach critical proportions' (Ffowlkes, 1973 — emphasis added). Although the spokesman self-consciously rejected the charge that this strategy amounted to 'blackmail', it certainly amounted to an attempt to obtain economic concessions by means of threats concerning the use of US power in its broadest political and economic sense. Clearly economic pressures were not leading automatically to the social and political changes required to defuse them. Rather competitive pressures were revealed as operating through channels which are politically constituted, and subject to change. In short, what appeared to be an economic problem turned out to be a problem of political economy.

The trade talks failed and the next two years witnessed the greatest instability of exchange rates since 1945 (Schmidt, 1979), the grain crisis[6], and the oil crisis. As a result, the US balance of payments position eased in the mid-1970s but, with underlying productivity trends unchanged, by the end of the 1970s the balance of payments had slid even lower than its 1973 level, and this without the burden of the Vietnam war. In response, the late 1970s saw: a major export drive with respect to military goods, greater use of defence as a bargaining lever with the end of detente; a second round of oil price increases, which still effects the US's competitors much more than it does the US, although the difference is now smaller with an increased proportion of imports in total US oil consumption.

By October 1979 the US's balance of payments position was deemed so difficult that the traditional remedy for deficit countries was sharply applied. With the introduction of strong deflationary policies (Volcker monetarism) in spite of an imminent presidential election campaign, the US seemed to have become just another economy, no longer able to ignore its external deficits because of the 'poisonous privilege' of dollar exports. When, in the first quarter of 1980, GDP fell at an annual rate of almost 10 per cent there was a policy reversal that halted the decline in output but left the balance of payments to find its own level, namely a deficit of \$38 billion. The lesson was that in the US the changes required by international competitive pressures were politically unacceptable, so that the problem was once more covered up by a dollar export. In the short run the problem has been further obscured by the use of high interest rates to attract a larger share of the extensive international liquidity now seeking safe investment outlets in an unsafe world, but this may well increase foreign liabilities, fuel inflation, strengthen the dollar and inhibit long-term investment, thus reducing the chance that long-term productivity trends will be reversed. However, if these are not reversed, relative economic decline will either have to be accepted in social and political terms or the rules of the game will have to be changed even more violently, with dangerous and unpredictable economic and political results.

Certainly by the end of the 1970s it had become clear that the greater economic dynamism of the main challengers — Japan, West Germany and France — was not simply a consequence of reconstruction nor of the rapid acquisition of already existing technologies. Although after twenty-five years the potential effect of reconstruction on the average age of capital would have diminished to negligible levels, in these economies that average age remains significantly lower than it is in the US (or the UK). Furthermore, although these challengers reached the technological frontier in many sectors there is as yet no evidence of a reversal of the long-term productivity trends.

This problem must be considered against the background of the second long-term trend emerging within the OECD from the late 1960s. This has involved falling rates of profit, increasing levels of industrial overcapacity (relative to effective demand at prices yielding minimum acceptable profits), increasing inflation and rising levels of unemployment. These changes undermined, both in theory and in practice, the foundation on which trade liberalization had been based. If full employment was not in prospect, then trade would inevitably become more divisive since it would now allocate unemployment, and not merely the commodity mix to be produced in any one economy.

While an exploration of the deeper causes of this trend goes beyond the scope of this paper (Mandel, 1980; Barr, 1979; Nordhaus, 1974; Rostow, 1978; MacEwan, 1975), a major contributory cause of this downturn was the overinvestment (in relation to what could actually be realized) encouraged by the long period of sustained economic expansion (Forrester, 1976), especially because credit mechanisms allowed early warning signals to be effectively obscured (*Business Week*, 1974; *Monthly Review*, 1975), and the running of a persistent trade surplus — as in Japan and Germany from 1967 — allowed individual economies to sustain relatively more favourable investment climates (Bienefield, 1980; Schlupp, 1980). This suggests correctly, these conditions were always likely to reassert the 'nationality' of capital, as nation states sought to secure advantages for 'their capital'.

Indeed, the emerging problem of industrial overcapacity was undoubtedly exacerbated in the late 1960s by the entry of Japan as a full fledged competitor into many major international markets for manufactured goods. Its shape of global manufactured exports increased from 4.8 per cent in 1965 to 7.8 per cent in 1970 (UNIDO, 1979:37). The impact was particularly great, partly because it was the result of strategic, long-range decisions (Ojimi in Singh, 1978b) involving the installation of very large, high-technology capacities whose viability had to be established against existing competitors through lower unit costs, and partly because Japan's imports of manufactured goods remained at a relatively very low level.

By 1967, with profit rates falling, with the full implication of Japan's expansion becoming apparent, and with both Japan and West Germany pursuing aggressive balance of payments policies, competitive pressures intensified. In response, the other major western industrial countries witnessed significant changes in economic structure in the shape of a remarkable wave of mergers. In Britain during 1967 and 1968 alone 'more than a quarter of the companies registered at the beginning of 1967 with a value of £10m. or more were taken over' (Tugendhat, 1973: 87), and similar though less dramatic changes occurred in the US (Dowd, 1977: Ch.3), France, Italy, Sweden and other smaller European economies over the mid-1960s.

Meanwhile the most dynamic major economies, Germany and Japan, concerned themselves less with the simple creation of size and more with the creation of a context in which longer range decisions could achieve an increase in the degree of intersectoral coherence within the national economy. In Japan, the symbiosis between state and corporations, both financial and industrial, achieved this result most effectively. In Germany, the fact that 'much of the economy is controlled by the big three banks' and that 'the country has a strong tradition of companies working together through co-operative agreements and understandings' (Tugendhat 1973: 91) contributed to a similar result. France, with its extensive state ownership of commercial banks and its indicative planning capacity, has sought to develop in a similar direction, though with many difficulties (Rehfeldt, 1980).

As competitive pressures intensified, such macroeconomic rationality became more important than ever. Increasingly, economic success depended on the maintenance of a favourable investment climate to sustain rapid innovation, combined with co-ordinated and effective national policies concerned with marketing, exchange rates, subsidies, foreign aid and education/technology. In the absence of such an environment the mere creation of big firms is no solution.

The overcapacity which emerged reduced productivity sharply in some sectors and firms, but also led to a decline in expansionary investments and an increase in rationalizing investment (Meier, 1977). The result was to destabilize the previously stable relationship between output and employment (Verdoorn's Law) in the OECD countries (Clark, 1979; Dean, 1979). As unemployment rose, the adjustments demanded by mounting international competitive pressure became more and more difficult to achieve, and the danger of economic or political confrontation grew.

Currently, this danger is increasing as the irresistible force of international competitive pressure bears down on the sluggish and complex social reality of the countries enmeshed in the system, and produces an escalation of class struggle, while polarizing choices around two options: that of 'market radicalism' or that of state or 'social radicalism'.

The market radicals essentially treat the changes in the social conditions of production necessary (as they see it) to re-establish competitive equilibrium as dependent variables, which 'must' adjust to 'the facts of economic life' at whatever cost. Unfortunately, under present economic circumstances ('Zero-sum society' — Thurow, 1980) this approach further intensifies the competitive struggle, with protagonists pushing each other towards more and more extreme positions.

The consequences of such a strategy depend on the assumption that through such an adjustment process the competing countries can, in the foreseeable future, regain full employment 'equilibrium' and general economic expansion. So long as prospects for that are remote, the danger of such strategies lies in the explosive and unpredictable social and political situations which will arise if they are dogmatically pursued irrespective of short- or medium-term costs.

The 'social radicals' propose to resolve these contradictions differently. On the assumption that the scale of social adjustment required to reconcile current economic disparities in a competitive context is neither feasible nor desirable, especially given the measures which an attempt at implementation would require, they argue that it is necessary to reduce the influence of the competitive principle through state intervention in trade and production. Using as much trade protection as is required to allow the effective domestic mobilization of resources and investment, they would seek to increase growth *and* trade. The feasibility of this option rests ultimately on the actual (technical, political, administrative) capacity to mobilize domestic resources in such a context.

Certainly both of these options may by now lead to a dangerous intensification of international economic conflict. While that danger is rooted in the the current crisis, it has been increased by rising trade ratios. Here it is interesting and potentially disquieting to note that the degree of intra-OECD interdependence (as measured by share of imports in total consumption of manufactures) had by the late 1970s just returned to the levels prevailing in 1913, at the end of the first great period of free trade (Batchelor *et al*, 1980). Since such high trade dependence increases the impact of changes in international competitive conditions and affects an economy's ability to respond to such changes in an orderly and effective manner the increase in these ratios, when combined with an international economic downturn, multiplies the danger of instability and conflict. It is this combination of circumstances which threatens to transform the competitive principle from a stimulant to growth and international convergence within the OECD, to an incitement to conflict and political crisis.

In this context it is necessary to consider the third long-term trend mentioned at the outset: namely, the pressure of sustained economic growth on the supply of certain strategic raw materials, which will lead into the next section, concerned with the developing world.

Although some eminent theorists have long pleaded that non-renewable resources should be placed at the centre of economic analysis (Georgescu-Roegen, 1971), the issue was generally neglected, obscured by strong assumptions about factor and product substitutability and by faith in technical progress. Only more recently in the context of the oil crisis has it received more attention (Dasgupta and Heal, 1979). In contrast, politicians and policy-makers working in a national context have always had a greater appreciation of the potential importance of this issue. While Europe and Japan have long been centrally concerned with this question, for good reason (Vaitsos, 1978a), even the US, with its high degree of resource self-sufficiency, has accorded it a lot of attention, especially more recently, when its degree of self-sufficiency had declined significantly (Dean, 1971; USGAO, 1976). As early as the 1950s a semi-official report[7] pointed out ominously that its 'conclusion that there is no general resource shortage problem for the balance of the century applies specifically to the United States ... [and] cannot be extended automatically to other countries' and that especially for the less developed countries the availability of materials to support 'a sustained increase in living levels can by no means be guaranteed with the same assurance' (Dean, 1971: 143). This was a considerable irony in view of the fact that a significant proportion of these materials are located in the developing countries.

In a critical sense this report proved prescient. When the supply of energy became scarce the bulk of the developing world found itself in a desperately weak position in the ensuing scramble, and for many there have been sharp reductions in living standards. In other respects, however, the report was mistaken. It significantly underestimated the growth of Japanese demand for raw materials; it mistakenly ruled out the possibility of accelerating industrialization in some developing countries; and it erred in assuming the continued hegemony of the US. As a result, the crunch came earlier than anticipated, and when it came it generated more serious problems for the US economy. Even so it remains true that in this conflict the political power of the US has been most evident and most effective in helping it to compensate for its economic weakness. Indeed, that advantage could still prove decisive, as the report assumes. When the energy crisis came it was closely linked to the two long-term trends already discussed. It shifted competitive advantage strongly against the US's main competitors in the shortrun, which unquestionably contributed to its timing and form. It also contributed to the problem of global industrial overcapacity, by slowing down growth and widening the gap between actual economic magnitudes and those anticipated by investors.

Meanwhile in the short run it probably helped to ease a central structural problem in the western economies by diverting income into demand for producer goods — purchased either by OPEC itself, or by borrowers using internationally recycled funds for industrial expasion. However, because these debtors had to export much of the consequent output to the OECD to meet their hard currency financial obligations, the longer term effect was much the same as if these productive capacities had been built in the OECD economies where overcapacity had restricted investment opportunities. In a sense this process became merely a further stage in the creation of global industrial capacities exceeding potential effective demand under existing economic and social conditions, and/or exceeding the levels of production possible, in view of existing or imminent bottlenecks in the supplies of certain critical inputs.

The Progress of the South: Diversity in a Rapidly Changing World

The political and economic weight of the South increased over the past thirty-five years, but it remains relatively small. Its share of the global production of manufactures has increased a few percentage points, but its share of population has increased more and, if one excludes oil, its share of global production and consumption has failed to rise. Furthermore, its aggregate influence is even less than this would imply, because its weight is divided between such a large number of heterogeneous countries. At the same time that heterogeneity has allowed a small number of developing countries to become more significant individual actors on the global stage.

Although the trends which emerged in the developing countries, during the thirty-five years since 1945, were powerfully affected by developments in the OECD, there is no doubt that they add a separate and additional dimension to the global process of development and change.

For the developing countries a focus on their links to the international market is particularly appropriate, not only because it is a useful starting point for the consideration of national interdependence in a global market, but because the wide absolute gap in income and technology between today's industrialized and developing countries, is the definitive characteristic of underdevelopment, and because this disparity creates a powerful and continuous tension between the almost unlimited number of internationally produced goods, which (apart from the ability to pay) the underdeveloped countries would find more useful and desirable than domestically produced goods, and conversely, the small and restricted number of their domestically produced goods which can be sold on the international market. Indeed this tension is such a dominant characteristic of modern underdevelopment that the way in which a country seeks to deal with it must be regarded as a central feature of its development.

For any particular developing country this focuses attention on the relationship between the economy's capacity to export, and the extent to which such production for export can utilize available labour. However, in a competitive context, underdevelopment may best be defined as a situation where even physical subsistence wages are unable to produce anything approaching full employment, so that reliance on the market will always produce (though to differing degrees) a common result, variously characterized as dualism, the preservation of pre- and non-capitalist forms of production, marginalization or overpopulation. This implies the need to create protected areas of production which allow the productive utilization of the available labour, even when that production does not meet current standards of international competitiveness.

Such policies frequently produce the now familiar import substitution crisis, but they may also lay the technical, organizational and social foundations, either for a relatively more self-reliant socialist strategy, or for an eventual export-oriented strategy in which export diversification and unprotected import substitution permits the achievement of full employment, at which point it is possible to make a good case that analytically such a country should no longer be characterized as underdeveloped, but should be simply analysed as a capitalist economy, though that would by no means imply its permanent capacity to sustain full employment.

In general, the post-war period has witnessed a significant differentiation between developing economies, with OPEC and the NICs coming to occupy a more and more distinctive position. While OPEC's rise was closely related to the enormous increase in oil rents and hence to the trends discussed in the earlier sections, the NICs deserve attention because they have been widely presented as generally applicable models (Keesing, 1979) whose success is primarily based on their national economic policies, with special significance being attached to their free market orientation and their elimination of any discrimination between production for domestic consumption or for export (Bhagwati, 1978; Krueger, 1978; Westphal, 1978; Little, 1979).

A complete assessment of the NIC phenomenon must, however: consider it in the context of the post-war evolution of the development debate and of development policy; discuss the extent to which it must be understood as one dimension of the international developments outlined earlier; and explore the likely future relationship between NIC growth and evolving global trends.

The post-war period began with a strong consensus among analysts and policy-makers, that the high levels of underemployment within the developing countries had to be eliminated by means of active policy intervention (Nurske, 1953; Rosenstein-Rodan, 1943; Myrdal, 1957). This reflected the severity of problems in the developing countries, but was not unrelated to the fact that such views were fashionable even with respect to the developed countries (Lewis, 1948).

Protectionist import substitution policies were consequently all but universal in the independent (as opposed to the still colonial) developing world. In some they were further encouraged by the post-war difficulties encountered by many industries built up under the 'special protection' afforded by wartime disruption of production and markets.

In the course of the 1960s evidence accumulated to emphasize both the urgency of the problem and the limitations of this particular 'solution'. The urgency of the problem was revealed on one hand by the inadequate levels of labour absorption (Turnham and Jaeger, 1971), by the socially and economically unsustainable rates of urbanization (Hauser, 1961), by the consequent problems of 'marginalization' (Quijano, 1974), and by the increasing political polarization which attended these developments. Furthermore, it appeared that in contrast to the great trade expansion before the 1930s, now the growth of trade in primary commodities was lagging behind the growth of trade as a whole (Maizels, 1963). This increased the need for structural changes to increase GDP/Export ratios, or for regional customs unions, since only thus could GDP growth exceed that of primary exports. In principle this reinforced the demand for import substitution, at least so long as the developing countries were effectively restricted to the export of primary commodities.

At the same time, the accumulating evidence on import substitution revealed the limitations of that 'solution'. While import substitution did produce some shift in GDP/Export ratios (Maizels, 1963), the high levels of import content and the high capital-labour ratios found in most of the industrial projects which resulted meant that economies soon ran up against the foreign exchange constraint in a more binding form because import shortages now had a greater multiplier effect due to their importance in domestic production. To make matters worse, in many cases the growth of exports had probably been reduced by these policies, which cancelled any advantage gained from an increased GDP/Export ratio as far as overall growth was concerned (McKinnon, 1965).

Furthermore, many of these new industries were inefficient, in that their operation did not yield the dynamic externalities which were their rationale (Singh, 1978a), although the debate about this was thoroughly confused by the fact that such inefficiency was frequently alleged on the basis of measures which defined it in relation to current international opportunity costs (Soligo and Stern, 1965; Krueger, 1966). Such measures did not so much assess import substitution, as deny the possibility that it could be a desirable policy, by assuming a level of project and *factor* divisibility and substitutability and an international market structure which made possible full employment under competitive conditions.[8] Without these assumptions their 'discovery' that import substitution industries were 'inefficient' by internationally competitive standards was obviously true 'by definition'. More disturbing was evidence showing that frequently such import substituting production actually consumed more foreign exchange that would have been required to import the finished articles. In time even those who assessed the general experience in more appropriate, dynamic terms, often came to pessimistic conclusions regarding the longer-term benefits of the policies, as they had generally been implemented (Lipton, 1976; Sutcliffe, 1971; Furtado, 1964; Amin, 1974).

However, if simple import substitution policies were at an impasse, this left three possible avenues for further advance, though these were not mutually exclusive. The first involved the search, or the demand, for significant increases in resource flows to the developing countries, either through aid (Pearson, 1969) or through some means of improving the effective terms of trade primary commodity exports (Prebisch, 1961; ECLA, 1963; Emmanuel, 1972; UNCTAD, 1974).[9] The second was based on the idea that a 'radicalization' or a 'nationalization' of import substitution programmes had the capacity to shift the economic structure substantially, and to release readily the productive potential residing in existing underutilized labour (Gurley, 1971; Amin, 1974; Thomas, 1974). The third emerged if one rejected the basic premise of the previous discussion, namely that the developing countries were effectively restricted to the export of primary commodities, and that under their circumstances the achievement of full employment was incompatible with export-oriented policies. By the mid-1960s the rejection of this premise was rapidly gaining support (McKinnon, 1965; Little *et al.*, 1970) partly because the belief in the benefits to be derived from free trade had grown much stronger in the light of OECD experience, partly because full employment in the industrial countries seemed to be permanently sustainable, and partly because only this third 'avenue' was really consistent with a reaffirmation of the international market as the primary mechanism for integrating the developing countries into the global process of economic growth as then dominated by the OECD countries.

In the event, the first avenue proved feasible for the OPEC countries which had their economic circumstances transformed by the dramatic change in their terms of trade, although unfortunately the benefits in growth were not always closely associated with development in a broader social sense (ILO/JASPA, 1981).

The second possible way forward, that of greater self-reliance, or of socialism, was espoused by an increasing number of nations in the 1960s. While the social benefits were often substantial (Horvat, 1974; US Congress, 1978) and economic growth was steady but not spectacular, all of these 'solutions' developed their own particular contradictions. In addition, economic performance was in all cases impaired by the international economic crisis of the mid-1970s since none of the countries concerned practised autarchy. In cases where the political and material basis for such a strategy was particularly weak, as in Tanzania and Ethiopia, these strains became virtually unbearable, while in others, such as Cuba, their dependence on favourable trade agreements with the socialist bloc increased sharply.

Whatever the ultimate lessons of these experiences may be, the fact was that in the latter half of the 1960s the option appeared increasingly attractive. Indeed it sometimes appeared as the only feasibile option in those countries which correctly saw the aid channel as hopelessly inadequate, which could envisage no massive improvement in their terms of trade, and which were not in a position to regard the suggestion that they should export diversified manufactures on a large scale as anything other than a rather bad joke, Hong Kong and Puerto Rico notwithstanding.

In general this trend towards 'self-reliance' was viewed with alarm by the OECD countries, since a reduction in the intensity with which the developing countries pursued the earning of foreign exchange could jeopardize essential raw material supplies, and worsen the prospects of realizing expected profits on past investments and of selling or investing profitably in future. Reactions included the Cuban blockade and the active assistance given to military *coups d'etat* intent on reversing such tendencies in Iran, Indonesia, Guatemala, Brazil and Chile, among others. More subtle efforts to achieve the same end were reflected in the US's counter-insurgency[10] and in the associated commitments to make alternative options viable through aid, as epitomized by the unhappy Alliance for Progress.

The simple fact was however that it seemed increasingly clear that no amount of repression[11] could contain the emerging social and political pressures as long as the manufactured export alternative did not become a more realistic option, at least in 'key' countries with particular geo-political significance.

Such 'political' considerations were not in themselves sufficient to allow the viability of this third alternative to be established, as illustrated by the total inadequacy of the aid flows which they generated directly. But they did create a context favourable to the emergence of a particular response to the contradictions developing within the OECD bloc. As competitive pressures between OECD producers intensified, the temptation for the lagging economies to improve their position (and hence sustain their profits and contain inflation) by taking advantage of cheap labour in the developing world became more and more irresistible. What the UK and the US had begun on a minute scale in Hong Kong and Puerto Rico, was now expanded dramatically to South Korea,

Brazil, Taiwan, Singapore, Mexico and the European periphery. In addition a growing number of Export Processing Zones were established as pure enclaves in a variety of countries (Froebel *et al.*, 1980; UNIDO, 1980).

In this context a relatively heterogeneous set of economies, all (except Mexico and Yugoslavia) under extremely authoritarian right-wing regimes, emerged more or less simultaneously as the NICs, to be eventually acclaimed as models which vindicated the market as an adequate, and indeed, the optimal engine of rapid development (Bhagwati, 1978; Krueger, 1978; Little, 1979). Their experience has become the basis for the militant application of equilibrium economics to development, as implicit in the use of cost-benefit techniques based on the practically unqualified use of international prices as relevant opportunity costs (Little and Mirrlees, 1968; Squire and van der Tak, 1975), and effectively ignoring the many earlier counsels that this frame of analysis was inappropriate to the development context (Seers, 1967; Nurkse, 1953; Myrdal, 1968; and many others). It is somewhat ironic that this should have happened just when the inadequacies of that frame of analysis have become most evident in the developed countries.

The new faith was immensely strengthened during the 1970s when a few of the smaller NICs — South Korea, Taiwan, Singapore, Hong Kong — attained effective full employment, and as a consequence saw real wages rise significantly in spite of continued political, and trade union, repression. This crucial evidence strengthened the argument that market-based policies which accepted initial inequalities could be economically and socially desirable in developing economies. The experience demonstrated once again that if the process of capitalist accumulation can be sufficiently concentrated in a particular economic space for an adequate period it has the capacity to generate full employment, and consequently to diffuse material benefits within that economic space. In this sense the notion of trickle down lives, as it has lived in Japan, and in the other industrialized countries before that. It still remains, however, to determine what conditions, both national and international, might allow such a concentration of accumulation to be sustained over time. In this respect the end of full employment in the industrial countries represents a strong warning against simplistic generalizations or undue optimism.

The international context which allowed this to happen in the NICs was therefore dominated by the growing contradictions within the OECD, and by the political crisis emerging in the developing world by the mid-1960s. It was in response to these contradictions that the latter half of the 1960s saw a significant shift of international economic patterns, spearheaded by the US and the UK, implemented by the multinationals and certain developing nations, and financed by the Eurodollar markets' explosive expansion based on the dollar glut resulting from the US deficits (Engellau and Nygren, 1979; Griffiths-Jones, 1980). The US took the lead in creating the three conditions most important for the emergence of the NICs, namely the provision of markets for NIC exports; the encouragement of investment and technology flows to the developing world; and the political and military support of regimes able to implement the new policies, against whatever domestic opposition this might create in the short run.

The early importance of the US (and to a lesser extent the UK) as markets for developing country exports of manufacturers is strikingly illustrated by the fact that by 1965, roughly 60 per cent of all such exports went to these two markets (Lary, 1968). Furthermore, these flows did not arise in response to a general trade liberalization granting freer access to exports from all developing countries, but appeared in the context of an extensive array of special import quotas granted to particular suppliers (as in the Multi-Fibre Agreement of 1973) or of measures like the US valued added tariffs 806 and 807.3, which levied import duties only on the difference between gross value and the value of inputs originating in the US (Helleiner, 1977). In other words, developed country markets were opened in a controlled and limited manner, and frequently to specific countries and particular products.

Meanwhile investment flows were encouraged by the effect of such market allocation, by the strengthening of government-backed export credit schemes, and by expanded investment guarantees. In this context the US banks were initially primarily responsible for mobilizing the Eurodollar pool for investment in the developing world. The resulting flow of funds was sufficiently large and sufficiently concentrated on a few economies (ten countries account for roughly 60 per cent of the total debts of developing countries — OECD, 1979c), to allow their import substitution crises to be overcome[12] by permitting the industrial structures to be rapidly expanded, modernized and export-oriented.

The military backing of the regimes in question has continued to be an important factor sustaining the confidence of the investor, and is probably stronger today than ever, in view of the significance these economies have attained for the international financial community.

While these international circumstances are essential for an understanding of the NIC phenomenon, that does not imply it was a process orchestrated by the OECD and passively endured by the respective developing countries. That this is not the case is illustrated clearly enough by the relevant country studies in this volume, and deserves special emphasis. In fact if one excludes tiny 'locations' like Ireland, Singapore or Hong Kong, which may have a reasonable chance of sustaining full employment by relying heavily on international capital flows, the extent of state involvement in generating and allocating investible resources in the most successful NICs is striking. Particularly in South Korea, the emphasis on long-term strategic investment criteria has strong similarities with the Japanese industrialization strategy (Hasan, 1976; Luedde-Neurath, 1980). The importance of this point is highlighted by one of the early architects of the Brazilian 'miracle', who suggested (Campos, 1980), that Brazil's current problems may have been made more intractable by an 'excessive use of foreign capital', particularly during its early import substitution phase. This contrasts sharply with the South Korean experience, where early import substitution was domestically based and where, as in Japan, the state has subsequently (at least until 1981) exercised strict control over direct foreign investment within the economy, so as to maintain effective domestic control over finance, and over 'strategic', or 'basic', industries (Kuznets, 1977; Hasan, 1976).

Indeed this dimension of the South Korean experience is so important that it may be placed alongside the Japanese, West German and French experiences, to reinforce the disturbing possibility that under the technological and economic conditions of the latter part of the twentieth century and especially in the context of general recession, the competitive process is beginning to reveal that the most 'efficient' form of social organization of production may be a capitalism organized in a relatively more corporate, more centralized form than was true of earlier periods. Furthermore, as the scale and the gestation periods of research and production projects increase, the formulation and co-ordinated implementation of strategic, long-term policies will become even more important, and may well erode that loose historical association between capitalism and liberal democracy, which, for all its shortcomings, has been a source of capitalism's strength in the past. The corporate state model effectively brings a much larger part of social life into the confines of what is, to all intents and purposes, one economic enterprise, and under capitalism, essentially authoritarian and hierarchical relations have always dominated within that sphere. The multinational conglomerates exhibit the same tenden-cies as they internalize markets, increase the share of 'non-arm's length transactions' (Helleiner, 1975; Vaitsos, 1978b) and extend their direct control over labour, but by now it seems more than likely that the corporate state will emerge as the more competitive form of capitalism because its range of powers over the social base on which production is organized is more comprehensive and more direct.

Meanwhile, in considering future prospects for the NICs themselves, three things must be centrally borne in mind. First, unless the problems of overcapacity, low profitability and underemployment can be resolved in the central economies, the prospects for the NICs must be gloomy as their capacities will add to the global problem, while their ability to expand domestic consumption will be limited by their need to balance their external accounts under increasingly difficult circumstances.

Secondly, the NIC's development of a significant capacity to export manufactures has thrown into direct competition economies with vastly different social conditions of production (as regards the social wage and the intensity of labour).[13] This, in itself, would ensure that the idyllic intra-OECD trade expansion of the 1960s would not be a good guide for predicting the consequences of trade liberalization in the new situation. Indeed, even within the OECD, the 'special' problems associated with Japanese competition, and the proliferating 'voluntary export restrictions' demanded of Japan, bear witness to the importance of this issue. In the case of the NICs, a freely operating competitive process in the context of high levels of unemployment would inevitably transmit signals which were so 'disruptive' that they would be either rejected, hence leading to protectionism, or enforceable only by means of increased political repression.

Thirdly, if one assumes that the competitive process could be extended internationally to its logical limits, so that the nation state was superceded as the effective social and political basis for capital, then in the absence of global full employment the conditions of labour would be equalized downwards, since in so far as labour was thrown into one large market suffering from excess supply the competitive principle would produce a progressive downward pressure on the wage (Bienefeld *et al.*, 1977) *irrespective* of the average productivity of labour, a conclusion which follows equally from neo-classical, classical or specifically Marxist perspectives.

In fact, of course, a pure labour market could never exist, because to treat labour as a pure commodity would be socially and politically inconceivable (Polanyi, 1957), so that in practice, sections of labour would always be able to separate 'their' labour market from the general labour market.[14] They would thus secure relatively better conditions for themselves,. and would be incorporated into the privileged enclaves which are such a central feature of the transnationalization thesis (Sunkel, 1973). However, if the above arguments are valid, then that process would not spread outwards from central economies, where the bulk of the population is within the 'privileged' enclave, to a developing world, where an expanding proportion of the population would be thus incorporated. Instead the proportion of the population thus incorporated in the industrial countries would decline towards a level which would vary little internationally, so that even there capitalism could no longer hope to generate a substantial social or political consensus and the type of liberal democracy associated with it. Everywhere the marginalized masses outside of the privileged enclaves would have to be dealt with harshly, and far from the industrial countries representing the model for the developing ones, the 'savage capitalism' (Andrade, 1982) of Brazil would become the vision of the future for the industrial countries.

For the time being this evolution is unlikely because much evidence suggests that, as in previous similar periods, the emergence of major contradictions at the international level is reinforcing the national character of capital. Indeed 'Japan Incorporated' seems to be proving the most competitive way of organizing production, but there are ominous signs to remind us that such economic success may have to be defended against increasingly strong political — and even military — pressures.

Apart from the NICs there are of course the 'other' developing countries, those with no oil and without the political or social conditions which might allow them to join the exclusive NIC club. For these economies the 1970s have been extremely disruptive and painful. With their balance of payments position shattered, most of them have had to reduce domestic levels of economic activity and consumption, to reduce imports and to allow more resources to be channelled into production for export. Meanwhile the fact that the bulk of international resources available to developing countries now flow through straight commercial channels means that their allocation simply reinforces the dictates of the market. Even though dwindling aid flows have been marginally diverted to the poorest countries in some cases, this hardly compensates for that effect, especially as non-commercial flows are declining further as the squeeze on the developed countries intensifies.

Prospects for these poorest economies are thus extremely bleak. For many, the capacity to diversify exports in an increasingly competitive international market is purely notional, while their traditional exports are being squeezed both by sluggish demand, and by the increased supply resulting from the generally intensified pressure to export, so that their ability to attract commercial international funds declines. In essence, they are being forced back to a more 'self-reliant' pattern of growth but under circumstances where the difficulty of sustaining a more self-reliant strategy economically or politically has risen dramatically.

On balance, in the developing world, the crisis of the 1970s has opened new (though possibly temporary) opportunities for some, and it has harshly disciplined others. With social and economic breakdown threatened in these latter economies, the industrial west and in particular the US, seems prepared to contain the resulting political upheavals by force, not so much because it has forgotten Vietnam, but because it has fewer options, because it probably considers the socialist bloc as less united and generally weaker, and because it feels that through the NICs it has consolidated its position in the most significant developing countries.

Conclusions, and Some Notes on the Socialist Bloc

This chapter has argued that there is a greater need than ever for national policies to be formulated in the context of an informed judgement about the nature of international development, because these are currently deeply contradictory and increasingly uncertain.

So far this discussion has concerned itself with developments in the capitalist world, and that is as it should be, since most underdeveloped countries are effectively part of that world. At the same time, developments within the socialist bloc clearly have a bearing on these trends and it is necessary to incorporate these into the discussion, although within this chapter, it has only been possible to indicate some of the major issues requiring further study and elaboration.

Economically the first thing to note about the socialist bloc is its phenomenal long-term growth, which has enabled it to increase its share of global manufacturing production, which was less than 10 per cent at the end of the Second World War, but rose from 18.1 per cent in 1960 to more than 27 per cent in 1975 (UNIDO, 1979), in spite of the fact that this was a period of historically unprecedented expansion in the capitalist world. By contrast the share of global manufacturing production located in the developing world, including the NICs, rose from 6.9 per cent to 8.6 per cent between 1960 and 1975.

This economic expansion was accompanied by an increase in political and military influence which, by the 1960s, had grown to the point where it could provide crucial support to regimes seeking to extricate themselves from their existing links with the international market, as in Cuba and Vietnam. While this represented an important new factor in the international situation, its significance has not continued to grow, partly because of rising international tension and partly because of the emergence of a range of internal contradictions within the socialist bloc itself.

The contradictions of socialism were partly political, reflecting the perpetual conflict between the democratic, participatory ideals of socialism and the need for a considerable degree of central authority to ensure the macroeconomic coherence necessary for continued growth. They were partly economic, reflecting the difficulty of planning an increasingly complex economy, the special problems of agricultural production in some of the countries, and the increasing attractiveness of western technology, especially as their technical levels rose far enough both to absorb it and to earn more of the foreign exchange needed to purchase it. They were partly social, or rather social psychological, in that the extensive responsibilities assumed by the state in such a system make it a ready focus of self-reinforcing discontent, particularly if and when economic difficulties appear.

Possibly the deepest contradiction of all, however, is that between the internationalism of socialist theory, and the fact that the actual socialist countries find themselves in a situation where painful and potentially divisive choices about relative prices or incomes are continually and necessarily made in a national context and must daily be justified on that basis. This reinforces nationalism and creates conditions for potential conflict between opposing national interests, which lead to difficulties in achieving a socialist international division of labour, in expanding collaboration with developing countries, and occasionally even to military conflict between socialist states.

As these tendencies have evolved in the different socialist countries, the socialist bloc has appeared to become a less attractive, and a less readily available, alternative context for development. It has become more and more efficiency, output and levels of employment, thus standing the import substitution argument on its head by asserting that the short-term costs associated with a strict adherence to market signals (in the presence of unemployment) should be accepted because that will produce long-term net benefits.

The 'terms of trade' debate has raged ever since, focused on disputes about the movement of nominal, barter, factoral or double-factoral terms of trade, and yielding a variety of outcomes depending on the choice of the period, the starting and end point of the series and the set of commodities included (Evans, 1979, IBRD, 1978; Thoburn, 1977; Spraos, 1980). As so often, this debate distorts the issue by considering only one aspect of the problem. The basic issue was a concern that primary exports could not yield the volume of foreign exchange required for rapid growth in the developing world. To discover that in the face of many arrangements to restrict production, and in the face of a heavy emphasis on import substitution, primary commodity prices have behaved in a certain way is therefore far from decisive. Even though for most primary products exported from developing countries, the post-war trends are not encouraging, the real question is what would have happened, or indeed what would happen now, if the developing world generally were to seek its salvation through primary exports above all else. Considered in this way it is difficult not to agree with those who thought this would lead to overproduction and worsening terms of trade for most primary producers, which does not, of course deny that individual exporters are always in a position to improve their incomes faster than implied by global price elasticities of demand, if they expand production relatively more rapidly and capture a larger share of the market. By the same token such gains are achieved at the further expense of the remaining exporters.

The essence of that strategy was to 'forestall' the need for military intervention, by intervening much earlier to prevent an explosive situation from emerging. This intervention was to be based on a combination of social/financial assistance and strengthening of the security apparatus.

A very high level of repression is apparently acceptable before support is withdrawn from regimes intent upon the reversal of unduly 'nationalist', 'self-reliant' or 'socialist' policies. The experiences of Vietnam, Indonesia, Chile, El Salvador, Guatemala, Haiti and others bear eloquent testimony to this fact.

In the longer term the proportion of NIC Gross Fixed Capital Formation which stems from foreign sources is relatively small, during certain early phases of strategy it was occasionally very high — as in South Korea where in 1964 over 90 per cent of total domestic savings came from foreign sources.

But this competition between economies with vastly different social conditions of labour does not produce trade of the *unequal exchange* variety but rather trade in competing goods (Evans, 1981a). As such it will not produce a situation involving implicit transfers of value or income, but rather an situation producing either adjustment or instability cum protection. Ricardian theory with its emphasis on distribution relations as major determinants of comparative advantage, and with its concerns for disequilibrium is highly relevant to the analysis of such situations.

It is of interest to note here that it has been recently suggested (Evans, 1980) that the lasting contribution of Emmanuel's intervention might well be his insistence on treating labour as heterogeneous rather than homogeneous in production relations.

This argument is a most interesting one. He rightly warns against the dangers of 'self-sufficiency' and indicates clearly that he sees it as a means to an end, not an end in itself. It is of some significance to our argument that he lays

heterogeneous and as individual economies within it have extended their trading and financial links with the capitalist world, they themselves have been increasingly exposed to the competitive pressures generated there. These developments have reduced the socialist bloc's importance as a potential context for alternative development strategies, although it does still play that role and at least a part of the reason for the current hotting up of the cold war is undoubtedly to reduce this option further in practice.

In general, developments within the socialist bloc (especially in Poland) further reinforce the earlier conclusion that the current international uncertainty makes it more important, though also more difficult, to define national development strategies on the basis of a realistic assessment of global tendencies.

To conclude, it is clear that while the specification of a desirable strategy must remain a matter to be defined for a particular place and time from a particular class perspective, there is little doubt that the historical importance of a strong nation state as the basis for a dynamic and politically viable process of expanded material production, has not diminished. Only the state can establish the coherent and sustainable set of social and political mechanisms which are necessary to facilitate expanded material production to some social purpose. Furthermore, that same state must seek to protect such internal coherence and dynamism from disruption by external change, and to reconcile that with taking advantage of the enormous benefits potentially to be derived from links with the external world.

How any particular state will perform those tasks depends on the resources at its disposal, the extent of influence it has over the allocation of those resources, and the interests is represents. In the world of the 1980s, as economic pressures intensify, the likelihood is that in ever more states, governments will be largely dominated by small minorities representing sections of private capital, desperately defending their material positions — often with international help — and effectively abandoning the idea of the nation as a significant economic or social unit, whose general political and economic strength it is in their interests to increase over time.

However, those states whose governments effectively represent the mass of their populations must, by definition, persevere in their attempts to stimulate a process of accumulation nationally with the capacity to produce growth while also diffusing social and material benefits and laying the social and economic foundations for the economic, social and political advance of the nation as a whole.

It is theoretically possible that such an objective could be achieved through capitalist accumulation in a relatively 'open' economy. In a few relatively small and relatively advanced developing countries this might even be possible in practice. However, our assessment of the experience of the 1970s, and especially of the larger NICs, suggests that this would generally require a strong, nationalist and highly interventionist state, which: liberalized trade gradually 'as it was able'; pursued an aggressive export strategy; organized the domestic acquisition of technological capabilities; maintained substantial control over financial flows and implemented an industrial strategy which reconciled long-term objectives with the need to balance the economy's external accounts in the interim. Moreover the possibility that even such a comprehensive strategy could succeed is receding because the favourable international conditions which allowed the NIC strategies to achieve such success for a period are now disappearing. Most particularly the critical availability of cheap (negative real interest rate) finance and of markets for exports is rapidly being eroded.

This leaves only the alternative of nationally oriented strategies capable of mobilizing domestic resources in a dynamic and effective manner on a national (or regional) basis, and trading with the outside world, in so far as that is possible without allowing the social conditions of production and the adequate (for economic survival) level of productivity to be determined by those established somewhere else, irrespective of short-term social or economic consequences. Within such a structure, just what role would be played by the market as an allocator of resources and by competition as a means of commensurating effort and reward would be a matter for considerable diversity. The essential requirements of such a policy would be political, namely control of the government by political forces effectively representing the broad interests of the working population (which still leaves much room for conflict of interests), and material, meaning sufficient control of the financial and material base of the economy to ensure that resources will be utilized within the context of the national strategy, although the types of ownership and control compatible with that objective would again be a matter for particular cases.

It is of some significance for this discussion that Keynes, who had written in 1923 that Free Trade was based on fundamental truths 'which, stated with their due qualificaitons, no one can dispute who is capable of understanding the meaning of the words', should write by 1933 that 'a greater measure of national self-sufficiency and economic isolation between countries than existed in 1914 may tend to serve the cause of peace, rather than otherwise' (Keynes, 1933), and that because 'there is no prospect for the next generation of a uniformity of economic system throughout the world ... we all need to be as free as possible of interference from economic changes elsewhere, in order to make our own favourite experiments towards the ideal social republic of the future' (Keynes 1933).[15]

That is not an argument against trade. It is an argument against the notion that the signals transmitted through the competitive process are always a desirable or acceptable judge of the adequacy of a country's social conditions of production. It is an argument to make trade the servant, and not the

master, of a responsible and democratically constituted sc policy.

Notes

1. This paper cannot enter into the theoretical controversy (free trade, but it should be noted that its discussion le Ricardian trade theory literature (Steedman, 1979a and challenged orthodox trade theory on its own ground and provided a theoretical basis for countering the 'free tr that body of thought. The themes of this paper, wh consequences of trade links between economies with technical conditions of production and in the contex ment disequilibrium, are also central concerns of the

2. In Marxian terms this refers to the extraction of ab said to dominate the early stages of capitalist a differentials are small and when labour is in excess

3. Some Marxists have used this concept of 'the misleading manner, as if it referred to some wage labour supply, represented a long-run optimal central contradiction of capitalism which rests (behaviour of individual capitalists does not ne of capital in general.

4. This refers of course to the 'social wage'. locational decisions may appear to be cap deductions from the total of social (private

5. Though the waters are occasionally mud example, that Japan's early development tariffs (Little *et al.*, 1970) but neglecting dominant in the Japanese case — i. nineteenth-century transport costs and as well as the well-known use of non-ec goods and finance, which are of such in

6. 'Food' was not a threat to be used agai Agricultural Policy, bu the *New York* study concerning food as a weapon Agriculture, was quoted to the e America's diplomatic arsenal'.

7. 'Resources in America's Future' pu the Future', funded by the Ford F work of the 'U.S. President's ('Paley Report') in 1952. W. S. helped to administer the new or

8. This is implicit in this discussi production for exports, resource efficiently into hard currency e for such export production (equalized in a context of full e additional domestic produc international efficiency. Of that the additional output

special emphasis on the point that 'finance be primarily national' largely because he argues that 'the structure of private enterprise is incompatible with that degree of well-being to which our technical advancement entitles us … [which] … may require a reduction of the rate of interest towards vanishing point within the next thirty years'. He then concludes that 'under a system by which the rate of interest finds, under the operation of normal financial forces, a uniform level throughout the world … this is most unlikely to occur' (Keynes, 1933).

Bibliography

American Economic Review (1980) 'Papers and procedings of the 92nd annual meeting', May, section on 'Current retardation in U.S. productivity growth', pp. 340–55.

Amin, S. (1973). *L'échange inégal et la loi de la valeur: la fin d'un débat, avec une contribution de J. C. Saigal* (Editions Anthropos-IDEP, Paris). English translation, excluding Saigal's contribution, in Section IV of S. Amin, *Imperialism and Unequal Development* (Harvester, Hassocks, 1977).

Amin, S. (1974). *Accumulation on a World Scale: a critique of the theory of underdevelopment*, 2 vols (Monthly Review Press, New York and Canada).

Amin, S. (1975). 'Accumulation and development', in *Review of African Political Economy*, No. 1.

Andrade, R., 1982, chapter in this volume.

Balassa, B. (1966). 'Tariff reductions and trade in manufactures among the industrial countries', *American Economic Review, LVI,* June.

Balassa, B. (1980). 'Structural change in trade in manufactured goods between industrial and developing countries', *World Bank Staff Working Paper No. 396,* Washington, June.

Barr, K. (1979). 'Long waves; a selective annotated bibliography', *Review,* No. 2 (Binghampton, New York).

Batchelor, R. A., Major, R. L., and Morgan, A. D. (1980). *Industrialisation and the Basis for Trade* (Cambridge University Press).

Bhagwati, J. (1978). *Foreign Trade Regimes and Economic Development Anatomy and Consequences of Exchange Control Regimes* (National Bureau for Economic Research, Cambridge, Mass.).

Bienefeld, M. A. (1979). 'Urban employment: A historical perspective', in R. Bromley and C. Gerry (eds.) *The Casual Poor in Third World Cities* (Wiley, Chichester).

Bienefeld, M. A. (1980). 'Externalising problems in a future EEC', in D. Seers and C. Vaitsos (eds.), *Integration and Unequal Development Re-experience of the EEC* (Macmillan, London).

Bienefeld, M. A., Godfrey, E. M., and Schmitz, H. (1977). 'Trade unions and the new internationalisation of production', *Development and Change,* **8,** No. 4, October.

Brandt Commission (1980). *North-South A Programme for Survival*, The Report of the Independent Commission on International Development Issues under the Chairmanship of Willy Brandt (Pan, London).

Braun, O. (1973). *Commercio Internacional e Imperialismo* (Siglo XXI Argentina Editores S. A., Buenos Aires).

Brenner, R. (1977). 'The origins of capitalist development: a critique of Neo-Smithian Marxism', *New Left Review,* No. 104, July–August.

Brett, E. A. (1981). *International Money and Capitalist Crisis: The Anatomy of Global Disintegration,* typescript, University of Sussex.

Business Week (1977). 'The debt economy', 12 October.

Campos, Ambassador Roberto de Oliveira (1980). 'Perspectives of the New Industrial Countries — Brazil', *Paper presented to the International Conference on Old and New Industrial Countries in the 1980s,* Sussex European Research centre, University of Sussex, 6–8 January.

CIA (1978). *Handbook of Economic Statistics,* Washington, October.

Clark, J. A. (1979). 'An Examination of the Historical Basis for some Recent Projections of Employment and Unemployment in the U.K.', *Paper to SSRC/IDS Conference on U.K. Employment Projections,* 22–25 May.

Dasgupta, P. S. and Heal, G. M. (1979). *Economic Theory and Exhaustible Resources* (Nibel, Cambridge).

Dean, A. (1979). 'Employment Forecasting and the Effect of Technological Progress', *Paper presented to a joint SSRC/IDS conference on U.K. Employment Projections,* Institute of Development Studies, Sussex, May.

Dean, H. (1971). 'Scarce resources: the dynamic of American imperialism' in K. T. Fann and D. C. Hodges (eds.), *Reading in U.S. Imperialism* (Paster Sargent, Boston).

Deyon, P. (1980). 'La proto-industrialisation: theorie et réalité', Programme for Session A.2., Huitième Congrès International d'Histoire Economique, Budapest 1982.

Diaz-Alejandro, C. F. (1978). 'Delinking North and South: unshackled or unhinged', in A. Fishlow, C. F. Diaz-Alejandro, R. R. Fagen, R. D. Hansen, *Rich and Poor Nations in the World Economy,* 1980's Project: Council on Foreign Relations (McGraw-Hill, New York).

Dowd, D. (1977). *The Twisted Dream: Capitalist development in the United States since 1776* (Winthrop, Cambridge, Mass.).

ECLA (1963). *The Economic Development of Latin America in the Post-War Period* (United Nations, New York, 1974).

Emmanuel, A. (1972). *Unequal Exchange: A Study in the Imperialism of Trade* (Monthly Review Press, New York).

Engellau, P. and Nygren, B. (1979). *Lending Without Limits: on international lending and developing countries* (Secretariat for Futures Studies, Stockholm).

Evans, H. D. (1979). 'International commodity policy: UNCTAD and NIEO in Search of a Rationale', *World Development,* **7**, pp. 259–279.

Evans, H. D. (1980). 'Emmanuel's theory of unequal exchange: critique, counter critique and theoretical contribution', *Discussion Paper No. 149* Institute of Development Studies, University of Sussex.

Evans, H. D. (1981a). 'Unequal exhcnage and economic policies: some implications of the Neo-Ricardian critique of the theory of comparative advantage' in I. Livingstone (ed.), *Development Economics and Policy: Readings* (George Allen and Unwin, London). (Originally published in the *IDS Bulletin* March 1975, and first reprinted in *Economic and Political Weekly,* **XI**, Nos. 5–7, Annual Number, February 1976).

Evans, H. D. (1981b). 'A critical assessment of neo-marxian trade theories', *Discussion Paper 12/81* (La Trobe University, Melbourne).

Ffowlkes (1973). 'Economic report: administration trade strategy taking shape to strengthen U.S. bargaining position', *National Journal,* Washington, 7 July cited in Y. Fitt, A. Faire and J. P. Vigier, *The World Economic Crisis* (Zed Press, London).

Forrester, J. (1976). 'Business structure, economic cycles and national policy', *Futures,* **8**, No. 3.

Froebel, J., Heinrichs, J. and O. Kreye (1980). *The New International Division of Labour* (Cambridge University Press).

Furtado, C. (1964). *Development and Underdevelopment* (University of California Press, Berkeley).

Gardner, R. N. (1956). *Sterling-dollar Diplomacy* (Clarendon Press, London).

Georgescu-Roegen, N. (1971). *The Entropy Law and the Economic Process* (Harvard University Press, Cambridge, Mass).

Griffiths-Jones, S. (1980). 'The growth of multinational banking, the Euro-currency market and their effects on developing countries', *Journal of Developmental studies*, January,

Grubel, H. G. and P. J. Lloyd (1975). *Intrta-Industry Trade* (Macmillan, London).

Gurley, J. G. (1971). 'Capitalist and Maoist economic development', in E. Friedman and M. Seldon (eds), *America's Asia* (Random House, New York).

Hasan, P. (1976). *Korea: Problems and Issues in a Rapidly Growing Economy* (Johns Hopkins University Press, Baltimore and London, for the World Bank).

Hauser, P. (ed). (1961). *Urbanisation in Latin America* Unesco, (International Documents Service, New York).

Helleiner, G. K. (1975). 'The role of the MNCs in the LDCs Trade in technology', *World Development*, **3**, No. 4.

Helleiner, G. K. (1977). 'Transnational enterprises and the new political economy of US trade policy', *Oxford Economic Papers*, **29**, No. 1, March.

Horvat, B. (1974). 'Welfare of the Common Man in Various Countries', *World Development*, **2**, No. 7, July.

IBRD (1978). *Commodity Trade and Price Trends*, report prepared by the Commodities and Export Projections Division, Washington DC.

ILO/JASPA (1981). *First Things First: Meeting the Basic Needs of the People of Nigeria* (Addis Ababa).

Jolly, R., de Kadt, E., Singer, H. W., and F. Wilson (eds) (1973). *Third World Employment: Problems and Strategy* (Penguin, London).

Kay, G. (1975). *Development and Underdevelopment* (Macmillan, London).

Keesing, D. B. (1979). 'Trade Policy for Developing Countries', *World Bank Staff Working Paper*, No. 353, Washington, August.

Keynes, J. M. (1933). 'National self-sufficiency', *New Statesman*, 8, 15 July.

Kiljunen, M. L. (1980). 'Regional disparities and policy in the EEC', in D. Seers and C. Vaitsos (eds), *Integration and Unequal Development: The Experience of the EEC* Macmillan, London).

Krueger, A. (1966). 'Some economic costs of exchange control: the Turkish case', *Journal of Political Economy*, *LXXIV*.

Krueger, A. (1978). *Foreign Trade Regimes and Economic Development: Liberalisation Attempts and Consequences* (Ballinger for NBER, Cambridge, Mass.).

Kuznets, P. (1977). *Economic Growth and Structure in the Republic of Korea* (Yale University Press).

Lary, H. B. (1968). *Imports of Manufactures from Less Developed Countries* (National Bureau of Economic Research, New York).

Lewis, W. A. (1948). *The Principles of Economic Planning* (Unwin University Books, London).

Lewis, W. A. (1951). *The Principles of Economic Planning* (Unwin, London).

Lewis, W. A. (1954). 'Economic development with unlimited supplies of labour', Manchester School, May, reprinted in A. W. Agarwala and J. P. Singh (eds), *The Economics of Underdevelopment* (OUP, New Delhi, 1975).

Lipton, M. (1976). *Why Poor People Stay Poor: A study of urban bias in world development* (Temple Smith, London).

List, F. (1904). *The National System of Political Economy* (Longmans, London).

Little, I. M. D. (1979). 'The Experience and Causes of Rapid Labour Intensive

Development in Korea, Taiwan, Hong Kong and Singapore and the possibilities of emulation', *Asian Employment Programme: Working Paper.*

Little, I. M. D., and J. Mirrlees (1968). *Manual of Industrial Project Analysis in Developing Countries,* 2 vols (OECD, Paris).

Little, I., Scitovsky, T., and M. Scott (1970). *Industry and Trade in Some Developing Countries: a comparative study* (Oxford University Press, London).

Luedde-Neurath, R. (1980). 'Export orientation in South Korea: how helpful is dependency thinking to its analysis?'. *IDS Bulletin,* **12** No. 1, December.

MacEwan, A. (1975). 'Changes in world capitalism and the current crisis of the US economy', *Radical America,* **9**, No. 1, January–February.

McKinnon, R. I. (1965). 'Review article: Maizels on industrial growth and world trade: implications for economic development', *Economic Development and Cultural Change. XIV*, No. 1, October.

Maizels, A. (1963). *Industrial Growth and Growth and World Trade,* for National Institute of Economic and Social Research (Cambridge University Press).

Mandel, E. (1964). 'The economics of neo-capitalism', in R. Miliband and J. Saville (eds), *The Socialist Register 1964* (Merlin, London).

Mandel, E. (1980). *Long Waves of Capitalist Development: The Marxist Interpretation* (Cambridge University Press).

Meier, H. D. (1977). *Der Konkurrenzkampf auf dem Wettmarkt* (Campus, Frankfurt).

Melman, S. (1965). *Our Depleted Society* (Holt, Rhinehart and Winston, New York).

Mendels, F. (1972). 'Proto-industrialisation: the first phase of the industrialisation process', *Journal of Economic History, XXXII,* , No. 1.

Monthly Review (1975). 'Review of the·Month', February, reprinted in an updated version as 'Banks: staking on thin ice', in *U.S. Capitalism in Crisis,* published by the Economic Education Project of the Union for Radical Political Economics, January 1978.

Murray, R. (1972). 'Underdevelopment, international firms and the international division of labour' in *Towards a New World Economy* (Rotterdam University Press)

Myrdal, G. (1957). *Economic Theory and Underdeveloped Regions* (Duckworth, London).

Myrdal, G. (1968). *Asian Drama,* 3 vols (Pantheon, New York).

Nordhaus, W. (1974). 'The Decline in the Rate of Profits', *Brookings Papers on Economic Activity,* Number 1 (Washington DC).

Nurkse, R. (1953). *Problems of Capital Formation in Underdeveloped Countries* (Blackwell, Oxford).

OECD (1977). *Towards Full Employment and Price Stability* (Paris) ('The McCracket Report').

OECD (1979a). *The Impact of the Newly Industrialising Countries on Production and Trade in Manufactures* (Paris).

OECD (1979b). *The Measurement of Profit,* by Peter Hill (Paris).

OECD (1979c), *External Indebtedness of Developing Countries, Present Situation and Future Prospects* (Paris).

Palloix, C. (1971). L'économie mondiale capitaliste (Maspero, Paris).

Pearson Report (1969). *Partners in Development,* Report of an Independent Commission on International Development (Chairman, Lester B. Pearson) (Pall Mall Press, London).

Perlo, J. (1973). *The Unstable Economy: Booms and Recessions in the US since 1945* (Lawrence and Wishart, London).

Phelps-Brown, E. H. and M. H. Browne (1968). *A Century of Pay* (Macmillan, London).

Polanyi, K. (1957). *The Great Transformation* (Beacon Press, Boston).

Prebisch, R. (1961). 'Economic development or monetary stability: the false dilemma', *Economic Bulletin for Latin America, VI,* No. 1.

Quijano, A. (1974). 'The marginal pole of the economy and the marginalised labour force', *Economy and Society, 3,* No. 4, November.

Rehfeldt, V. (1980). 'France' in D. Seers and C. Vatisos (eds), *Integration and Unequal Development: The Experience of the EEC* (Macmillan, London).

Rosenstein-Rodan (1943). 'Problems of industrialisation of Eastern and South-Eastern Europe', *Economic Journal,* June–September.

Rostow, W. W. (1978). *The World Economy: History and Prospects* (Macmillan, London).

Schlupp, F. (1980). 'Federal Republic of Germany', in D. Seers and C. Vaitsos (eds), *Integration and Unequal Development: The Experience of the EEC* (Macmillan, London).

Schmidt, W. E. (1979). *The US Balance of Payments and the Sinking Dollar,* International Center for Economic Policy Studies (New York University Press, New York).

Seers, D. (1967). 'The limitations of the special case', in K. Martin and J. Knapp (eds), *The Teaching of Development Economics* (Cass, London); first published in Bulletin of the Oxford Institute of Economics and Statistics, 1962.

Seers, D. (1972). 'What are we trying to measure?', *Journal of Development Studies,* **8,** No. 3, April.

Seers, D. (1981). 'Massive Transfers and Mutual Interests', *World Development,* **9,** No. 6, 557–562.

Senghaas, D. (1979). 'Dissociation and Autocentric Development: Concepts, Evidence and Implications', *Forschungsbericht No. 3, Projekt: Untersuchung zur Grundlegung einer Praxisoreinteirten Theorie Autozentrierter Entwicklung,* University of Bremen, February.

Singh, A. (1978a). 'The basic needs approach to development versus the new international economic order: the significance of Third World industrialisation', *World Development,* **7,** No. 6, June.

Singh, A. (1978b). 'The reconstruction of UK industry' in F. Blackaby (ed), *De-Industrialisation* (Heineman and the National Institute for Economic and Social Research, London).

Soete, L. (1981). 'Technological dependency: A Critical View', in D. Seers (ed), *Dependency Theory: A Critical Assessment,* (Frances Pinter, London).

Soligo, R. and J. J. Stern (1965). 'Tariff protection, import substitution and investment efficiency', *Pakistan Development Review,* Summer.

Spraos, J. (1980). 'The statistical debate on the net barter terms of trade between primary commodities and manufactures', *The Economic Journal,* **90,** March.

Squire, L. and H. G. Van der Tak (1975). *Economic Analysis of Projects* Johns Hopkins University Press, Baltimore).

Steedman, I. (ed.) (1979a) *Fundamental Issues in Trade Theory* (Macmillan. London)

Steedman, I. (1979b). *Trade Amongst Growing Economies* (Cambridge University Press, Cambridge).

Sunkel, O. (1973). 'Transnational capitalism and national disintegration in Latin America', *Social and Economic Studies,* **22,** No.1.

Sutcliffe, R. (1971). *Industry and Underdevelopment* (Addison-Wesley, London).

Thoburn, J. T. (1977). *Primary Commodity Exports and Economic Development* (Wiley, Chichester).

Thomas, C. (1974). *Dependence and Transformation* (Monthly Review, New York and London).

Thurow, L. (1980). *The Zero-Sum Society: Distribution and the Possibilities for Economic Change* (Basic Books, New York).

Tinbergen, J. (1962). *Shaping the World Economy* (Twentieth Century Fund, New York).

Triffin, R. (1960). *Gold and the dollar crisis* (Yale University Press, New Haven).

Tugendhat, C. (1973). *The Multinationals* (Pelican, London).

Turnham, and I. Jaeger (1971). *The Employment Problem in Less Developed Countries*, OECD Development Centre Studies, Employment Series No. 1 (Paris).

UNCTAD (1974). *An Integrated Programme for Commodities; Reports by the Secretary General:* TD/B/C.1/166, together with Supp. 1 Add. 1, Supp. 2–5, Geneva.

UNIDO (1979). *World Industry Since 1960: Progress and Prospects* (United Nations, New York).

US BLS (1977). US Department of Labour, Bureau of Labour Studies, 'Comparative Growth in Manufacturing Productivity and Labour Costs in Selected Industrialised Countries', *Bulletin No. 1958,* Washington DC.

US Congress (1978). A Eckstein, 'The Chinese development model', in *Chinese Economy Post-Mao,* a compendium of papers submitted to the Joint Economic Committee Congress of the United States, Vol. 1, Washington DC.

USGAO (1976). report to the Congress, *US Dependence on Imports of Five Critical Minerals: Implications and Policy Alternatives,* Washington, DC.

Vaitsos, C. (1978a). 'From a Colonial Past to Asymmetrical Interdependences: The Role of Europe in North-South relations', *Paper presented at the General Conference of the European Association of Development Research and Training Institutions,* Milan, September.

Vaitsos, C. (1978b). 'Regional Integration cum/versus Corporate Integration', *Report Prepared for the United Nations Center on Transnational Corporations,* New York, January.

Vernon, R. (1966). 'International investment and international trade in the product cycle', *Quarterly Journal of Economics,* **80**, May.

von Hayek, L. (1972). *A Tiger by the Tail* (London).

Wallerstein, I. (1979). *The capitalist World-Economy* Institute of Economic Affairs, (Cambridge University Press).

Warren, B. (1980). *Imperialism: Pioneer of Capitalism* (New Left Books, London).

Westphal, L. (1978). 'The Republic of Korea's experience with export-led industrial development', *World Development,* **6**, No. 3.

Woodham-Smith, C. (1968). *The Great Hunger* (New English Library, London).

The Struggle for Development:
National Strategies in an International Context
Edited by M. Bienefeld and M. Godfrey
© 1982 John Wiley & Sons Ltd.

Chapter 2

British Industrialization and the External World:
A Unique Experience or an Archetypal Model?

J. K. J. THOMSON*

> No other country had to make its industrial revolution virtually
> alone, unable to benefit from the existence of an already established
> industrial sector of the world economy, to draw on its resources of
> experience, skill, or capital. Both the extremes to which ... British
> social development was pushed (for example the virtual elimination
> of the peasantry and the small-scale artisan producers) and the highly
> peculiar pattern of British economic relations with the underde-
> veloped world may well be largely due to this situation
>
> (Hobsbawm, 1969:20–1).

> Whatever the national affiliation of resources used, any single
> nation's economic growth has its base somewhere outside its
> boundaries — with the single exception of the pioneering nation, and
> no nation remains the pioneer for long
>
> (Kuznets 1976:287).

It is Britain's industrialization which indubitably marks the beginning of what
Kuznets has described as the 'modern economic epoch' but many of the
generalizations which serve to define this epoch do not apply to Britain's case.
This is particularly so for the matter which concerns us, the links between
British industrialization and the external world. Thus Britain's industrializa-

---

*The author gratefully acknowledges the helpful comments made on an earlier draft of this
chapter by Manfred Bienefeld.

tion, unlike all others, as the quotation from Kuznets implies, was spontaneous, and did not have its 'base' in some other economy. In addition the innovations on the basis of which Britain's industrialization was achieved were not drawn from an international 'stock of scientific knowledge' but were rather self-generated and the fruit of a gradual accumulation of skills of an 'artisanal' nature. (This was the major reason both for the slowness of the diffusion of these innovations to other countries and for the low priority given to education, and particularly to scientific education, during Britain's industrialization.) And finally neither were immigration nor the import of capital significant contributory factors to Britain's industrialization, although Britain herself, once industrialized, was to become a particularly important source of both labour and capital (Kuznets, 1976: 1–15, 285–333). One aspect of Britain's industrialization was, however, in conformity with the observed characteristics of international economic interdependence in the modern epoch: a growth in overseas trade, it is clear, played an important role in Britain's economic growth. International trade grew exceptionally rapidly in the nineteenth century and Britain's response to this is gradually also regarded as exceptional. As Mathias writes in an essay devoted to a theme similar to that of this chapter, Britain's case was 'doubly unique': 'the national response was unique ... and it was a response to a unique historical context' (Mathias, 1979:20). Indeed so much was Britain's industrial success identified with the growth of her overseas sector that free trade (although it was in fact only fully introduced when this success had already been assured) became both national ideology and, for a crucial period in the mid-nineteenth century, a supposed essential preliminary for any successful industrialization.

Our discussion will thus be narrowed because a number of the issues raised by discussions of the relationship between internal and external factors in the development process are much less relevant to Britain. (This narrowness will make possible the greater degree of detail which it is necessary to provide in view of the extent of disagreement concerning the role of overseas trade in Britain's industrialization.) To assess this role we shall first provide a survey of Britain's commercial development over the approximate period 1550 to 1870.* Our survey will be divided into two parts, pre- and post-1780, as we shall be concerned with two different questions: the link between the growth in overseas trade and the Industrial Revolution's *inception* (pre-1780) on the one hand and its *consolidation* (post-1780) on the other. This will then be used to distinguish between the 'unique' and the 'archetypal' in industrializing Britain's relationship with the external world.

---

*In fact it will be the commercial development of England and Wales, rather than Britain, with which we shall be concerned until well into the eighteenth century since statistics for British trade only exist from the mid-eighteenth century, nearly fifty years after the 1707 union with Scotland.

Overseas Trade and the Inception of the Industrial Revolution, 1550–1780

The development of British trade in the period leading up to the Industrial Revolution can be divided into three major phases in each of which the major stimulus for growth came from a distinct source (Davis, 1969b; 110–13). Central to the first phase, which came to an end in approximately 1660, was the English reaction to disruptions in her staple export trade in broadcloth to north, central and east European markets. During the second phase, which lasted from approximately 1660 to 1725, and which has been dubbed the 'Age of the Commercial Revolution', the dynamism in English trade came primarily from the development of a large re-export trade in products obtained from outside Europe. The third phase, 1725–80, which it has been customary to link most closely to the inception of the Industrial Revolution, was characterized by the growing importance of extra-European markets for a widening range of manufactured goods other than textiles. These different phases we shall describe in turn.

1550–1660

Commercially England was on the periphery of the European economy until the seventeenth century. Illustrative of this position of subordination were both the presence on English soil of privileged groups of foreign merchants who handled a large share of overseas trade — the Venetians had colonies in London until 1533 and in Southampton until 1587 and the Hanse, a trading organization based in northern Germany, was only evicted from England in 1598 (Minchinton, 1969:2–3) — and also the fact that exports consisted almost entirely of a single item, woollen cloth and, what is more, largely of unfinished cloth which was dyed, pressed and dressed in continental commercial centres before being dispatched to its final destinations.

The commercial centre to which the majority of England's cloth production was exported in the first half of the sixteenth century was Antwerp. The abrupt decline of Antwerp and of the Brabantine cloth-finishing centres which depended on it, during the second half of the sixteenth century, as a consequence of a series of political misfortunes, occasioned the first major disruption to English trade (Davis, 1969b:110). Recovery was achieved through English merchants finding new northern European entrepôts to handle their cloth — Amsterdam, Hamburg, Emden, Middleburg and Stade amongst other places — and establishing direct contact themselves with their markets (Minchinton, 1969:6). However, the outbreak of the Thirty Years' War in 1618 gave rise to a more fundamental crisis since it not only disrupted those markets to which the bulk of English cloth was sent, but also disturbed the transcontinental trade routes which were the main arteries for the European trading system. The reaction to this second crisis was of necessity more radical and took various forms. First, English merchants ceased to depend on foreign entrepôts for the completion and commercialization of their cloth; the finishing processes were increasingly carried out in England (the proportion of cloth leaving England in a finished state rose from 30 to nearly 100 per cent during the seventeenth century); and direct contact was established with the majority of markets. Secondly, new types of cloth were devised and considerable successes were achieved with these in south European and Mediterranean markets (Davis, 1969b:110–11). By the mid-seventeenth century the Mediterranean area was absorbing as large a share of England's exports as her traditional north, central and east European markets (F. J. Fisher, 1969:68). Furthermore, as a result of direct contact with a wider range of markets the size of the English merchant fleet was increased — total tonnage grew from 101,000 to between 162,000 and 200,000 tons between 1609–15 and 1660 (Minchinton, 1969:10); new types of commercial organiza-tion were developed — joint-stock companies were necessary to finance direct trading with distant markets; and finally English merchants (though by no means to the same extent as the Dutch) took advantage of their personal contacts with a growing number of trading centres to develop their role as 'middlemen'. The growing importance of this element in English trade is apparent from Gregory King's calculation that England's 'invisible earnings' amounted to £3½ million *per annum* by 1688 (Deane and Cole, 1962:34). As F. J. Fisher noted, by '1640 Londoners were re-shipping East Indian wares to Russia, Germany, the Netherlands and even to Italy and the Levant; Virginia tobacco to Hamburg; Mediterranean produce to the Netherlands; European manufactures to Africa and America'. 'Re-exports' from London had grown to be equal in value to the export of all other goods than textiles (F. J. Fisher, 1969:75).

   This last development, significant though it was for the future, had done little to reduce both the predominance of cloth in English exports and the dependence on European markets: as late as 1640 between 80 and 90 per cent of total exports consisted of woollen cloth, and between 1663 and 1669 Europe was the source of 76 per cent of the goods imported to and the destination of 91 per cent of those exported from London, which handled between two-thirds and three-quarters of English foreign trade (F. J. Fisher, 1969: 65–8; Davis, 1969a: 96–7). The basis of this first phase in England's commercial expansion was thus a traditional one. In an economic world in which trading possibilities were limited by three major factors — the high cost of transport, the lack of comparative advantage obtainable within Europe on account of the negligible extent of technological progress, the similarity of climate and economic resources of countries in the European trading area and the deficiency of suitable return-products (apart from bullion and, to a certain extent only, woollen cloth) for trading with non-European economies, the only possibility for commercial expansion lay in extensive development (F. J. Fisher, 1969: 71–5). England between 1550 and 1650 had taken advantage of the disruption of overland trade routes, as well as of a general crisis in the industries of the traditional suppliers of southern markets, to achieve commercial expansion on this traditional basis (Sella, 1968: 106–26; Cipolla, 1968: 127–45).

1660–1725

There were clearly limits to the extent to which this policy of extensive development could be pursued and could act as a source of commercial expansion. Not only did new markets, in their turn, become saturated, but also the foreign competition, which had been temporarily handicapped by political and social disturbances, revived, particularly in view of the increased emphasis being placed on industrial expansion by governments in this period.

   By the mid-seventeenth century these factors combined to check the growth in English woollen exports. There was no absolute decline but, as Davis noted, momentum was lost, 'woollen export neither advanced nor retreated — it hung fire' (1969b: 111). It was at this point that the second phase in England's commercial development began, with new forces for growth, already present in embryonic form in the 1640s, taking over the leading role from cloth exports. England's, and above all London's importance as an international entrepôt grew rapidly. The most significant element in this renewed commercial expansion was the growth in the re-export trade from extra-European territories: a variety of products unobtainable in Europe were imported to England, processed if necessary, and then distributed to European markets. Most prominent among these products were tobacco, sugar and Indian calicoes, whose consumption grew at rates which were revolutionary when the stability of the demand for European products in this period is borne in mind. England's consumption of tobacco, for example, rose from a mere 50,000 lbs in 1615 to 13 million in 1700, and a further 25 million lb of tobacco were being re-exported to continental markets by this date. The speed of this expansion is to be accounted for more by a rapid fall in price than by any sudden rise in European purchasing power. Tobacco, for example, was a luxury at the beginning of the century, costing twenty to forty shillings a lb. By the 1670s the price for the same quantity was less than a shilling. Sugar, likewise, was halved in price between 1630 and 1680, and sugar imports to London rose from 148,000 cwts in 1663–69 (annual average) to 371,000 in 1699–1701. It was the cheapness of Indian calicoes too which caused their consumption to rise from insignificant levels before the Restoration to 861,000 pieces in 1699–1701, two-thirds of which were re-exported. Davis notes that there are clear parallels between the expansion of this demand for colonial imports with that for cotton textiles after the technological breakthrough achieved by Hargreaves,

Arkwright and Crompton in the 1760s and 1770s. Both were based on a rapid decline in production costs.

The importance of these new products to the development of English trade during this period is revealed by comparing trading statistics for the turn of the eighteenth century with those just provided for the 1660s. The share of woollen cloth in English exports had been reduced to 47 per cent, that of re-exports had grown to nearly 31 per cent and that of non-woollen manufactured goods to nearly 8.4 per cent. The geographical pattern of trade had, likewise, been altered, though less markedly: Europe's share of English exports and imports had fallen to 85 and 68 per cent respectively. Clearly at this stage the extra-European areas were more important as a source of supply for products with which to trade within Europe than as a market (Davis, 1969a: 79,96–7). The expansion in England's role as an entrepôt had also occasioned further growth in the size of the English merchant fleet — from an estimated 180,000–200,000 tons in 1660 to 340,000 in 1686 (Minchinton, 1969: 12) and both this development and the increase in the re-export trade had been encouraged by the Navigation Acts of 1651 and 1660 which were designed to give a trading monopoly to English merchants and shippers in the colonial areas.

It is this second phase in England's commercial development which represented a decisive rupture with the past in so far as a definite diversification away from cloth exports occurred. Until this period 'changes in the character of English foreign trade always left untouched its central feature ... wool or woollen cloth constituted almost the whole of English exports' (Davis, 1969a). The release from dependence on cloth exports was achieved not by industrial expansion but by a concentration on commercial activities — a 'large investment in commerce not accompanied by industrial investment' — and it is for this reason that Davis favoured the use of the term 'Commercial Revolution' for these developments. 'Before the diversification of industry had made a substantial impact on foreign trade', he wrote 'and four generations before technical changes created an entirely new basis for commercial expansion, the English merchant class was able to grow rich, to accumulate capital, on middlemen's profits and on the growing shipping industry which was needed to carry cheap sugar and tobacco, pepper and saltpetre on the ocean routes' (1969a: 93–5).

1725–1780

Revolutionary though the developments of the 1660–1725 phase may have been in terms of England's commercial past they were by no means unprecedented in terms of the commercial development of Europe as a whole: London's new role had been anticipated by that played by Venice for the European economy until the end of the sixteenth century and that which Amsterdam had been playing since the collapse of Antwerp. The scale was larger because London, and Amsterdam, were now playing the role of entrepôt for an extra-European, as well as European economy. But no more than the Venetians were the English assured of continuous commercial expansion on the basis of these developments. In addition that very quality which justifies the title 'Commercial Revolution', the primacy of commercial over industrial investment in the period, caused the economic benefits of this phase of England's commercial development to be largely confined to her trading ports.

By the beginning of the eighteenth century the dynamism which had been provided by the expansion in re-exports was beginning to fade, in part as a consequence of the intrusion of new competitors in the trade — the French above all — and in part on account of the prohibition of calico imports in most countries (Davis, 1969b: 112). What is more, the tendency noted in the previous phase, for the extent of competition in European cloth markets to rise was becoming more marked. Most European countries, England included, were pursuing policies designed to encourage and protect domestic industries and it was only the tardiness of Portugal and Spain in applying such policies to their domestic and colonial markets which prevented a net decline in English cloth exports during the first half of the eighteenth century (Davis, 1969b: 101–2; H. E. S. Fisher, 1969: 144–83). As a result England's European trade was increasingly confined to areas on the periphery of the European economy and above all to countries bordering on the Baltic and Mediterranean. England's extra-European trade, however, was beginning to benefit notably from a new stimulus, namely the American colonies, which were gradually developing an additional function to that of acting as a source for tropical products for re-export. As their populations grew, from a few hundred thousand at the turn of the century, to some three million by 1774, and as their wealth grew, probably even more rapidly, they became an increasingly important market for the whole range of English manufactured goods. And this was a market in which there was no danger of either foreign competition or import substitution, for the Navigation Acts both forbade foreign intervention and restricted colonial industrial development (Davis, 1969b: 105–6).

Thus the central force in this third phase of England's pre-1780 commercial development lay in the growth in trade with her American colonies. A further boost to demand came from the (likewise protected) markets of Ireland, West Africa and India but the bulk was assured by America and, as Davis noted, England's economic growth from the second quarter of the eighteenth century 'was to an important extent a response to the colonial demands for nails, axes, firearms, buckets, coaches, clocks, saddles, handerkerchiefs, buttons, cordage and a thousand other things' (Davis, 1969b: 106). This new demand for industrial goods not only supported the quantitative growth in England's trade, but accelerated that process of change in its commodity composition and geographical pattern, already observable in the previous phase. Thus the total trade of England and Wales grew at a rate of 1.2 per cent per annum between

1700 and 1730, 1.5 per cent between 1730 and 1760, and between 1760 and 1790 *British* trade grew at 1.8 per cent per annum (Deane and Cole, 1962: 29). The share of woollen cloth in England's total exports (including re-exports) continued to fall — to a level of just under 27 per cent in 1772–74. There was no absolute decline but it is evident that the cloth industry had not participated in the general expansion. Re-exports, on the other hand, did share in the growth even though their relative position improved only marginally — from the 31 per cent recorded in 1699–1701 to 37 per cent in 1772–74. Finally, and all importantly, the category 'general manufactures', with woollen cloth excluded, expanded impressively, greatly improving its relative position to account for over 27 per cent of total exports by 1772–74 (Davis, 1969b: 120). For the first time not only in England's commercial history but also in that of Europe as a whole a substantial and dynamic market had been found for the whole range of pre-industrial manufactures. At the same time the change in the geographical pattern of trade also accelerated. By 1772–74, the extra-European areas had become the main suppliers of imports — their share of the trade having grown to just under 53 per cent, but the greater discontinuity was the rise in their role as a market (we have noted above the previous shortage of suitable products for extra-European markets): they were absorbing nearly 38 per cent of total exports by this date (Davis, 1969b: 119).

Thus if the second phase of the commercial expansion had been characterized by the growth in England's role as entrepôt, and by the primacy of commercial over industrial investments, the third had been distinguished, above all, by the growth in the export of manufactured goods to extra-European markets. The growth in exports was clearly a major factor enabling a significant enlargement of Britain's industrial sector. An important step had been taken towards Britain's becoming 'the workshop of the world'. No better illustration could be provided of this than the details of changes in the commodity composition of English imports: in 1699–1701 the shares of manufactures and raw materials in total imports were 33 per cent and 42 per cent respectively, but by 1772–74 the share of the former category had shrunk to a mere 15 per cent whereas that of the latter had risen to 61 per cent (Davis, 1969b: 104).

Trade Growth and the Conception of the Industrial Revolution: the Traditional View

But did this last phase in Britain's commercial expansion, or indeed any of the three phases which we have described, contribute significantly to the Industrial Revolution? We shall first consider the arguments in favour of such a linkage and then those against.

As we have already noted neither the first nor the second phases of the commercial expansion had led anywhere unusual and they had, besides, been anticipated by the experiences of other commercial centres. The third phase did, however, we have emphasized, have unique characteristics in so far as it was based on an unprecedented rise in the demand for the whole range of industrial goods produced within the pre-industrial economy. Effectively England had developed a new type of relationship with the extra-European world. Extensive geographical areas had been transformed to fit in with the requirements of the English economy and thereby two of those major shortcomings of the pre-industrial trading system described earlier had been overcome — the range of goods which could be traded within Europe had been boosted by the growth in re-exports, and the problem of the lack of return-products for trading with extra-European economies had been solved by the creation of settlements in the New World which required the whole range of European manufactured goods. Britain's commercial advance was in consequence particularly widely-based, the ports of Bristol, Liverpool and Glasgow sharing in the general expansion. England's was the first case of a national economy, rather than of a trading city, achieving predominance in the world economy and this distinction was of significance. Trading cities had *participated* in the world economy but a national economy's combination of commercial, industrial and political power provided scope for a *domination* of world trade.

Despite all that was new and dynamic in the English commercial expansion, however, contemporaries had doubts about the possibility of its continuation. The growth had been in great part dependent on the enforcement of a monopolistic trading system between Britain and her colonies and the breaking of this monopoly would, it appeared, occasion a commercial collapse, for there was no evidence of the existence of any fresh source for expansion, in embryonic form, as there had been during the previous phases of commercial growth. With the American War of Independence, which was fought by the colonists in part to escape their commercial subjection, these doubts appeared to be on the point of being realized. 'The prospects for trade based on privilege and non-economic influences', Davis noted, 'were becoming gloomy indeed during the last quarter of the eighteenth century' (1969b: 117). The war was lost by Britain, of course, but the expected commercial collapse *did not occur*. And here lay the major grounds for linking the growth in overseas expansion with the Industrial Revolution. It was apparent that British industries had outgrown the need for special protection and it seemed self-evident that it was production for overseas markets which had made possible such a coming of age. The new industries which were to figure prominently in the Industrial Revolution had 'cut their teeth' on the basis of overseas demand: they had achieved economies of scale, received the necessary incentive to mechanize, and thereby been liberated from the need for protection. Davis himself originally subscribed to this viewpoint. 'By the time privilege was threatened', he wrote, 'towards the end of the century, England's cotton and metal industries had transformed themselves out of all recognition; they were poised ready to invade not only the European but all other markets with their irresistible bundles of products of the

Industrial Revolution' (1969b: 117). The final major limitation on commercial expansion in the pre-industrial period had been removed: a continuous growth in trade could now take place on the basis not of monopoly but of reductions in costs.

The Traditional View Challenged

This view of the centrality of overseas trade both to Britain's overall growth process in the eighteenth century and to the actual conception of the Industrial Revolution has been held by many. 'If a spark was needed this is where it came from', E. J. Hobsbawm concludes after presenting figures which show an 'export-industries' ' category to have grown at some ten times the speed of a 'home-industries'' one in the period 1700 to 1780 (1969:48). But in recent years the idea of an export-stimulated, or of a predominantly export-stimulated, Industrial Revolution has been subjected to considerable criticism. In this subsection I shall provide a résumé of the basic quantitative evidence which relates to this issue and then summarize these recent criticisms of the idea of a 'foreign trade hegemony' (Thompson, 1973: 94) in the conception of the Industrial Revolution, leaving to the final subsection of this first half of the chapter the formulation of my own position in this debate.

On first appearance quantitative evidence seems to support the traditional view. Thus Deane and Cole's calculations show that the expansion in exports was a faster rate than that of national income in the eighteenth century — a fivefold to a threefold increase — and that as a consequence the share of exports in national income grew considerably during these years — from between 5 and 6 per cent in 1688, to around 14 per cent between 1780 and 1810 (1962:28). This improvement in their relative position in national income implies, of course, that exports may have played a leading role in Britain's economic growth and this possibility becomes all the more probable when figures are disaggregated and the growth of exports is related purely to the industrial sector of the economy. Manufactured goods predominated in domestic exports, forming 85 per cent of the total, and one-third of Britain's total industrial production was exported. The correlation between the growth in trade and that of industrial output is sufficiently close for Deane and Cole to feel justified in using the better recorded trade figures 'in conjunction with other indicators ... to form some impression of the speed and directions of [total] industrial change' (Deane and Cole, 1962: 42). If the industrial sector, in turn, is disaggregated then the links between trade and growth appear yet more emphatic. Industries dependent purely on the domestic economy for their raw materials and sales grew far more slowly than those participating in overseas trade: Mathias, using Deane and Cole's figures, calculated that whereas the former had grown from an indexed base of 100 in 1700 to 152 by 1800, the latter had more than quintupled to a figure of 544 over the same period (1969: 103–4).

The timing of the (considerable) fluctuations in the rate at which overseas trade grew would seem, too, to provide support for the hypothesis of a trade-induced industrialization. And this is the case whether one attributes the beginnings of the Industrial Revolution to the 1740s (as Deane and Cole are inclined to), or to the 1780s (the decade favoured by most historians), since an acceleration in the rate of expansion in exports occurred in both decades. Between 1745 and 1760 the growth rate rose to 3.9 per cent per year (in contrast to the low rate of 0.5 per cent per year recorded between 1700 and 1745) and between 1779 and 1802 the annual rate of increase was even higher, 4.9 per cent (Deane and Cole, 1962: 49).

The immediate impression which these figures provide of an overwhelmingly strong link between trade and economic growth in the eighteenth century needs to be qualified, however, on two major accounts. First, the progress illustrated by the figures was from a relatively low starting point and Britain's export/national income ratio, until the 1780s, when a rapid improvement began, stood at levels which would be judged low if comparisons were made with those recorded by underdeveloped countries beginning their industrialization in this century. It is true that at the end of the century the ratio had grown to 14 per cent according to Deane and Cole, and even higher, to nearly 18 per cent, according to Crouzet, who in a very recent article has argued that the British economy was export-led at this stage, but it is important to emphasize that this higher ratio was a temporary phenomenon only, which was reversed after 1810 (the significance of this will be discussed in the second half of this chapter), and that this growth — and this according to all accounts — occurred *after* the conception of the Industrial Revolution and, if we accept Crouzet's arguments, was largely in *consequence* of the technological breakthrough in textile production (Crouzet, 1980: 48–93). The second qualification which needs to be registered concerns the distinction made both by Mathias and Hobsbawm between export- and home-industries. This division is a confusing one for inclusion in the former category requires mere *participation* in, not total concentration on, export trade and thus a large part, though unfortunately an unquantifiable part, of its impressive growth would have consisted of production for the home market. As for the home market category, in this case the dice are stacked in the opposite way, for a grouping which excludes all industries involved in foreign trade inevitably catches the most sluggish elements in the economy, such as the food-processing industries. These sluggish sectors of the economy, however, were not necessarily the least significant quantitatively. Indeed, in contrast to the 'export-industries' the starting point for these lagging 'home-industries' was without doubt a high one.

Some 'editing' of the quantitative evidence is thus, it is apparent, necessary if a balanced view of the role of overseas trade in the conception of the Industrial Revolution is to be obtained. This type of 'editing', though, has possibly been taken to an extreme by Paul Bairoch. In a recent article he has subjected what

have always been regarded as the two principal links between overseas trade and
the Industrial Revolution — in terms of capital and demand — to most
exhaustive quantitative assessment and reached conclusions on both issues
which are far removed from the traditional position. The relative unimportance
of the capital-accumulation link he demonstrates in two ways — first, by making
macroeconomic calculations of the maximal profits which could have resulted
from the expansion in trade, he shows that, even on the unlikely assumption that
all commercial profits were invested in industry, the proportion of this
investment to total domestic capital formation would have been small; and
secondly he emphasizes how unrealistic such an assumption would be in view of
the fact that the majority of studies on capital formation during the Industrial
Revolution show that the importance of capital of commercial origin was small in
comparison with that proceeding from self-finance through the ploughing back
of profits (Bairoch, 1973: 545–51). The export-led industrialization thesis
Bairoch attacks in a similar manner from two angles. He emphasizes, first, that in
the eighteenth century, in contrast to the modern world, industrial units did not
need to be particularly large in order to achieve economies of scale. The same point
has been made by others (Davis, 1979: 67) and it should be noted for it is another,
major, example of the distinctiveness of economic circumstances for an early
industrializer. In the context of Bairoch's argument its significance is fairly self-
evident: the contribution of overseas trade was not needed to provide that
(relatively low) level of demand necessary for the achievement of economies of
scale. And secondly Bairoch shows, with the help of some elaborate macro- and
microeconomic calculations, that the share of exports in total demand was very
small. Again Bairoch is not alone in asserting the pre-eminence of the domestic
market in the conception of Britain's industrialization (John, 1969: 165–83;
Eversley, 1967: 220–5) but his calculations give a degree of precision to the issue
which was previously lacking: the internal market, he shows, was responsible for
a minimum of 88 per cent and a maximum of 96 per cent of the overall increase in
national income between 1700 and 1780, and he thus feels justified in concluding
that 'the influence of overseas markets was very limited, marginal we might add',
and he makes this statement with all the more certainty in so far as his analysis of
certain key sectors of English industry suggests, too, that there has been a
tendency to overrate the importance of overseas demand. In the expansion of
the iron industry, he shows, the demand contributed by overseas trade was an
important, but not the preponderant influence; in that of woollen cloth he
demonstrates that there was an 'inverse proportion between expansion of
production and expansion of exterior markets'; and even in the case of cotton,
always regarded as the classic example of trade-induced growth, he shows that,
although growth was to become dependent on overseas sales, this was only after
1790, and that the early expansion and, crucially, that which led to the major
technological breakthroughs, was based on the domestic market (Bairoch, 1973:
553–71).

The 'extremity' of Bairoch's position results from his reliance, above all, on an aggregate, national income approach in his analysis of the links between exports and demand and capital formation. The danger of failing to relate the size of the export sector to that of the economy as a whole has just been stressed, but Bairoch's reluctance to disaggregate results in another type of bias, for in all aggregate figures the influence of the agricultural sector, still the largest sector in the English economy, was inevitably preponderant. If the industrial sector is isolated, and there clearly is some justification for such an isolation since it is the transformation of this sector which is of primary concern when the conception of the *Industrial* Revolution is under discussion, then the link between the expansion in overseas trade and the economic growth of the eighteenth century becomes more apparent. Bairoch discounts, too, most non-quantitative links between overseas trade and Britain's growth. Thus he argues that there was no connection with the growth of banking, the British banking system having developed *after* the Industrial Revolution. But this view, it would seem, involves some oversimplification, for a formal banking system was anticipated by a complex, informal credit network to which merchants involved in overseas trade were certainly important contributors, both with respect to the supply of capital and commercial expertise. Likewise Bairoch neglects the role played by imports from extra-European areas in stimulating new consumption habits among Europe's population and thus reinforcing that growth in domestic demand to which he attributes such prominence. Consumers became accustomed to the availability of a wider range of consumption goods and altered their expenditure patterns in accordance. De Vries has argued that the 'demonstration effect' of these non-Western imports was possibly more important than the benefits obtained from growing colonial demand for traditional European products in so far that not only was social behaviour changed but efforts were made by European manufacturers to develop imitations. There is no more important example of such an 'imitation', of course, than the English cotton industry, an imitation which was facilitated by government prohibition of the import of printed Indian calicoes from 1720 (de Vries, 1976: 145–6). Similarly Bairoch's point about economies of scale requires some refinement. It is true that these, in so far as they related to manufacturing costs, were achieved at a fairly low level of production by individual industrial concerns but economies of scale in the transactions sector of the economy were not so easily obtained. It was only on the basis of handling a large and growing trade over many years that the English economy gradually came to rival the Dutch as an entrepôt and provider of commercial services and the possession of an advanced, and competitive, transactions sector certainly lowered costs for English manufacturers with respect to the provision of credit, access to market knowledge, insurance, transport and raw material supply.

The criticisms of the traditional view presented so far have been mainly related to the *size* of the stimulus provided by exports to the British economy in the eighteenth century. Deane and Cole, however, by relating movements in the terms of trade between Britain and the protected trading zone to fluctuations in the rate of growth of British exports, throw light on another question, the *source* of the dynamism in the overseas sector. It emerges from their analysis that the major bursts of expansion in British exports followed unfavourable movements in the terms of trade which increased the purchasing power of the Atlantic trading partners. The implications of this are clear. The roots of the growth in overseas trade have to be sought 'at home rather than abroad' (1962: 82–8). Acceptance of Deane and Cole's hypothesis does not, of course, entitle us to discount the role of overseas trade in Britain's industrialization. Even if the main stimulus to the growth of trade did come from internal dynamism it was the possession of large and protected markets which ensured that the British economy did not run up against supply and market limitations such as those which had stunted previous commercial expansions in European history. The issues does serve to remind us, however (and this, clearly, is one of the 'unique' characteristics of industrializing Britain's relationship with the external world) of the still limited scope for commercial expansion that existed during this period. In the absence of a more advanced economy, demand from which might have served as an exogenous stimulant to economic growth, industrialization was ultimately dependent on internal forces. The centrality of this factor, isolation, to the exceptional form which industrialization took in Britain, is well expressed by Hobsbawm in the quotation with which this chapter is headed.

Wherever the 'motor' for the trade growth was situated, however, Deane and Cole's quantitative evidence, as we have noted, does illustrate, at least, a definite parallelism between movements in exports and progress in the economy as a whole and this synchronization might itself seem an important argument for those who believe in a significant export role in Britain's economic growth in the eighteenth century. It is largely on this ground that Ralph Davis, in a most important study which he completed just before his death, separated himself from the views of Bairoch and Eversley. 'I cannot wholly agree', he wrote, 'with the reasoning of those writers who have approached the matter from the side of demand, for the modest industrial expansion of the middle decades of the eighteenth century did ... derive a good deal of its support from export trade. 'But if Davis disagreed with Bairoch and Eversley on this question it was not to revert to the traditional view of a largely export-conceived Industrial Revolution. On the contrary, he had other reasons, which were both more subtle and final than those of Bairoch, for rejecting such an approach. The mid-century expansion, he argued, quantitatively significant though it may have been, was not of a nature to 'lead to the Industrial Revolution'. Involved were traditional industries, using traditional techniques: economic growth but not industrialization. By contrast the expansion of the 1780s was of a different kind, since it was based on the rapid expansion of a new industry, using a new technology and organization of production, with new customers, and the progress of this industry set 'in motion a movement towards a new kind of industrialism in other spheres which in time engulfed the whole of economy and society'. But this expansion, in *contrast* to that of the mid-century whose consequences Davis believed were unrevolutionary, was *not* linked to a previous expansion in overseas trade. The stimulus came from the supply side, 'from technical change in the manufacture of cotton', the lack of link with any previous commercial expansion being revealed by the fact that it was 'an industry which hitherto had been almost negligible and one which with its old techniques would have remained so'. And even after the technological breakthrough had been achieved the stimulus for expansion in the early years came (and Davis agreed with Bairoch on this) from the home market (Davis, 1979: 9–10).

Conclusion on the Role of Overseas Trade in the Conception of the Industrial Revolution

Ultimately, it has become apparent, the nature of the decision about the importance of overseas trade in Britain's Industrial Revolution depends on definitions. If it is to Deane and Cole's 'Industrial Revolution' that credence is given — an Industrial Revolution which began in the 1740s, accelerated in the 1780s, and whose defining characteristics were that 'for the first time in English history, population began to expand continuously without being checked by an output barrier' (Habbakuk and Deane, 1963: 68) — then, it is evident, and Davis's research would support this, that overseas trade played a crucial role. 'This was the sector', write Habakkuk and Deane, 'which developed increasing returns by carrying the products of British industry to mass markets, which reaped the advantages of new resources and technical progress in primary producing countries and which created a world demand for new products' (1963: 77). If, on the other hand, it is the definition of the Industrial Revolution to which Davis evidently subscribed that is favoured, a definition in which the emphasis is placed on the economic and social discontinuities consequent upon major technological changes in a small selection of industries (Davis, 1979: 10, 62), then overseas trade's role was at the most only an indirect one. The source of the discontinuity came from the supply side, the main market produced for in the early years was the domestic, and the external world's contribution was limited to the provision of the essential raw material, cotton (an important role, of course, but not a dynamic one) and to the fact that it had been a 're-export' from the east, Indian calicoes, which had contributed to fostering this domestic demand (de Vries, 1976: 146). Rather than representing a continuation of mid-century trends Davis's Industrial Revolution represented a reversal, for not only did the main source for growth shift from the export to the domestic market but there was also a revival in the share of textiles in total trade (this had been declining until 1772–74 we have noted) and advance was on a narrow front (it was the wide range of the industrial demand for all types of manufactured goods which had distinguished the mid-century expansion). 'The Industrial Revolution', Davis wrote, 'in fact involved a movement on to quite different paths of industrial development from those that were being successfully followed' (1979: 64–5).

Which definition is the more acceptable? That which has found most favour, and in the opinion of this writer justifiably, is the one to which Davis subscribes, for the type of economic growth which, for Deane and Cole, represents the beginning of the Industrial Revolution was not unprecedented — in previous periods of European history prolonged economic expansions had occurred and indeed such an expansion was occurring in other parts of Europe, as well as in Britain, in the mid-eighteenth century without leading to technological change. Deane and Cole themselves seem aware of this weakness in their definitions: 'if we were to judge by the only national output series dating right back to the Middle Ages ... the statistics of tin output,' they note, 'we should have to set the beginnings of the upward movement in the middle of the seventeenth century' (1962: 60). The in-considerable-part-trade-induced industrial growth of the mid-century was growth of the old kind, extensive and capital-widening, rather than intensive and capital-deepening, and it was to continue as such well into the nineteenth century. This Davis emphasized: 'the industries that had been in the van of progress in the 1770s in making buttons, locks, nails, firearms, cutlery, tools and the like changed little over the following 80 years ... The Industrial Revolution passed them by, and they were not transformed before the latter part of the nineteenth century, and then often by imitating American or European examples' (1979: 65). Hobsbawm, once again, has made the same point most concisely: 'What was needed was not any kind of expansion, but the special kind of expansion which produced Manchester rather than Birmingham' (1962: 50).

If we accept, then, the definition of the Industrial Revolution to which Davis subscribed the role of foreign trade in its conception appears to be secondary. The overseas expansion was an enabling factor 'without which the industrial take-off might not have proceeded so fast or gone so far' (1979: 10).

Trade and the Consolidation of the Industrial Revolution, 1780–1870

If, as we have just seen, there are reasonable grounds for questioning the importance of overseas trade in the inception of Britain's Industrial Revolution there are none for doubting its importance in its consolidation. This Davis himself conceded: 'once home demand ceased to be sufficient to maintain the momentum of growth of the most advanced industries, around 1800,' he wrote, 'overseas trade did begin to play an absolutely vital direct part in their further expansion' (1979:20). Again, though, as we shall see, the *extent* of the importance of overseas trade has been a matter of dispute.

In this section we shall first present the quantitative evidence about the performance of Britain's overseas sector between 1780 and 1870. This done, we shall interpret this growth, identifying the distinct sources of commercial expansion which, as in the period 1550–1780, predominated at different stages of Britain's industrialization. Finally we shall assess the importance of overseas trade in the consolidation of the Industrial Revolution before returning to the question posed in the title of this chapter.

The Figures

As mentioned in the previous section, an acceleration in the rate of expansion in overseas trade coincided with the period which has been selected by most historians as representing the beginning of the Industrial Revolution. It should be noted, however, that the rapidity of the growth in exports during these years is in part to be explained by the fact that trade had stagnated in the 1770s on account of the American War of Independence and if growth rates over the period 1771–1802 are averaged then a lower figure of 2.6 per cent (in contrast to the 4.9 per cent registered between 1779 and 1802) is arrived at (Deane and Cole, 1962: 49). Growth rates for different periods between 1801–80 are as follows: 1801–31, 2.9 per cent; 1811–41, 4.0 per cent; 1821–51, 4.7 per cent; 1831–61, 4.5 per cent; and 1841–70, 4.9 per cent (Deane and Cole, 1962: 311). The overall pattern is comparatively clear. After the exceptionally rapid expansion of the 1779–1802 period growth rates settled at a rather lower level for some thirty years and then accelerated gradually from the mid-1830s to reach a peak in the 1870s. It was only with this acceleration that the growth rate of exports came to exceed that of national income and so the ratio of exports to national product remained virtually constant during the first half of the century at between 9 and 11 per cent (a slight decline from the figure of 13–14 per cent recorded at the end of the eighteenth century), before rising steadily to a peak of 23 per cent in the 1870s (Deane and Cole, 1962: 29). The mid-century expansion in exports was all the more significant in so far as it occurred at a time of decline in the rate of population growth. Thus the annual average growth in the volume of exports per head increased from 1.8 per cent between 1800–4 and 1830–34, to 4.0 per cent between 1830–34 and 1843–47, to reach 5.9 per cent between 1843–47 and 1857–61 (Bairoch, 1976: 192).

That gradual shift both in the commodity composition and in the geographical pattern of British trade which we have traced from the mid-seventeenth century continued during these years, as is revealed by tables 1 and 2. By the turn of the century, it is apparent, the general manufacturing category had achieved predominance and extra-European markets were on the point of

Table 1   Commodity composition of British exports and re-exports 1784–86 to
1854–56

	Woollens %	Re-exports %	Other Manufactures %	Foodstuffs %	Raw Materials %
1784–6	22.6	20.9	42.4	7.5	6.6
1804–6	13.3	19.3	57.8	5.6	4.0
1834–6	11.9	18.1	62.7	2.8	4.5
1854–6	7.1	17.0	60.2	4.7	11.0

Source: Davis, 1979: 94–109

Table 2   Geographical pattern of British exports and re-exports 1784–86
to 1854–56

	Europe, including Near East %	Outside Europe %
1784–6	53.0	47.0
1804–6	50.3	49.7
1834–6	46.5	53.5
1854–6	45.8	54.2

Source: Davis, 1979: 88–91

doing so. The share of re-exports in total trade declined, however, to levels
below those recorded in the second half of the seventeenth century, and that
steady, relative decline in the share of woollens in British exports, which
originated in the mid-seventeenth century, continued.

Disaggregation of the 'manufacturing' category in British exports reveals the
predominant role played in the growth by a small number of particularly
dynamic industries. Thus the export of cotton goods, which had been minimal
before the 1780s, came to account for nearly one-half of all British exports
during the first half of the nineteenth century, and largely on the basis of
overseas demand, with the share of overseas sales in total production rising
steadily, from 15 per cent in 1784–86, to 61 per cent in 1849–51, to reach a peak
of 79 per cent in 1899–1901 (Davis, 1979: 66; Deane and Cole, 1962: 187). If
other types of textile production, including woollens, are added to the totals for
cotton then it becomes apparent that the textile sector exercised an extraordinary dominance over British trade during this period, accounting in 1834–36 for
79 per cent of all manufactures exported (Davis, 1979: 25 n.1). In the 1830s,
however, cottons attained their peak of relative importance and that gradual

acceleration in the growth rate of British trade which can be traced to this decade was occasioned by a certain broadening in the range of exports. The share of other types of textiles in total trade was growing and the export of metal products, which had grown but modestly until 1830 (the share in total exports of the iron and steel industries between 1814–16 and 1830 had only risen from about 6 to 10 per cent), began to expand rapidly. Thus the share of *all* metal industries in total exports grew from 12 per cent in 1814–16, to 19 per cent in 1844–46 and to 27 per cent in 1854–56, and that of iron and steel grew from the 10 per cent recorded in 1830 to 14 per cent in 1870, by which date exports were accounting for over 40 per cent of the gross product of this industry. This growth in the exports of metal products was largely a consequence of the rise in overseas demand for refined metals, semi-finished and constructional goods and industrial machinery — these categories experienced an eightfold rise in overseas sales between 1814–16 and 1854–56 — and as such (in line with Davis's arguments) it represented a break with the mid-eighteenth century metallurgical expansion which had been based largely on the export of finished metal goods. Exports of these did continue to rise, but at a slower rate, a mere doubling of overseas sales being achieved between 1814–16 and 1854–56 (Deane and Cole, 1962: 31, 255; Davis, 1979: 25–7).

One general trend which characterized most branches of British exports was the declining share of finished goods in total trade. Thus the share of raw materials and textile yarns in all exports and re-exports increased from 10 per cent in 1784–86, to 21 per cent in 1824–26, and to 31 per cent in 1854–56 and, if trade with Europe is isolated, then this trend becomes all the more marked, the percentages for these three dates being 18, 37 and 57 respectively (Davis, 1979: 34). The commodity composition of British imports changed too with that movement away from manufactured goods in favour of raw materials, which we have noted in the eighteenth century, being sustained. The share of manufactured goods declined continuously, both in relative and absolute terms, until approximately 1820 and then experienced a slight recovery, but only to some 5 per cent of the total by the 1850s, and the share of raw materials grew continuously until 1834–36, to reach a peak of just over two-thirds of the total trade. The third major category, that of foodstuffs, shrank continuously too (but less sharply and not absolutely) until about 1830 and then recovered to account for 36 per cent of total imports by 1854–56. This recovery is to be accounted for not by a rise in the consumption of luxury foods (the cause for growth of this category in the seventeenth and eighteenth centuries) but by a rise in the import of what Davis refers to as 'temperate foodstuffs' — grain, meat and dairy produce — as a consequence of the rapidity of population growth. The share of this category in total food imports, which had stood at around 10 per cent for many decades, rose to 31 per cent in 1844–46 and 43 per cent in 1854–56. This increase, and its timing, as we shall emphasize, were of some significance. 'It was ... from the middle of the nineteenth century', Davis wrote, 'that Britain finally moved to the kind of import-dependence in which starvation, rather than inconvenience or even poverty, became the alternative to importing' (Davis, 1979: 36–8, 51–2).

One category, and an increasingly important one, which does not appear in Table 1, is invisible earnings. We have noted a steady growth in these for earlier phases in Britain's commercial expansion and there was an acceleration in the pace of this advance during these years. The primary element in the growth consisted in earnings from shipping. Britain's success in this field was overwhelming and the dominance achieved in the age of steam was to be even greater than that of the age of sail — by the last decade of the century Britain possessed more tonnage than the rest of the world put together. In some ways this success represented an inheritance from the entrepôt trading cities of the pre-industrial period. As Peter Mathias remarks, 'one of the essential objectives behind the Navigation Acts of the seventeenth century, of reserving British trade for British ships, was thus continued with increasing success into the hey-day of the free trade economy'. The 'export' of commercial, financial and insurance services followed naturally from the rise in the importance of British shipping. It is no coincidence, Mathias notes, that 'Leadenhall Street and Gracechurch Street in the City (the location of many shipping line headquarters) are immediately adjacent to Lombard Street and Cornhill'. Earnings from the provision of these services were supplemented, and supplemented to a growing extent, by interest paid on overseas investment: by the mid-century some £200 million had accumulated, and by the outbreak of the First World War the figure had grown to £4000 million and the interest on this sum by then was sufficiently large, Mathias suggests, to compensate for 'even quite a marked degree of failure in the competitive standards of some British export industries' (Mathias, 1969: 314–16).

Interpreting the Figures

It is from the varying commodity composition, rather than the rates of growth, of British overseas trade that the changing role of the external world in Britain's industrialization is best perceived. If the last phase of the pre-Industrial-Revolution commercial expansion was characterized by a gradual broadening of the range of industries involved in overseas trade as a consequence of the opening up, and expansion, of new markets in the New World — in other words an extensive type of commercial development similar to that undertaken between 1550–1650 — that of the period 1780–1840 was a consequence of the transformation of the supply situation in a narrow range of British industries, and above all in textile production. Advance was on a narrow front, and based on a combination of cost-cutting and monopoly. Technological change, for a short period only, had given Britain a comparative advantage over all other nations. As Davis wrote, 'the Industrial Revolution ...

involved the rapid creation of a unique set of material factor endowments in Britain — factories and machinery, labour specialised to serve them and entrepreneurs with skill in organising them — a generation before other countries had them' (1979: 72). It was on the basis of these exceptional advantages that overseas trade kept pace, but only just, with rising national income until about 1840. The growth rate in exports then accelerated until the mid-1870s and this acceleration, we have noted, was a consequence of some diversification in British trade and a renewed dynamism in overseas markets. The major cost reductions had been achieved but British exports were boosted as a consequence of the rising demand from other countries which themselves were not industrializing. As Davis wrote, the diversification of export trade, which had been interrupted towards the end of the eighteenth century, was resumed again on the basis of the rolling mill, the steam hammer and the locomotive engine' (1979: 29). The dynamic element in British exports was increasingly the demand for goods needed by industrializing countries — raw materials, semi-finished goods and machinery. Capital exports, as a response to the same phenomenon, were increasing too, we have noted. It was not that Britain had ceased to be 'the workshop of the world' but rather that to that role had been added those of hardware store, merchant's warehouse, banker and shipper, and for Europe at least, we have seen, these new roles had already become predominant by the 1840s.

The Importance of Overseas Trade to the Industrial Revolution's Consolidation

The growth of British overseas trade had kept pace with that of national income until the 1840s and had exceeded it (considerably) between the 1840s and the 1870s. By this stage 'the sheer weight of foreign trade in the sum total of British economic activity gave it a dominant role' (Deane and Cole, 1962: 311). But was the role of overseas trade likewise 'dominant' during the years 1780–1840, the 'heroic' period of the Industrial Revolution? This is less evident for two major reasons. The size of the export sector remained, we have noted, small in comparison with that of national income and, as we have already emphasized, the domestic market provided a more than adequate basis for achieving economies of scale in the industries whose technologies were changing. The first point is made forcefully by J. Mokyr who, having shown that the ratio of exports both to the national product and to industrial product actually declined during these years, concludes that, 'had export demand been the one factor that singled out Great Britain as the economy most suitable to industrialisation, one should observe that the role of exports increased when industrial growth was fastest, that is, after the Napoleonic wars' (1977: 987).

Mokyr's point is a convincing one and it would clearly be unreasonable to argue that British industrialization was trade-led during these years. Nonetheless, as we shall attempt to show, the contribution of overseas trade was

absolutely essential to economic growth during these years, more apparently so
when this sector's contribution is judged in terms of the limitations which
existed on *any type* of economic progress at this precocious stage of modern
economic growth rather than in terms of those utilized by economists in this
century — foreign trade proportions, economies of scale, comparative
advantage etc. In this section we shall first demonstrate how the exceptional
circumstances in which Britain industrialized limited the possibilities of growth
in her export sector and then demonstrate how this growth, limited though it
was by these circumstances, was indispensable to Britain's industrialization.

An insight into the exceptional nature of the international economic
circumstances at the time of Britain's trade expansion is provided by an analysis
of her terms of trade with her trading partners. The most notable characteristic
of these was that there was a steady movement in her trading partners' favour
throughout the century, particularly so during the period which concerns us.
The change was no less than 100 per cent between 1800 and 1860. As Mathias
writes, 'industrialization did not produce accumulating surplus, but a mounting
deficit on trade right up to the 1914–18 war' (1969: 304). The explanation for
this sustained deterioration is quite simple — the large productivity gains on
which the export successes of Britain's leading industries were based were not
matched in those countries from which she was importing. Raw materials (by
far the major item in the import bill as we have noted) continued to be
produced in the same way, experiencing only a slight decline in price during
these years. The phenomenon underlines the importance of 'invisible earnings'
which more than served to balance trade; it underlines too the extent of the
achievement of Britain's leading export industries in financing the majority of
imports despite falling prices. Our figures for exports have been based on
value, rather than volume, and the rise in the latter was many times more
impressive than that of the former. To take just one example, the 'official' value
of the export of cotton fabrics (in the formulation of which no allowance was
made for price reductions) rose from £18,235,000 in 1814–16 to £132,816,000 in
1854–56 whereas the declared values (actual values) only rose from £16,378,000 to
£27,601,000 during these years (Davis, 1979: 17). Above all, though, thephe-
nomenon provides an insight into the unique circumstances in which Britain
industrialized, circumstances which conditioned the nature of her industrialization process. First, it is clear, these circumstances severely limited the extent to
which Britain could specialize in industrial activities. As the supply of imports
from trading partners was relatively inelastic and not, apparently, liable to any
considerable economies of scale, there was clearly a limit on the
extent to which specialization could be carried without causing severe
balance-of-payments problems. Of necessity, then, Britain's industrialization was broadly-based and relatively balanced — hence the importance to it
of a continued expansion (which was noted by Davis) in that wide range of
industries which had been developing on the basis of old techniques since the

mid-eighteenth century, and which depended, increasingly, on domestic demand; hence too, and yet more crucially, the importance of that gradual increase in agricultural productivity which can be traced back to the same period. Indeed no better example could be found of an 'industry' in which supply from international sources was relatively inelastic, and liable to few economies of scale, than agriculture, and it is clear that the achievement of British agriculture in feeding the majority of a rising population until the 1840s — when 'temperate' food imports began to rise, we have noted — was a quite essential element in Britain's industrial success. Total demand for food remained vastly greater than that for any other commodity and large imports of food would have placed an impossible burden on Britain's balance of payments (even relatively slight grain deficiencies, such as those of 1829–31, were extremely costly). In fact, as Davis emphasized, 'it is unlikely that European surpluses would have been found, at any possible price, to supply the needs of such a fast-growing population in Britain': in other words if British agricultural productivity had not increased 'the Industrial Revolution would have been stopped in its tracks by failure to feed its urban masses' (1979: 40–1, 63, 71).

The major reason for the limited extent of the growth in overseas trade during the period 1780–1840 has thus been revealed. It was the backwardness of the rest of the world which gave Britain an industrial monopoly but the same quality severely limited the extent to which international economic specialization could be carried. But why was this limited export expansion indispensable to Britain's industrialization? In view of what has just been written it might be inferred that the resources which were devoted to the boosting of production for export would have been better utilized in the development of import-substitutes and in industrial diversification for the home market. This issue too was raised by Davis. Having listed the gains accruing from the overseas trade expansion — the acceleration of the movement of the labour force from low- to high-productivity sectors of the economy, the important contribution to the maintenance of the pace of Britain's industrial advance, particularly in the new sectors, which made possible a continuous modernization of techniques, the contribution to maintaining relatively high levels of employment at a time of most rapid expansion in the labour force and the gains (apparent from the rising overseas capital holdings) from the positive balance of payments — Davis questioned whether similar, or better, results could not have been attained by a broader domestic investment programme and a policy of import-substitution. But as he pointed out such a question assumes that import substitution was possible and that alternative domestic investment opportunities existed, but neither, it seems, was the case. Thus of the 80 per cent of the imports which can be classified in terms of substitutability only about one-sixth, Davis calculated, were substitutable by British goods in 1784–86 and a bare tenth in 1814–16 and 1854–56. And alternative, high-yielding investments simply did not exist. The major economic problem in this period, as it had been in the eighteenth century, was one of a shortage of investment opportunities, and of capital surplus rather than scarcity. The range of new, high-yielding investments was extremely narrow before the Railway Age. The 'modern' section of the British economy was a minority one still and the alternative to investing in it (for the sake of export expansion) would have involved capital widening in a large range of low-productivity industries. As Davis wrote, 'from 1815 until the railway age was well under way, Britain was again an under-employed economy, with both savings and labour in excess supply. The mechanism for transforming savings into investment which could then provide employment worked very imperfectly'. The contribution of overseas trade to Britain's industrialization is thus only properly understood if the severe limitations on any type of economic growth in a period in which the extent of technological progress was still most limited is borne in mind. Without the growth in overseas trade it is doubtful whether Britain would have been able to employ her factors of production fully and achieve continuous growth in national income per head despite the rapidity of the growth of population (Davis, 1979: 71–6). Britain's monopolization of world export markets, for textile production above all, during the period 1780 to 1850 made possible a maximization of the limited possibilities that existed at this stage in Europe's industrialization for modern industrial development.

It might appear that we have been guilty of inconsistency in so far as we have stated that Britain's growth during this period was of necessity balanced and widely-based, with agriculture and a wide range of traditionally organized industries participating most vitally, and yet we have insisted too on the indispensability of the contribution of overseas trade, which was the leading influence behind the unbalanced growth of a small range of new industries. But this apparent paradox, rather than being a consequence of our inconsistency, is an illustration of how the nature of Britain's industrialization was conditioned by the limited possibilities existing for economic growth at the time. Growth in such restricted circumstances could only be achieved by maximizing the growth possibilities available both for new industries *and* old. Rather than favouring one type of Industrial Revolution over another, that of Rostow and Davis over that of Deane and Cole, it should be recognized that Britain experienced both varieties of economic growth during these years, and needed both to achieve a large degree of her industrialization before the Railway Age. It required the technological breakthroughs in textiles, in iron production and in the provision of steam power; it required too that steady, broadly-based industrial and agricultural expansion on the basis of old techniques which can be traced back to the early eighteenth century. That all these forces only resulted in a slow rate of economic growth — 'in the end', write Habakkuk and Deane, '... the most striking characteristic of the first take-off was its gradualness' (1963: 82) — is yet one more proof of the strength of the barriers to economic growth which continued to exist in this period.

Unique or Archetypal?

As has gradually emerged from our analysis there was far more of the unique than of the archetypal in industrializing Britain's relationship with the external world. Not only, as we noted at the beginning of this chapter, are certain, frequently important types of international economic link quite absent from Britain's case —technological transfer, capital movements, immigration — but also in most aspects of growth in respect of which comparisons can be made Britain's experiences look diametrically opposed to those of later industrializers, and in particular to those of underdeveloped countries in this century. This is hardly a cause for surprise. The major international problem encountered by Britain was the exact reverse of those encountered by underdeveloped countries in the process of industrialization today. Whereas the latters' difficulties derive from the extent of their backwardness in relation to the already industrialized nations, Britain's, we have noted, came from the extent of her advance over other economies, and the solution was provided when her isolation was broken as a consequence of other nations industrializing. Predictable though these contrasts are, however, we shall list the principal ones. Whereas in Britain's case, we have noted, a major restriction on growth was the limited range of investment opportunities and the lack of a backlog of inventions to be drawn from the 'worldwide stock of useful knowledge' (Kuznets, 1976: 285), in the case of underdeveloped countries 'the range of possibilities open to investors ... is seemingly infinite' and the choice so wide that confusion and misallocation of resources can and have resulted (Hirschman, 1978: 19–20). Capital shortage was evidently not a problem during Britain's industrialization, but neither is it, some development economists now believe, the prime obstacle to the early stages of growth in underdeveloped countries. If the ability to invest, or entrepreneurial skill (Hirschman, 1978: 1–6, 11–28) is regarded as a limiting factor, in this connection, once more the nature of Britain's problem was quite different. There was no shortage of entrepreneurial ability, to judge from the breadth of the economic advance, but there was an evident lack of scope for the exercise of this ability because of the limited extent of technological development. The social and cultural preparations for industrial growth had, it is evident, *preceded* (rather than *followed* as may be the case in underdeveloped economies) the technological ones. And finally the problems which beset Britain in connection with her trading relationship with the external world were quite the reverse from those which tend to arise in the cases of underdeveloped countries in this century. The extent of the growth of Britain's trade, we have noted, was limited by the inability of new trading partners to achieve economies of scale in their exports and in some crucial cases, it seems probable, to provide goods at any price. Underdeveloped countries, on the other hand, tend to find that whereas they can obtain any imports which they require from overseas suppliers at competitive and stable prices they have difficulty in developing export products of their own which are subject to economies of scale and disposable in international markets. Hirschman, on these grounds, compares the situation of underdeveloped countries unfavourably with that of 'pioneer industrialisers who could — and can — always find foreign markets for the output of their newest inventions and creations', but he neglects to consider that, in the case of the first industrial nation at least, the growth of overseas trade was limited by one difficulty not encountered by late-industrializers — the high price, and possible non-availability, of imports (Hirschman, 1978: 171–2)

The nature of Britain's industrialization, our analysis suggests, was unique and thus provides little basis for direct comparisons. Above all it was unique for two reasons: the fact that the means for achieving economic growth were so restricted — it was this which was the basic cause for Britain's industrialization being gradual and widely-based; and the fact that Britain's advance was so solitary. The extent of Britain's industrial lead over the rest of Europe had widened, not narrowed, by 1850 (Crouzet, 1972: 104–9) and, as Mathias notes, a lead of this kind was unprecedented and has not been repeated (1979: 18). It is this second factor which is the cause of modern theories of trade having only a limited application to Britain's case. It was on the basis of comparative advantage that Britain traded during these years but it was a comparative advantage of an unstable and temporary kind. She enjoyed an advantage in the manufacturing of textiles and it was largely on the basis of this that exports progressed between 1780 and 1840, but this advantage did not provide a permanent basis for specialization. And that acceleration in the rate of growth of exports after the mid-1830s was a consequence, too, of unusual and temporary factors. Central to it was a demand for equipment and resources from other industrializing economies and in so far as the process of equipping was successful such an expansion could not last long. In fact only one characteristic of British trade during these years was to show powers of endurance — 'invisible exports', which were growing in importance through-out these years, have continued to play a crucial role for the British economy to this day and it is London's role as a world financial centre that more than anything else has continued to symbolize that internationalism which it is believed characterized British industrialization from its inception. The survival of this aspect of Britain's Industrial Revolution, whereas other elements have proved more evanescent, is comparatively easily explained. Those industries on which Britain's international success was based during the early stages of the Industrial Revolution had characteristics which made their introduction into other countries relatively easy — the cost of their capital equipment was low and economies of scale could be achieved by comparatively small plants. By contrast the scale of activities necessary to achieve significant economies of scale in that wide range of commercial activities which contributed to invisible earnings was far larger. Britain, by first obtaining a dominating position for herself in world markets, and then by servicing the commercial and industrial needs of other countries during their industrialization processes, built up an almost unassailable comparative advantage in these fields. In this case at least, then, the role of the external world in Britain's industrialization had a consequence of a permanent nature. The phenomenon again, however, is an isolated and unusual one and there have been few modern imitators who have developed this specialization. Parallels are more likely to be found in the pre-industrial period — the continuance of Amsterdam's commercial predominance as Europe's major entrepôt until the disruption of the 1789–1815 period, and long after the decline of the importance of Holland as an industrial centre, being probably the closest one.

Bibliography

Bairoch, P. (1973). 'Commerce international et genèse de la révolution industrielle anglaise', *Annales E.S.C.* **28**, 541–71.

Bairoch, P. (1976). *Commerce extérieur et développement économique de l'Europe au XIXe siècle* (Montin, Paris).

Cipolla, C. M. (1968). 'The economic decline of Italy', in B. Pullan (ed.) *Crisis and Change in the Venetian Economy in the 16th and 17th Centuries* (Methuen, London), pp. 127–45.

Crouzet, F. (1972). 'Western Europe and Great Britain: "catching up" in the first half of the nineteenth century', in A. J. Youngson (ed.), *Economic Development in the Long Run* (George Allen and Unwin, London).

Crouzet, F. (1980). 'Toward an export economy: British exports during the Industrial Revolution', *Explorations in Economic History*, **17**, 48–93.

Davis, R. (1969a). 'English foreign trade, 1660–1700', in W. E. Minchinton (ed.), *The Growth of English Overseas Trade in the 17th and 18th Centuries* (Methuen, London), pp. 78–98.

Davis, R. (1969b). 'English foreign trade, 1660–1700', in W. E. Minchinton (ed.), *The Growth of English Overseas Trade in the 17th and 18th Centuries* (Methuen, London), pp. 99–120.

Davis, R. (1979). *The Industrial Revolution and British Overseas Trade* (Leicester University Press).

Deane, P. and Cole, W. A. (1962). *British Economic Growth, 1688–1959* (Cambridge University Press).

Eversley, D. E. C. (1967). 'The home-market and economic growth in England, 1750–1780', in E. L. Jones and G. E. Mingay (eds.), *Land, Labour and Population in the Industrial Revolution* (Edward Arnold, London), pp. 208–59.

Fisher, F. J. (1969). 'London's export trade in the early seventeenth century', in W. E. Minchinton (ed.), *The Growth of English Overseas Trade in the 17th and 18th Centuries* (Methuen, London), pp. 64–77.

Fisher, H. E. S. (1969). 'Anglo-Portuguese trade, 1700–1770', in W. E. Minchinton (ed.), *The Growth of English Overseas Trade in the 17th and 18th Centuries* (Methuen, London), pp. 144–64.

Habakkuk, H. J. and Deane, P. (1963). 'The take-off in Britain', in W. W. Rostow (ed.), *The Economics of Take-Off into Sustained Growth* (Macmillan, London), pp. 63–82.

Hirschman, A. O. (1978). *The Strategy of Economic Development* (W. W. Norton, New York).

Hobsbawm, E. J. (1962). *The Age of Revolution 1789–1848* (Mentor, New York).

Hobsbawm, E. J. (1969). *Industry and Empire: An Economic History of Britain since 1750* (Penguin, London).

John, A. H. (1969). 'Aspects of English economic growth in the first half of the eighteenth century', in W.E. Minchinton (ed.), *The Growth of English Overseas Trade in the 17th and 18th Centuries* (Methuen, London), pp. 165–83.

Kuznets, S. (1976). *Modern Economic Growth: Rate Structure and Spread* (Yale University Press).

Mathias, P. (1969). *The First Industrial Nation* (Methuen, London).

Mathias, P. (1979). 'British industrialization: unique or not?', in P. Mathias, *The Transformation of England* (Methuen, London), pp. 3–20.

Minchinton, W. E. (1969). 'Introduction', in W. E. Minchinton (ed.), *The Growth of English Overseas Trade in the 17th and 18th Centuries* (Methuen, London), pp. 1–63.

Mokyr, J. (1977). 'Demand vs. Supply in the Industrial Revolution', *Journal of Economic History*, **37**, 981–1008.

Sella, D. (1968). 'The rise and fall of the Venetian woollen industry', in B. Pullan (ed.), *Crisis and Change in the Venetian Economy in the 16th and 17th Centuries* (Methuen, London), pp. 106–26.

Thompson, A. (1973). *The Dynamics of the Industrial Revolution* (Edward Arnold, London).

Vries, J. de (1976). *The Economy of Europe in an Age of Crisis, 1600–1750* (Cambridge University Press).

The Struggle for Development:
National Strategies in an International Context
Edited by M. Bienefeld and M. Godfrey
© 1982 John Wiley & Sons Ltd.

Chapter 3

The Japanese Development Model Re-examined: Why Concern Ourselves with Japan?

MARTIN BRONFENBRENNER

Japan is a developed country, and has been one for the greater part of the twentieth century. It may therefore seem strange or at least antiquarian to consider Japan as a usable model for present-day developing countries in Asia and elsewhere.

But Japan remains the outstanding if not the only case of sustained economic growth under capitalism by a non-European country without European colonization, and without unhealthy or paralytic dependence on the West. For this reason there is continuing interest in Meiji Japan (1868–1912) as a possible development model. (Contemporary Japan, meaning Japan since the Second World War, is admittedly much less relevant.)

What Japan Did: General Aspects

A conventional view is that Japan, during the reign of the Meiji Emperor, maintained an average growth rate of 3.5–4.0 per cent annually. This long reign, whose dates we have already given, includes a Rostow 'take-off' period for the Japanese economy, a period sometimes specified as 1885–1905. By modern standards, the annual average growth rate is less impressive than the time span which it covers, within which business cycles were few and relatively mild. Since population was growing too, the per capita growth rate was perhaps 1 per cent lower on average.

Prior to 1905, according to the analysis of Ohkawa and Rosovsky, Meiji era growth was not dualistic. That is to say, Japan's traditional industries, such as agriculture and handicrafts, shared in the overall growth. After that approxi-

93

mate date a certain degree of dualism developed, with traditional industries declining while modern ones advanced at increasing rates.

A newer view, howeever, stems from Nakamura's work on Japanese agriculture in the Meiji period. It is on balance less laudatory than the conventional one we have just outlined. Nakamura has found no structural or technological base for any rapid growth in agriculture, which was then the major part of the economy. He believes that the base-period agricultural output (at the beginning of the Meiji era) was higher than estimated — the underestimate resulting from tax-evasion considerations on the part of the peasantry. If Nakamura is more nearly right than his several critics, the 'conventional' growth rates, both total and per head, are from 1.0 to 1.5 per cent too high per year, and there may have been no Rostow-type 'take-off' at all.

What Japan Did: International Aspects

Whatever stand we may take on the 'Nakamura controversy', there is significant agreement on the international aspects of Japanese growth in the Meiji era.

First, even at that time Japanese growth was not and could not be resource-based. Japan had a trained labour force, some coal and water-power, but little more on-shore natural resources. Even Japan's arable land area is variously estimated at only 15 to 18 per cent of the total, although mulberrry leaves for silkworms can be raised on slopes too steep for ordinary agriculture. At the start of the Meiji era, Japan had considerable copper and some silver and gold — which were largely exhausted early in the development process. The western motives for forcing the opening of Japan to trade were not resources in the ordinary sense but the provision of food, water and rest for ships and crews engaged in Pacific whaling and in the profitable China trade, including protection from storms and foul weather.

Secondly, Japanese growth was 'into' and not 'out of' the international economy, from which Japan had been deliberately insulated for 250 years of Tokugawa shogunal rule. In fact, Japanese growth was export-led, violating to some extent the precepts of Adam Smith's *Wealth of Nations* (Book III), which proposes that agriculture and domestic industry should precede trade in any growth process. As a result of unequal treaties imposed by the western powers, moreover, Japanese import tariffs were limited to 5 per cent until 1899, approximating a full free trade regime. No foreign aid was offered at any time, and foreign loans were minimal until after the Russo-Japanese War (1904–05). While some of these loans were strategic — for example, Japan's first railroad, a twenty-mile line connecting Tokyo and Yokohama, was financed with British capital — debt service charges were never a burden.

Japanese Advantages

As far as I have yet been made aware, no western critic or commentator of 1860 or 1870 vintage considered *ex ante* the 'fantastic' possibility of Japanese economic development outpacing that of India or China. It seems to have required the Sino-Japanese War (1894–95) to awaken the West in general to what had been taking place on the 'far side' of the Pacific Ocean. But historical hindsight now displays to us *ex post* a number of important developmental advantages possessed by Japan at and before the Meiji 'restoration' of 1868, advantages not available to most of today's developing countries more than a century later. We shall discuss seven of these advantages.

First, Adam Smith's optimism on the subject of development is summarized in a passage from a lost lecture which antedates the *Wealth of Nations,* but which is reproduced in Cannan's introduction to his classic edition of that volume:

> Little else is required to carry a state to the highest level of opulence from the lowest barbarism, but peace, easy taxes, and a tolerable administration of justice, all the rest being brought about by the natural course of things.

(I should myself argue, in common with many contemporary writers, that more is required than Smith realized, particularly by way of population control and socio-psychological self-confidence, but this is not the issue here.) It further seems that, in the Smithian trio of 'peace, easy taxes, and a tolerable administration of justice', the first is by all odds the most important, especially if the peace is maintained domestically and not imposed by some foreign 'imperialist'. Japan had had in 1868 more than 250 years of peace, enforced by the Tokugawa family of *shoguns* rather than by foreign invaders (as in India), and managed to survive the Meiji restoration (of imperial rule), plus the disturbed decade which followed the restoration, with only sporadic, superficial and local disturbances of the peace. The contrast with many Latin American or African countries is revealing, the more so as Japan's taxes were not particularly 'easy', and Japan's administration of justice was not particularly 'tolerable', either before or immediatley after the restoration.

A comparison with Mao's China may also be in point. Mao's accession to power in 1949 ended some 110 years of almost unbroken civil and international warfare in China. It has been followed by remarkable developmental achievements. These are often ascribed to Chinese Communism and particularly to those aspects of Maoism embodied in the *Little Red Book.* Adam Smith's analysis, and the Meiji record in Japan, both suggest that Chairman Mao's economic achievement may be due less to his ideology than to his prior accomplishments of unification and pacification.

Secondly, Japan's geographical position was at the end of the line connecting Western Europe with India, Southeast Asia and South China. This meant, given the transportation and communication systems of past centuries, that the West came to these other countries before coming to Japan. When westerners arrived, or at any rate shortly thereafter, the Japanese were already aware of their conquests and depredations in India and Southeast Asia, and did not underestimate the intruders as the Indian, Chinese and other Asian rulers had done. During the century ending in 1650 the main Japanese concern was with the threat from Spain and Portugal. In the nineteenth century the major menace was perceived to be Russia, either by itself or in alliance with China. (The nationalist Yoshida Shoin saw the Russians, from Siberian strongholds, as invading Japan either as a forward base from which to conquer China or alternatively in a joint Russo-Chinese expedition after China had been conquered directly.) Great Britain was also seen as a threat, following the Opium War with China (1840) and the establishment of a colony and base at Hong Kong.

Thirdly, during the centuries following the extirpation of Spanish and Portuguese influence, the Japanese had retained watchful contact with the West. Japan's so-called 'Christian Century' (1543–1638) had left a miniscule Dutch base at Nagasaki, or rather at Deshima, then a small island in Nagasaki harbour. This residual 'window on the West' had attracted a small group of *Rangakusha* or 'Dutch scholars'. Their immediate interest was the Dutch language, through which they obtained insight into not only Dutch but general western European culture. Their special interests seem to have been mathematics, astronomy, medicine, gunnery, history and geography; many of them became, both before and after the Meiji restoration, advocates of westernization, both for its own sake and as a defence against western imperialism.

Fourthly, Japan was a beneficiary of certain special historical circumstances in the world history of 1850–75, which drew the western powers' attention away from colonization in Japan at the time when it might easily have succeeded. In the Russian case, we may mention the Crimean War (1854–55) and the Russo-Turkish War (1877–78). In the British case, in addition to the Crimean War, there was the Indian Mutiny (1857). In the France of Napoleon III, the Crimean War again entered, followed by the rise of Italy and Prussia, France's unfortunate intervention in Mexico, and the final debacle of the Franco-German War (1870–71). The United States could hardly have been a threat in any case, but for completeness' sake we might mention the Civil War of 1861–65 as further minimizing American freedom of action in the Pacific.

Fifthly, the middle third of the nineteenth century was a period of low tariffs and minimal non-tariff protection. The Cobden–Chevalier Treaty between Britain and France can be called the high-watermark of the Free Trade movement. Near-freedom of trade permitted Japan to take full advantage of its principal competitive advantage in export trade, namely its low wage level, and export enough to pay for capital goods and technical assistance on a commercial basis without gifts or loans. (Japan did not become a net food importer until the 1890s.) Japan's principal exports became silk and silk fabrics, which alone sufficed to finance some 40 per cent of Japan's imports.

Indeed, Japan became as monocultural in silk as Colombia or Brazil would later become in coffee, Bangladesh in jute, Thailand or Burma in rice, Cuba in sugar, or any 'banana republic' in bananas.

Sixthly, in addition, a number of special circumstances favoured the expansion of the Japanese silk industry. In the first place, the increased availability of cotton imports from the United States and India freed marginal 'waste land' for the growing of mulberry trees as food for silkworms. At the same critical period, the competitive silk industries of China, France and Italy were temporarily incapacitated, permitting the Japanese to rise to a dominant position in world markets. In the Chinese case, the problem was the major fifteen-year civil war known as the Taiping Rebellion, centred in the Yangtze Valley, which was also the centre of China's export trade in silk. In the French and Italian cases, the problem was a silkworm disease called *pébrine*, whose eventual conquest is associated with the researches of the great French chemist and bacteriologist Pasteur. Finally, artificial fibres (especially rayon) had not yet been developed. (It is interesting to speculate upon what the economic history of Meiji Japan might have been like had rayon been developed a half-century, or even a quarter-century, before it actually was!).

Finally, demography was also on Japan's side, and in two respects. While Japan's population roughly doubled in the forty-five years of the Miji era (the reign of the Meiji Emperor Mutsuhito) the annual rate of increase was slow, and the farm population was maintained. There was therefore no pile-up of unemployables, intellectual or otherwise, in the Japanese cities of the Meiji era. There might of course have been such a pile-up — in fact, one can hardly imagine the pile-up having been avoided — had Japanese labour been organized to demand high wages. In fact, no labour aristocracy developed in Meiji Japan, which has become a type case for the so-called Lewis–Ranis–Fei theory of growth with large supplies of unskilled workers. (Japan grew because wages remained low; India failed to grow, and developed chronic under-employment, because urban wages rose.)

It is important, in considering Japanese labour history, to realize that no viable alternative to the capitalist pattern of growth was visible, except for reversion to Tokugawa feudalism. No socialist alternative to capitalism was available outside books. (Once again, it is interesting to speculate on the consequences for Japanese labour history and economic growth had the Russian revolution occurred, say, immediately after the assassination of Czar Alexander II by Narodnik revolutionaries in 1881.)

Returning to the facts: far from the dangerous combination of a labour aristocracy and a mass of urban unemployables, Japan was fortunate enough to develop labour shortages in its skilled trades in the early twentieth century, as a concomitant of the definitive shift of the Japanese economy from 'traditional' to 'modern' sectors. It appears to have been as a reaction to the resulting shortages of skilled and semi-skilled labour in the modern sector that Japan developed what has become a distinctive 'Japanese' pattern of permanent employment, seniority and other aspects of industrial relations. Far from being, as was once believed, a feudal residue, this pattern apparently made good economic sense almost from the outset.

Basic Decisions

At this point in the analysis, it is important to thread our way between two opposing errors. One error is to regard the accomplishments of Meiji Japan as nothing more than the passive acceptance of the advantages of Japan's peculiar position in world geography and history in the middle third of the nineteenth century. The opposite and more frequent error is to ascribe these accomplishments to a group of unified and doctrinaire supermen or philosophers — meaning either the Japanese people as a whole or the 'Meiji statesmen' (*Meiji no Genkun*) in particular.

The facts appear to be rather that without certain basic decisions — we shall list six of these — having been made decisively and correctly, the Meiji era political and economic affairs might have failed miserably despite all Japan's advantages. And at the same time nothing in the record suggests either that the Japanese were supermen or that the Meiji statesmen — any more than their American equivalents, the 'founding fathers' of 1770–1800 — were a unified or doctrinaire body of political or economic geniuses. 'National-character' explanations of historical events are always tempting but always tautological, and the Meiji statesmen were a group of practical pragmatists fired by private, class and regional ambitions along with their patriotic nationalism, and unified in little beyond their desires to oust the Tokugawa shoguns and avoid western political (but not necessarily cultural) domination.

Of the six decisions mentioned above, the most important, looking back from a century later, seems to have been less economic than political in nature. This was the decision to centralize the Japanese government and with it the Japanese economy. A multitude of squabbling, fighting, and protectionist feudal lords or *daimyo* had preceded the Tokugawa shogunate. Any return to that system, which in one form or another had prevailed from 1100 to 1600, would have imperilled Japan's internal peace, and certainly invited appeals for foreign intervention, as had occurred in India.

A second, and related, set of primarily political decisions resulted not only in the reconciliation of the *samurai* élite in the process of economic modernization but also in their actual enlistment in the economic effort. These *samurai* or *bushi* were Japan's highest social class, traditionally warriors but largely converted (under peacetime conditions) to bureaucrats with military training. They were supported by rice rations from the particular lord or *daimyo* to whom they had pledged their loyalty; the sale of whatever rice a *samurai* family did not itself eat provided additional (low) incomes. While the merchant class was at the bottom of the social hierarchy, it had been gaining in economic power and prestige throughout the Tokugawa period, while the proud *samurai* had been losing relative (and possibly even absolute) status during the last century of Tokugawa rule. The great majority of the Meiji statesmen were 'lower' *samurai*; the overthrow of the Tokugawa shogunate should not be regarded as equivalent to a western-style class or social revolution by which merchants 'overthrew' feudal lords.

As an aspect of centralization, the first basic decision mentioned, the *daimyo* were persuaded to cede their fiefs to the central government and to the Emperor. But what was to happen to the subordinate *samurai* that these *daimyo* had supported? At first the central (imperial) government simply took over the *daimyo* obligations. Later the ration was shifted from rice to money; then it was commuted from money income to wealth in the form of a lump-sum 'payment' of national bonds. These bonds were denominated in national currency, which was depreciating in consequence of overissue in what would later become the typical developing-country pattern, but even as wasting assets they were usable as business and particularly financial collateral.

Armed with these bonds and their superior status, many *samurai* swallowed their pride and went into business and finance as managers and entrepreneurs. Many, perhaps most of them, failed, but many of Japan's rising financial oligarchy were of *samurai* origin. (Other *samurai* joined the armed services, the police, the bureaucracy, the educational system and the free professions.) All of this contrasted with other societies in which business was left to religious, racial, immigrant and other low-status minorities, and in which the upper classes remained aloof from or even hostile to the development process.

Meiji Japan's third basic decision was to set up pilot plants for industrial activities at public expense, and for the benefit of the rising capitalist class. Japan had no Mahatma Gandhi and no abstract fear of 'the machine'. The need for some degree of industrialization seemed obvious, both in the military and civilian economies. But mere transplantation of foreign plants and methods had already been found counterproductive. Japan's wages were lower than western wages and Japan's capital costs were higher, and so some form of intermediate or 'appropriate' technology was sought. No doctrinaires for private enterprise or laissez-faire, the Meiji statesmen and their subordinates took over the start-up losses of adjustment. They selected and hired foreign experts on short-term bases and always subordinate to native Japanese executives. They selected (mainly from *samurai* families) Japanese students for foreign training, and financed this training themselves. They imported capital equipment, either to be used as imported for production or as models for modification. The first Japanese railroads, textile mills, shipyards and arsenals were founded in this way. Private plants which were founded subsequently could profit by the pilot plants' experience and avoid the pilot plants' mistakes; in some fields the pilot plants themselves were later sold to favoured capitalist concerns at substantial losses during peiods of budgetary stringency, and not without suspicions of corruption.

Similar pilot-plant methods, incidentally, were later used during and after the Second World War by the United States government in the production of synthetic rubber, nuclear power, communications satellites, etc., where what had to be 'transferred' were not foreign methods but primarily impractical laboratory prototypes. During the Second World War, also, the American military paid special attention to captured Japanese blueprints involving American products and patents which of course the Americans already had. Why this interest? Because both Japan and America were faced with raw material shortages, but the Japanese had surpassed the Americans in many fields as regards problems of design and process modification to meet these shortages as they developed.

The fourth major decision on our list is the provision of industrial capital from public sources. While Japan had developed high private saving and investment rates well before the Meiji 'restoration' — during the Tokugawa quarter-millenium of peace and security — the Meiji government supplemented these private resources by gifts and loans, by operating public plants at a loss, and by 'infrastructure' investments in railroads, roads, harbour facilities, schools, hospitals, etc. Rosovsky had estimated that approximately 40 per cent of physical capital investment during the Meiji era was public rather than private; the percentage rises to 50–55 if military capital equipment is included in the computations.

But capital is not created out of thin air, and the question naturally arises: How was all this financed, without aid from abroad and without a crushing burden of debt service?

Almost all the public financing was domestic, and only a relatively small part represented the 'forced frugality' of inflationary financing of public budgetary deficits. (True, the Japanese price level roughly doubled during the forty-five years of Meiji; this inflation is relatively slow by contemporary standards!) Japan's frequent budget deficits were financed primarily by non-inflationary sales of public securities, chiefly to the rising financial oligarchy. (Both bonds and currency, incidentally, were backed by gold after the Chinese War of 1894–95 had yielded Japan a large gold indemnity.)

But the main source of public finance was taxation, and the principal tax source was a land tax. Tax theory tells us that such a tax falls on landowners — including, in Japan, the small peasant family farmers. And even in the 'large landlord' cases, land taxes could in fact be shifted back to the tenant cultivators, because the land market was usually a disequilibrium one. That is to say, the demand for land at going rentals characteristically outran the supply, giving landlords a wide choice of tenants. This excess demand for rented land made tax shifting to the cultivator almost automatic, despite the analysis of equilibrium economic theory. What this account adds up to, in economic terms, is that publicly furnished capital for Japanese industrialization came from the Japanese peasantry, either as landowners or as tenant farmers.

From physical capital we pass to human capital. In a public-policy context, this means primarily the nature and efficiency of the educational system. The fifth basic decision of the Meiji statesmen, then, was the encouragement of an extensive (but élitist) educational system. Actually it was a dual system, with both public and private facilities at most stages. One basic aim was universal literacy for both sexes; the requirement of six years of compulsory education was well enforced for boys, less so for girls, particularly in rural areas.

Above the elementary level, educational segregation took over, partly on an academic basis and partly on an economic one. For poor children, particularly the children of poor farmers, there was a two-year terminal programme. For the élite there was a pyramid of middle schools, high schools, and a very few colleges and universities, with Tokyo Imperial University at its apex. More important perhaps, there arose a network of technical schools, both public and private, for a wide variety of technical specialities and with entry at various points. The upper ones included some university-grade academic work in a limited range of subjects; the higher normal schools and commercial schools are examples. This network of specialized technical training schools is described by Passin as the best such system in the world — better even that the German system on which it was modelled. After the Second World War it was abolished by the American Occupation in the interests of educational democracy, but Premier Hayato Ikeda tried vainly to revive it during the 1950s in the interest of *Hito-zukuri* (the creation of manpower).

Not the least of the advantages gained by Meiji Japan from its system of technical schools and colleges was the avoidance of the 'labour aristocracy' problems which have plagued many developing countries. The system reduced the need for apprenticeships, which are often controlled by trade unions on a restrictive basis.

The last of our six decisions of the Meiji statesmen — and the one which provoked the deepest divisons among and between them — was the avoidance, or rather the postponement, of military adventurism. In view of Japan's later history, we shall discuss this decision in more detail than its direct economic importance may warrant.

Japan's most acute foreign-policy issue of the late 1870s was a proposal to invade and dominate Korea. In disgust with the decision against such an invasion, many disafffected *samurai*, commanded by the general (Saigo Takamori) of the anti-Tokugawa forces in the Meiji restoration itself, rebelled in 1879 and were suppressed in a short but bloody civil war fought mainly on the southern island of Kyushu and known as the Satsuma rebellion.

Korea had long been an invasion route between continental Asia and the Japanese islands. The Mongol Emperor Genghis Khan had used it in the twelfth century with an invasion force largely composed of conscript Chinese and Korean soldiers and sailors. In the late sixteenth century, the Japanese warlord Toyotomi Hideyoshi had used the Korean route in an ill-advised attempt to overthrow the Ming dynasty and conquer China. Now, in the nineteenth century, there was widespread fear of Russia and/or Chinese invasion through Korea before Japan was ready to repel it. The Korean invasion was proposed as a preventive measure aimed at gaining time.

Meanwhile a decadent Korean kingdom, unconscious of its own economic and military weakness, had been openly scornful of Japanese westernization. Japanese ambassadors to the Korean court at Seoul had in fact been insulted for yielding to western pressure. The desire to use Japan's modern weapons to invade Korea and teach the Koreans a lesson was ostensibly prompted by these insults. Perhaps more important economically, however, was *samurai* under-employment in the 1870s — despite out second decision above — and the desire of the *samurai* to restore their pre-Tokugawa military glory.

The majority view of the Meiji statesmen, however, was that Japan was not ready for any such adventures. Japanese forces might be bogged down in Korea (as Hideyoshi's had been 300 years before). The invasion might attract Chinese or Russian intervention and become a larger scale war than Japan could manage. Perhaps more important still in the eyes of the anti-war factions, the concentration of Japanese military and naval forces in a Korean adventure would leave the Japanese mainland open to invasion by whichever foreign powers might wish to attempt it.

From the viewpoint of economic development, it is certain that a Korean war in the late 1870s would have delayed the economic progress of the Meiji era by concentrating Japan's limited resources on military glory. In the longer run it might have weakened rather than strengthened Japan even if it had been militarily successful. This argument too was not overlooked by the peace party among the Meiji statesmen.

The Standard of Living

Two key questions are often asked by economists who discuss Meiji Japan, both in my own country (the United States) and in the developing countries of the twentieth century:

(1) What if anything (beyond statistics) did Meiji-era growth mean to the living standard of the ordinary Japanese, whom we shall call Taro Suzuki?

(2) How was the Meiji-era pattern of Japanese growth related to Japanese imperialism, which indeed began during the Meiji era and continued afterwards?

Let us consider these questions in order: The Japanese working-class living standards, estimated as real per capita consumption, appears to have begun to rise in urban areas no later than the 1890s. The increase in the countryside appears to have begun a generation later (First World War or the 1920s). However, since the cities absorbed all the increase of Japanese population (which roughly doubled during the Meiji era), and since the measured urban living standard was higher than the measured rural one throughout the period, the overall measured standard of living rose quite steadily. But for a representative rural Suzuki family either a move to the city or a fifty-year wait would have been necessary for its living standard to rise above its 1868 level, despite Meiji growth. This holding down of the rural living standard accords, as we have already pointed out, with Lewis–Ranis–Fei prescription for development with 'unlimited' supplies of labour, and also avoids the labour 'dualism' which developed in many countries, where an organized urban labour force, or at least the employed portion thereof, forms a labour aristocracy.

The question is sometimes asked whether Japanese peasants were forced off the land by any analogy to the Western European enclosure movements. The answer is that there were neither enclosures nor widespread agricultural mechanization. Population growth, plus primogeniture, produced a constant stream of younger family members from the countryside to the towns and cities, quite as though there *had* been enclosures or mechanization. But to complicate the matter further, those leaving the countryside seldom *felt* forced out. Many elder sons, in fact, wanted to leave but could not, because of traditional Japanese standards of filial piety. To some extent, also, the migrants were self-selected on a meritocratic basis, with the brightest of the children going to the city for schooling or jobs and seldom returning.

The official Japanese attitude toward the people's living standards was an ambivalent one. The official line expressed pride in westernization, civilization, progress, culture. But it also expressed pride in the Japanese ability to flourish under lower standards and greater hardships than effete westerners could endure. The armed services, as in other countries, preferred country boys to city boys for military training — including officer candidacy. (They also favoured natalism and opposed family planning — again, like military services in other countries with neighbours more populous than themselves.) The various Meiji governments opposed trade unions and strikes in Japanese industry, and tolerated conditions which conventional economists call both 'monopoly' and 'monopsony' exploitation. Low wages and docile workers of course held down costs, increased export competitiveness, and decreased Japan's import dependence for finished goods. More important perhaps, a docile labour force avoided or postponed class conflicts which would have diluted partiotism and national unity.

Imperialism and War

Our second question is about imperialism and war. We shall subdivide it further as between Meiji-era wars and later ones, and we shall claim that the peculiar Meiji-Japanese pattern of development had little to do with either.

Both of the Meiji-wars were originally about the control of Korea. (We have seen that the Meiji statesmen had decided against an invasion of Korea as early as the late 1870s.) The Sino-Japanese war of 1894–95 was ostensibly to secure Korean independence from a Chinese 'protectorate'. The Russo-Japanese war of ten years later decided which of the two powers would include Korea in its sphere of influence. (Japan did not annex Korea formally until 1910, five years after the end of the war with Russia.)

It is certainly true that Japan wanted Korea as a source of cheap rice, as an outlet for 'surplus' population, and as a dumping ground for consumer goods in periods of recession. (Japan's increasing population had made it a net rice importer in the early 1890s, and at the same period the recovery from the so-called 'Matsukata' deflation of the 1880s seemed delayed by a lack of markets at home.) So far as I am aware, there was no thought of Korea *ex ante* as an important outlet for Japanese capital investment or as a source of cheap labour within Japan itself.

But at the same time there were also many non-economic factors, unconnected with the details of Meiji-era growth, prompting Japanese ambitions on the Korean peninsula. We have mentioned Korea's geographical position as a potential invasion route from the Asian continent to Japan. There was also a long history of Japanese-Korean rivalry and hostility. At the crucial period of the Meiji era (1890–1910) a particularly backward and corrupt Korean court was seen as an invitation to intervention by acquisitive powers hostile to Japan (meaning first Ching China and then Czarist Russia).

Patriotic Korean students in American universities sometimes bring with them what appears to be a conventional Korean history-textbook interpretation of Japanese growth in the Meiji era as intended primarily to provide an economic basis for the late-Meiji military conquest of Korea. (In Maoist terms, this would be a case of 'politics in command' of economics.) With all due respect to the natural Korean view of Korea's importance to the world at large, this position appears to be a highly ethnocentric view of Meiji Japan, and there seems to be no good reason for accepting it or even taking it seriously.

When it comes to Japan's later wars, Japanese motivation both economic and non-economic appears so easy to explain by post-Meiji forces that there seems little point in going back to the Meiji era development pattern for further explanation.

On the economic side, a key factor was the Great Depression of the 1930s, which led to increased protectionism in the West as a 'beggar-my-neighbour' remedy for unemployment. It is difficult to prove from the trade figures that Japan was actually hurt by either the American Smoot–Hawley tariff or British imperial preference, but the Japanese had anticipated injury in seeking and securing a 'yen bloc' or a 'co-prosperity sphere' of its own to ensure against either a cutting off of its essential imports or a denial of the export earnings to pay for them.

Even before the 1929 crash, western trade discrimination against Japanese exports was strengthening the military and imperialistic forces within Japan. Increasingly unable to compete with Japan in the production of labour-intensive goods, particularly textiles, western governments were yielding to their trade unions and accepting the International Labour Office doctrine of 'social dumping'. Under this doctrine, discrimination was to be legalized against exports from any country paying less than internationally standard wages, so that low-wage countries like Japan would be denied the benefits of a principal source of export competitiveness. Also related to the same revulsion against wage competition, but reinforced by considerations which can only be characterized as racist, were western refusals to accept immigrants from Japan; the key legislation here was the American Exclusion Act of 1924.

Another economic problem which Japan faced in the 1930s — and which the Japanese blamed on European and American interference rather than on Japan's own 'forward policies' — was discriminatory treatment and even boycotting of Japanese exports by the Kuomintang government of China in the important Chinese market. Trade with China then comprised nearly 40 per cent of Japan's total import and export volume. China had become Japan's major source of iron ore, coking coal, salt (for chemical fertilizers), and soybeans (for protein in the Japanese diet). China was also the major market for Japan's light industry — for textiles particularly — and the main investment outlet for Japanese multinational enterprise, particularly in Manchuria and in the Shanghai area.

On the political and social side, there were also major forces pushing Japan in an expansive direction during the same crucial period. There was exaggerated self-confidence arising from success in Japan's prior wars, including the First World War which had been won with relatively small losses and with no damage to the Japanese homeland. Like the Korean situation of the 1890s, the disordered Chinese situation was too tempting to resist, particularly since it might not last after the anti-Japanese Kuomintang had consolidated its power with Anglo-American support. There was racial pride, as already mentioned; resentment of Anglo-American anti-Oriental attitudes in the Orient itself, expanded into the 'reverse-racist' notion of a Japanese Imperial 'mission' to save first China, and then all East Asia, from white arrogance and domination. There was fear of Soviet Communism, less perhaps because of its ideology than its association with past Russian aggression, exercised both directly and through an anti-Japanese China. And finally, as events developed in the later 1930s, there was a feeling, inspired by failure of the western powers to check German and Italian aggression elsewhere in the world, that a 'wave of the future' belonged to military Fascism and that Japan would do well to climb on the surfboard and claim its share of the spoils.

We need not, therefore — and so I believe we should not — go back two generations and ascribe to the economic-development pattern and expedients of Meiji Japan the aggressive outbursts of Japanese militarism in the current reign of the Meiji Emperor's grandson.

Conclusion: Irrelevant — But Why?

I have been 'teaching Japan' more or less regularly for a generation to Development and Area Study classes in the US. These have included many citizens of one or another developing country, and also many devotees of the Third World and its causes. On leaving my classes, these students have usually seemed disappointed at the paucity of the helpful hints which they have derived from my presentation of the Meiji experience in Japan. I have agreed with them, however reluctantly, that little more can be learned by the Third World development strategist from Japanese development, let alone from contemporary Japan, than from the British, the American or the Continental European development experiences. Let me, however, suggest why I think this is so. There are, I think, four main reasons — none of which has anything to do with the putative Japanese 'national character'. These reasons are interrelated, and none should be interpreted as applying uniformly to all Third World countries in Asia or anywhere else.

(1) For the first of these I return to Adam Smith, to 'peace, easy taxes, and a tolerable administration of justice'. Today's developing countries by and large lack Japan's advantage of domestically-maintained peace and tranquillity, with its encouragement of saving and education and its accompanying provision of social infrastructure — roads, harbours, public health, and all that. Their historical records alternate between internal strife and dependence on the hated colonialists or imperialists to knock the tribes' or other factions' heads together. (Of all the forms *dependencia* may take, this neglected one may be the most blighting.)

(2) Today's developing countries — including those with zero or negative measured growth rates — lack free access to the most important northern or western markets, in which they can utilize in open competition their advantages of cheap labour and natural resources, including land. What is missed above all else is the British free-trade institution of Japan's Meiji era or, alternatively, the rise of some other reliable free-trade and low-tariff country to a position like Victorian Britain's prominence (together with its Empire) in world markets. (The high tariff in being is currently less of a menace, in my view, than the presence and the constant threats of quotas, 'voluntary' export restrictions, and 'orderly' marketing arrangements.)

(3) Adlai Stevenson's 'revolution of rising expectations' has carried the day in the Third World; it was unknown in Meiji days. What is now not only

wanted but assumed as an ethical entitlement is not only greater measured growth than anyone would have considered possible (had figures been available!) a century ago, but also more rapid diffusion among the poorer classes of society. In particular, one finds refusal to tolerate one or more generations of increasing income inequality as the probable price of accumulating capital and maintaining export competitiveness while awaiting decline in the population growth rate.*

(4) Accompanying if not causing the revolution of rising expectations in the Third World, a number of development theories, from Fabianism and the Welfare State to Marxism and *dependencia*,** have left the leadership groups or power élites of these several countries eager for high wages, western and/or 'appropriate' technologies, and social welfare institutions here and now, without waiting for even the Meiji Japanese level of development. These are to be financed from aid or concessionary loans by the richer countries (and their corporations' Third World facilities and branches) here and now, as quasi-reparations for the donor countries' past and sometimes present sins of inperialism, colonialism or what have you. The West's guilt feelings have played their part here; so has the short-term success of OPEC. But can anyone imagine such statements as 'They are rich *because* we are poor' from the mouths of even the most nationalistic or prematurely-militaristic of Japan's Meiji statesmen?

Bibliographical Appendix

We have refrained from footnoting our references to Japanese economic history, in favour of collecting a number of the more useful English-language sources in this Appendix. They are separated into two groups, 'general' economic and business histories and 'more specialized' sources on the specific subjects indicated in the title. Few of these sources, of course, deal exclusively with the Meiji era; most contain spill-overs both back to Tokugawa days and forward to the period after the death of the Meiji Emperor in 1912.

---

*For the view that some such period of increasing inequality is probable, see Simon Kuznets, 'Economic Growth and Income Inequality', *American Economic Review* (March **1955**), reprinted in Kuznets, *Economic Growth and Structure*. The World Bank, in particular, has sought growth policies which avoid this 'Kuznets effect'. Compare Hollis Chenery *et al.*, *Redistritution With Growth*, and more recently Chenery, *Structural Change and Development Policy*.

**Which has been most important in this regard, Fabianism or Marxism? An interesting dialogue on the point may be found in the pages of *Commentary* magazine (March and August, 1975). D. P. Moynihan, 'The U.S. in Opposition' stresses the role of the Fabians and particularly of Harold Laski in the March issue. A letter from P. T. Bauer takes the opposite view in the August issue. Both contributions are reprinted in Karl Brunner (ed.) *The First World & The Third World*, chs. 5–6.

General

Allen, G. C. (1946). *Short Economic History of Modern Japan* (Allen & Unwin, London).

Halliday, Jon. (1975). *Political History of Japanese Capitalism* (Pantheon, New York).

Hirschmeier, Johannes and Yui, Tsunehiko. (1975). *Development of Japanese Business* (Harvard University Press, Cambridge, Mass).

Lockwood, W. W. (1954). *Economic Development of Japan* (Princeton University Press).

Kelley, Allen and Williamson, Jeffrey (1974). *Lessons from Japanese Development* (University of Chicago Press).

Ohkawa, Kazushi (1957). *Growth Rate of the Japanese Economy Since 1878* (Kinokuniya, Tokyo).

—— and Rosovsky, Henry (1973). *Japanese Economic Growth: Trend Acceleration in the 20th Century* (Stanford University Press).

Sumiya Mikio, and Taira Koji, (1979). *Outline of Japanese Economic History* (University of Tokyo Press).

Tsuru, Shigeto (1958). *Essays on Japanese Economy* (Kinokuniya, Tokyo).

Yoshihara, Kunio (1979). *Japanese Economic Development* (Oxford University Press).

More Specialized

Dore, R. P. (ed.) (1967). *Aspects of Social Change in Modern Japan* (Princeton University Press).

Emi, Koichi (1963). *Government Fiscal Activity and Economic Growth in Japan* (Kinokuniya, Tokyo).

Lockwood, W. W. (ed.) (1965). *The State and Economic Enterprise in Japan* (Princeton University Press).

Marshall, B. K. (1967). *Capitalism and Nationalism in Prewar Japan* (Stanford University Press).

Nakamura, James (1966). *Agricultural Production and the Economic Development of Japan* (Princeton University Press).

Norman, E. H. (1940). *Japan's Emergence as a Modern State* (Institute of Pacific Relations, New York).

Passin, Herbert (1965). *Society and Education in Japan* (Teachers College Press, New York).

Patrick, H. T. (ed.) (1976). *Japanese Industrialization and Its Social Consequences* (University of California Press, Berkeley).

Roberts, J. G. (1973). *Mitsui., Three Centuries of Japanese Business* (Weatherhill, New York).

Rosovsky, Henry (1961). *Capital Formation in Japan* (Free Press, New York).

Shinohara, Miyohei (1962). *Growth and Cycles in the Japanese Economy* (Kinokuniya, Tokyo).

—— (1970). *Structural Changes in Japan's Economic Development* (Kinokuniya, Tokyo).

Smith, T. C. (1965). *Agrarian Origins of Modern Japan* (Stanford University Press).

—— (1955). *Political Change and Industrial Development in Japan* (Standord University Press).

Taira, Koji (1970). *Economic Development and the Labor Market in Japan* (Columbia University Press).

Yamamura, Kozo (1974). *Study of Samurai Income and Entrepreneurship* (Harvard University Press).
Yanaga, Chitoshi (1968). *Big Business in Japanese Politics* (New Haven, Yale University Press).

The Struggle for Development:
National Strategies in an International Context
Edited by M. Bienefeld and M. Godfrey
© 1982 John Wiley & Sons Ltd.

Chapter 4

Why Did China Fail to Follow the Japanese Road?

GORDON WHITE

Introduction

When the Communist-led revolutionary movement swept to power in China in 1949, the country exhibited the classic symptoms of economic backwardness, social debility and exploitation, and political weakness. It had an overwhelmingly agricultural economy characterized by stagnant productivity, negligible technical change, heavy demographic pressure, a generally low level of 'intensive' or 'modern' commercialization, a low level of gross investment, static income levels (GDP *per caput* was 113 *yuan** in 1912, 123 in 1933 and 115 in 1952), substantial rural tenancy and inequality in land tenure (50 per cent of the rural population were involved in some form of landlord-tenant relationship, and rents in kind averaged 43 per cent of the value of the main crop), squandering of the rural surplus on unproductive expenditure and a high level of rural indebtedness (in 1935, 44 per cent of farm households were in debt, mainly for consumption not investment). Though modern forms of economic enterprise had taken root, they grew in narrow enclaves, which mostly clustered along the coast and were dominated by foreigners; import surpluses were chronic and exports were mainly primary products in unpredictable markets characterized by unstable or deteriorating terms of trade. Social life had not yet recovered from decades of war and famine; the Nationalist government had been weak and divided, combining administrative incompetence with systematic corruption and harsh repression.

The reality was almost a caricature of politico-economic underdevelopment; poverty, inequality, exploitation, social anomie and inertia, political paralysis

---

*Yuan is the Chinese dollar.

and dependence.* How had this come about? Why had economic development** — whether of the 'natural evolutionary' kind based on a rising bourgeoisie or of the state-sponsored kind characteristic of the 'late developers' — not taken place? Why was it that China had stagnated while another Asian nation, Japan, which one hundred years earlier seems to have less favourable preconditions for national development, had been able to mobilize its internal resources so effectively that, from the turn of the century onwards, it was able to rival the western powers at their own imperialist game? Were the key constraints on Chinese development largely *external*, namely the impact of western and Japanese imperialism, or were they *internal* — the dead hand of bureaucratic rigidity, ideological conservatism and a static social structure? Moreover, if both sets of factors constituted a causal constellation, what form did this take and what were its dynamics? These are the basic questions I shall pursue in this paper.

The analysis of pre-Liberation China may seem to sit somewhat uneasily in a volume which is mainly concerned with the possibilities for national development within the evolving context of global politico-economic relations after the Second World War — a period when modes of international domination became more informal and less ineluctable. The Chinese experience analysed in this paper belongs to the earlier colonial period of imperialism when hegemonic ambitions were pursued and implemented by more directly coercive and administrative methods. China's historical experience before 1949 is certainly a fruitful context for investigating the mechanisms and impact of this earlier stage of imperialism, but it is also relevant to debates about the post-war period since China was never fully incorporated into any empire — in the words of Chinese nationalism, it was 'semi-colonial' — and there are important areas of continuity between the pre- and post-Second-World War situations. Many of the mechanisms of foreign penetration and control — economic, political and cultural — can be compared to those current in other Third World countries in later decades. By the 1930s, certain features of China's emerging political economy resembled — in embryonic form at least — patterns of penetration and dependence familiar to observers of the post-War scene. However, the Japanese invasion and the successful Communist revolu-

---

*Unless otherwise specified, I am using the terms 'underdevelopment' and 'dependence' in a loose sense, not to denote the precise characteristics embodied in Frank's theory of 'underdevelopment' and 'dependency'.

**My notion of economic development has three basic components: (i) autarchy or self-reliance, i.e. national control over the basic dimensions of economic life; (ii) structural integration of different economic sectors; and (iii) a self-sustaining process of capital accumulation and rising living standards. Economic development is not synonymous with 'development' which has certain key political, social and cultural features. In this chapter, however, I shall concentrate on the economic dimensions of development but, as my analysis suggests, any simple 'distinction' between 'economic' and 'non-economic' variables is treacherous and misleading.

tion ruptured these trends and consigned the question of China's ability to achieve autonomous capitalist development to the Cloud-Cuckoo-Land of counter-factual conjecture.

The structure of the paper is as follows: first, I shall review the various theories commonly used to analyse and explain the Chinese failure to develop before 1949; second, I shall present my own analysis of Chinese history during the century from the Opium War to Liberation and use my findings to evaluate the utility of contending theories; third, in a brief conclusion, I shall discuss the implications of China's earlier experience for the pattern and process of Chinese socialist development after 1949.

Competing Analyses of China's Developmental Failure before 1949

There are numerous analytical approaches to the question 'Why did China fail to develop before 1949?' In discussing them, I shall focus on the central theme of this volume, i.e. 'the interaction between internal and external factors, as these combine to define the trajectory of socio-economic systems'. Two sets of distinctions can be made: first, between analysts who assign prime importance to *external* factors, economic and non-economic, as constraints on Chinese development and those who argue that *internal* factors were primary; second, in evaluating the role of external economic factors, there are 'positivists' who argue that the net foreign economic impact was beneficial by laying the technical, attitudinal and organizational foundations of modern industrial growth in China, (Chang, 1969; Dernberger, 1975) as opposed to 'negativists' who argue that it was harmful, by inhibiting Chinese entrepreneurs, draining surplus out of the country and disrupting handicraft and agricultural production. These two sets of distinctions overlap to some extent: the 'externalists' tend to have a critical view of the impact of western and Japanese imperialism, but the 'internalists' vary, some viewing the foreign economic impact as benign, others as detrimental. Unsurprisingly, these differences seem to have ideological roots: liberal or conservative western analysts — protestations of methodological innocence notwithstanding — are more likely to take a rosier view of the foreign impact while western radicals and Chinese nationalists, Communist and non-Communist, share a critical perspective. In the review which follows, I shall focus mainly on western (mainly North American) analyses — systematic Chinese accounts are few and mostly inaccessible to the non-Chinese reader.

The Argument for the Primacy of External Causes

The view that imperialism was the main constraint on twentieth-century Chinese development is shared, in more or less systematic terms, by the vast majority of modern Chinese commentators and many foreign scholars, particularly younger historians who have attacked the 'modernization' mystique of their elders (Peck, 1969; Esherick, 1972). They argue that, though imperialism did bring elements of modern economy to China, this impact was geographically confined and sectorally skewed to serve foreign interests, producing a distorted and superficial form of 'false modernization' (Esherick, 1972: 14). Though imperialism increased foreign trade, it made the Chinese economy dependent on unstable foreign markets, cemented China into a typical pattern of exchanging primary for manufactured products in a context of deteriorating terms of trade, and severely disrupted the traditional economy, notably its handicraft sector. Moreover, by hampering the emergence of indigenous Chinese entrepreneurs through their superior resources and competitive pressure (both 'fair' and 'unfair'), foreign interests prevented the development of a strong industrialization process led by a progressive bourgeoisie; by undermining successive Chinese states and tying the hands of national policy-makers, they prevented the emergence of a political structure capable of organizing a programme of national development.

Perhaps the most coherent statement of the 'externalist' position is that of Frances Moulder (Moulder, 1977). Comparing the historical experiences of China and Japan, Moulder argues that Japan's success in national regeneration should not be attributed mainly to its unique 'traditional' society, but to its position of relative autonomy in the international political economy of the late nineteenth century which gave it a crucial 'breathing space'. China was unable to organize a similar response because it was more tightly incorporated into the world political economy, being swamped by successive waves of imperialist expansion first from the West and later from Japan. Moulder's argument is distinctive in that she emphasizes the impact of imperialism on the ability of the Chinese *state* to mobilize resources for national industrialization in ways comparable to other 'late developers' such as Germany, Russia and Japan: '[the] major way in which incorporation contributed to underdevelopment in China was the impact on the state' (Moulder, 1977: 200). In consequence, China has been able to industrialize rapidly 'only since the Community revolution decisively broke the ties that chained China to the imperialist system' (Moulder, 1977: viii–ix) and established a strong state. More broadly, the lesson of Japan and China for Third World nations is that 'if national industrialisation is to occur, revolutionary Communist movements will be necessary to bring it about' (Moulder, 1977: ix).

The Argument for the Primacy of Internal Forces

The arguments which place primary stress on internal factors as constraints to development are rather more diverse, reflecting different analytical and ideological perspectives. We can order them into three main groups.

Traditional society theories. These theories emphasize the obstacles to industrialization posed by certain unique facets of China's pre-industrial social system which, unlike Japan's feudal system, made it unreceptive to external stimuli towards modernization. Thus, for example, the doyens of East Asian historical scholarship in the United States, Fairbank and Reischauer, argue that 'the requirements of modernisation ran counter to the requirements of Confucian stability' (cited in Peck, 1969: 53), whereas Japanese society 'was receptive to innovations based on Western ideas and institutions' — in their view, the external impact on the two countries was basically similar.

The factors identified as constraints are many and various: the nature of the traditional Chinese family system, a breakdown in basic social controls (Levy, 1953), a conservative bureaucracy and ruling ideology, a parasitic élite, restraints on the power, prestige and prosperity of merchants, fatalistic attitudes among the population, and so on (for example, see Levy, 1953 — Moulder, 1977: 206–7 provides a comprehensive bibliography). Most of these approaches lie within the tradition of western 'modernization theory' and share its assumptions, notably that the western impact provides a necessary and ultimately beneficial 'exogenous shock' which can initiate a process of cumulative endogenous growth, that indigenous development is unlikely or impossible without exogenous pressure and the success or failure of a country's development effort mainly depends on its specific response to that pressure: Japan responded well, China poorly. They tend to a 'positivist' view of imperialist economic penetration and increasing economic integration with the international political economy. Even when their view is negative, imperialism tends to be deodorized as an ineluctable historical force, a painful medicine which must be swallowed for national progress. Fairbank, for example, has argued that China was the victim not so much of the Western powers but of 'world civilisation', not of 'Western imperialism' but the 'modern world's dynamic expansion' (Peck, 1969: 44–5). This kind of analysis, which Lippit labels 'pre-industrial stage theory' (Lippit, 1978: 269–71) has its parallels in certain analyses within the Marxian tradition, notably those which stress the progressive function of western imperialism and the conservative impact of the 'Asiatic mode of production' or 'Oriental despotism'.

The technological approach. This is a version of the above, but puts the major stress on the constraining effects of traditional technology. It usually rests on the concept of the 'high-level equilibrium trap' (Elvin, 1972; Dernberger, 1975:24–7) i.e. by the end of the nineteenth century Chinese agriculture had exhaused available opportunities to increase farm productivity to meet growing population demands. A major transformation was required in both techniques and organization of production — without such a revolution in agriculture, national industrialization was highly unlikely. But since industrialization was a *precondition* for transforming traditional technology, the necessary impetus would have to come from abroad — the 'exogenous shock' once again. Since the impact of western technology on China as a whole was relatively superficial and particularly so on agriculture, China was unable to break out of the trap and move, as Britain had done, from agricultural to industrial revolution (for critiques of this theory, see Riskin, 1975; Lippit, 1978:289–94).

'Distributionist' theories. These exist in various degrees of articulation and they share a common emphasis on the size and utilization of the economic surplus and its potential role as the engine of economic development. Riskin argues that proponents of the 'technology school' who maintain that surplus ('potential surplus above mass consumption') was minimal or non-existent in the rural sector in late nineteenth- and early twentieth-century China are wrong. A potential surplus existed in China before 1949 but, instead of being channelled into productive investment, it was wasted in unproductive consumption. The reasons were various: a tradition of conspicuous consumption among the rural élite, widespread social inequality, foreign incursions and recurrent wars and political instability (Riskin, 1975). Lippit takes this argument further, arguing forcefully that, though external influences were inimical to Chinese development, they were not primary because 'the process had deeper roots in the domestic economy' (p. 275). He identifies the primary constraint in the nature of Chinese class structure (Lippit, 1978). Economic surplus existed but was not invested productively because of the parasitic nature of the ruling class in general and its political élite in particular. In consequence, China set itself up as a victim for western aggression when its own élite class successfully thwarted the forces of development (Lippit, 1978: 321).

The relative salience of internal and external factors aside, however, 'internalists' have differed in their evaluations of the developmental impact of imperialism. Distributionists such as Riskin and Lippit, arguing in a neo-Marxist framework, have emphasized the damaging political and economic impact of imperialism while relegating this to secondary importance. Adherents of the other two schools, most clearly liberal North American economists and historians such as Eckstein, Nathan and Dernberger, have tended to argue that, despite the reprehensible political and military behaviour of the imperialists, their economic impact was beneficial: by jerking China out of its allegedly millennial lethargy, increasing the size of markets and the flow of goods, providing scarce capital and modern technology, educating Chinese entrepreneurs in the skills of modern business and establishing some of the basic infrastructure of modern economic growth.

These simplified summaries of the different approaches should not lead one to underestimate their sophistication — some analysts combine elements from different streams (for example, Feuerwerker, 1958; Fairbank *et al.*, 1960). They are not polar theories, posing internal and external variables as either/or, nor are they, in most cases, monocausal, exalting one 'cause' or 'factor' above all others. Though they rest their conclusions on historical data, however, the more articulated theories tend to be ahistorical, abstracting from the historical process in two basic ways: either by selecting certain 'factors' as more or less primary or by imposing certain restrictive 'ideal types' (such as Marxist sequences of modes of production) or particular theories (such as Schultz's theory of traditional agriculture which is the basis of the 'equilibrium trap'). Detailed empirical studies by historians suffer from an opposite defect, invoking a plethora of causal factors and failing to organize them in a systematic form of explanation. In our analysis, it is important to differentiate historical factors and rank them in their degree of importance but this must be done within a dynamic and holistic analytical framework. On the one hand, we need to trace the dialectical interaction of factors as they move over historical space; on the other hand, we must avoid isolating factors *in vacuo* without relating them systematically to other facets of social structure and social change — this is particularly important in dealing with the relationship between politics and economics. I hope to follow these prescriptions in the analysis which follows and, in so doing, to establish the relative utility of the competing theories outlined above.

Imperialism and China's Modern Development Experience: 1840–1949

The Opium War to the Collapse of the Qing Dynasty: 1840–1911

Though the nineteenth century was a period of internal challenges to the imperial Chinese regime, the main source of change and dislocation was external. With the surge of western, notably British, economic expansion in the Far East in the early nineteenth century under the impetus of the industrial revolution, the Chinese government came under increasing pressure to accede to 'normal' principles of political and economic interaction between nations. Though there had been trade relations between China and western nations prior to mid-century, this was on Chinese terms, was regarded as a generous gesture by the Emperor and not a natural right of foreigners, and was severely restricted in scope and location. The British government sought greater access for British merchants and demanded that the barriers to commercial penetration be dismantled. These obstacles were all the more irritating to British traders since formerly unsatisfactory terms of exchange with China in the late eighteenth century had improved dramatically with the expansion of an illicit opium trade, spearheaded by the British East India Company and abetted by corrupt Chinese officials. The widespread acceptance of this commodity in China meant that Chinese exports (notably porcelain, silk and tea) no longer had to be paid for in Mexican silver — in fact, silver was increasingly draining out of China. It was the Chinese government's ill-starred attempt to clamp down on this illegal trade which brought its defeat in the Opium War (1839–42) and the signing, under *force majeure*, of the Treaty of Nanking in 1842 which was the thin end of the wedge of foreign penetration. This began a succession of conflicts between China and various foreign powers throughout the latter half of the century. After each major conflict, China's defeat and humiliation were formalized in a treaty — cumulatively, these formed the 'unequal treaty system'. Each treaty legitimized and extended the range of foreign economic penetration and political domination and, conversely, eroded the economic and political autonomy of the Chinese nation. Through the 'most favoured nation' clause, moreover, the advances of each foreign power were generalized to the rest.

The impact of foreign depredations was multi-faceted, and intensified as interimperialist rivalry icreased towards the end of the nineteenth century. At the *political* level, foreign powers directly appropriated sections of Chinese territory: Britain took Hongkong after the Opium War and Japan colonized the island of Taiwan after the Sino-Japanese war of 1894–5. The latter conflict sparked off the 'struggle for concessions' as each power sought to consolidate its foothold in China by establishing a territorial sphere of influence, which fell short of formal colonization, or control over key transportation routes: the Germans in Shandong province in the north, the British in the lower Yangtse in central China, the French in the southern province of Yunnan, which bordered their recently acquired colonies in Indochina, and the Japanese and Russians competing for control over Manchuria in the northeast.

Successive treaties opened more and more Chinese ports to foreign trade — they came to be known collectively as the 'treaty ports'. Many of them contained 'concessions': areas under direct foreign administration — the most famous of these were in Shanghai and Tientsin — thus establishing the principle and reality of 'extra-territoriality'. China was also deprived of the right to adjust her tariff rates, administer her customs and appropriate her customs revenues. Foreign factories established in the treaty ports after the Sino-Japanese war enjoyed special tax privileges for their products. After the Boxer Rebellion in 1900, moreover, the foreign powers imposed a heavy indemnity on the Chinese government. This cumulation of foreign pressure and privilege led to a decline in the authority of the Chinese imperial government, precipitating a process of institutional decay and growing resistance which hastened the end of the dynasty in 1911.

At the *economic* level, foreign trade expanded substantially in the latter part of the nineteenth century (sevenfold between 1870 and 1911) and diversified in terms of commodity and trading partner. Progress was made in substituting for certain imports, notably opium and cotton piece-goods, but exports were still predominantly primary products, notably silk and tea, and there was a chronic import surplus from the late 1880s on. By the end of the dynasty, however, foreign trade was still a very small proportion of GNP, it was still highly concentrated in a number of key treaty ports and its basic mechanisms (notably the banks) remained almost wholly in foreign hands, with Chinese compradors as intermediaries. Financial flows from abroad increased after the Sino-Japanese war in 1895, when the Treaty of Shimonoseki allowed foreigners to set up factories in the treaty ports. The largest area of investment was in mining, followed by foodstuffs, textiles, and public utilities. Official loans to the imperial government also increased, particularly during its belated and abortive attempt at crash modernization in the first decade of the twentieth century. But by the end of the dynasty modern industry — whether foreign or Chinese capitalist or state-managed — was little developed. For instance, of 20,749 'factories' in operation in 1912, only 363 (1.7 per cent) used mechanical power and there were only about two pieces of mechanized equipment for each of these 'mechanized' enterprises. Modern industry was also restricted geographically to a few cities and regions. Moreover, though some sectors of the traditional handicrafts industry had suffered from foreign competition (notably cotton-spinning), other sectors were able to adjust to the foreign challenge (notably cotton-weaving, using a mixture of imported and domestic yarn) (Feuerwerker, 1969: 17–31). There is evidence, moreover, that the growing foreign presence stimulated native Chinese enterprise, in both commercial and manufacturing sectors (notably textiles and foodstuffs), though this still remained relatively small-scale — the few large-scale enterprises relied heavily on official support and protection — and overshadowed by the competitive advantages and superior resources available to foreign firms. The special status of foreign firms, moreover, meant that they often attracted indigenous investment, notably by Chinese compradors and merchants, to the detriment of Chinese concerns. China's lack of tariff autonomy, moreover, meant that the government was unable to provide protection for 'infant' indigenous industries.

In terms of purely economic indicators, one could argue that by 1911 there were some signs of movement towards a model of economic dependence: increasing foreign trade and thus vulnerability to foreign markets; a nascent bourgeoisie heavily dependent on foreign capital and skewed towards commerce rather than industry; chronic trade deficits; increasing financial dependence and debt-service ratios and foreign control over international economic transactions. At the same time, however, this process was still little advanced — the impact of foreign economies on the Chinese economy was very limited, both sectorally and geographically. The vast agricultural sector had been little affected, whether in land utilization, organizational forms or level of technology.

It was in the political realm that China's dependence was most marked. Imperialist pressure had a crippling effect on the capacity of the Chinese imperial *state* to emulate Russia and Japan by mobilizing domestic resources, strengthening class forces conducive to comprehensive economic development and reducing or eliminating the burden of foreign economic privilege. The Chinese state and political forces generally should not be seen as passive victims during this period. The reaction to imperialist pressure passed through several stages, each of them initiated by a traumatic event, and culminated in two officially sponsored efforts at national regeneration. The four basic steps can be categorized as resistance, reconciliation, restoration and 'self-streng-thening', and reform — their failure led to the rise of a revolutionary alternative which toppled the dynasty in the Republican Revolution of 1911.

The early period of resistance, which culminated in the debacle of the Opium War, foundered on China's gross inferiority in the techniques and organization of contemporary warfare. The policy of diplomatic reconciliation from 1842 to 1960, resting on the principle of 'playing barbarians off against each other', was undermined by collusion among the foreign powers, each of them gaining from the concessions extorted by the others. This period culminated in a march on the sacred city of Peking and the imposition of a still more humiliating settlement. The Chinese political élite responded by attempting to revitalize Confucian ideology and institutions (the Tongzhi Restoration of 1862–74) and, at the same time, under the prodding of progressive officials, to inaugurate a process of slow, cautious modernization — the watchwords of the time were 'self-strengthening' and 'Chinese learning as essence, Western learning for practical use', implying techical change but institutional conservatism. Activity was concentrated in the fields of military technology (the construction of arsenals and steamships) and translations of western technical and scientific works. Western experts were employed and a small number of Chinese students were sent abroad to acquire the Promethean fire. Between 1878 and 1894, the government went further by developing a limited programme of industrial growth, the so-called *guandu shangban* (literally 'official supervises, merchant manages') system, whereby the government sponsored private industrial and commercial concerns (Feuerwerker, 1958).

Even these limited moves towards modernization were opposed by conservative officials with the result, for example, that few large enterprises were sponsored under the *guandu shangban* system and returned students were not put to full use — it was felt that they had been contaminated by foreign culture and had lost their 'Chineseness'. But the tentative technical progress of the 'self-strengthening' movement was halted by yet another traumatic event, the resounding military defeat by the parvenu imperialist power Japan in 1894–5. This strengthened the hand of those members of the political élite who favoured more far-reaching reforms, including economics, education, politics and administration. They obtained a brief victory in the Hundred Days of Reform in 1898 but were crushed by conservative opposition under the Empress Dowager. The victory of the conservatives was shortlived, however, since there followed an even more devastating conflict, the Boxer Rebellion of 1900, which brought the combined weight of eight foreign armies down on the imperial government and the imposition of yet another set of humiliating terms, notably the right to station troops in the legation quarter of Peking and the demand for a large indemnity which the Chinese government could ill afford to pay. The Boxer Rebellion and its consequences had two conflicting effects: it galvanized the imperial government into a last-ditch programme of comprehensive modernization (including support for indigenous industrialization, notably in railways and textiles) and it stimulated the emergence of a revolutionary movement, notably the embryonic form of the later Nationalist Party (Kuomintang or Guomindang) organized by a Cantonese doctor, Sun Yatsen.

Viewing the period as a whole, it is clear that though the imperial government was initially slow to respond to foreign incursion, it did make two more or less systematic attempts to develop the country and regain lost sovereignty, tasks which were seen as inextricable. Though the political élite was divided, the social forces of reform relatively weak, and the internal ideological and institutional obstacles very great, the historical record suggests that the crucial factor which foreclosed the option of a Japanese solution was the damaging political impact of western and Japanese imperialism. This was decisive in two respects: first, by whittling down the decisional autonomy of the Chinese government in areas of key developmental importance (notably control over taxation, tariffs and customs revenues) and by weakening state authority through successive political and military defeats, the imperialist powers undermined the state's capacity to organize a successful programme of defensive modernization. Second, and more specifically, when the imperial government at last girded up its loins for an all-out effort for national salvation after 1900, it was a virtual Gulliver, pinned prostrate by many closely meshed cords of imperialist domination, not least the crippling indemnities imposed after the Boxer Rebellion which pre-empted a large share of the financial resources required for national development.

In sum, therefore, considering this first process of foreign incursion and national response, imperialism precipitated a national effort for 'strength and wealth' but stifled the infant in its cradle. On the other hand, the impact of the foreign presence on the Chinese economy, social structure and values gradually generated the socio-political basis of a more radical anti-imperialist programme of national salvation and development in the post-dynastic era. While the previous dialectic of challenge and response had been between imperialism and traditional forces desperately trying to defend and adapt, in the next phase the stage was set by imperialism itself — it was pitted against new forces of its own creation: new ideas of progress, science, democracy and self-determination; new social classes or groups, most notably an emerging Chinese bourgeoisie, incubated and hatched in the treaty ports and growing within the shadow of foreign economic dominance; new military men trained abroad (notably in Japan) who saw a modern army as an essential precondition for national sovereignty and socio-economic progress; a new generation of dedicated youth, educated in foreign-style schools and colleges, who wished to turn their new-found knowledge against its progenitors, particularly through the instrument of revolution (Wright, 1968). We now turn to the Repulican period, the era of revolutions.

The Republican Period: 1912–1949

At the political level, this period saw a repetition of the earlier pattern of imperialist challenge and nationalist response. After a phase of political anarchy under the warlords following the collapse of the 1911 Revolution, a strong nationalist movement arose in the major cities and coastal provinces which led to the establishment of the Kuomintang government in 1928. Although the new Nationalist government, under Chiang Kai-shek, had shed its more radical adherents in a brutal *putsch* in 1927, it still maintained a (more restrained) anti-imperialist stance, seeking to claw back national sovereignty from the imperialist powers and organize a programme of national development dominated by state industry. During the 1920s and early 1930s, however, the shadow of Japan lengthened over China: the north east provinces were detached and after the faked Mukden Incident of September 1931 a Japanese puppet-state, Manchukuo, was established in 1932. Over the next few years, the Japanese penetrated further south and in 1937 swept into the interior. This ended the Nationalist party's attempt to consolidate its rule and lay the foundations of a national development programme. Since the ensuing period was one of war (1937–45) and civil war (1945–9), it seems sensible to concentrate our attention on the period of Kuomintang hegemony from 1928 to 1937.

In the economic realm the post-dynastic period was one of gradual, though uneven, expansion and greater international integration. Industry expanded gradually, as Table 1 shows. The annual rate of industrial growth was 5.6 per cent between 1912 and 1949 and between 1931 and 1936 was as high as 9.3 per cent. But this movement took place from a very low base and had little cumulative impact on GDP per head or on the basic structure of domestic production — modern industry increased from 3 to 4.2 per cent of domestic production between 1931 and 1936. Moreover, the rate of accumulation remained low (5 per cent gross in 1933). Factories were heavily concentrated in the coastal cities or along the Yangtse and employed only 2.4 per cent of the non-agricultural workforce compared with 25.9 per cent in handicrafts. With the exception of Manchuria (where the Japanese established a heavy industrial war economy in the 1930s and 1940s) most factory production was of consumer goods, predominantly in small and technologically backward workshops. Foreign firms dominated more strategic sectors of the economy, as Table 2 shows (Hou, 1965: 127–30; Feuerwerker, 1977: 36–7):

But the 1920s and 1930s did see a gradual but uneven expansion of Chinese-owned industrial enterprise — by 1933, 90 per cent of 'factories' were Chinese-owned and they produced nearly 70 per cent of total modern industrial output,

Table 1 Index of industrial production of mainland China, 1912–1949 (15 commodities, 1933 = 100)

Year	Gross value of output	Net value added
1912	11.9	15.7
1913	15.6	19.2
1914	20.1	24.0
1915	22.5	26.1
1916	24.0	27.7
1917	26.9	32.0
1918	27.8	32.2
1919	31.1	36.9
1920	40.2	42.9
1921	42.4	42.4
1922	34.7	39.0
1923	41.6	45.6
1924	46.9	50.5
1925	55.7	60.1
1926	59.0	61.0
1927	66.6	66.3
1928	72.1	70.5
1929	76.9	75.2
1930	81.6	80.1
1931	88.1	86.5
1932	91.6	90.3
1933	100.0	100.0
1934	103.6	106.8
1935	109.7	119.5
1936	122.0	135.0
1937	96.0	112.3
1938	76.2	104.1
1939	88.2	120.7
1940	94.1	137.6
1941	109.2	161.2
1942	115.7	176.1
1943	105.6	157.1
1944	91.8	140.9
1945	62.0	94.1
1946	90.7	93.6
1947	115.1	116.8
1948	96.7	101.1
1949	105.6	119.2

Source: John K. Chang, *Industrial Development in Pre-Communist China: A Quantitative Analysis* (Edinburgh University Press, 1969), pp. 60–1.

considerable evidence, as Lippit concludes, that 'Chinese-owned factories were not as a group replaced by foreign ones but grew apace with them' (Lippit, 1978: 264). Chinese enterprises were mostly small-scale, technologically backward and labour-intensive — they accounted for less than 40 per cent of total industrial capital. Building on a platform established during and

Table 2 Foreign share in the modern sector of the chinese economy (percent)

Year	Total shipping	Yangtse shipping	Cotton yarn spindles	Coal	Iron ore	Pig iron
1897	77	–	41	–	–	–
1902	83	–	37	–	–	100
1903	–	73	37	–	–	100
1907	84	–	34	–	–	100
1914	–	77	46	90	100	100
1918	77	79	43	77	100	100
1922	76	–	37	78	100	100
1924	79	76	40	76	100	100
1928	78	77	43	78	99	96
1930	83	78	43	76	99	99
1934	–	77	43	80	99	96
1936	–	82	46	66	99	97

Source: Chi-ming Hou, *Foreign Investment and Economic Development in China* (Harvard University Press, 1965), p. 128.

immediately after the First World War, when it benefited from a decrease in foreign competitive pressures, Chinese capital was able to achieve a certain degree of success in import substitution: for example, domestic for foreign cigarettes and cotton piece-goods (Chang, 1969: 39–42 and Eckstein, 1977: 21–3). But this success was not generalized, even in the consumer-goods sector: for example, although Chinese flour-milling enterprises flourished during the First World War, when flour supplies from Europe and North America were interrupted, the return of foreign competition after 1920, coupled with the inability of the Chinese government to raise duties on imported flour, led to a decline in the industry. It did not revive until 1932 when the Kuomintang government was able to impose import duties (Chang, 1969: 42–4). Lack of control over tariff policy was indeed an important factor in weakening the indigenous challenge to foreign goods. For example, the Chinese match industry was severely inhibited by successive waves of foreign competition (Japanese between 1895 and 1918 and Swedish after 1927). In the mid-1920s, it benefited from boycotts of foreign goods, but the crucial turning point was 1931 when the Nationalist government imposed a 40 per cent tariff on imported matches, resulting in a rapid decline in imports and rapid growth in domestic production.

In more technologically advanced or capital-intensive sectors of industry Chinese capital found the going much harder. Chang argues, for example (1969: 52–3) that, though the Chinese machinery industry expanded rapidly during the first World War as the indigenous consumer-goods sector boomed, it was unable to expand later in the face of foreign imports unencumbered by protective tariffs and a general preference on the part of Chinese businessmen for foreign machines, even when they were more expensive. On the other hand, Rawski (1975:207–10), who focuses on the development of a textile machinery concern, argues that individual firms were in fact able to reach critical technical thresholds by the 1930s and that 'this evolutionary growth, similar in nature to the growth of engineering in nineteenth and early twentieth century Europe and America, could have continued to gather momentum in a China free of foreign and civil war and political revolution' (p.213). His argument is weak in that it is based on the record of a few successful firms rather than a whole industry. Moreover, he does not view the ferrous metallurgical industry with the same optimism — this was hampered by indivisibilities, technological dependence, business fluctuations and capital shortage, opening the industry up to foreign control.

Direct investment in manufacturing industry, however, was a small portion of the foreign economic presence. Foreign investment was skewed towards foreign trade and its ancillary services: in 1936, for example, 16.8 per cent went directly into import-export trade, 20 per cent into banking and other financial services linked to trade, 25 per cent into transport and only 19.6 per cent into manufacturing. Much foreign manufacturing was also closely linked to trade: for example, cigarette factories which used imported US tobacco. The foreign economic system was pervaded by a mercantile mentality: foreign banks tended to be speculative rather than productive, commercial rather than industrial. Thus, the pattern of investment reinforced a pattern of trade which contributed little to indigenous industrialization, with imports consisting mainly of consumer goods and exports of agricultural and mining commodities which had few backward or forward linkages with the rest of the economy. There was also a net outflow of capital during most of this period (Feuerwerker, 1977: 93), though this deficit was made up by remittances from overseas Chinese. Focusing on state liabilities, Lippit calculates that debt repayments on largely unproductive loans and indemnity claims accounted for about 30–40 per cent of government expenditures between 1931 and 1934. In his view, this financial burden 'left little room for discretionary measures in support of industrialisation' (Lippit, 1978: 264).

Although foreign investment increased substantially between 1914 and 1936, it still played a small role in the total economy, providing about 1 per cent of GNP in the early 1930s. In relation to population, it was relatively insignificant, amounting to about US $7 per head in 1936, compared with $20 in India, $86 in Latin America and $23 in Africa (excluding South Africa). On the other hand, it did provide a considerable proportion (20 per cent) of total gross investment (Dernberger, 1975: 30). But it was highly concentrated in enclaves and the degree of concentration increased from the turn of the century, as Table 3 indicates. In 1931, for example, 61.4 per cent of all foreign capital was in either Shanghai or Manchuria. This pattern in turn attracted agglomerations of Chinese investment: for example, 62 per cent of all new Chinese firms were

Table 3 Geographical distribution of foreign investments in China, 1902, 1914, 1931 (US $ millions)

	1902		1914		1931	
Shanghai	110.0	14.0%	291.0	18.1%	1,112.2	34.3%
Manchuria	216.0	27.4	361.6	22.4	880.0	27.1
Rest of China	177.2	22.5	433.1	26.9	607.8	18.8
Undistributed	284.7	36.1	524.6	32.6	642.5	19.8
Total	787.9	100.0%	1,610.3	100.0%	3.242.5	100.0%

Source: Carl F. Remer, Foreign Investments in China (New York, 1933), p. 73.

in one province, Jiangsu, where Shanghai is situated. In the rural sector, technology and productivity levels changed very little except in some commercializing areas in the hinterlands of enclaves where cash crops were planted for export (Skinner, 1965; Moulder, 1977: 31–4). However, such regions suffered heavily from the contraction of export markets during the world depression between 1931 and 1935.

Similarly, though foreign trade expanded during this period, it was still a small proportion of total economic activity. Chronic trade and current account deficits continued. Although Chinese exports diversified from their earlier reliance on silk and tea, they were still mainly primary products. Export performance also suffered from unstable or shrinking markets, notably reflecting competition from tea plantations in South Asia and from synthetic fibre against Chinese silk. Terms of trade also seemed to move adversely: the ratio of export to import prices was 76.5 in 1870, 100 in 1913 and 122.9 in 1935.

In sum, one can agree with most analysts that, in the context of the Chinese economy as a whole, little progress was made in the process of modern industrialization by the late 1930s. The foreign economic impact was relatively superficial on the total economy but important in the small modern sector, where it dominated the more strategic and sophisticated branches. Although foreign enterprise stimulated Chinese entrepreneurship in certain sectors, it also inhibited indigenous capital, particularly in the producer-good sector. Evolving patterns of foreign trade and investment reinforced the skewed and dependent type of development which had emerged in embryonic form in the last years of the Qing Dynasty: a pattern of trade with minimal benefits for indigenous accumulation and a highly concentrated spatial distribution which left most of the economy relatively untouched. In class terms, a Chinese bourgeoisie was emerging in the treaty ports but was weak vis à vis the conservative landowning élite in the countryside. The rural area was a double constraint: first, as distributionists correctly point out, because the surplus-controlling élite was largely parasitic, thus wasting a potentially powerful source of domestic industrialization; second, by failing to raise rural productivity and purchasing power, which could have widened the market for domestic consumer goods produced behind the more effective tariff walls of the 1930s.

Given this conjuncture, the galvanizing, organizing role of the state was crucial: to abolish or reduce external dependence, both economically and politically; to aid progressive class forces against internal and external opposition; to mobilize and direct capital for a balanced development programme and to break the shackles on farm productivity through technical change and social reform. Without such vigorous and thorough-going state intervention, the chances for a 'natural' evolutionary process of development, based on a dominant bourgeoisie or a progresive class alliance, were slim.

Like the nineteenth and early twentieth centuries, 1928–37 was a period in which the Chinese state made a systematic effort to lay the foundations of comprehensive national development. Like its predecessor, the Kuomintang state defined the major developmental constraint as external — the recovery of national sovereignty was seen as crucial to allow the government a free hand to restructure the national economy. Some significant successes were in fact achieved: tariff autonomy was regained in 1928, tariffs rising in consequence from 8.5 per cent in 1929 to 30 per cent in 1935; the unequal treaties were abolished during the wartime alliance with the West against Japan. Internally, the Nanking regime sought — at the declaratory level at least — to develop heavy industry through public enterprises, to stimulate agriculture through programmes of education and technical change, and to rationalize the financial system. But these programmes of technical and economic modernization were promoted within a framework of ideological and social conservatism, resuscitating the corpse of Confucianism and resisting major social and institutional reforms.

However, the record suggests that the Kuomintang government did not succeed in moving the nation decisively into the early stages of industrialization, sustained economic growth, technological progress and economic independence. Though this failure can be attributed in part to the internal and external pressures of the time — notably civil war, Japanese encroachment and the world depression — it is generally agreed that the Kuomintang state was divided, corrupt and ineffectual and that its action fell far short of its proclaimed intention and its impact far short of its action. It was a regime of paper plans, laws in letter only and large but incompetent bureaucracies. It failed to tackle the problems of agricultural stagnation: agrarian reform programmes were abandoned and agriculture received little financial attention — total agricultural production rose a mere 1 per cent between 1932 and 1936 (Bianco, 1971: 112). Though there were some successful programmes of agricultural modernization in a few localities, they were directed by progressive local interests, owed little to the central government and had marginal impact on the economy as a whole. Though some progress was made in financial rationalization and communications, the Kuomintang made little direct or indirect contribution to indigenous industrialization: policies towards private business were ambiguous and the much-vaunted state sector of the economy, established under a general slogan of 'controlled economy' (*tongzhi jingji*), tended to become the private preserve of influential party members who ran it for personal or sectional profit (Bianco, 1971, 113–115; Paauw, 1964). Internal defects apart, moreover, the Kuomintang state was weakened by its inability to establish and maintain a united and progressive class base: its relationship to domestic capitalists remained ambiguous, and, where it received solid support — for example among the rural élite — it rested on the most conservative elements of society; it also failed to reconcile the contradictions of interest between its rural and urban constituencies.

Though there many factors *within* Chinese society and the state mechanism which accounted for this weakness, however, the force which converted a weak state into a moribund one was *external* — viz. politico-economic rivalry between the imperialist powers, notably the Japanese encroachment and eventual invasion of China. The parallel with the last decades of the Qing dynasty is clear: the imperialist powers tolerated a weak and dependent Chinese state but resisted its attempts to strengthen national sovereignty as a precondition to or as part of a programme of national regeneration, undermining its power and legitimacy through political, military and economic pressure; then a final crisis, the Boxer Rebellion of 1900 (a defeat inflicted by interimperialist collaboration), and the Japanese invasion of 1937 (precipitated by interimperialist rivalry) brought the demise of the regime and in each case stimulated the emergence of a new generation of anti-imperialists, the republican revolutionaries of 1911 being succeeded by the communist revolutionaries whose movement flourished during the years of anti-Japanese struggle and gained from the decay of the Kuomintang.

Conclusions

Given this historical record, the logic of the 'externalist' argument for the prime importance of external factors as a constraint on Chinese development is very compelling. Among the various theorists, Moulder's emphasis on the devastating impact of imperialism on the capacity of the Chinese *state* is particularly cogent — as a 'late developer', this was especially crucial given the importance of state action in successful cases of national development, notably Germany and Japan. While imperialism created the need and the desire for social, economic and political development in China, it frustrated its achievement without revolution. 'internalists' have tended to argue that the Chinese state was unable to 'react favourably to the forces of modernisation' (for example, Dernberger, 1975: 47) because of domestic institutional limitations. Though they are correct in identifying certain domestic constraints, they mystify 'the forces of modernisation' and underestimate the devastating impact of imperialist politico-military pressure on the main attempts at national mobilization before 1949 (Chang, 1969: 113).

What of those who argue as follows: yes, we all know that imperialist political and military activity in China was damaging and reprehensible, yet you must admit that the net economic benefits of the foreign presence were beneficial? Some North American analysts, for example, separate the economic aspects of foreign penetration from 'imperialism' which is defined in exclusively political terms. Thus Dernberger (1975: 38), discussing the impact of direct and indirect foreign control over China's railroad system, states: 'Despite the "imperialist", i.e. political, aspects of these foreign investments and loans, they must be considered one of the major direct contributions of the foreigner to China's economic development'. Such arguments are both overstated and ill-put. First, after one hundred years of foreign economic penetration, China had precious little of the substance of economic development and still less of its benefits. Second, where pockets of economic progress did flourish, they were dominated by foreign economic concerns and directed towards foreign interests. The embryonic pattern of development stamped upon China was highly uneven and dualistic, technologically and financially dependent and skewed towards unproductive forms of commercial exchange. Through a series of economic and administrative privileges, foreign economic concerns succeeded in binding the hands of successive Chinese governments and weakening the competitive power of the emergent Chinese bourgeoisie. True, Chinese capitalists did emerge as a historical force 'because of' the foreign presence, but they also developed *in spite of* it, and remained weak in consequence. Third, the argument for 'net economic benefits' is poorly put — indeed heavily self-fulfilling — in its concentration on economic and sometimes purely technological factors. It tends to lead logically to the conclusion that any net addition to domestic output or any new technique is 'positive', regardless of its economic function, political purpose and social consequences. Moreover, this method dismantles history into disconnected parts and subjects each to cost-benefit analysis. I feel this is analytically unsound — the imperialist impact was an organic process with many aspects, economic, technological, cultural, ideological, political and military, the underlying logic of which was domination, the urge to restructure Chinese reality in accordance with the politico-economic needs of the competing powers. If we assign levels of causation within this constellation, moreover, the major constraints on Chinese developmental capacity were *political* rather than economic.

From this perspective perhaps the most 'positive' contribution of imperialism as a system was to start a process in China which culminated in its own destruction — it changed the constellation of social, economic and political forces within the country and instilled the faith among Chinese across a wide political spectrum that the only way to achieve national regeneration was to create a counter-state capable of destroying foreign dominance.

Economic and technical facts about the foreign presence should be analysed within this matrix. From this perspective, the facts of the foreign economic presence only became potentially 'positive' when the matrix was broken. One can thus argue for the 'retrospective functionality' of the pre-1949 imperialist economic impact *after* the success of the Communist revolution. Imperialism did bring certain progressive economic changes to China — new ideas, entrepreneurial and technical skills and methods of organization — but this Promethean fire was sealed in the casket of foreign dominance. After 1949, the new regime could open the casket and utilize the accumulated capital and skills as an important underpinning for the comprehensive development programmes which began with the First Five Year Plan in 1953. Indeed, it has been estimated that over two thirds of the increase in industrial output in the 1950s came from an expansion in the production of existing enterprises (Feuerwerker, 1977: 39–40). The existence of a base of consumer goods production helped to soften the impact of concentration on producer goods after 1949 and provided valuable foreign exchange (notably through textile imports).

Analysts viewing the Chinese experience before 1949 in the context of the post-Second-World War global system and the post-colonial patterns of integration and dependence which have developed during this era might argue that the Chinese case is of dubious relevance to present development debates. Freed from the depredations of classical coercive imperialism, they might argue, and integrated into a basically benign post-war international political economy, China could have achieved the balanced and autonomous development which eluded it for so long. The counterfactual path is treacherous but, given an assumption of a strengthened state and an expanded Chinese business class, such a hypothesis would not be far-fetched. As we have seen, there were clear signs of the latter in the 1930s. But the historical record of successful 'late development', whether in its earlier (Japan or Germany) or later (South Korea, Singapore) phases, argues strongly for the thesis that the 'original' pattern of evolutionary development based on an atomistically organized bourgeoisie is not feasible in a world political economy already dominated by major capitalist powers. The role of the state is crucial, both externally in achieving political and economic freedom of manoeuvre and internally in changing institutions, reorganizing class forces, mobilizing surplus, restructuring the economy and maintaining socio-political stability. On this account, the hypothetical prospects for capitalist development in China are much less favourable. The Kuomintang state — particularly in its later years — was politically divided, administratively incompetent and socio-economically regressive; its calamitous situation in 1947–9 has been vividly described by the US academic and journalist Barnett (Barnett, 1963). It was unwilling and unable to implement the basic ownership reforms necessary for progressive economic change (notably in rural ownership). Given this pervasive political weakness and even assuming that international pressures were less damaging, it would have been difficult for China to break out of the developmental pattern and structure of class relations current in the 1930s. Thus if capitalist development had taken place, it would have been likely to share certain features familiar in many other Third World countries: foreign dominance in key economic sectors; uneasy coexistence between various fractions of the bourgeoisie in the cities and a conservative landowning stratum in the countryside an enclave pattern of industrialisation anchored in the eastern cities and provinces with increasing disparities between regions and between cities and countryside with the usual pattern of migration, rural stagnation and social degradation, with the fruits of development growing in the orchards of the few; and pervasive corruption in the public life of a 'soft state'.

Comprehensive, balanced and humane development demanded both political sovereignty and a major change in domestic class relations — the key to both was a strong and genuinely revolutionary state. Through the Communist revolution of 1949 China was able to break decisively with the dependent capitalist option and establish the political and social basis for a form of development tailored to the needs of China as a nation and of the majority of its people. First, by breaking the ties of international economic and political integration and dependence the Chinese government was at least in a position to determine, to a large extent, in consideration of the national interest, the nature of its relations with the international economy, both capitalist and socialist. China benefited from a large-scale transfer of Soviet technology in the 1950s (Heymann, 1975) and, by the time reintegration with the major capitalist economies came about, tentatively in the early 1960s and more boldly in the late 1970s, the Chinese state had the capacity to define the terms and establish the parameters of interaction; it was not entangled in a complex web of external economic constraints which limited its freedom of action or skewed its decisions in the interests of foreign powers or corporations. In short, the establishment of a strong, autonomous state provided the political precondition for ensuring — with a margin for miscalculation — that international economic ties were more likely to be beneficial, as classical economic theory and modern development economics have promised.

Secondly, the break with an externally-oriented development pattern and with a regime which failed to change the status quo in Chinese relations led to the adoption of a development strategy oriented towards the interests and aspirations of the vast majority of the population. This strategy reflected the revolutionary socialist programme of the new regime which sought far-reaching socio-economic redistribution and emphasized the need to provide for the basic welfare requirements of all the population as an underpinning for industrialization. Though the developmental practice of the Chinese Communist Party (CCP) regime has often been inconsistent and authoritarian, this basic difference in class orientation marks a sharp contrast between the post-1949 development pattern and its predecessor (or hypothetical alternative).

Though this analysis has emphasized the role of external factors in inhibiting Chinese development before 1949, this does not imply that 'internalist' arguments are without foundation. The Communist revolution of 1949 was anti-imperialist, but it was also a response to the stagnation, poverty and injustice of the 'old society'. On the one hand, the new government was able to meet 'distributionist' obstacles by transforming patterns of ownership in cities and countryside and mobilizing a significant surplus for investment in the new programme of heavy industrialization. On the other hand, the CCP has wrestled constantly with other major constraints identified by 'internalist' analysis before 1949, notably the need for a breakthrough from traditional to modern technology in agriculture and the need to prevent rapid population growth from eroding the benefits of growth. Moreover, though the new regime has achieved considerable success in delivering both growth and equality, it has many pervasive problems of its own — political instability, administrative rigidity, economic incompetence and persistent social conflict. Clearly a decisive break with the international political economy does not 'solve' all the problems of national development; it may, however, establish a more favourable political and economic context within which other major constraints and problems — familiar to students of development economics, sociology and politics — can be tackled, more or less successfully.

References

Barnett, A. Doak (1963). *China on the Eve of Communist Takeover* (Praeger, New York).

Bianco, Lucien (1971). *The Origins of the Chinese Revolution 1915–1949* (Stanford University Press).

Chang, John K. (1969). *Industrial Development in Pre-Communist China* (Edinburgh University Press).

Dernberger, R. F. (1975). 'The role of the foreigner in China's economic development, 1840–1949', in Perkins (1975), pp. 19–47.

Eckstein, A. L.. (1968). 'The economic heritage', in A. Eckstein, W Galenson and J-c Liu, *Economic Trends in Communist China* (Aldine, Chicago), pp. 33–85.

Eckstein, A. L. (1977). *China's Economic Revolution* (Cambridge University Press).

Elvin, Mark, 'The high-level equilibrium trap; the causes of the decline of invention in the traditional Chinese textile industries', in W. E. Willmott (ed.) *Economic Organization in Chinese Society* (Stanford, Stanford University Press, 1972).

Fairbank, J. K., Eckstein, A. L., and Yang, L. S. (1960). 'Economic change in early modern China: an analytical framework', *Economic Development and Cultural Change*, **IX**, I (October 1960), 1–26.

Fairbank, J. K., Reischauer, E. O., and Craig, A. M. (1965). *East Asia: The Modern Transformation* (Houghton and Mifflin, Boston).

Feuerwerker, Albert (1958). *China's Early Industrialization* (Harvard University Press).

Feuerwerker, Albert (1969). *The Chinese Economy ca. 1870–1911* (Ann Arbor: University of Michigan Centre for Chinese Studies), Paper No. 5.

Feuerwerker, Albert (1977). *Economic Trends in the Republic of China, 1912–1949* (Ann Arbor: University of Michigan Centre for Chinese Studies), Paper No. 31.

Heymann, Hans Jr. (1975). '"Self-reliance" revisited: China's technology dilemma', in B. G. Garth (ed.), *China's Changing Role in the World Economy* (Praeger, New York), pp. 15–35.

Hou, Chi-ming (1965). *Foreign Investment and Economic Development in China 1840–1937* (Harvard University Press).

Levy, Marion J. (1953). 'Contrasting factors in the modernisation of China and Japan', *Economic Development and Cultural Change*, 2, 161–97.

Lippit, Victor D. (1978). 'The development of underdevelopment in China' *Modern China*, 4:3 (July 1978), 251–328.

Moulder, Frances V. (1977). *Japan, China and the Modern World Economy* (Cambridge University Press).

Nathan, Andrew J. (1972). 'Imperialism's effects on China', *Bulletin of Concerned Asian Scholars*, 4:4 (December 1972), 3–8.

Paauw, Douglas S. (1964). 'The Kuomintang and economic stagnation, 1928–1937', in A. Feuerwerker (ed.), *Modern China* (Prentice-Hall, Englewood Cliffs), pp. 126–35.

Peck, James (1969). 'The roots of rhetoric: the professional ideology of America's China-watchers', *Bulletin of Concerned Asian Scholars*, 2:1 (October 1969), 59–69.

Perkins, Dwight H. (1975). *China's Modern Economy in Historical Perspective* (Stanford University Press).

Rawski, Thomas G. (1975). In Perkins (1975), pp. 203–34.

Riskin, Carl (1975). In Perkins (1975), pp. 49–84.

Skinner, G. W. (1965). 'Marketing and social structure in rural China', *Journal of Asian Studies*, XXVI:2 (February 1965), 211–28.

Tawney, R. H. (1932). *Land and Labour in China* (Allen and Unwin, London).

Wright, Mary C. (1968). 'Introduction: the rising tide of change', in Wright (ed.) *China in Revolution: The First Phase, 1900–1913* (Yale University Press, London), pp. 1–63.

Chapter 5

India: Capitalist Industrialization or Structural Stasis?

T. J. BYRES

> Now, India , we are bound to be industrialised, we are trying to be industrialised, we want to be industrialised, we must be industrialised.
>
> Jawaharlal Nehru, Address to the special silver jubilee convocation of Lucknow University, 28 January, 1949 (Nehru, 1958: 368)

> ...as soon as the factory system has attained a reasonable space to exist in, and reached a definite degree of maturity, and in particular as soon as the technical basis peculiar to it, machinery, is itself produced by machinery, as soon as coal-mining and iron-mining, the metallurgical industries, and the means of transport have been revolutionised; in short, as soon as the general conditions of production appropriate to large-scale industry have been established, this mode of production acquires an elasticity, a capacity for sudden extension by leaps and bounds, which comes up against no barriers but those presented by the availability of raw materials and the extent of sales outlets.
>
> Karl Marx, *Capital,* Volume 1 (Marx, 1976: 579)

The Problematic; The Development of Capitalism in India and Industrialisation

The problematic to which this chapter relates is that of the development of capitalism in India. The issues at stake may be stated clearly and briefly enough: they are the manner and the extent of the development of capitalism so far, the nature of any obstacles in its path, the degree of its maturity, the prospects for its further development and its likely future course. Put thus baldly, our task possesses a certain stark simplicity. But it entails matters of formidable complexity, which can be adequately addressed only on a basis of carefully posed theoretical formulations (which are likely to be contentious, however scrupulous their posing), in conjunction with 'concrete analysis of a concrete situation' (which, we recall, was for Lenin 'the living soul of Marxism', and which, if pursued seriously, is likely to be a task of awesome proportions). Such analysis needs to be firmly rooted in detailed and sophisticated historical scholarship, which is emerging for India but which leaves much to be done. Serious treatment of the contemporary situation, with such perspectives, is now considerable, and is very much more in evidence than it was even a decade ago. It is, however, uneven in its coverage of the relevant questions. Thus, our problematic's terrain must be both countryside and town: both capitalism's penetration of agriculture (the agrarian question) and the kind of industrialization which a particular urban bourgeoisie and a particular state are capable of setting in motion. Town and country are, of course, inextricably linked, with changes in one critically dependent upon changes in the other (as we shall see). Nevertheless, the peculiar and quite distinct problems which adhere to each have an autonomy which demands separate treatment: a treatment that will be no more straightforward for the one than for the other. The analysis, moreover, cannot be satisfactory unless there is parity of treatment. Yet, curiously, there has been among Indian Marxist scholars a quite disproportionate concentration upon the countryside. So far, there has been no equivalent for industry of the extensive and rich mode-of-production-in-agriculture debate that raged throughout the 1970s and continues unabated, although there have been individual contributions of major importance.

In the brief compass of this chapter I cannot aspire to the rigour of a full treatment. My fairly limited purpose is to try to identify, in terms of the stated problematic, the major characteristics of the industrialization that has proceeded in India since 1947. It is an industrialization that has, indeed, been pursued with the seriousness suggested in the statement by Nehru quoted at the head of this chapter. The crucial question, however, is whether that industrialization has met, or seems likely to meet, the criteria contained in the passage by Marx: whether it has created, or is poised to create, a factory system with the 'reasonable space to exist in', the 'definite degree of maturity', 'the general conditions of production appropriate to large-scale industry', 'the elasticity, a capacity for sudden extension by leaps and bounds, which comes up against no barriers', that would signal a deeply rooted and healthily functioning capitalism. We start by tracing the antecedents of the problem to their origins in colonial India.

The Colonial Economy; Marx's Prediction, Structural Stasis and the Indigenous Urban Bourgeoisie

It was Marx himself who, when India was still virtually untouched by modern industry, first raised the issue of the likely course of industrialization there. In his journalism of the early 1850s, in a famous passage, he made a bold and optimistic prediction. Marx was at pains to stress 'the misery inflicted by the British on Hindustan', in his article, 'The British Rule in India', published in the *New York Daily Tribune* on 10 June, 1853 (Marx and Engels, no date: 33), and the narrow and selfish interests followed. Yet, the British bourgeoisie, in pursuit of those very interests and, to be sure, 'dragging individuals and peoples through blood and dirt, through misery and degradation' (in his article, 'The Future Results of British Rule in India', published in the *New York Daily Tribune*, 22 July, 1853 (Marx and Engels, no date: 88)), would 'lay down the material premises' for capitalist industrialization:

> I know that the English millocracy intend to endow India with railways with the exclusive view of extracting at diminished expenses the cotton and other raw materials for their manufactures. But when you have once introduced machinery into the locomotion of a country, which possesses iron and coals, you are unable to withhold it from its fabrication. You cannot maintain a net of railways over an immense country without introducing all those industrial processes necessary to meet the immediate and current wants of railway locomotion, and out of which there must grow the application of machinery to those branches of industry not immediately connected with railways. The railway system will, therefore, become, in India, truly the forerunner of modern industry. (*Marx* and *Engels*, no date: 87)

There is, perhaps, an anticipation here of Marx's celebrated *De te fabula narratur!* injunction to the German readers of *Capital* (Marx, 1976: 90). He is careful to add that 'the Indians will not reap the fruits of the new elements of society scattered among them by the British bourgeoisie... till the Hindus themselves shall have grown strong enough to throw off the English yoke altogether', and that 'the regeneration of that great and interesting country' lies in a 'more or less remote period' (Marx and Engels, no date: 88). Still, the thrust of his argument is quite unmistakable: the British, albeit as the 'unconscious tool of history' (Marx and Engels, no date: 39), would unleash an irresistible process of industrialization: a process which, when India achieved independence, would gather force and lead to her full regeneration as an industrial power. Our concern here is with the 'more or less remote period' which was inaugurated in 1947, when the British left. We must, however, underpin our treatment of that era with some consideration, however jejune, of the extent to which the predicted unleashing actually materialized and of the conditions that were created. Our understanding of what has happened in post-1947 India will depend upon that.

Marx's *De te fabula narratur!* was triumphantly vindicated with respect to Germany. But in India of 1947 it was impossible to sustain the view that 'the railway system... [had] become...truly the forerunner of modern industry', in the sense suggested by Marx. The railways were built, and some industrial development did ensue, as a result of accumulation by both British capital and, against the odds, an emerging Indian capital: without benefit of protection until 1914 (until then British interests dictated completely free trade); with the help of some 'discriminating protection' in the interwar years, which benefited industries like iron and steel, cotton, sugar, paper, chemicals; and with some stimulus from the circumstances of war between 1939 and 1945 (Government of India, *First Five Year Plan*, 1952: 420–1; Gadgil, 1971: Ch. XVI; Bagchi, 1972: 5, 7). The colonial state limited its support of industrial development — after its earlier active opposition — to belated and grudging protection. There was no public sector activity: 'Modern industry in India meant, barring a few ordnance factories and a few pigmy-sized demonstration factories, private industry' (Bagchi, 1972: 4). Marx's *New York Daily Tribune* readers might have expected those industries which he was later to categorize as Department 1 to play a central role in industrial development in India. This was not so. Marx underestimated the capacity of the British urban bourgeoisie to ensure that British Department 1 industries would be the beneficiaries of railway building and accumulation in India: it turned out to be less the 'unconscious tool of history' than the conscious tool of its own interests. Had there been a concentrated development of Department 1 industries, then, indeed, the unleashing of productive forces and the upsurge of capitalist industrialization would have taken place. It was not to be, however. Let us consider the broad outline of what happened.

It is possible that between about 1815 and 1880, with the ruining of traditional handicrafts and little compensating growth of modern industry, there was a 'major shift from industry to agriculture' in India (Thorner and Thorner, 1962: 70–1, 77) — the so-called 'de-industrialization' of India — although 'we do not have the kind of data which would allow us to say with any assurance whether or not this actually took place' (Thorner and Thorner, 1962: 77). Certainly, it seems a likely hypothesis on the basis of what evidence there is. Thereafter, the figures on occupational distribution reveal a situation far from the industrial transformation envisaged by Marx. The all-India figures for 1881 to 1951 are reproduced in Table 1. In his *magnum opus, The Development of Capitalism in Russia,* Lenin observes:

> ...the development of commodity economy *eo ipso* means the divorcement of an ever-growing part of the population from agriculture, i.e. the growth of the industrial population at the expense of agricultural population... .One cannot conceive of capitalism without an increase in the commercial and industrial population at the expense of the agricultural population, and everybody knows that this phenomenon is revealed in the most clear-cut fashion in all capitalist countries. (Lenin, 1964: 40)

We will comment later on the crucial role that such a shift plays in the creation of the home market that is essential to the development of capitalism in general and to the full unleashing of industrialization in particular. Here we note that if, indeed, over a sufficiently long time-span, shifts of labour of the

Table 1   Workers in agriculture and manufacture per hundred workers: India, 1881 to 1951. Males and females

Year	Agriculture Males	Females	Manufacture Males	Females
1881	70	69	–	–
1891	–	–	–	–
1901	72	78	–	–
1911	74	77	11	11
1921	75	79	10	10
1931	74	78	10	9
1941	–	–	–	–
1951	69	80	11	7

Note: The figures have been calculated from Census data and there was no Census in 1941. They are for the Indian Union (i.e. they exclude Burma and Pakistan).
Source: Thorner and Thorner (1960: 13).

kind postulated are not taking place then we may justifiably doubt whether structural change of a fundamental kind is in motion: whether, indeed, capitalism is developing healthily. The period in question is surely long enough. The Indian figures show that 'throughout the period...agriculture ...has claimed the great bulk of the Indian working force' (Thorner and Thorner, 1960: 13). There was no net shift between agriculture and industry, such as one would expect in circumstances of industrial transformation. Between 1881 and 1951 the proportion of the male working population in agriculture remained more or less the same (and actually increased in intervening decades), while the proportion of the female working population in agriculture rose significantly. The picture of structural stasis is confirmed by the figures for the proportion of the working force in manufacturing. These are not available on an all-India basis before 1911. Data for a large number of provinces do exist, however, and these (too detailed to reproduce here — they may be seen in Thorner and Thorner, 1960: 16–17), along with the full information for 1911 and thereafter, indicate 'that for India as a whole the relative number of male workers in manufacture decreased from 1881 to 1901 and remained practically unchanged thereafter...[while] with regard to female workers the fall in the proportion assigned to manufacture continued...right through 1951' (Thorner and Thorner, 1960: 15). Our interest is in modern manufacturing industry and the industrial base which had been created by 1947. Clearly, there was a growth of modern manufacturing industry between 1880 (or earlier) and 1947, with the possible 'de-industrialization' of a previous period replaced by a different situation, in which 'whatever new employment was created by the introduction of textile mills, rice dehusking plants, and other modern industrial establishments may have been roughly offset by an

Table 2 The structure of modern industrial employment in India at independence

Industrial activity	Numbers employed (thousands)	Proportion of total industrial employment (%)	Proportion of total working population (%)
(a) Railways	901	23.4	
(b) All mining	519	13.5	
of which coal-mining	345		
(c) Factory employment			
cotton textiles	653		
jute textiles	222		
general and electrical engineering	136		
railway workshops	108		
ordnance	84		
iron and steel	60		
chemicals	18		
other	1153		
Total factory employment	2434	63.2	1.7
Total Industrial employment (a + b + c)	3854	100	2.8
Total working population	139500		100

Sources and note: The working population figure is for 1951 and is from Thorner and Thorner (1960: 4). All other figures are for 1949 and are from Bhagwati and Desai (1970: 31), which takes them from Myers (1958: 22). Very little is lost by expressing the 1949 figure as a proportion of the 1951 one.

equivalent falling off in handicrafts' (Thorner and Thorner, 1962: 77). We may now focus our attention upon 'modern industrial establishments'.

Table 2 shows that at Independence the *total* 'modern sector' — including therein employment in railways and in mining as well as in strictly factory employment — absorbed only 2.8 per cent of India's working population. Moreover, the structure of this small 'modern sector' was noteworthy, inasmuch as 23 per cent were in railways and 13 per cent in mining (two-thirds of the latter in coal-mining, which *had* been stimulated by the railways). Thus a mere 1.7 per cent of the work force gained their livelihood in the 'modern manufacturing sector' (i.e. excluding railways and mining) — see Table 2 — and this sector produced only 6.6 per cent of India's national income (Government of India, *First Five Year Plan*, 1952: 420): tiny figures, representing a reality far from the Industrial Revolution that Marx foresaw. The anatomy of the 'modern manufacturing sector', as shown in Table 3, is yet more revealing. Department 1 was represented to any extent only by iron and steel, and even then the representation was meagre. On the indicators tabulated, iron and steel — developed, essentially, by the Parsi, Jamsetji Tata (for a biography see Harris, 1958), and located mainly at Jamshedpur, in Bihar — constituted a lowly 5 to 9 per cent of the sector. Its output was minute in relation to India's total population (see Byres and Nolan, 1976: 17), for figures on steel and other industries and a comparison with China, which shows a close similarity between the two countries in the early 1950s), although there were clear signs of efficiency (Johnson, 1966: 12). The polyglot general engineering, a crucial branch of Department 1, achieves recognizable proportions only through a process of agglomeration. Given the wide range of activity it covered, its share of only 5 to 8 per cent in this sector underlined the extremely meagre nature of its constituent parts. Heavy machinery and machine tools were hardly in operation: with pride of place taken by two locomotive manufacturing works, one at Chittaranjan (in West Bengal), the other at Tatanagar (in Bihar) (Government of India, *Programmes of Industrial Development, 1951–56,* 1953: 41–7, 53–60). There were also plants producing, in very small quantities, among other things, agricultural machinery, auto-mobiles, ships, textile machinery, ball and roller bearings, and electrical engineering products (see above: 25–116). The dominating elements in the 'modern manufacturing sector' were, in fact, a group of predominantly consumer-good industries: cotton textiles, the most 'mature' of India's industries (by 'mature' meaning able both to meet home demand and compete abroad) and the domain of Indian capital; jute textiles, largely the product of foreign investment; sugar, another area of Indian activity; and vegetable oils and rice-milling, both started and organized by Indians. Together, these five industries constituted 69 to 76 per cent of the 'modern manufacturing sector': cotton was undisputedly pre-eminent, with 36 to 50 per cent of the sector; and cotton and jute between them had 50 to 66 per cent, so that one writer has

Table 3 Structure of India's manufacturing sector in 1946. Percentage share of leading industries in productive capital, employment, salaries and wages, production, and value added of total sector

Industry	Productive capital employed	Number of persons employed	Salaries and wages	Production (value)	Value added by manufacture
1. Iron and steel[a]	8.6	4.8	6.7	5.6	7.6
2. General engineering[b]	6.3	7.4	7.9	4.5	5.4
3. Cotton textiles[c]	35.6	43.0	50.3	–*	46.0
4. Jute textiles	13.7	21.1	15.8	14.7	17.5
5. Sugar	8.3	6.2	3.8	6.3	3.7
6. Rice milling	5.0	3.3	1.3	5.8	0.7
7. Vegetable oils[d]	6.3	2.4	1.9	10.0	3.5
8. Total 3 to 7 inclusive	68.9	76.0	73.1	–*	71.4
9. Other industries[e]	16.2	11.8	12.3	–*	15.6

* not available
[a] Iron and stell smelting, rolling and rerolling.
[b] Including electrical engineering, but not the generation and transformation of electrical energy.
[c] Cotton textiles, spinning and weaving.
[d] Vegetable oils, oil seed crushing and extraction, and processing of vegetable oils.
[e] Wheat flour; biscuit-making; fruit and vegetable processing; distilleries and breweries; starch; paints and varnishes; soap; tanning; cement; glass and glassware; ceramics; plywood and tea chests; paper and paperboard; matches; woollen textiles; chemicals; aluminium, copper and brass; bicycles; sewing machines; producer gas plants; electric lamps; electric fans.
Source: Calculated from data in Bhagwati and Desai (1970: Table 3–1, 39–42). Their data are calculated from Directorate of Industrial Statistics, Cabinet Secretariat, Calcutta, Ten Years of Indian Manufactures (1946–55). This in its turn is a summary tabulation of the results of the Census of Manufacturing Industries. The Census was confined to establishments employing twenty or more workers and using power.

observed of the years 1900 to 1939 that 'once we have accounted for investment in the jute and cotton manufacturing industries, we have accounted for the major part of changes in aggregate industrial investment' (Bagchi, 1972: 7). In the shadow of the dominating industries which we have noted existed a large number of industries (for a full list see Table 3, note *e*), each of microscopic importance. They included such 'strategic' industries as cement, fertilizers, heavy chemicals, and petroleum products. Of these, cement, along with various other industries like paper, showed a fairly marked tendency to grow during the interwar years and especially during the war, and heavy chemicals a rather milder tendency, but it was the early growth of embryos. The demand for petroleum products was growing fairly sharply, but at independence India imported 95 per cent of her requirements, the remaining 5 per cent being met by the Assam Oil Company's refinery at Digboi, based on the exploitation of crude petroleum in the neighbourhood (Government of India, *Programmes of Industrial Development, 1951–56*, 1953: 191–2).

All in all, important as individual industries admittedly were *per se* (especially cotton, but also jute and coal) and as signs of what potential might lie unrealized in India (especially iron and steel), Indian modern industries amounted, in the total social formation, to a trifling industrial base. India, in 1947, was an overwhelmingly rural society, dominated by a backward agriculture. Her miniscule manufacturing sector (miniscule in relative terms) produced, for the most part, consumer goods. Her capital good industries, to the extent that they existed at all, were severely attenuated. The criteria by which one might judge whether or not successful industrialization had taken place or was under way (which Marx suggested in *Capital*, and which we have pointed to) were so far from being met that it seems reasonable to characterize the years between the early 1850s and 1947 as an era of 'stunted industrialisation' (Bagchi, 1972: 440–3) or 'thwarted industrialisation' (Bagchi's phrase used by Banaji, 1972: 2501). Why this was so is one of the central questions of Indian economic history. Here we may simply record the outcome of the developments that did take place. If India were to be industrialized, she had a long way to go. Massive accumulation would be needed before the necessary industrial sinew could be created.

What was to happen subsequently, in Marx's 'more or less remote period', would depend upon a range of factors, forbidding in their scope and intricacy, some of which will be discussed in the analysis that follows. Among these strategic influences, of central importance would be the nature of India's urban bourgeoisie and its capacity, through its own efforts and through the mediation of the post-colonial state (if, indeed, there was to be mediation with respect to a serious bid to industrialize), to set in motion and maintain the requisite massive accumulation. What kind of bourgeoisie was it? Attention has been drawn to the 'peculiarly complex, bewildering character of the bourgeoisie in India' (Banaji, no date: 1), and the roots of its perplexing contemporary quality need, assuredly, to be traced to the pre-1947 period. Part of the problem lies in the need to identify different fractions of the urban bourgeoisie: which at one level have an obvious unity of interests — in relation, for example, to subordinate classes; but which at another may have significantly divergent interests (though non-antagonistically so) — in the context of this chapter, in the area of accumulation for industrial development. Thus, we may distinguish an industrial (or manufacturing) bourgeoisie and a financial/commercial bourgeoisie. The interests of the former are certainly geared to the rapid development of manufacturing industry, and its predominance is essential if industrialization is to proceed. Within it, however, one may single out two further subfractions, the bigger sections of capital and medium/smaller capital, which, again, may be at variance. We may say that the unfettered development of capitalism probably requires that the latter should not be constrained. The financial/commercial bourgeoisie includes property and asset holders of various kinds, those with interests in trade and financial manipulation, and so on. For them, it is important that their capital be tied up for relatively short periods, and it is likely, therefore, that it will go into essentially unproductive spheres. In a pre-capitalist social formation, and especially one dominated by a colonial power, conditions will favour this fraction, and the relevant rate of profit is likely to be very high compared with the rate of profit on industrial capital, because, for example, of the limited size of the domestic market (which is not necessarily to attribute any sort of primacy to this factor) and a host of impediments to industrialization including overt as well as more subtle discrimination against indigenous capital. Nor is this all. The complexity is compounded by the fact that the bigger sections of capital embody an extensive overlapping of interests, within which one or other tendency, the manufacturing or the commercial/financial, dominates. Such is only to hint at the complexity in question, in an excessively schematic fashion. We may pursue it a little further in more concrete terms.

That India had not experienced an industrial transformation should not blind one to the fact that, unlike many other poor countries in the wake of decolonization, she did have an indigenous, industrial bourgeoisie. This bourgeoisie had existed as an identifiable class since the 1880s; had grown since the end of the First World War; and had, in the face of severe obstacles, generated some industrial development, which, although tiny in relative terms and distorted, had achieved, because of India's great size, significant absolute proportions. It was a class which was not concentrated in one small part of the country, but was spread throughout India, which was possessed of considerable class coherence, and which

> was well-organized…via a whole plethora of business organizations: the Delhi Factory Owners' Association, the Indian Mining Federation, The Indian Colliery Owners' Association, the Indian Sugar Mills' Association etc., and the apex organizations unifying the capitals of various industries, the Federation of Indian

Chambers of Commerce and Industry and the All-India Manufacturers' Organization. (Banaji, no date: 5; I am indebted to Banaji's unpublished paper for some of the foregoing points in this paragraph.)

It was a class, however, which had taken naturally, and with relish, to that unique creation of British capital in India, the managing agency system, which allowed control over a remarkable range of activities, both industrial and otherwise, and which accentuated any tendency there might be 'towards financial manipulation rather than production performance' (Gadgil, 1955: 461). This was so inasmuch as it placed

> control of the productive organization primarily in the hands of financiers...[and gave rise] to agglomerations and combines of a peculiar type...[not] either horizontal or vertical combines round a central productive activity...[but] because of the operation of the managing agency, large financial combines with a very mixed composition, since the link between the various members of the group...[was] not...technical production or trading considerations but financial opportunity. (Gadgil, 1955: 462)

Indian capital did not experience an era of competitive capitalism, but almost from its birth took a monopoly form (Chandra, 1979: 1270), so that by 1947 monopoly groups like Tata and Birla had accumulated massive resources and controlled vast areas (Chandra, 1979: 1267). An industrial bourgeoisie there was — at once sophisticated, powerful and well-organized — one that dwarfed medium/smaller capital and stifled its growth and, from the viewpoint of industrial transformation, had its industrial character excessively overlaid by financial/commercial considerations.

The Indian urban bourgeoisie has been variously categorized: at one extreme as a comprador bourgeoisie, and at the other as a national bourgeoisie. Neither of these categories, however, captures its complex reality. Thus, far from having those organic links with foreign capital which would have subordinated it financially and economically and given it a thoroughly comprador character, it had, to a considerable extent, grown in spite of, in opposition to and independently of foreign capital (Banaji, no date: 1). It felt threatened and overshadowed by foreign capital, and was hostile to the colonial state. During the independence struggle, the Indian urban bourgeoisie was to an important degree anti-British, anti-foreign capital, and pro-nationalist, and provided, indeed, most of the funds that sustained the nationalist movement (Kidron, 1965: 65–9): although perfectly capable of collaborating with the colonial state and with foreign capital, where this was possible and where its interests seemed to be furthered, as, for example, Birla, Kirloskar and Dalmia, and others, on occasions did (Kidron, 1965: 69–72). Its subsequent relationship with foreign capital would be important. If, however, the Indian urban bourgeoisie did not possess that abject dependence on foreign capital which would have constituted it as a comprador class, then neither did it have the strength and the capacity to accumulate on a sufficiently large scale that the national bourgeoisie characterization appears to connote (for an excellent critical account of the national bourgeoisie notion — in general terms and not with specific reference to India — which focuses upon its political content see Gordon (1973): Gordon stresses the rather shadowy nature of the notion). It was clearly conscious of this weakness, and already, before 1947, in for example, the famous Bombay Plan, actively supported the idea of state planning and control and the creation of a public sector, especially for new and 'difficult' industries (such as Department 1 industries), upon which industrial transformation, they realized, would depend (Kidron, 1965: 72–3; Mukherjee, 1976). The state would be necessary to relieve the urban bourgeoisie of much of the burden of this formidable task. The role of the state in subsequent accumulation would be crucial.

The Post-colonial Economy; (a) Sources of Accumulation and an Active Post-colonial State

The capacity to accumulate, whether realized in the private sector or the public sector, would have to include, critically, in an economy still overwhelmingly dominated by agriculture, an ability to mobilize an agricultural surplus (through taxation, or the terms of trade, or the lending of savings, or direct investment): in any major effort to industrialize, the countryside would be a necessary, primary source of accumulation (the details of this I argue elsewhere and will not repeat here, see Byres, 1972; 1974: 224–7; 1977: 258–9). A second source of accumulation, to which the industrial bourgeoisie would reach relentlessly, in the event of the first proving recalcitrant, with the active support of any state intent upon capitalist industrialization, would be the urban proletariat: via an enhanced extraction of surplus value, which would require stagnating real wages and a probable onslaught upon organized labour. Then, thirdly, given the likely inadequacy of the first two sources, recourse might be had to foreign capital, whether aid or private foreign capital, although the scale of the flows necessary to facilitate sufficient accumulation in a large country like India would be forbiddingly large, while their form would be crucial to the nature of the accumulation that took place. We cannot, however, concentrate exclusively on the surplus mobilization necessary to permit accumulation. Whether or not accumulation on a large scale, and hence industrial transformation, was worthwhile, either for the urban bourgeoisies or the state, would be influenced, for a large country in which foreign trade plays a relatively small role, by the size of the home market: there would be initial scope for import substitution (in both Department 1 and Department 2) and the creation of Department 1 could, in its early stages, create its own market through a process of self-expansion, but, ultimately, and certainly before any industrial transformation could be completed, capitalist industrialization would require a broadly-based home market. In the remainder of this chapter we will examine what has been attempted in India since 1947 and with what success.

In marked contrast to the colonial state, in post–1947 India the state has played an active role in seeking to secure India's industrial transformation via: a carefully articulated and consistently pursued industrialization strategy; the creation of a large public sector, in which the 'difficult' industries might be established and made to grow to adequate dimensions; the attempted mobilization of resources, through taxation, public enterprise surpluses, deficit finance, foreign aid and a controlled inflow of private foreign investment; stringent protection of both public sector and private industries; the control of organized labour; the establishing of a large array of financial institutions to extend long-term credit to private industry; and a whole host of other measures. This state intervention on a large scale has always had the clear aim of securing capitalist development in India. There was a clear commitment from the outset to the state's playing a major role in making possible the necessary massive accumulation (the First Plan, for example, stressed that 'the State must itself raise, to the extent possible, through taxation, through loans and through surpluses earned on State enterprises a considerable proportion of the savings needed' (Government of India, *First Five Year Plan*, 1952: 41) and a use of socialist rhetoric (still uttered as a ritual incantation, however hollow the sham). It may usefully be described as state capitalism (cf. Chattopadhyay, 1970). There has never been any doubt that Indian state power has been geared, in part, to serving the needs of the urban bourgeoisie, although, to the extent that the state has been the representative, too, of dominant rural classes, a powerful constraint has existed (a theme to which I have given attention in previous writing — see below for references). Very quickly after independence, the need for industrialization was stressed in the Resolution on industrial Policy of 1948 (as it had been in much pre-independence Indian writing and statements) and in the First Five Year Plan (1951–2 to 1955–6). It was not, however, until the Second Five Year Plan (1956–7 to 1960–1) that a determined attempt at rapid industrialization was set in motion by the Indian state. It was at this juncture that the decisive effort to break with the past came. The major thrust was towards the laying of a heavy industry base (iron and steel, heavy engineering, machine tools, heavy chemicals etc.) — Department 1, which, as we have seen, barely existed — on the grounds that the capacity of the economy to grow, and any ultimate industrial transformation, depended upon the creation of the essential productive base of capital goods. For as long as the economy in general and the industrial sector in particular continually came up against a barrier formed by an inability to secure capital goods, industrialization would be frustrated. India, with her lagging exports and chronic shortage of foreign exchange, lacked the wherewithal to import them. And even if she could import them, a fully-formed domestic Department 1 would impart to the economy a resilience and an elasticity which it otherwise would not have.

Moreover, as Marx had stressed a century previously, India was richly endowed with the raw materials (coal and iron ore) necessary to manufacture them (more richly endowed than Marx knew). She might even have oil, though in the mid-1950s little had been discovered (and hardly any prospecting had been done). We cannot here trace the vicissitudes of the Second Plan period or the details and vagaries of subsequent plans. Suffice it to say that the stress upon industrialization and the efforts to achieve it have remained a central preoccupation of the Indian state. What we must now try to do is assess the outcome of a concerted attempt to industrialize that has been in operation for a quarter of a century.

Our task of assessment — of seeking to identify the underlying tendencies at work — is not an easy one. One has to be careful to separate short-run phenomena from long-run tendencies, cyclical movements from persistent trends, uneven and disproportionate development (ever a feature of capitalism) from structural change. Sufficient time has now passed, however, at least to give the attempt some meaning. We may start with the important features of India's industrial growth since the early 1950s.

The Post-colonial Economy: (b) Inadequate Industrial Growth, Paralysis of Department 1 and Continuing Structural Stasis

A quite definite break in the course of India's industrial development may be identified in the mid-1960s: a marked deceleration of growth and a change in the pattern of growth. Indian industry seems, fairly quickly, to have reached the limits of modest growth and to have entered a period of virtual stagnation. Not only that, but Department 1 especially appears to have been so afflicted — by a kind of paralysis, most notably in certain key branches — although industries producing mass consumption goods have been badly hit too. Disquietingly, the structural stasis that characterized the colonial economy continues to a surprising degree.

Table 4 shows that in the period 1947 to 1965 production in the modern industrial sector (in factory enterprises) displayed an accelerating trend: growing at a compound rate of 4.8 per cent per annum between 1947 and 1951 (the years which preceded the initiation of planning), 5.7 per cent per annum between 1951 and 1955 (the First Five Year Plan period, before the industrialization strategy began in earnest), 7.2 per cent between 1955 and 1960 (the Second Plan period), and 9 per cent between 1960 and 1965 (the Third Plan period). It was growth which, especially from 1956 onwards, was dominated by Department 1: by what the Indians term 'basic industries' (which include coal, cement, finished steel, electricity generated, etc.) and 'capital goods industries' (which include machine tools, heavy engineering, textile machinery, commercial vehicles, railway vehicles, etc.), which grew, after 1951, in the respective plan periods, at 4.7, 12.1 and 10.4 per cent, and at 9.8,

Table 4 Annual compound growth rates in index numbers of industrial production in factory enterprises: overall and by group

Groups	1947 to 1951	1951 to 1955	1955 to 1960	1960 to 1965	1965 to 1970	1970 to 1976	1965 to 1976
Use-based or Functional Classification							
Basic industries	—	4.7	12.1	10.4	6.2	6.8	6.5
Capital goods industries	—	9.8	13.1	19.6	−1.4	6.0	2.6
Intermediate goods industries	—	7.8	6.3	6.9	2.6	3.3	3.0
Consumer goods industries	—	4.8	4.4	4.9	4.1	2.9	3.4
(a) Consumer durable goods	—	—	—	11.0	8.5	4.3	6.2
(b) Consumer non-durable goods	—	—	—	—	2.8	2.9	2.8
Input-based Classification							
Agro-based industries	0.3	4.0	3.8	4.0	1.7	1.8	1.7
Metal-based industries	4.5	7.5	14.1	18.2	0.7	5.1	3.1
Chemicals-based industries	26.2	8.5	12.2	9.0	9.8	7.3	8.4
Classification based on Sectoral Indicators							
Transport equipment and allied industries	—	—	—	14.4	−2.2	4.8	1.6
Electricity and allied industries	—	10.4	14.7	14.4	11.8	6.8	9.1
General Index	4.8	5.7	7.2	9.0	3.3	4.7	4.1

Source: Shetty (1978: 9).

Table 5   Index of manufacturing production and annual percentage
increases in India, 1974–1979

Year	Index of manufacturing production (1970 = 100)	Percentage increase over previous year
1974	113	–
1975	116	0.9
1976	128	10.3
1977[a]	135	5.5
1978[a]	144	6.7
1979	149	3.5

[a] Provisional
Source: Tata Services Limited, Statistical Outline of India, 1978, p.61 and
Statistical Outline of India, 1980, p.63.

13.1 and 19.6 per cent. Consumer-good industries grew at a steady 4 to 5 per
cent per annum. In the planning period, these rates were consistently less than
those targeted (see Raj, 1976: 223), and for individual industries this was often
significantly so (as a perusal of the plan documents quickly reveals); and, given
the considerable investment that was devoted particularly to Department 1
industries, and the relatively low base from which growth started, they were
hardly spectacular. Moreover, such overall figures tell one nothing about the
underlying structural characteristics. Still, for all the dangers of a kind of index
fetishism (anything that goes up represents an inexorable drive towards the
triumph of capitalism), the overall growth of industry at 7 to 7½ per cent per
annum achieved between 1951 and 1965 (see Byres, 1966: 94), and the initial
upsurge of growth in Department 1 did suggest the possibility, if no more, of
the first strides along a path that might lead to industrial transformation.

After 1965, however, Indian manufacturing industry entered a period which
several commentators have described as one of 'stagnation' (for example, Raj,
1976; Patnaik and Rao, 1977; Nayyar, 1978). The former acceleration came to
a halt, and between 1965 and 1976 industrial production grew at 4.1 per cent
per annum (Table 4). Indeed, including 1976 may give the post-1965 industrial
growth something of an upward bias, inasmuch as the increase in that year
appears to have been unusually high, to be followed by a gravitating towards
the diminished growth in subsequent years (Table 5). If we take the years 1964
to 1975, overall industrial growth was 3.5 per cent per annum compound
(Kelkar, 1977: 2133), or half the rate recorded between the early 1950s and the
mid-1960s, and this may be a more accurate indicator of the trend from 1965
through to the present (i.e.to the early 1980s). Patnaik and Rao observed
apropos of 1976 that 'it is too early to say that the economy is poised for
sustained growth' (Patnaik and Rao, 1977: 121), and that observation seems to
have been valid. Moreover, deceleration was particularly marked in Department 1 industries (two branches of which we will discuss in a little more detail

below), with consumer goods in general slowing down, but by nothing like so much. What happened *within* consumer-goods industries is, however, worthy of note. While the production of mass consumption goods lagged behind, with cotton textiles, and within cotton textiles the coarser varieties of cloth, very badly affected (Shetty, 1978: 14) (see also Patnaik and Rao, 1977: 124; Kelkar, 1977: 2133), that of luxury goods proceeded apace. It is the case that

> many industries which directly or indirectly cater to the requirements of the rich and upper middle sections of the community have registered phenomenal growth rates...disproportionately large increases in the output of manmade fibres, beverages, perfumes and cosmetics, commercial, office and household equipment, watches and clocks, finer varieties of cloth — all signify the emergence of an output structure that was getting increasingly élite-oriented. (Shetty, 1978: 18)

The same author mentions 'tooth-paste and tooth powder, baby food, radio sets, refrigerators, room air conditioners...scooters' (Shetty, 1978: 18).

There are features of India's industrial performance with profound structural implications: which suggest that structural or industrial transformation have not taken place to a degree or in a manner that would indicate a healthily functioning capitalism, and that India faces formidable barriers to her successful traversing of the capitalist path. These are at the level of the forces of production and relate to the inadequate development of Department 1, and in particular to two strategic elements, machine tools and oil. In each case a brief comparison with China proves illuminating.

In the Indian industrialization strategy that prominence has never been given to machine tools which their key role in an economy's capacity to produce would suggest as desirable. K.N. Raj has pointed to Dobb's powerful insight here (see, for example, Dobb, 1960) and his stress upon

> the peculiar ability of the machine-tools branch within the capital goods sector to initiate and sustain a circular production process of its own and of thus 'breaking out of the determinism' laid upon the sector by the existing structural relations. (Raj, 1967: 218)

Mahalanobis, the architect of India's Second Plan, did emphasize the distinction between capital goods for the manufacture of capital goods (which Dobb, for convenience, termed the 'machine-tool sector' (Raj, 1967: 217) and capital goods for the manufacture of consumer goods (Mahalanobis, 1963: Ch. 6), as Raj points out (Raj, 1967: 217). This did not, however, produce any particular focus upon machine tools within the Second Plan's general espousal of the development of capital goods industries, with only 1 per cent of total planned investment in the public sector allocated for machine-building industries and a similar allocation for private industry (Raj, 1967: 221), Thereafter, some further attention was given to the machine-tool sector in the Indian literature (Raj and Sen, 1959, 1961; Naqvi, 1963), and the Third Plan accorded it a somewhat more prominent place. But it never attained a place of central importance and, indeed, in both Second and Third Plan periods it was subject to 'considerable...shortfalls in performance' (Raj, 1967: 221). China, which started off at a very similar level of industrial development to India in the early 1950s but whose industrial performance has far outstripped that of India since then (Byres and Nolan, 1976: 16–17, 51–4), by contrast

> has attached very high priority to machine-building, and to the 'machine-tool sector' within it, from the very beginning of its development programme (Raj, 1967: 219)

allocating in her First Plan more than 5 per cent of her capital construction investment (which was analogous to India's planned investment) to machine-building (Raj, 1967: 220). It is a 'very high priority' that has continued (Rawski, 1980: 51–2, 65–6, 95–7). Thus, at about the time that the watershed I have identified with respect to industrial growth in India was reached, in the mid-1960s, Raj could point out that, while China could produce herself at least 85 per cent of her requirements of machinery and equipment, India could meet only 55 per cent of her needs from domestic production (Raj, 1967: 220–2). At that time, Raj was impressed by the far greater range of products and the greater sophistication in production which China seemed capable of (Raj, 1967: 221). Since then China's progress has continued to be impressive (Rawski, 1980: 65–6) and, indeed, Rawski cites the report of a team of American machine-tool specialists (published in 1975) to the effect that in China in the early 1970s

> the appearance is that of Japan in 1959–60 when she began her big push in the machine tool business.(Rawski, 1980: 66)

In India, however, no greater priority has been given to machine tools since the mid-1960s, and Shetty singles out mechanical engineering industries, and within them machine tools, as among those whose poor performance since 1965 constitutes strong evidence for 'structural retrogression' in the industrial sector (Shetty, 1978: 14, 18). To give some idea of one dimension of the problem, for the Fifth Plan period (1974–79) it was projected that the category 'metal products, machinery and transport equipment' (i.e. capital goods, more or less) would constitute 21 per cent of India's massive import bill (Government of India, *Fifth Five Year Plan*, 1976: 49, 114). India continues to labour under the constraint upon her industrial growth imposed by her inability to manufacture her own machinery and equipment. She has not been able to break out of Dobb's 'determinism of existing structural relations'.

When, in the 1950s, India and China embarked upon their respective programmes of industrialization, neither had any known deposits of oil of any importance. In neither had exploration that was anything other than cursory taken place. Oil, one need hardly add, is extremely important for the development of modern manufacturing industry. In India, it is still the case that known deposits are of minor importance, and India currently is heavily dependent upon imports of crude oil and badly hit by an increase in its price. An authority on India's oil industry tells us:

> Excepting for a brief period under the direction of K.D. Malaviya, the exploration programme of the Indian government has always been half-hearted, unimaginative and lop-sided. This is despite a large prospective oil-bearing area of 400,000 square miles of which three-quarters lie outside Gujarat and Assam, the two states which together accounted for one-third of 22.6 million tons of crude oil needed by Indian refineries in 1972. So far 95% of the drilling efforts have been confined to these two states, and the extent of geological knowledge about the huge sedimentary area is negligible. (Dasgupta, 1977: 71)

The Fifth Plan estimated that between 1974 and 1979 POL imports (petroleum products, crude oil and lubricants) would be a massive Rs. 6280 crores, or 22 per cent of total imports: the biggest single item on the projected import bill (Government of India, *Fifth Five Year Plan*, 1976: 49, 114). Of China, in the late 1950s, 'it was generally believed...that lack of domestic oil would be a major bottleneck to Chinese development' (Chen and Galenson, 1969: 78). In 1959, China imported about half the petroleum products she consumed from the Soviet Union (Chen and Galenson, 1969: 77) and was especially dependent on the Soviets for crude oil (Eckstein, 1977: 126). The Chinese were very concerned about this and in the 1960s

> a very active programme of geological exploration was launched which led to the discovery of significant new oil deposits. As a result, China became self-sufficient in crude oil and most oil products and by the 1970s became a supplier of oil to other countries, notably Japan. (Eckstein, 1977: 126)

The reasons for the divergence in practice and results between the two countries, with oil as with machine tools, are obviously several and complex, and our concern here is not with the details of the comparison. I would suggest that, for oil, one difference at least lies in the contrasting capacities to generate the large resources necessary for exploration and development; while for machine tools, too, as we have seen, a contrast in the scale of accumulation has been obvious.

Turning next to the structure of the labour force — to the level of relations of production and, in particular, to the formation of an industrial proletariat — one notes a feature of wide-ranging significance. I have already stressed that as an index of whether structural change is taking place the sectoral composition of the labour force is of obvious importance, and I have pointed to the structural stasis that characterized India before 1947. Again, the period since independence is sufficiently long for one to expect any tendency towards structural change to manifest itself. Table 6 reveals that the industrial growth

Table 6 Share of agriculture in the male
working force of India, 1911–1971
(%)

Year	Share
1911	66.7
1921	67.7
1931	65.9
1941	66.5
1951	64.9
1961	65.02
1971	67.40

Source: Krishnamurty (1972: 117).

of 7 to 7½ per cent per annum between the early 1950s and the mid-1960s and
the 3½ per cent per annum between the mid-1960s and now has had no impact
whatsoever upon the structure of India's working population. This is so at least
until 1971: it is unfortunate that this is being written before the results of the
1981 census would allow an updating. Astonishingly, the proportion of the
male working force in agriculture was the same in 1971 as it was in 1911 (and,
indeed, 1881: we note that the figures in Table 6 are calculated on a different
basis to those in Table 1, but that this does nothing to invalidate the point
made). There are, to be sure, greater absolute numbers in industry in general,
and more especially in manufacturing industry, and to that extent an industrial
proletariat has been formed. It is the case, however, that since the mid-1960s
any such absolute increase has slowed down and that of the 'niggardly
employment growth' (Shetty, 1978: 36) that has taken place in non-agricultural
activities since then

> the bulk has been in non-manufacturing activities like banking and insurance and
> Government administration. Manufacturing activities and even important infras-
> tructural activities like transport and communications have hardly absorbed any
> significant quantum of additional employment. (Shetty, 1978: 36)

The 1981 figures are unlikely to show any structural shift. The shifts postulated
by Lenin have not taken place in India. India continues to be in the constricting
grip of structural stasis.

The Post-colonial economy: (c) The Urban Bourgeoisie, the Public Sector, and the Crisis of Accumulation

We must now consider the two essential agents of accumulation: in the private
sector the urban bourgeoisie, and in the public sector the state. Such an analysis
is revealing. First, the urban bourgeoisie.

Starting with those two fractions of the urban bourgeoisie which I distinguished earlier, the manufacturing or industrial bourgeoisie and the commer-
cial/financial bourgeoisie, one notes a crucial implication. Looking at the
whole period from the early 1950s until the early 1970s, on a basis of the
available data one writer tells us:

> [the] ... share of re-investible profits in output seems to have declined, and the
> incremental output has benefited the recipients of non-work incomes — the
> property and asset holders ... . Re-investible profit margins do not seem to have
> increased on account of increasing prices of raw materials and intermediate goods.
> Margins in trade and business, profits on agricultural surplus and contract incomes
> are some of the major categories of incomes which seem to have been swelled
> during the period of steep rise in prices. A large part of these incomes have also a
> tendency to be spent on purposes other than productive investment either on
> account of their doubtful legal antecendents or a high tendency for conspicuous
> consumption among their holders. (Papola, 1973: 2299–300: Papola cites Ranadive,
> 1973 and Shetty, 1973.)

Very clearly, the commercial bourgeoisie has gained more than the manufacturing bourgeoisie and would seem to be in the ascendancy, a fact that bodes
ill for the full success of industrialization in India and for the development of
capitalism. The discomfiture of the manufacturing bourgeoisie is borne out by
other evidence. Thus, a study of twenty-one manufacturing industries
between 1946 and 1965 — including both Department 1 and Department 2
industries —appears to show a tendency for the rate of profit to decline over
the period (Chattopadhyay, 1977: 24–8, 26–7, 30–1); while another, which
examines the Reserve Bank of India data on profits after tax for a sample of
both public and private limited liability companies between 1960–61 and
1970–71 concludes that:

> while profits as a proportion of capital employed have increased in one or two
> activities since 1960–61, the overall picture is one of general stagnation, if not of
> general decline in the rate of return. (Mitra, 1977b: Ch. 10.)

These are tendencies which we must assume to have been accentuated in the
years which followed, in view of the evidence presented for the post-1965 era.
The only industries exempt from them are that small group producing luxury
products which we have noted has experienced substantial growth after 1965.
Private manufacturing industry in India is characterized by a deep-seated
accumulation crisis: accumulation, which has never proceeded on an extended scale, has slackened off to very low levels because it has become
decreasingly worthwhile.

If we look at the urban bourgeoisie along another line of division, that of
the bigger sections of capital or monopoly capital and medium/smaller
capital, further disquieting features emerge. The old managing agency system

was legislated out of existence in the early 1960s (Chandra, 1977: 1405), but the underlying reality of a powerful monopoly capital, of which, ultimately, it was but a surface expression, remained untouched. Hazari, in his path-breaking study, identified, in the 1950s, twenty large houses, which exercised a remarkable degree of control over the private corporate sector, in a wide diversity of fields (Hazari, 1966), with

> an interest of one kind or another in 983 companies with a share capital of Rs.236 crores in 1951 and 1073 companies with a share capital of Rs.352 crores in 1958 ... . These companies accounted for 29.2 and 32.4 per cent of the share-capital of nongovernment companies in 1951 and 1958 respectively. (Government of India, *Report of the Mahalanobis Committee*, 1964: 41; a convenient summary of Hazari's findings and of his data may be seen in this report, pp. 39–43.)

That monopoly power which Hazari showed to be on the increase in the 1950s has been the subject of subsequent study: by the Monopolies Inquiry Commission for 1964 (Government of India, *Report of the Monopolies Inquiry Commission*, 1965); by the Industrial Licensing Policy Inquiry Committee for 1966 (Government of India, *Report of the Industrial Licensing Policy Inquiry Committee*, 1969); by Dutta for 1966 (Dutta, 1970); by various official agencies for 1971 (cited by Ghose, 1974), 1972 (cited by Oza, 1977), and 1973, 1974, 1975, 1976 (cited in Chandra, 1979); and by Chandra (Chandra, 1979). It has been the subject of monopoly legislation (the Monopolies and Restrictive Trade Practices Act of 1969) and is now under the scrutiny of a Monopolies Commission (Chandra, 1977: 1405 *et passim*). Chandra examines this body of data, with its differing conceptual bases, is an excellent guide across an often bewildering terrain, and concludes that if one looks at the 'monopoly share' of private corporate assets for the whole period 1951 to 1975 it certainly reveals 'no decline in the share of the monopoly houses' (Chandra, 1979: 1261). His conclusion errs on the side of caution. His carefully compiled index of monopoly share shows a quite definite increase between 1951 and 1971, a levelling off thereafter, and over the whole period a perceptible rise in concentration (see Table 7). The nature of monopoly capital is of great significance for our problematic. Obviously, its power to accumulate is great. But that power has not been mobilized to secure India's industrial transformation. On the contrary, its very existence, given the characteristics of Indian monopoly capital, is an obstacle to successful industrialization via the private sector. Chandra argues:

> monopolists in India have generally been able to retain or expand their market power not so much by superior economic efficiency, but by controlling the supply of raw materials and intermediates through their intimate links with the state machinery at various levels, restrictive selling practices designed to shut out smaller firms, and an easy access to cheap industrial finance. On the other hand, such credits, despite the nationalisation of banking and insurance are effectively denied to the vast majority of

Table 7 Index numbers of the share of monopoly houses in the assets of the private corporate sector in India, 1951–1975

Year	Index
1951	100
1958	113
1964	100
1966	106
1968	117
1969	119
1971	120
1972	115
1973	116
1974	112
1975	119

Source: Chandra (1979: 1257). See there for the methodology and the statistical manipulations upon which the index numbers are based.

small capitalists who have to fall back either on their own limited resources or on usurious moneylenders. (Chandra, 1979: 1270)

The bigger sections of capital in India continue to veer towards financial manipulation rather than productive performance, and they are effective in preventing the productive activity of medium/smaller capital being translated into a major engine of accumulation. Chandra concludes:

...monopoly capitalism in India bears a closer family resemblance to pre-industrial monopolies than to contemporary monopoly capitalism in the West, and constitutes *ipso facto* one of the major obstacles...to the transformation of India along capitalist lines. (Chandra, 1979: 1270)

At the very least, this is a hypothesis that deserves the closest attention.

If India's urban bourgeoisie has not been such as to secure an industrial transformation which might meet, even remotely, Marx's criteria, what of the public sector — that most important and tangible site of state capitalism, where the state can itself accumulate directly and develop the forces of production, in the necessary direction and to the requisite extent? The state has, indeed, attempted to develop Department 1, and most Department 1 industry is located in the public sector. Moreover, public sector activity has achieved a position of dominating influence in the Indian industrial domain: already, by 1966, making 50 per cent of total domestic investment and 75 per cent of investment in organized industry (Shetty, 1978: 65). Thus, the public sector has occupied a position of strategic importance with respect to those industries whose development was most meagre in India but which are central to any attempt at industrial transformation; and not only that but by virtue of this very position

> the level of investment in the public sector plays a catalytic role in sustaining and accelerating the overall level of capital formation in the economy (Government of India, *Economic Survey, 1971–72*, 1972: 40, (cited in Shetty, 1978: 65)

with crucial repercussions upon the private sector. Our earlier discussion indicates that the results have been disappointingly inadequate and that these industries have performed badly after 1965. We singled out machine tools and oil and showed public sector performance here to have been particularly weak (the Chinese comparison underlining the extent of the weakness). The responsibility undertaken by the state to create the essential sinews of modern industry — a responsibility assigned to the state from the very outset by an urban bourgeoisie conscious of its own weakness — has not been successfully discharged. India's incapacity in this most fundamental area remains a striking source of weakness. Part, at least, of this failure of state capitalism — failure in terms of the imperatives of successful industrial transformation — may be traced to the process of accumulation itself and to the public sector's inability to give it shape on the massive scale that is needed. A recent study tells us that, for the years following 1965, while the public sector's share in net domestic product rose steadily (from 11.8 per cent in 1964–5 to 17.1 per cent in 1975–6) its share of net domestic saving declined significantly (from 30.2 to 21.7 per cent over the same period and with far lower proportions in intervening years — for example 12.1 per cent in 1967–8), and with it the proportion of net domestic product in the public sector saved (from 25.7 to 20.9 per cent, going lower in other years — for example, to 10.2 per cent in 1967–8): implying a negative marginal rate of saving in the public sector (Shetty, 1978: 41, Table 35; 49–50). The same study documents, in some detail, 'the most glaring financial profligacy and indiscipline' (p. 50), with smaller and smaller proportions of total outlays going to productive investment: and not, either, as is sometimes suggested, because of rising defence appropriations, but rather as a result of the disproportionate growth of non-development expenditure other than defence (p. 51). Moreover, public enterprises incurred

> enormous amounts of losses...through inefficient working as well as through uneconomic pricing policies. (p. 61)

These artificially low prices represented an indirect subsidy to private enterprise, but not one that could be justified in terms of any sustained accumulation in the private sector. Indian industry — both in the public and the private sectors — has been characterized by significant underutilization of capacity (Raj, 1976: 233–6; Shetty, 1978: 8). That should not, however, be taken to imply the absence of the need to accumulate. On the contrary, it is arguable that large investment in public sector Department 1 industries would have had the effect of removing that underutilization and inducing net investment elsewhere in the economy. But India's public sector has, by its very nature, proved incapable of generating such accumulation.

Conclusion: In Lieu of a Full Analysis of Essential Underlying Causes

In a sense, to argue that sustained public sector investment might have lifted India from her industrial 'stagnation' and arrested her 'structural retrogression', and might, indeed, have impelled her towards that industrial transformation predicted by Marx 130 years ago, is analogous to our comparison with China. It points not, in any immediate sense, towards *possibilities*, for such possibilities have as their prerequisite fundamental social and political change. It is precisely the unlikelihood of the suggested action being taken that constitutes India's dilemma: India's crisis of accumulation. Rather, it points towards the essential underlying causes. Analysis of these causes is beyond the scope of this chapter. But the roots of India's crisis of accumulation surely lie deep in her history, which we have touched upon; in the processes of class formation, in town and country, some of which we have hinted at; and in the relationships she has forged with international capital, which we have so far ignored. We may finish with the briefest of outlines, in lieu of a full analysis.

I have argued in several previous papers that in India the town-country relationship has been of central importance in impeding the development of Indian industry: with an inadequate flow of marketed surplus from country to town, terms of trade unfavourable to industry since the late 1950s, and a marked inability on the part of the Indian state to tax agriculture (Byres, 1972b; 1974; 1979; 1981). I think that this most certainly has been of crucial importance. Adverse terms of trade have contributed to the declining rate of profit in manufacturing industry; the failure to tax agriculture has been a large part of the state's lack of success in mobilizing resources on a scale sufficient to generate the requisite level of accumulation; while an inadequate agricultural surplus and the general insufficiency of agriculture as a source of accumulation have driven the Indian state on the one hand in the direction of foreign aid and private foreign capital and on the other towards a concerted attack on organized labour. I have treated the neo-colonial relationships inherent in aid and private foreign investment elsewhere (Byres, 1972c), and suggested that, far from alleviating any crisis of accumulation, they serve, in a variety of ways, to exacerbate it. Aid, for example, by taking pressure off the state to mobilize resources domestically and (to the extent that it contributes only to the most partial of industrial transformations) by postponing such action simply makes it more difficult to achieve in future, through the entrenching of interests that is thereby permitted. Private foreign investment secures some development of the productive forces, but a development that is inappropriate and undesirable: it has, for example, contributed to the post-1965 upsurge of growth in luxury industries that we have noted (cf. Shetty, 1978: 19); and it imparts an excessive degree of capital-intensity, which minimizes employment creation and so intensifies the structural stasis which characterizes the Indian economy. Neither aid nor private foreign investment has brought about the adequate growth of Department 1 and, in particular, they have failed to destroy the barrier to industrial transformation inherent in a weak machine-tool sector and an absence of oil. I have also pointed to the success of the urban bourgeoisie in keeping the real wages of the urban proletariat constant (Byres and Nolan, 1976: 66) and the deploying of the coercive power of the state against a weak and divided urban proletariat (Byres, 1976: xi–xii; 1981). While this has given the urban bourgeoisie a little more room for manoeuvre, it has assuredly not constituted a source of accumulation anything like sufficient to relieve the crisis of accumulation. Indeed, inasmuch as it narrows the home market even further it may worsen that crisis.

This takes us to a final issue: to what extent can one attribute India's industrial 'stagnation', and, more generally, her failure to create a factory system such as to meet Marx's criteria, to the 'problem of the home market'? Several writers have suggested that this might be so, with varying degrees of emphasis (Bagchi, 1970; Raj, 1976; Mitra, 1977a, b; Nayyar, 1978; Chakravarty, 1979). That such a problem is important is obvious. We recall Lenin's statement apropos of the postulated necessary shift out of agriculture:

> It need hardly be proved that the significance of this circumstance as regards the problem of the home market is enormous, for it is bound up inseparably with the evolution of industry and with the evolution of agriculture; the formation of industrial centres, their numerical growth, and the attraction of the population by them cannot but exert a most profound influence on the whole rural system and cannot but give rise to a growth of commercial and capitalist agriculture. (Lenin, 1964: 40–1)

It is the shift of labour that creates the home market, both in the mass market constituted by a growing wage-earning proletariat in the cities and in the market formed by a thoroughly commercialized, capitalist agriculture. Such a shift has not taken place in India. To the extent that the bulk of the population continues, persistently, to be 'trapped in agriculture' (to use Sheila Bhalla's evocative phrase, Bhalla, 1977: 1903), in circumstances of low productivity, for the most part, and very unequal distribution, and to the extent that urban real wages are relentlessly kept down and urban distribution of income is grossly unequal (see Byres and Nolan, 1976, for a treatment of some of the evidence on unequal distribution in both town and country), then there must, indeed, be a serious problem of realizing surplus value. It is a problem which, for a country of India's size, cannot possibly be resolved through exports, however much of an export boom one might conceive of as possible (cf. Chandra, 1977: 1412–14;

and see Nayyar, 1978: 1276 and Nayyar's authoritative and exhaustive study of Indian exports in the 1960s, Nayyar, 1976). But does the 'home market problem' constitute the essence of India's blocked industrialization? I would suggest not. It is itself the product of a failure of accumulation. Only accumulation could generate the necessary shifts of labour. And if, tomorrow, the 'home market problem' were to disappear — let us say through the sudden emergence of limitless export markets — the roots of India's accumulation crisis would remain undisturbed. Indian industry, if we may revert to the passage from Marx with which we started, continues to come up against formidable barriers which are logically prior to 'those presented by the availability of...sales outlets'.

References

Bagchi, Amiya K. (1970). 'Long-term constraints on India's industrial growth, 1951–1968, in E.A.G. Robinson and Michael Kidron (eds.), *Economic Development in South Asia* (Macmillan, London).

Bagchi, Amiya K. (1972). *Private Investment in India, 1900–1939* (Cambridge University Press).

Banaji, Jairus (1972). 'For a theory of colonial modes of production', *Economic and Political Weekly*, 23 December, **VII**, no. 52.

Banaji, Jairus (no date). 'The Indian Bourgeoisie and Congress'.

Bhagwati, Jagdish N. and Desai, Padma (1970). *India, Planning for Industrialization: Industrialization and Trade Policies since 1951*, (Oxford University Press).

Bhalla, Sheila (1977). 'Agricultural growth: role of institutional and infrastructural factors', *Economic and Political Weekly*, 5, 12 November, **XII**, nos. 45 and 46.

Byres, T.J. (1966). 'Indian planning on the eve of the Fourth Five Year Plan', *The World Today*, March, **22**, no. 3.

Byres, T.J. (1972a). 'Industrialization, the Peasantry and the Economic Debate in Post-Independence India', in A.V. Bhuleshkar (ed.), *Towards the Socialist Transformation of the Indian Economy* (Popular Prakashan; Bombay).

Byres, T.J. (1972b). 'The dialectic of India's Green Revolution', *South Asian Review*, January, **5**, no. 2.

Byres, T.J. (1972c). 'The white man's burden in a neo-colonial setting', in T.J. Byres (ed.), *Foreign Resources and Economic Development* (Cass, London).

Byres, T.J. (1974). 'Land reform, industrialisation and the marketed surplus in India: an essay on the power of rural bias', in David Lehmann (ed.), *Agrarian Reform and Agrarian Reformism* (Faber and Faber, London).

Byres, T.J. (1976). 'Introduction', in Ashok Mitra, *Calcutta Diary* (Cass, London).

Byres, T.J. (1977). 'Agrarian transition and the agrarian question', *Journal of Peasant Studies*, April, **4**, no. 3.Byres, T.J. (1979). 'Of neo-populist pipe dreams; Daedalus in the Third World and the myth of urban bias', *Journal of Peasant Studies*, January, **6**, no.2.

Byres, T.J. (1981). 'The new technology, class formation and class action in the Indian countryside', *Journal of Peasant Studies*, July, **8**, no. 4.

Byres, T.J. and Nolan, Peter (1976). *Inequality: India and China Compared, 1950–70* (The Open University Press, Milton Keynes).

Chakravarty, Sukhamoy (1979). 'On the question of home market and prospects for

Indian growth', *Economic and Political Weekly*, August, Special Number, **XIV**, nos. 30–32.

Chandra, Nirmal K. (1977). 'Monopoly legislation and policy in India', *Economic and Political Weekly*, August, Special Number, **XII**, nos. 33–34.

Chandra, Nirmal K. (1979). 'Monopoly capital, private corporate sector and the Indian economy: a study in relative growth, 1931–76', *Economic and Political Weekly*, August, Special Number, **XIV**, nos. 30–32.

Chattopadhyay, P. (1970). 'State capitalism in India', *Monthly Review*, March, **21**, no. 10. Reprinted in S.A. Shad (ed.), *Towards National Liberation. Essays on the Political Economy of India* (Montreal, 1973).

Chattopadhyay, Suhas (1977). 'Falling tendency of the rate of profit in Indian manufacturing industries', *Social Scientist*, January/February, **5**, no. 6/7 (no. 54–5).

Chen, Nai-Ruenn, and Galenson, Walter (1969). *The Chinese Economy under Communism*, (Edinburgh University Press).

Dasgupta, Biplab (1977). 'World oil, development, and India', *Social Scientist*, January/February, **5**, no. 6/7 (no. 54–5).

Dobb, Maurice (1960). *An Essay on Economic Growth and Planning* (Routledge & Kegan Paul, London).

Dutta, B. (1970). *Company News and Notes*, May.

Eckstein, Alexander (1977). *China's Economic Revolution* (Cambridge University Press).

Gadgil, D.R. (1955). 'Indian economic organization', in Simon Kuznets, Wilbert E. Moore, Joseph J. Spengler (eds.), *Economic Growth: Brazil, India, Japan* (Duke University Press, Durham, NC).

Gadgil, D.R. (1971). *The Industrial Evolution of India in Recent Times, 1860–1939*, 5th edition (Oxford University Press, Bombay).

Ghose, Aurobindo (1974). 'Joint sector and "control" of Indian monopoly', *Economic and Political Weekly*, 8 June, **IX**, no. 23.

Gordon, Alec (1973). 'The theory of the "progressive" national bourgeoisie', *Journal of Contemporary Asia*, **3**, no. 2.

Government of India (1952). *The First Five Year Plan* (New Delhi).

Government of India (1953). *Programmes of Industrial Development, 1951–56* (New Delhi).

Government of India (1964). *Report of the Committee on Distribution of Income and Levels of Living, Part 1: Distribution of Income and Concentration of Economic Power (Report of the Mahalanobis Committee)* (New Delhi).

Government of India (1965). *Report of the Monopolies Inquiry Commission* (New Delhi).

Government of India (1969). *Report of the Industrial Licensing Policy Inquiry Committee* (New Delhi).

Government of India (1972). *Economic Survey, 1971–72* (New Delhi).

Government of India (1976). *Fifth Five Year Plan, 1974–79* (New Delhi).

Harris, Frank (1958). *Jamsetji Nusserwanji Tata. A Chronicle of His Life* (Blackie, Bombay).

Hazari, R.K. (1966). *The Structure of the Corporate Private Sector* (Asia Publishing House, Bombay).

Johnson, William A. (1966). *The Steel Industry of India* (Harvard University Press, Cambridge, Mass.).

Kelkar, Vijay Laxman (1977). 'Growth possibilities in the Indian economy', *Economic and Political Weekly*, 24 December, **XII**, no. 52.

Kidron, Michael (1965). *Foreign Investments in India* (Oxford University Press).

Krishnamurty, J. (1972). 'Working force in 1971 census. Some exercises on provisional results', *Economic and Political Weekly*, 15 January, **VII**, no. 3.
Lenin, V.I. (1964). *The Development of Capitalism in Russia, Collected Works*, vol. 3 (Progress Publishers, Moscow).
Mahalanobis, P.C. (1963). *The Approach of Operational Research to Planning in India* (Asia Publishing House, London).
Marx, Karl (1976). *Capital*, Volume 1 (Penguin Books, London).
Marx, Karl and Engels, F. (no date). *On Colonialism* (Foreign Languages Publishing Company, Moscow).
Mitra, Ashok (1977). 'Industrial growth and income distribution', *Social Scientist*, January/February, **5**, no. 6/7 (no. 54–5).
Mitra, Ashok (1977b). *Terms of Trade and Class Relations* (Cass, London).
Mukherjee, Aditya (1976). 'Indian capitalist class and the public sector, 1930–1947', *Economic and Political Weekly*, 17 January, **XI**, no. 3.
Myers, C. (1958). *Labour Problems in the Industrialisation of India* (Asia Publishing House, Bombay).
Naqvi, K.A. (1963). 'Machine tools and machines: a physical interpretation of the marginal rate of saving', *The Indian Economic Review*, February, **VI**, no. 3.
Nayyar, Deepak (1976). *India's Exports and Export Policies in the 1960s* (Cambridge University Press).
Nayyar, Deepak (1978). 'Industrial development in India: some reflections on growth and stagnation', *Economic and Political Weekly*, August, Special Number, **XII**, nos. 31–3.
Nehru, Jawaharlal (1958). *Jawaharlal Nehru's Speeches, volume 1, 1946–1949* (Government of India, New Delhi).
Oza, A.N. (1977). *The Illustrated Weekly of India*, 18 September.
Papola, T.S. (1973). 'Income policies for India', *Economic and Political Weekly*, 29 December, **VIII**, no. 52.
Patnaik, Prabhat and Rao, S.K. (1977). '1975–76: beginning of the end of stagnation?', *Social Scientist*, January/February, **5**, no. 6/7, (no. 54–5).
Raj, K.N. (1967). 'Role of the "machine-tools sector" in economic growth. A comment on Indian and Chinese experience', in C.H. Feinstein (ed.), *Socialism, Capitalism and Economic Growth. Essays Presented to Maurice Dobb* (Cambridge University Press).
Raj, K.N. (1976). 'Growth and stagnation in Indian industrial development', *Economic and Political Weekly*, February, Annual Number, **XI**, nos. 5–7.
Raj, K.N. and Sen A.K. (1959). 'Sectoral models for development planning', *Arthaniti*, May, **II**, no. 2.
Raj, K.N. and Sen, A.K. (1961). 'Alternative patterns of growth under conditions of stagnant export earnings', *Oxford Economic Papers*, February, **13**, no. 1.
Ranadive, K.R. (1973). 'Distribution of income concept of justice and the right to property', paper read at Golden Jubilee seminar, Department of Economics, University of Bombay.
Rawski, Thomas G. (1980). *China's transition to Industrialism. Producer Goods and Economic Development in the Twentieth Century* (University of Michigan Press, Ann Arbor).
Shetty, S.L. (1973). 'Trends in wages and salaries and profits of the private corporate sector', *Economic and Political Weekly*, 13 October, **XIII**, no. 41.
Shetty, S.L. (1978). *Structural Retrogression in the Indian Economy Since the Mid-Sixties* (Economic and Political Weekly, Bombay).
Thorner, Daniel and Thorner, Alice (1960). *The Working Force of India, 1881–1951,*

Part One, Trends in Size and Industrial Distribution, mimeo, Bombay, Census of 1961 Project: India Statistical Institute.

Thorner, Daniel and Thorner, Alica (1962). '"De-industrialization" in India, 1881–1931', in their *Land and Labour in India* (Asia Publishing House, Bombay).

The Struggle for Development:
National Strategies in an International Context
Edited by M. Bienefeld and M. Godfrey
© 1982 John Wiley & Sons Ltd.

Chapter 6

Brazil: the Economics of Savage Capitalism

REGIS DE CASTRO ANDRADE

In a metaphorical sense, Brazil is a frontier of the capitalist world. It is the empty lands to be conquered by the gun and turned into profitable business. In a more analytical sense, it is a young industrialized country where capital has spread in a blind rush, without developing the self-consciousness and institutions which could have attenuated its socially unacceptable effects. In any sense it is a case of savage capitalism. But is it a success? From the point of view of growth, yes. The GDP grew at an average compound rate of 7 per cent a year from 1947 to 1977. From the point of view of the wellbeing of the Brazilian population, no. The 'unprivileged half' of the population has never been so unprivileged. The majority of those with relatively stable jobs earn less today than they did twenty years ago.

While growth and persistent poverty are one of the dominant features of the Brazilian case, it is nevertheless true that Brazil is also one of the rare instances of a successful transition from backwardness to capitalist modernity in the last few decades. How has this been possible in the hostile international environment of the twentieth century?

This paper provides some elements for a discussion of these general questions. However, the socio-political and, more generally, the broad historical conditions of development are not dealt with here in a direct way. Instead of taking the Brazilian case as an illustration of a general thesis, the paper focuses on the specific mechanisms and structures of capital accumulation in the country.

The first section contains an introductory description of the origins of the modern Brazilian economy, from 1930 to the economic crisis of 1962–67. The next section analyses the 'Brazilian model'. The third section deals with the economic boom of 1968–73 (the 'Brazilian miracle'), and with recent developments. The last section discusses the prospects now opened for the Brazilian economy in the light of the previous analyses.

A Brief Historical Introduction

The industrial era in Brazil started in 1930, with the collapse of the international coffee market. The sudden contraction of external trade which followed the 'crack' of 1929 was partially offset by Government purchases of unsaleable coffee. This policy, and favourable conditions created by import difficulties, stimulated industrial investments and sustained the economy during the worst years. Total output fell off by less than 10 per cent in the early depression years, and by 1933 had recovered to the level of 1929. Such a combination of external constraints and economic policies reinforced the internal factors of development. Industry gradually became the leading sector of this process. The internal market became more attractive than the external one (Furtado, 1963).

The revolution of 1930, led by Getulio Vargas, strengthened the federal state to the detriment of the local systems of power. This would, in itself, have paved the way for industrial development in so far as it reduced the influence of the old oligarchic politicians linked to export interest. But until the mid-1930s, industry was not directly fostered by the state.

In 1937, following the anti-imperialist uprising of 1935, Vargas assumed full dictatorial powers. The previous authoritarian and centralizing tendencies were consolidated into strong politico-administration structures. The alliance, never to be broken, between the urban bourgeoisie and the rural oligarchies was by then cemented. The local oligarchies would be removed from the central spheres of Government in exchange for social peace and for maintenance of their local political and economic power. The industrial bourgeoisie emerged as the most influential class in government.

In Brazil, the industrial bourgeoisie rose at a time when the material basis of oligarchic rule had been weakened by the world crisis; but so long as the old politicians still retained the levers of local power throughout the country, the rising bourgeoisie could only consolidate its supremacy over the oligarchy, on the one hand, and over the popular movement, on the other, by controlling a powerful state (Andrade, 1979).

Undisputed rule by the executive power in economic matters is a central characteristic of the capitalist order in the country. Several economic agencies of the state, empowered to formulate and implement sectoral policies, were created during the *Estado Novo*. The new democratic constitution of 1946 did not alter this administrative structure.

The early development of industry in Brazil was favoured by the crisis of the industrialized economies in the 1930s and in the Second World War years. From 1945 onwards international competition increased. Strong foreign exchange controls involving multiple exchange rates were established in 1947. Coffee income, swollen by rising international prices, was partially appropriated by the state and transferred to industry. Subsidized exchange rates for intermediate and capital goods and high rates for consumption goods generated a protected market for the latter. This system discouraged the vertical integration of industry as a whole. Traditional industries modernized rapidly.

President Juscelino Kubitschek's 'Plan of Targets' (1956–61) was an attempt to correct the industrial imbalances generated in the previous period (Lessa, 1964). This period constitutes a turning point in the economic history of Brazil. Substantial changes were introduced in the scope and magnitude of state intervention, in the industrial structure and in the pattern of relations with the industrialized countries. Public investments jumped from 25.8 per cent of total investments in 1952–56 to 35.6 per cent in 1956–60, largely by virtue of state investments in electric power and transport infrastructure programmes (Escritório de Pesquisa Econômica Aplicada (EPEA), 1966). The large financial resources required for accelerated development were extracted from the economy through fiscal and monetary instruments, including the printing of money. An array of development institutions was mobilized or created to deal with tariff, monetary, financial and sectoral development matters. Among those institutions, the Executive Groups were in charge of defining guidelines and standards for the development of the main industrial sectors, as well as of granting or recommending incentives to particular investment projects (Martins, 1976). Such powerful institutional machinery operated largely outside democratic controls. It sheltered the interests of industrial big business in the country, both national and foreign.

Extremely liberal policies regarding foreign capital were initiated in 1953 and reinforced by Kubitschek. They comprised preferential exchange rates for profit remittances, favourable rules concerning the registration of capital, the right to import capital goods without exchange coverage by the authorities and tariff exemptions or reductions. Other internal tax and credit benefits completed the set of measures which made conditions highly attractive to foreign investors. In quantitative terms, results were impressive, as shown in Table 1. Direct investments from abroad concentrated on large industrial enterprises, especially in the following sectors: motor vehicles, shipbuilding, engineering, heavy electrical equipment and steel industries.

Direct foreign investments raised the degree of monopoly in Brazilian industry. All new dynamic sectors had an oligopolistic structure. Big assemblers faced a cluster of suppliers in a situation of oligopsony. Consequently, productivity gains generated almost anywhere in the economy tended to be transferred, through price mechanisms, either to the final stage of production, or to the basic capital goods industries. This could eventually have reduced the dynamic impulse of the new big investments. However, the forward and

Table 1   Inflow and outflow of foreign capital, 1947–61
(US$ million)

Capital flows[a]	1947–55	1956–61
Average yearly inflow	265.3	707.8
Financing	204.0	561.8
Direct investments	61.3	146.0
Average yearly outflow	203.7	489.5
Amortizations	85.3	340.5
Profits and other	118.4	149.0
Average yearly balance	61.6	218.3

Source: Brazilian Balance of Payments, Superintendencia da Moeda e do Credito (SUMOC) and Central Bank Bulletins.
[a] Compensatory loans not included.

backward complementarity of these investments, in the context of a previously expanding economy, enhanced their net development effects during the first years of the cycle.

In the medium run, overaccumulation was predictable. The highly oligopolistic structure of industry meant that falling rates of industrial growth would severely hit the smaller units; this, in turn, would lead to further industrial concentration. Serious problems of dynamic instability were thus inherent in this pattern of development. At the same time, problems of profit realization appeared. The reduced possibility of making profits in a situation of excess capacity leads to increased profit remittances in periods of low activity, with negative effects on the balance of payments (Tavares, 1977).

Strictly speaking, the cluster of foreign investments of the late 1950s did not denationalize Brazilian industry in so far as they inaugurated new product lines. For the same reason, the rising degree of monopoly did not imply, at the beginning, the disappearance of smaller firms. Everybody benefited from this 'bunching' of investments with a large component of foreign capital. Wages rose until 1959, although at a lower rate than productivity. Industrial employment also rose significantly, although urban expansion reached even higher rates. Hence this development strategy did not provoke immediate reactions from the nationalist popular movement. However, strong nationalist opposition emerged in the early 1960s under President Joao Goulart.

During this period there was no absolute reduction of the real income of any stratum of the urban working population. Income concentration occurred, however, as the natural result (i) of the new pattern of industrialization in the context of an abundant supply of labour; and (ii) of a very fast expansion of demand for white-collar labour both in the private and public sectors (Oliveira, 1977).

A crisis emerged in 1962–63. Estimated capacity utilization in the capital goods industry fell to 60 per cent in the early 1960s (Reischstul and Goldenstein, 1980). In the sector of heavy engineering products the relation of estimated demand to capacity was under 30 per cent in steam generators, electrical turbines, step-up transformers, metal structures and direct-fired horizontal furnaces (Economic Commission for Latin America (ECLA), 1963). The annual rate of increase in output of the capital goods sector as a whole fell from 20 per cent in 1962 to 2.6 per cent in 1963, and decreased in the following years (Leff, 1968). Arguably, the crisis could have been attenuated by increased investment efforts by the state. Financial resources, however, were particularly scarce. Budgetary deficits had already reached the high level of 4.2 per cent of GDP in 1963. External credit, which was required in large amounts given the high import coefficients of state investments, was limited, due partly to the ill-feeling and/or scepticism displayed by international agencies during those years of high inflation, partly to the nationalistic policies of the Brazilian government and partly to the general political unrest in the country (Belluzzo and Cardoso de Mello, 1977).

In the consumer durables industry, the effects of product differentiation and sales promotion efforts may have been strengthened by the Government's decision to expand consumer credit. This had been timidly attempted, with moderate success, in those years of recession. The annual average sectoral rate of growth declined from 24 per cent (1955–62) to 4.1 per cent (1962–67).

Budgetary deficits — partly caused by the precariousness of the existing financial system — accelerated the inflationary process up to almost 100 per cent in 1963–64 despite diminishing wages (Kahil, 1973). A political decision by the nationalist government of President Goulart not to give up development policies was behind that process. Thus, structural and conjunctural as well as economic and political factors must be taken into account in the explanation of the 1962–67 crisis in Brazil.

A military *coup d'état* in March 1964 deposed Goulart's government. An authoritarian regime was set up in which congress and the unions played virtually no role. However, this was not a mere military dictatorship. The new regime expressed the increasing political power, in the executive, of the big business community associated with the high state technocracy and military officers.

To reduce inflation was target number one of the new government. Notwithstanding the severity of the stabilization programme — especially with regard to wages — results were neither immediate nor satisfactory. Production fell; but prices were not affected to the same degree. The ability of the oligopolistic sectors to translate all cost increases into final prices is one of the main causes of unresponsiveness to orthodox anti-inflationary therapy (Fishlow, 1974).

The 'Brazilian Model'

The Autonomy of the 'Model'

The development of industrial capitalism in Brazil cannot be dissociated from the development of world capitalism. But it would be naïve to think that the Brazilian economy is *nothing but* a local department of a single global system, thereby assuming that by knowing the laws of international capitalism one knows the laws of capitalism in Brazil. Specific historical evidence — the gist of which has been given in the last section — shows that fast industrialization incorporating foreign capital required the *previous* consolidation of the state of Brazil.

In other words, it required the political organization of local social forces and aspirations, of particular economic conditions and potentialities which, under bourgeois leadership, would provide the institutional framework and motivation for development. Whatever the influence of foreign powers in its constitution, the national state expresses the peculiar historical identity of a country.

Development, in Brazil, is an ambivalent process. It did not remove the element of domination inherent in centre-periphery relations; it just changed its forms and mode of operation. But in so far as development presupposed the constitution of a local system of power, fighting, at the international level, for the control of an increasing wealth, it brought the national question to the fore. Some dream of a future Great Power. Others react against the subordination of the national productive efforts to multinational interests.

Economically, Brazil has developed into a relatively autonomous system. Its economy is now diversified and to a considerable extent, self-determined, in the sense that its cyclical fluctuations are largely explained by endogenous variables. Even the powerful attempts by multinational corporations (MNCs) to achieve complete domination of the economy are mostly *internal* to the Brazilian policy-making process. This is clearly shown by some case studies describing the negotiations between the Government, MNCs and national capital over major projects involving strategic choices on technology and resource allocation (Tavares and Dick, 1974).

The endogenous nature of the cycle had already been stressed in the early 1970s (Singer 1965). More recently, emphasis has been put on sectoral imbalances in industrial structure which characterize late capitalist countries. In particular, the relatively small size of the capital goods and durables industries explains their instability. These industries are characterized by high rates of growth during periods of general expansion, followed by severe contractions. In this perspective, external imbalances and inflation are not primary factors in crises. They are symptoms of declining rates of expansion. When the pace of economic activity slows down, the struggle for the diminishing mass of profits inflates prices. Non-invested resources are transferred to the financial circuit. Foreign credit required for external equilibrium becomes more expensive (Tavares and Belluzzo, 1979).

The Economic Role of the State

The economic activity of the state has strong dynamic and stabilizing effects on the economy as a whole. The state's share of total fixed investment is very substantial, rising from about 38 per cent in 1970 to 43 per cent in 1978. It has been estimated that 35 per cent of the total demand for locally produced capital goods in 1975 was generated by public investments (Suzigan, 1976). In 1974, the state controlled 68.5 per cent of assets in mining, 72.6 per cent in steelworks, 96.4 per cent in oil production and 34.8 per cent in chemicals and petrochemicals. It monopolizes railway transport, communications, generation and distribution of electric and nuclear energy, and other public services. All these productive activities have been supported by the state's unorthodox financial structure. Besides the budgetary resources, the state stimulates private long-term savings through fiscal and credit benefits; it collects forced saving in the form of compulsory contributions by all wage and salary-earners to government-controlled social funds; and it manipulates huge amounts of resources through the open market, kept busy by high rates of monetary indexation and interest.

The state's productive activity affects the industrial sector as a whole in four main ways. First, it generates external economies to be appropriated by the private sector. Research carried out in 1977 on a sample of 1261 leading firms of all sectors revealed that the state's productive sectors contributed 7 per cent of total industrial output; scale of production and capital intensity were higher in the public sector than in the private sector; but profits in the state's productive sector were well below average by virtue of its low-price policies (Tavares and Facanha, 1977). Secondly, the state attenuates the cycle in the capital goods sectors by keeping demand at a high level in difficult years. Thirdly, the state has a decisive influence on employment and on demand for mass consumption goods through its control over the building industry. Large public works and housing programmes carried out by the state are strategic instruments of the government's stabilization policies. Fourthly, the state's financial transactions remunerate the private sector and help to sustain private returns in hard times.

Income Concentration, the State and Industrialization

As mentioned before, rapid industrialization in the Brazilian context naturally promotes income concentration. From 1964 onwards such a tendency was reinforced by government policies.

Table 2   Personal income distribution, 1960, 1970 and 1976

Strata of economically active population[a]	Share of total income (%)		
	1960	1970	1976
Low (50%)	17.7	14.9	11.8
Middle-low (30%)	27.9	22.9	21.2
Middle-high (15%)	26.7	27.4	28.0
High (5%)	27.7	34.9	39.0
Total (100%)	100.0	100.0	100.0
Gini coefficient	0.50	0.56	0.60

Source: Reichstul and Goldenstein (1980). Data for 1960 and 1970 from the National Censuses. For 1976, from Pesquisa Nacional de Amostra por Domicilio.
[a] Population from 10 to 65 years-old.

Real basic wages (of unskilled workers) were severely cut. The official minimum wage fell steadily, in real terms, by 48 per cent between 1960 and 1979 (Departmento Intersindical de Estatistica e Estudos Sócio Econômicos (DIEESE), 1979). About 60 per cent of the total wage-earning labour force were directly affected. Average real wages remained constant from 1963 to 1970 (Wells, 1975); they rose somewhat during the boom and seem to have declined in recent years. In any event, average wages have not incorporated the huge productivity gains generated in the last years.

The increased mass of surplus value — or total profit — has been redistributed along lines determined both by market conditions and by government policies to the benefit of the high-income strata. Thus, income concentration has been positively affected by the scarcity of managerial skills and by the government's almost unlimited ability to put pressure on basic wages; by the government's efforts to ensure the loyalty of the public bureaucracy, the armed forces and the security services; and by widespread corruption; by the concentration of capital and property, as well as by the exacerbation of the 'ethics of the jungle' among Brazilian ruling, entrepreneurial and upper-middle classes (Table 2).

The history of Brazilian industrial expansion is a history of a series of economic discontinuities. The 'laws of the market' have repeatedly been waived. Administrative controls of foreign exchange, enormous subsidies and credit at negative rates of interest, periods of deliberate monetary and financial disequilibrium, and the strict control of wages: these are some of the instruments used to remove barriers to accumulation, against the wisdom of the market and the advice of orthodox economists. But this apparently arbitrary process is subordinated to another kind of logic. Industrialization is not the 'fortunate' outcome of an irrational process. That 'different logic' can be perceived in the peculiar mechanics of equilibrium in Brazilian industrialization.

In the 'Brazilian model' the principle of equating current aggregate demand with current production does not play the role of absolute *prima donna*. The observation of recurrent overbuilding of capacity in large, modern units has led some economists to a different formulation of the problem; for instance, Tavares has spoken of a dynamic equation of actual productive capacity with fast-growing demand (1977). Actual productive capacity is to a considerable extent determined by financial and technological costs regardless of current demand. For instance, the ability to innovate technologically at near-zero marginal cost (by bringing in used equipment from abroad) and the availability of local working capital at negative interest have been largely responsible for initial investments in the 'modern' sectors. Tax incentives are also an important factor in investment decisions. Demand forecasts, on the other hand, are not made on a *ceteris paribus* assumption. The probability of changes, deliberately provoked or not, in some structural parameters of the economy in the short or medium run is also taken into account.

Possibly, such low rates of capacity utilization as have been observed in the leading sectors would have been economically unacceptable in slow-growing, mature economies. In Brazil, however, excess capacity is reabsorbed in the medium run by the dynamic forces operating in the economy and by Government policies designed to foster the modern sector. First, positive rates of growth (even during crises), accompanied by rapid income concentration, make prospects bright enough for the durables industries to justify large investments at favourable moments, despite insufficient current demand. Secondly, the reallocation of credit resources and/or the creation of new credit instruments in an ever-changing financial market controlled by the government can cause the sudden expansion of the product marked in threatened 'strategic' sectors. Thirdly, state investments operate as a relatively independent variable in the capital goods market. True, the Government's expenditure on capital account is not continuous with regard to individual industries. Different sectors are activated at different times. But the overall impact of state investment is very strong, and permanent. Indeed, these investments are not just palliative instruments to be employed at this or that moment. They are essential components of the complex mechanics of growth in all its phases.

It should not be concluded from the above remarks that the problem of excess capacity has somehow been 'solved' in Brazil. Our purpose has been to draw attention to some interesting features of the recent twelve-year period of growth in the country and, in particular, to certain peculiarities of the investment function which are not usually considered in macroeconomic analysis. But already cyclical aspects of long-run trends loom large here, associated, among other things, with the increasing capital intensity of investments. These aspects will be considered later in the chapter.

The Expansion of Multinational Corporations

Available data show that MNCs' penetration is massive and economically widespread. MNCs grew faster than the rest of the economy in the boom and seem to have kept their position in recent years. Their power is enhanced by their oligopolistic character and technological superiority. The report to the subcommittee on MNCs of the US senate (1975) points out that 'with close to half of industry under foreign control, MNCs' conduct is a critical determinant of Brazilian economic performance. Moreover, as many foreign firms are oligopolists, denationalisation is linked to concentration in product markets. Market concentration confers additional power on those MNCs freed from the discipline of the competitive market place' (Newfarmer and Mueller, 1975).

The weight of local capital has diminished in relation to that of multinational and state corporations, both in terms of numbers of firms and share of total assets. From 1966 to 1972, the number of private Brazilian manufacturing firms among the largest 300 (by magnitude and capital) fell from 156 to 139. Assets of Brazilian corporations in those top 300 fell from 36 per cent in 1966 to 28 per cent in 1972. There is no reason to believe that this trend has been reversed since 1972. In fact, both multinationals and state corporations have maintained high rates of investment throughout the decade. A recent report of the Ministry of Planning revealed that between 1970 and 1977 assets of public enterprises as a whole rose from 47.5 per cent to 53.3 per cent of the total assets of a sample of 1069 firms. The yearly average of MNCs' investments almost trebled from 1969–73 to 1974–78 (Central Bank of Brazil (CB) Reports).

Nobody questions the positive impact of MNCs on Brazilian industrialization. But the overall impact of foreign capital is diversely assessed. The local bourgeoisie has always been favourable to foreign direct investment in the country as a means of incorporating advanced technology. Empirical research has detected no significant nationalistic component in local entrepreneurial ideology (Cardoso 1972; Diniz and Boschi, 1978). However, many voices within and without the state apparatuses call for more effective control of MNCs' actions in the country, and for harder bargaining with them. The popular opposition blames the whole of the capitalist class in Brazil for the high social costs of development. Some denounce the cultural and economic alienation of the country. But hopes based on the political action of a progressive national bourgeoisie have disappeared.

Industrialization and International Relations

The structure of the Brazilian balance of payments has been deeply changed in

Table 3   Balance of payments
(US$ million — yearly averages)

Current and capital transactions (excl. compensatory loans)	1965/68	1969/73	1974/78
Trade balance	333	−5	−2,248
Exports	1,718	3,629	10,304
of which:			
manuf. and semi- manuf. goods	430	957	4,323
Imports	−1,385	−3,634	−12,552
of which:			
capital goods	−482	−1,347	−3,440
oil-crude and by- products	−124	−427	−3,470
Services (net)	−477	−1,080	−3,740
of which:			
profits and dividends	−54	−136	−376
Interests	−160	−318	−1,729
Royalties and other	−107	−65	−249
Current transactions (net) (incl. unrequited transactions)	−81	−1,066	−5,961
Capital flows (net)	146[a]	2,147	6,748
Inflow[a]	645	3,899	10,770
of which:			
Investments	66	401	1,099
Loans and financing (more than 360 days)	435	2,657	8,974
of which: currency loans	285	2,007	6,852
Outflow	−499	−1,752	−4,022
of which:			
Loans and financing	−267	−978	−3,280

Source: Monthly Bulletins and Annual Reports of Central Bank
[a] Yearly averages of capital flows for 1964/68, from the Central Bank Annual Report of 1969.

the last fifteen years (Table 3). During this period the integration of the local economy to the international capitalist system was strongly encouraged by all governments.

The sudden expansion of trade in 1969–73 — breaking an old tradition of low figures on this account — is clearly the most significant change in that period. It reflected both the increase in Brazilian industrial power and a deliberate attempt by the authorities to foster international trade for development purposes. But trade equilibrium plus a larger services deficit required extra capital resources. Extremely favourable conditions were created in the country for external finance, which poured in mostly as currency loans taken by private and public firms. The net magnitude of this flow indicates that the equilibrium of current transactions was not the only, and perhaps not even the most important, explanation for the policy of external indebtedness initiated in 1969–73. Foreign resources fed the internal financial system and augmented, at the same time, the Central Bank reserves of foreign currency, paving the way for further daring expansionist policies.

These trends persisted in 1974–78, and new ones became apparent. A substantial trade deficit was caused by the government's deliberate attempt not to compensate for the rocketing oil costs by cutting other imports, especially of capital goods. Manufactured and semi-manufactured goods now represented 46 per cent of total exports against 26 per cent in the previous method. Notwithstanding this performance, high import figures, combined with a bad evolution of the services account, generated a huge deficit of current transactions. The total balance remained positive, thanks to the truly massive inflow of foreign resources, which again were absorbed mostly by private and public firms. The ratio of capital income and amortizations to exports fell a little in 1974–78. But future tensions were obviously building up. The painful effects of the financial burden would soon be felt. The total external debt jumped from about US $12 billion in December 1973 to US $43 billion in 1978.

Technological dependence increased throughout the period, but this is not sufficiently clear in the balance of payments. despite its impressive magnitude, the value of capital goods fell as a proportion of total imports. The import coefficient of total investment also seems to have fallen (central Bank Report, 1978). The internal production of capital goods grew faster than the external supply. However, the problem of local development of technology remained acute: a recent survey carried out by a research team of the Ministry of Planning among local producers of capital goods led to the conclusion that

> if the present guidelines of industrial policy are maintained, the perspectives of technological development in the national capital goods industry are bleak. Technological dependency will be aggravated, eventually leading to the marginalisation of national producers in the market and to a growing denationalisation of the sector.

As local firms diversify and sophisticate their product lines, foreign licensing becomes more and more economic from the point view of the individual producer. The process is self-sustaining. It has also been observed that heavy dependence on licensing makes the local producer vulnerable to foreign pressure for capital-sharing (Erber et al., 1974).

The Country and the Cities: the Other Side of the Coin

The effects of this style of industrialization on the agricultural sector were complex and ambiguous. Stimulated by the government policies of taxation,

Table 4   Average annual growth in agricultural production

Products	1950/59	1960/69	1967/78
Rice	3.61	3.23	3.21
Beans	2.92	4.19	−1.60
Manioc	3.33	6.07	−1.63
Potatoes	4.84	4.34	1.73
Onions	5.36	3.48	5.91
Corn	3.30	4.75	2.47
Wheat	3.48	5.89	10.64
Soya	8.18	16.39	29.78
Coffee	6.62	−6.94	−3.91
Sugar cane	5.42	3.63	5.69
Cotton	1.31	1.61	−2.30
Oranges	3.02	6.02	11.88

Source: Homem de Mellow, F.B., 'A Politica Economica e o Setor Agricola no pos-guerra'.

minimum prices and subsidized credit, primary exports regained momentum. In those sectors affected by the export boom agricultural machines and other inputs 'modernized' the methods of cultivation, mostly in the rich Centre-South States. Production of the main food staples (beans, rice, manioc and potatoes) was displaced and either increased little or declined in the last decade (Table 4).

Capitalization of middle-sized and large holdings in the Centre-South required the extension of labour legislation to the rural areas. This has been done indiscriminately since the early 1960s, and as a consequence resident labourers (*colonos*) were expelled from the farms. Of these part went to the cities and part stayed in smaller towns, working the land at a wage as a seasonal labour force (*bóias frias*).

Permanent wage-earners are relatively few; they work on large farms, doing all sorts of jobs between seasons. Although the number of *bóias frias* and wage-earners has increased, family units (smallholdings and sharecropping) still predominate throughout the country.

Most of these units are *minifundia*, which play a crucial role in the Brazilian economy. They serve as subsistence plots for rural families; they generate marketable surpluses of food staples at very low prices; and finally they keep a labour reserve to be mobilized by the neighbouring *latifundia* during the planting and harvesting seasons (Sá, 1973; Oliveira, 1972).

The capitalization of agriculture occurred in only a few areas near the industrial centres. Otherwise, the rural economy was not substantially affected by industrialization: land ownership remains very concentrated and subsistence agriculture is widespread. The monetary income of rural permanent wage-earners is only 60 per cent of the official minimum wage in Rio de Janeiro (Bacha, 1976). Local politics is still based on local clientelism. Such structures of the rural economy persist since government credit, fiscal and land-distribution policies benefit the big landowners and neglect the smallholders, thus contributing to the preservation of the *status quo*.

Such a global situation generates growing tensions as the economy develops. First, social tensions in the cities are aggravated by migratory flows and lack of industrial jobs. Secondly, land speculation develops as the agricultural frontier expands. Serious conflicts multiply all over the country between the tenants of non-registered land (*posseiros*) and the invading agents of economic groups.

The cities sum up the country. Industrial workers, domestic servants, unemployed, semi-employed, they are all one huge, ever-growing mass of people within and around the cities. They are not transitional social groups, as some would have it. Rather they represent the particular articulation of pre-capitalism and capitalism in the context of Brazil's history. Here vertical social mobility is illusory, and urban poverty merely recycles rural destitution.

The weighted rate of unemployment in the four largest industrial cities of Brazil (Sào Paulo, Rio de Janeiro, Belo Horizonte and Porto Alegre) was 6.4 per cent in May 1980 for all persons over fifteen-years-old. The rate for the semi-employed — those not working full time or earning less than one minimum wage a month — was about the same (Instituto Brasileiro de Geografia e Estatistica: IBGE). The population of the urban areas of Sâo Paulo and Rio de Janeiro has been expanding at 4.5 per cent yearly in the last decade; the total population grew approximately 2.9 per cent during the same period. The growth of total employment in the country averaged 7.3 per cent in 1971–73 and 2.3 per cent from 1974 to 1979 (IBGE). These figures suggest a tendency for the 'marginal sector' to expand whenever industrial growth falls below 7–8 per cent yearly.

The 'Brazilian Model': a General Assessment

Development in Brazil is by and large the manifestation and the consequence of the internationalization of the Brazilian economy. The three main aspects of internationalization are the following: first, the 'internalization' of foreign capital, whereby MNCs integrate the local productive system — defined by technical and economic complementarities — and produce mostly for the internal market. Secondly, the Brazilian economy plays a specific role in the international division of labour: it is an exporter of cheap manufactured goods and an importer of advanced equipment and technology. Thirdly, the realization of a growing proportion of locally generated profits depends on their conversion into international currency (Oliveira, 1977). A continuous expansion of exports and external financing becomes imperative.

This model is different from the traditional export model. Exports are now diversified and instrumental to local accumulation and realization of profits. It also differs from the 'central economies' model, either in the sense of an imperialist country or in the ECLA sense of a fully industrialized, structurally diversified and integrated economy. Brazil is an industrialized economy in which strategic means of production — technology and oil — are externally produced *and* whose industry is not competitive enough to incorporate those inputs without serious socio-economic strains and cyclical instability.

The internationalization of the Brazilian economy has not implied economic stagnation. On the contrary, it has been the basis of rapid capital accumulation in the country. It is also far from certain that it has led to complete submission to MNCs or to foreign governments during this period of fast growth. A sort of dialectic internationalization seems to have operated here: accompanied by the strengthening of local (if not national) interests.

Historically, in Brazil a modern diversified industrial structure was attached to a previously expanding internal market. This particular formation became a (relatively) independent, competitive system in the international context. As foreign stakes in the country grew bigger, and the local economy became more and more integrated into the international economy, the scope for arbitrary foreign pressures narrowed.

In the context of Brazil's unfettered capitalism, the state tends to stand aloof from excessively particularistic pressures, and not necessarily for reasons which would confer credit on its civic virtue. In effect its relative autonomy (or unresponsiveness) is fostered by the impossibility of granting everyone's demands. Where the struggle among large corporations for government favours is so savage, and broader industrial and urban conflicts are so severe, a strong and 'relatively independent state' is a necessary counterweight, not to a 'loosely organised society', but to an intensely competitive one. The Brazilian state is not the servant of this or that particular group. It is the fulcrum of a normative order which reflects, through complex ideological mediations, the long-run interests of the dominant classes as a whole.

To what extent is development via internationalization of the economy in the sense described above viable in the not-so-long run, given the liabilities it generates during its early stages? Of course this question does not have a straight answer and, whatever it may be, the answer must take into account internal and external, economic and political, controllable as well as uncontrollable variables. If these remarks seem too vague to be useful, they at least may convey the suggestion that 'yes' or 'no' types of answer could not be derived from the analysis of some kind of ineluctable process. In a way, this chapter is a systematic account of the pressures building up in the Brazilian economy: monopolization, complete lack of R & D either public or private, foreign indebtedness, income concentration, maintenance of traditional structures in the rural areas, mushrooming cities, etc. In a broad sense, all these features are liabilities. However, it would be too easy and indeed unwise to stop the analysis at this point. From the viewpoint of capital accumulation as a total process, these liabilities can be turned into assets. Deep internationalization can mean that returns to foreign capital become more and more dependent upon the expansion of the internal market. Heavy unemployment or semi-employment can keep wages low and unions weak. Traditional agriculture can be a source of cheap food. Income concentration can soothe the middle classes. Heavy external indebtedness can trigger off big new investment projects which otherwise would not be considered, and so on. Of course, all this has to do with the historical prospects of survival of the system, not with the cyclical behaviour of capitalist economies, nor with the debate about capitalist irrationality.

The 'Brazilian Miracle'

From 1964 to 1966 a process of 'natural selection' took place in the country with a little help from the government's austerity policies. Credit to the private sector declined in real terms and budgetary equilibrium was restored. 'Excess' capital was eliminated: many small or medium-size firms went bankrupt; many were incorporated by larger firms. The number of new MNC affiliates formed by acquisition of local firms grew from 24 in 1945–65 to 39 in 1966–72, whereas those newly formed fell from 89 to 29 in the same periods. Concomitantly, the 'reformist imagination' of the government was brought into effect. An impressive set of measures laid the ground for the 'miracle':

(1) A policy of wage restraint reinforced a natural process of property and income concentration. This policy was forcefully implemented. Strikes were virtually forbidden, 425 unions were closed, union militancy was repressed. Official minimum wage indices were fixed substantially below the rate of inflation.

(2) Exports were encouraged by an impressive battery of tax, credit and foreign exchange incentives. As a result, exporters of manufactured goods enjoyed gross subsidies allowing them to place their products abroad at FOB prices from 40 to 60 per cent lower than the domestic prices of the same goods. Later, production for exports would also be boosted by powerful incentives such as exemptions from taxes on income, profit remittances and certain imports. Tax and credit benefits were also extended to trade companies (Doellinger et al., 1974).

(3) The financial system was drastically reformed. The basic innovation was the indexation of assets (long-term deposits, bills of exchange, public bonds and savings deposits). Protected against inflation, voluntary savings increased rapidly and were channelled to the building industry and to consumer credit. Institutional forced savings were also increased through the creation of large social funds, financed by deductions from wages.

(4) The tax system was also formed with a view to increasing the federal revenue.

(5) Subsidies to public services were suppressed, paving the way for the expansion of the electrical equipment and building industries associated with a vast energy programme.

Stimulated by these policies and by favourable external conditions, industry boomed. Already in 1965–67 the durables sector had started moving. From 1967 to 1970, the motor industry expanded at 24 per cent yearly, while the production of capital goods grew at 14 per cent. According to Financiadora de Estados e Projetos (FINEP) estimates, for the period 1971–73, the average rates were 21 per cent for durables and 39 per cent for capital goods. The growth rate for all manufacturing industries from 1967 to 1973 was 13 per cent *per annum* (Table 5). The inflation rate was brought down from 40 per cent in 1966 to 16 per cent in 1972–73.

A comparison with the previous boom (1957–61) illuminates some aspects of the so-called 'miracle'. During the Kubitschek years foreign investments concentrated on new product lines, particularly in the capital goods sector. The industrial structure was greatly altered. The impact on general industrial productivity was so big that all classes of income increased in real terms. The commercial balance and the primary sector were not affected. The lack of a proper financial market led the government to finance its investments through forced institutional savings and budgetary deficits: external finance was modest.

In the late 1960s the durables (transport and domestic electrical equipment) and building industries took the lead, initially on the basis of existing capacity. The industrial structure was not changed. Low wages and income concentration became policy targets. A financial market was attached to the industrial structure, collecting voluntary savings and cheap external resources. The state strengthened its grip on investment flows through its control over the financial system and over decisive phases of the productive process. The public and private economic sectors became more integrated and, consequently, risks for big investors were partly covered by the state. The economy flew higher than ever, and lost its breath.

A substantial gap between accumulation and demand opened up. The durables industry, unable to keep up its formidable pace, flinched first and suffered most. The capital goods industry resisted for a longer period, thanks to public investments; but its rate of investment later also declined (Tavares and Belluzzo, 1979).

From 1974 onwards public investment grew at a higher rate than private investment (Table 6). This was true even for 1976, when the government attempted to restrain inflationary tendencies and improve the position regarding the internal and external debt. High rates of public investment involved considerable financial strains. State corporations were encouraged to look for resources in the Euromarket. Big state projects proceeded.

Table 5 Industrial production by sectors — Annual rates of growth, 1949–77

Periods	Capital goods	Consumer durable	Non-durable goods	Intermediate goods	Total
1949–55	11.0	17.1	6.7	11.8	8.8
1955–62	27.0	24.0	6.6	12.1	11.3
1962–67	−2.6	4.1	0.0	6.3	2.7
1967–73	18.1	23.6	9.4	13.5	13.3
1973–77	8.4	5.5	4.2	8.7	6.6

Source: Reichstul and Goldenstein (1980).

Table 6 Gross capital formation in the private and
public enterprises — Annual rates of growth,
1975–78

Years	Private sector	Public enterprises
1975	5.3	18.0
1976	5.7	9.7
1977	1.5	15.0
1978	4.0	10.5

Source: Reichstul and Coutinho (1980)

Since the mid-1970s economists have been pointing out that the economy is in serious trouble and many talk about a crisis. Nevertheless the GDP has been growing at 6–7 per cent a year from 1974 to 1980. For this reason, the focus of such economic analyses has shifted from aggregate growth to what can be called the 'paradox of growth in recession'. Indeed, the crisis in Brazil is unique in many ways.

After the astounding three year investment boom of the 'miracle', by all standards industry was set for recession. The overall position was aggravated by the fact that overheating occurred when oil prices were raised and the world economy slowed down. Growth rates fell; but recession did not happen. Profits remained healthy enough throughout the economy and no extravagant figures on bankruptices were recorded. It is true that the rate of inflation was going up. But the Federal budget was balanced, wages were under control and the *cruzeiro* did not collapse despite the galloping external debt.

The dynamic effects of public investments, already mentioned, were partly neutralized by powerful depressive factors, namely: excess capacity, rocketing oil prices, the newness of a considerable proportion of industrial equipment and high levels of consumer indebtedness. The recent development of the Brazilian economy must be described in terms of the interaction of these opposite factors.

In a depressed oligopolistic industrial structure, the lack of investment opportunities liberates financial resources. However reduced, profits from production are still larger than investment requirements, given the expected behaviour of demand. These financial surpluses enter into the financial system and are partly absorbed by the government's investment projects. Of course, this is made possible by generous and high interest rates. Such a market is an irresistible invitation to financial speculation. Three consequences derive from this. First, speculation and investment compete, and financial mechanisms conceived to stimulate production gradually develop into obstacles to economic recovery. Secondly, returns to big corporations now include a monetary component. The interdependence between the state and private interests becomes more complex and complete. Thirdly, public resources become scarce. The internal public debt, inflated by indexation, subsidies and interest, absorbs an increasing proportion of the government's total resources. To keep things going, external finance becomes indispensable. Massive currency loans are contracted by private and public corporations. This is one of the main factors behind the extraordinary magnitude of the external debt. The total cost of money rises, and a growing share of the GDP is appropriated by the financial sector.

Inflation is accelerated by these mechanisms. The possible impact of government expenditure on prices is apparent not in the fiscal budget but in the monetary budget. To individual firms such a financial roundabout is, at one end, a source of monetary gains and, at the other, a factor in their higher costs. From then on, inflation tends to get out of control. Marking up (over production costs) by oligopolistic firms penalizes competitive sectors and consumers, at the same time guaranteeing large returns to the big corporations.

At the roots of the processes described above there is a sort of bargain made between the government and big business. The government asks the corporations and external creditors not to repatriate capital and profits, not to give up investment plans, not to be intransigent about conditions and terms of loans, not to lay off too many people, not to become jumpy about inflation, not to withdraw political support. In exchange, the government makes sure that money capital is conveniently reproduced until real solutions are found and a new period of rapid expansion begins.

Prospects

Oddly enough, inflation, running at 100 per cent in July 1980, does not seem to be the government's main concern in the short run. The idea behind present policies is that the public sector must avoid bankruptcy and keep investment going. This is consistent with the regime's economic ideology: development, perceived by the rulers as the building up of a Great Power, must proceed.

The Brazilian economy has been running its course in the last four years as if the internal and external debts could increase forever in so far as real output also grew. Speculative gains of the industrial and financial sectors in the financial roundabout could be realized at any moment in the foreign exchange market. Thus the essential link between the internal and external debts reinforced the monetary spiral. But interest rates went up with increasing risks in all markets. The government found itself short of money and, what is worse (and indeed unbearable for the ruling team), unable to rule. 'Confidence' in the government — expressed in terms of private investment and lending — became more and more expensive.

Since December 1979, a set of strong measures has tried to reverse the situation. First, the government clamped down on the financial system: interest rates came under strict control and were reduced; ceilings for indexation and for global lending were established for 1980, in such a way as to keep them lower than the expected rate of inflation; the financial transactions tax was extended to imports; the income tax rate for the highest income strata was raised. Secondly, it reinforced controls over prices. Thirdly, it eliminated subsidies to exports and decreed a devaluation of 30 per cent. Fourthly, it liberated the prices of public services. These two latter measures aimed at provoking a 'corrective' inflation. It was thought that their short-run inflationary impact would be offset by medium-run beneficial effects on the government's financial position and on the balance of payments.

It has been estimated that this set of measures raised the state's share of the GDP by 3–4 per cent. This seems to be the only lasting effect of such policies. Indeed, all other objectives are being gradually eroded by inflation and strong pressures from various interest groups. The government tries hard to keep the upper hand; but no sector is prepared to give up part of its profits, and all feel discriminated against.

Most observers agree that the government is at a crossroads. One road leads to still greater administrative and economic state control over the economy as a whole. In this scenario, the short-term components of both internal and external debts are 'negotiated' into longer term loans and oligopoly margins are reduced by direct price controls. The financial system is, for all practical purposes, nationalized. Wages are kept under strict control and the state's share of total investment increases.

The other road leads to conventional austerity policies. This is what has been recently proposed by the IMF in a study prepared for the Brazilian government. Here, the market is restored as a means of improving resource allocation. In particular, the structure of interest rates is not interfered with; 'safer' financial ratios are selected so as to reduce non-monetary assets; export subsidies and official wage indexation are eliminated. Government spending is cut down. Foreign exchange controls are loosened. Unemployment and wage cuts, bankruptcies, negative rates of growth, etc. are seen as necessary evils on the road to economic salvation through free enterprise.

The first scenario makes the business community nervous. They approve of the 'Brazilian model': the state has been doing a good job. But they fear a still more powerful and autonomous state. In particular, they greedily dislike the panache of ever-growing state corporations. On the other hand, a straightforward depressive strategy would have unpredictable consequences, both political and economic. The international crisis and the highly oligopolistic structure of the economy would reduce the efficiency of the conventional anti-inflationary therapy, aggravate recession and delay recovery. There is no apparent way out of this dilemma. Therefore a hybrid solution is bound to be adopted. Public investment will be somewhat reduced, but energy programmes (hydroelectrics, alcohol, oil and nuclear plants) will not suffer. Internal credit will be cut back; the external debt will be renegotiated. Recession seems to be unavoidable. The question mark is: how serious will it be? This question is certainly very grave, because in any event the working masses will be asked to pay most of the bill.

The government has not outlined a long-run strategy of development. But capitalism in the country is very much alive and already concocting plans for the turbulent years to come. A first line of attack will probably be the capitalization of the primary sector, both in agriculture and mining, with heavy participation by MNCs. The Metal Amazon Project is a US $30,000 million integrated project involving the exploitation of the huge reserves of iron, copper, aluminium, manganese and gold ores of the Caraja region; the local development of a large metal industry; agricultural and cattle-raising projects covering an area of 7 million ha; a new road and railway network and a big new port near São Luiz. MNCs of all industrialized countries are now negotiating their shares of the project. A second line will be the development of the energy, armaments and national integration (roads and communications) programmes, which embody the power politics of the industrial-military complex. A third front is the motor industry. Brazil hopes to take advantage of the international 'rationalization' of that industry, consolidating its position as a producer country. This does not seem to be a wild dream: Volkswagen will export 120,000 vehicles in 1980. Fourthly, the substitution of alcohol for oil as a source of engine fuel is under way. Finally, commercial relations with Latin American, African and socialist countries are expected to improve. In Latin America, and in particular in the South Cone, two circumstances may give substance to such expectations: the aggressiveness of Brazilian industrial power and the economic liberalism of the military regimes in neighbouring countries.

If such tendencies gather momentum, and if the main levers of the previous expansion (income concentration, wage reductions, external indebtedness, etc.) cannot operate as in the past, then Brazil may be entering a new stage in which *external* factors become relatively more important. External factors mean here, in the first place, the foreign control of crucial phases (oil and technology) of the productive process in Brazil. These phases cannot be easily internalized because (i) the gap between internal technological requirements and capabilities has not been reduced by industrialization; (ii) with industrialization, technology becomes more expensive and internal resources to buy it or develop it become relatively smaller; (iii) Brazil has not sufficient oil reserves. Secondly, external factors mean investment decisions which are not related to the internal market but rather determined by entirely multinational strategies. It would follow that a higher proportion of the locally produced surplus would be transferred abroad and natural resources would be depleted at a faster pace.

Whatever may be the future of capitalist development in Brazil it will not take place in a political vacuum. Social and political strains seem to be on the increase. Nuclear plants, a high degree of industrial pollution, decreasing quality of life for the majority of the Brazilian people: all these tend to reproduce the 'model', and will be opposed by the great majority of the population. But there is no conclusive evidence that savage capitalist expansion in Brazil is coming to an end. Political and economic instability are bound to continue.

Bibliographical References

Andrade, Regis de Castro (1979). 'Perspectivas sobre o Estudo do Populismo no Brasil', *Encontros com a Civilacao Brasileira,* no. 7, Rio de Janeiro.

Bacha, Edmar (1976). *Os Mitos de Uma Década* (Paz e Terra, Rio de Janeiro).

Belluzzo, Luiz Gonzaga M. and Cardoso de Mello, João Manuel (1977). 'Reflexôes sobre a Crise Atual', *Escrita Ensaio,* no 2, Sao Paulo.

Cardoso, Fernando Henrique (1972). *Empresário Industrial e Desenvolvimento Econômico no Brasil* (Difel, Sao Paulo).

Departamento Intersindical de Estatística e Estudos Sócio Econômicos (DIEESE), (1979). 'Salário Mínimo', *Revista DIESSE,* April.

Diniz, Eli and Boschi, Renato R. (1978). *Empresariado Nacional e Estado no Brasil* (Forense Universitária, Rio de Janeiro).

Doellinger, Carlos von Castro, Hugo B. de, Cavalcanti, Leonardo C. (1974). *A Política Brasileira de Comércio Exterior e seus Efeitos,* IPEA, Relatorio de Pesquisa, no 22.

Erber, F. S., Tavares Jr., J. Alvos, S. F., Reis, I. G. and Redinger, M. L. (1970). *Absorcão e Criacão de Tecnologia na Indústria de Bens de Capital,* Financiadora de Estudos e Projectos (FINEP), Série Pesquisas No 2, Rio de Janeiro, March.

Economic Commission for Latin America (ECLA) (1963). 'Basic equipment in Brazil', *The Manufacture of Industrial Machinery and Equipment in Latin America,* Vol 1 (New York).

Escritório de Pesquisa Econômica Aplicada (EPEA) (1966). 'Situacão monetária, creditícia e do mercado de capitais', *Plano Decenal de Desenvolvimento Econômico e Social,* May.

Fishlow, Albert (1974). 'Algumas reflexões sobre a política econômica Brasileira após 1964', *Estudos CEBRAP,* No 7, São Paulo, January–March.

Furtado, Celso (1963). *The Economic Growth of Brazil: a survey from colonial to modern times* (University of California Press, Berkeley).

Kahil, Raouf (1973). *Inflation and Economic Development in Brazil, 1946–1963* (Clarendon Press, Oxford).

Leff, Nathaniel H. (1968). *The Brazilian Capital Goods Industry, 1929–1964* (Harvard University Press, Cambridge, Mass.).

Lessa, Carlos (1964). 'Fifteen years of economic policy', *Economic Bulletin for Latin America,* **IX**, no 2, November.

Martins, Luciano (1976). *Pouvoir et Développement Economique* (Anthropos, Paris).

Newfarmer, R. S. and Mueller, Willard F. (1975). *Multinational Corporations in Brazil and Mexico* (Report to the Subcommittee on Multinational Corporations, US Senate), Washington, August.

Oliveira, Francisco de (1977). *A Economia da Dependência Imperfeita* (Graal, Rio de Janeiro).
——(1970) 'A economia Brasileira: crítica à razão dualista', *Estudos CEBRAP,* no 2.
Paiva, Ruy Miller (1966). 'Reflexões sobre as tendências de producão, da productividade a dos precos no setor agrícola do Brasil'. *Revista Brasileira de Economia,* June–September.
Reichstul, Henri-Philippe and Goldenstein, Lidia (1980). 'Do complexo cafeciro à industrialização', *Gazeta Mercantil,* Edição Especial, 29 April.
Sá Jr., Francisco (1970). 'O desenvolvimento da agricultura nordestina e a função das atividades de subsistencia', *Estudos CEBRAP,* no 3, January.
Silva, Sergio (1977). 'Formas de acumulacâo e desenvolvimento do capitalismo no campo', *Capital e Trabalho no Campo,* Pinsky, J. (ed.) (Hucitec, Sao Paulo).
Singer, Paul (1970). 'Ciclos de conjuntura em economias subdesenvolvidas', *Revista Civilização Brasileira* I(2), May.
Suzigan, Wilson (1976). 'As empresas do governo e o papel do estado na economia brasileira', *Aspectos da Participacão do Governo na Economia,* Instituto de Planejamento Economico e Social (IPEA), Monografia no 26, Rio de Janeiro.
Tavares Jr., José and Dick, Vera M. (1974). 'Governo, empresas multinacionais e empresas ncaionais: o caso da industria petroquímica', *Pesquisa e Planejamento Econômico,* December.
Tavares, Maria da Conceição (1977). *Acumulação de Capital e Industrialização no Brasil* (Tese de Livre Docencia, Faculdad de Economia e Administracao, Rio de Janeiro).
Tavares, Maria da Conceição and Belluzzo, Luiz Gonzaga M. (1979). 'Notas sobre o processo de industrialização recente no Brasil', *Revista de Administração de Empresas* **19**(1), January–March.
Tavares, Maria da Conceição and Serra, José (1972). 'Alem da estagnacao' *Da Substituição de Importacoes ao Capitalismo Financeiro* (Zahar, Rio de Janeiro).
Tavares, Maria da Conceição and Facanha, Luiz Otávio (1977). 'A presença de grandes cmpresas na estrutura industrial Brasileira', Rio de Janeiro, December (mimeo)
Wells, John (1975). 'Distribuição de rendimentos, crescimento e a estrutura de demanda no Brasil na década de 60', *A Controversia sobre Distribuicao de Renda e Desenvolvimento,* Tolipan, R. and Tinelli, A. C. (eds.) (Zahar, Rio de Janeiro).

The Struggle for Development:
National Strategies in an International Context
Edited by M. Bienefeld and M. Godfrey
© 1982 John Wiley & Sons Ltd.

Chapter 7

South Korea: Vision of the Future for Labour Surplus Economies?

TONY MICHELL

Introduction

The experience of South Korea since 1960 is of great interest to all developing countries for four main reasons. First, it has been outstandingly successful judged by two criteria: a rapidly rising GNP, averaging 9.3 per cent per annum between 1962 and 1979, and a relatively equal distribution of income. The former criterion is undisputed, the latter will be qualified later. Secondly, this success is believed to have been achieved through the export of labour-intensive manufactures. Thirdly, there appears to be a close relationship between growth and economic planning. Fourthly, Korea appears now to have reached a structural transition which shows both the problems of rapid growth and the potential limitations of the strategies developed between 1960 and 1980.

From the point of view of other countries wishing to learn from Korea's experience the obvious question is whether there is a Korean model which can be transferred to other economies, or whether Korea forms a special case. The conventional view of Korea's development, laying heavy stress on factors which are both endogenous and susceptible to appropriate government economic and social policy, encourages the belief that there is a Korean model of development. It is obviously impossible to do justice to the complexity of the Korean experience in a short chapter, but I shall argue that, while other economies may have much to learn from Korea's experience, a failure ro recognize what was unique in Korea and unlikely to be replicable and the overriding importance of exogenous factors negate many of the arguments made for the existence of a Korean model.

The Conventional View of Korean Economic Development

The conventional view has been summarized recently by Joel Bergsman (1980), a sophisticated and detailed version of the conventional view is given by Westphal (1978) and many variants can be found both in official Korean publications or ministerial speeches and in articles written by non-Koreans. According to this view, in the early 1960s Korea seemed a hopeless case with an income per head of $82 ($241 at 1975 prices). The post-Liberation division into two Koreas had split a naturally complementary economy into the north, with heavy industry and natural resources, and the south with most of the agricultural land. The Korean war of 1950–53 perpetuated the division, while devastating the south. Despite initial recovery, the whole country was grinding to a halt by 1960, with a population increase of 3 per cent per year outstripping economic growth. Finally, the fall of Synghman Rhee brought a period of political instability. 'A new military government took office in 1961. During its first year in office, the strategy of Korea's growth was changed to export-oriented industrialisation, a path it has followed ever since' (Bergsman, 1980). Exports rose from 5 per cent of GNP at current prices in 1962 to 34.1 per cent in 1978.[1] The industrial sector grew by 17 per cent per year over the same period and agriculture by about 4.7 per cent. 'Korea's policies to export manufactures and to keep her labour cheap were perfect complements to her lack of natural resources, modest internal market, but well educated and willing labour force' (Bergsman, 1980, drawing on data from Kubo and Lewis, 1978).

Despite policies to 'keep her labour cheap', Korea maintained a very equal distribution of income. Although there are signs of a slight deterioration in the 1970s, the extremely egalitarian land reform carried out before and during the Korean war and deliberate government measures to support the agricultural terms of trade — including the widely publicized Saemaul movement — resulted in continued equality in the rural sector and a relatively equal distribution between rural and urban areas. For Korea, therefore, the same policies which promoted growth also promoted equity, Korean experience thereby suggesting that if the growth rate is high enough the benefits of growth can indeed trickle down.,

According to this view, the basic ingredients in the Korean model are the concentration on manufactured exports, a responsive government strongly committed to growth and a highly educated and well-motivated labour force. Through the choice of a harmonious package of policies and incentives the government was able to stimulate the private sector in such a way as to optimize investment and exports. These ingredients are all directly amenable to government direction. Indeed Korean government policy since early 1979 has been aimed at recovering those conditions which it is felt were lost in the 1970s and which, once restored, would ensure continued rapid growth.

Central to the conventional view is the importance of export-led growth. Based on countries such as Korea, Taiwan and Singapore a substantial amount of research has gone into export-promotion policies and export incentives which are seen as holding the key to development in a considerable number of developing countries. Accordingly Korea becomes a potential vision of the future for labour-surplus countries. In view of this interest it is all the more important to examine the caveats that attach to the conventional view.

Exogenous Factors in Korean Development

The most obvious missing factor in the account of Korean development described above is the state of the world economy between 1960 and 1979. Clearly this was outside the control of Korean policy-makers. Nevertheless the shape of the world economy during this time was exceptionally favourable to Korean development. As a period of unparalleled expansion of world trade and of growth in the developed countries, along with relatively stable international financial conditions and limited barriers to trade, conditions between 1960 and 1973 were highly beneficial to any country specializing in labour-intensive manufactures.

Such circumstances applied to all developing countries. Only a few had advantages in their relationship with the United States and Japan comparable to those enjoyed by Korea. The rapid recovery from the oil crisis of 1973–4 was the direct result of recovery in Korea's two major markets. Correspondingly the recession in Japan and the US since 1979 has compounded Korea's recent economic difficulties.

Relatively little research has been directed towards a full assessment of the relationships between Korea and the United States and Japan. Consequently it is impossible to do more than sketch the broad outlines. First, however, it is important to confront a basic assumption of many critics of Korea.

Despite the close trade relations between the three countries exemplified in Table 1, the amount of Korean industry directly owned by US or Japanese interests is relatively small. Koreans have consistently borrowed capital for investment in preference to permitting foreign investment. Where foreign investment is permitted it has nearly always been subject to a joint venture in which the Koreans had a controlling interest. Only 7 per cent of foreign funds entering Korea between 1961 and 1978 was in the form of direct investment (*Handbook of Korean Economy*, 1979: Table 65). This figure is misleading, however, in that all amounts are in current dollars. Westphal (1978: 362) states that foreign firms accounted for 15 per cent of Korea's manufactured exports in the mid-1970s. Korea was slow to create a free trade zone (at Masan in 1970) and by 1980 it was underutilized.

In the absence of large-scale foreign ownership of Korean industry the linkages must be sought on different levels. One area is US aid. Korea is said to

Table 1 Growth of exports and imports and major markets

	Exports				
	Amount (in million $)	Index (1975 = 100)	Growth rate (%)	USA (%)	Japan (%)
1962	54.8	1.1	34.0	21.9	42.9
1963	86.8	1.7	58.4	28.0	28.6
1964	119.1	2.4	37.3	29.9	32.1
1965	175.1	3.5	46.9	35.2	25.1
1966	250.3	5.0	42.9	38.3	26.5
1967	334.7	6.7	33.7	42.9	26.5
1968	486.2	9.7	43.3	51.7	21.9
1969	658.3	3.2	35.4	50.1	21.4
1970	882.2	17.6	34.0	47.3	28.1
1971	1,132.3	22.6	28.3	49.8	24.5
1972	1,675.9	33.5	48.0	46.7	25.1
1973	3,270.8	65.4	95.2	31.7	38.5
1974	4,515.1	90.2	38.0	33.5	30.9
1975	5,003.0	100.0	10.8	30.2	25.5
1976	7,814.6	156.2	56.2	32.3	23.4
1977	10,046.5	200.8	28.6	31.0	21.4
1978	12,710.6	254.1	26.5	31.9	20.7
	Imports				
1962	390.1	5.8	37.8	52.2	25.9
1963	497.0	7.4	27.4	50.7	28.4
1964	364.9	5.5	26.6	50.0	27.2
1965	415.9	6.2	14.0	39.3	36.0
1966	679.9	10.2	63.5	35.4	41.0
1967	908.9	13.6	33.1	30.6	44.5
1968	1,322.0	19.8	45.5	30.7	42.7
1969	1,650.0	24.7	24.8	29.1	41.3
1970	1,804.2	27.0	9.3	29.5	40.8
1971	2,178.2	32.6	20.7	28.3	39.8
1972	2,250.4	33.7	3.3	25.7	40.9
1973	3,837.3	57.5	70.5	28.3	40.7
1974	6,451,9	96.7	68.1	24.8	38.3
1975	6,674.4	100.0	3.4	25.9	33.5
1976	8,405.1	125.9	25.9	22.4	35.3
1977	10,523.1	157.0	24.8	22.6	36.3
1978	14,491.4	217.1	37.7	20.3	40.0

Source: Handbook of Korean Economy 1979

have received the largest amount of non-military aid of any LDC on a per head basis, but it is not clear that this necessarily helped the economy much. Most of the aid arrived in the 1950s when it bridged the gap between imports and exports, and went a long way to supplying the government budget. This not only prevented the government from adjusting to economic reality, but through extensive food aid appears to have been partly responsible for the slowdown in economic growth in the later 1950s by creating an agricultural depression.

On the other hand, US military aid has released Korean government funds for investment in infrastructure, industry and other important areas of the economy while keeping the level of taxation relatively low. In view of the perceived hostility of North Korea, South Korea would have had to spend a much higher percentage of GNP on defence in the absence of US forces and aid.[2]

Koreans are reluctant to discuss the Japanese dimension of their development (see, however, Lee, 1979: 89–113; Suh, 1979: 67–93). Any account which laid considerable stress on the role of the Japanese would be heavily criticized by the Korean academic community, and for Koreans there can be no question of any benefits from the colonial occupation by Japan between 1910 and 1945. Legally Japanese direct investment could not begin until the treaty of 1965 settling differences outstanding since 1945. Synghman Rhee had first cut off all trade with Japan on the creation of the Republic of South Korea by the American Military Government. Limited trade was resumed out of sheer necessity during the Korean war, but only on the fall of Rhee in April 1960 was freer trade restored.

The result was immediate. In 1960 exports rose by 21 per cent at 1975 prices and 63 per cent of Korea's exports went to Japan.[3] The following year exports rose by 28 per cent, and 47 per cent of the total was exported to Japan. The importance of these figures is that they show the inherent vitality of the Korean economy before the implementation of the First Five Year Economic Plan 1962–66 and the export-oriented set of policies presumed under the conventional view to have initiated growth. (Limited measures to promote exports had been taken in 1959.)

Despite the fact that US involvement at official levels was much more intimate than the official Japanese links, most of the foreign investment between 1965 and 1974 was Japanese. Kiyoshi Kojima (1979: 15–18) has contrasted 'American style investment' with that made by the Japanese. The former is styled 'anti-trade oriented', concerned with penetration of the domestic market, while Japanese investment is 'trade oriented', concentrating on processes or subassemblies which are required in Japan or overseas, but which are becoming too expensive in the domestic economy. Therefore the predominance of Japanese investment was in itself important in the early growth of exports.

But this understates the importance of the Japanese and Americans. During the 1950s Japan had been growing rapidly and Japanese businessmen were beginning to look for overseas bases where labour would be cheaper. Korea therefore entered the world market at an advantageous time. The nearest non-communist countries to Japan were her two earliest colonies, Korea and Taiwan. Most Korean businessmen in the early 1960s spoke Japanese, some had even been in business with the Japanese prior to liberation. Legal direct investment was often not necessary. A simple subcontracting arrangement often suited the Japanese better since it left them free to change suppliers. Even if Korean businessmen had no direct contacts with Japan, in the intensely competitive situation that rapidly developed they could copy what their rivals were doing and then seek a Japanese customer.

The symbiosis between the Japanese and Korean economy taught Koreans to manufacture what would sell and gave them access to one of the largest and least penetrable domestic markets in the world. By comparison with, say, the EEC Korea has a colossal share of the Japanese market, 3.2 per cent of total imports compared with 7.5 per cent for the nine countries of the EEC in 1978 (UN, 1978). Naturally with such a close relationship between businessmen of the two countries, Japanese manufactures had a natural advantage in the Korean market. Thus, since 1961, the balance of trade between the two countries has remained heavily in Japan's favour.

The American subcontractors came to Korea later than the Japanese. It was not until the later 1960s and early 1970s that the large mail order houses began to handle considerable quantities of Korean clothing manufactures. Nevertheless US agencies did everything in their power to promote exports to the US from the early 1960s.

It is unlikely that any labour-surplus economy wishing to follow the Korean model could recreate the external conditions of the early 1960s in the 1980s, even by combined collective action for a new economic order, nor could it replicate the close relations with Japan and the US. Whereas in the early 1960s Japan was suffering from a labour shortage and there was no objection to the transfer of jobs to Korea, no developed country in the 1980s is expected to have full employment. The growth of quotas, tariffs and the general decay of the GATT system all make the adaptation of the Korean experience more difficult. During the 1960s the government of Korea could act as though the crude interpretation of Say's law that overproduction was impossible would always be true. One of the major problems of the current Korean economy is that investment proceeded throughout most of the 1970s on the same basis.

The principles of the systematic application of comparative advantage through a 'stages approach' advocated by Bela Balassa, and previously studied in some of its dimensions by Sharpston, Keesing and others are now well-known (see Balassa, 1977; Sharpston, 1974: 14–135; Keesing, 1979). Unfortunately these studies have concentrated on production and the need for free trade and restructuring in developed countries, and neglected the all-important stage of marketing and distribution. Through the close contacts with Japan and the US, Korea avoided this problem, since for the first twelve years of rapid growth marketing was handled by foreigners. This may help to explain the phenomenon noted by Chenery and Keesing (1979: 13) that 'the bulk of manufactured exports come from a small number of industrially relatively advanced LDCs'. In these circumstances the government merely had to achieve a system which encouraged manufacturers to focus on foreign markets and not the hitherto more profitable domestic market. For Korea the problem of marketing only began to emerge as the nation developed more sophisticated products in the more difficult world economy of post-1974. The nature and the degree of the success of the Korean solution to this problem is discussed below in connection with the problems of transition.

The Successful Promotion of Manufactured Exports

Contrary to the conventional view, the Korean government was not working in a totally unfavourable domestic environment in the early 1960s (Michell, forthcoming). Although the agricultural sector was depressed the manufacturing sector was growing at 10 per cent per annum in the late 1950s and early 1960s (Bank of Korea (BOK), 1978) and exports grew rapidly in 1960 and 1961.

The importance of the high educational standard of Koreans is stressed in the conventional view as a resource that the government could draw on. In 1965, Koreans had an educational level three times that of the norm for countries with Korea's level of per capita income (McGinn *et al.*, 1980: 62). However, for most of the labour-intensive occupations created by exports only a minimal education was required. This is confirmed by the importance of young women in the Korean manufacturing sector. As important as literacy was responsiveness to discipline. In the Korean context it is difficult to be sure whether discipline is acquired through socialization in the neo-confucian family structure and reinforced by the highly regimented educational system, or vice versa. On the other hand, when looking at the role of entrepreneurs, the significance of a large number of unemployed graduates in the early 1960s for whom there were insufficient places in the civil service — the avenue of advancement of traditional Korea — is certainly important.

The evolution and behaviour of the Korean entrepreneur has been inadequately investigated. It is an essential ingredient in the Korean model without which the best government policies could have failed. The Korean cultural milieu encouraged a desire amongst educated Koreans to be independent businessmen rather than employees. In the context of the 1960s not only were there unemployed graduates but also many unemployed senior civil servants and military officers, dismissed by the democratic government or the military regime. Most of these had amassed a certain amount of capital, and all had excellent contacts with their former subordinates who were still in the government. Finally, the land reform had greatly reduced the possibility of investment in agricultural land, which became technically illegal, encouraging investment in business.

The major decision the government faced was on the form of development to pursue. In the early 1960s export-led growth was a novel concept. Accordingly export promotion, contrary to the conventional view, was not a fundamental aim of the First Five Year Economic Plan. Indeed the drafts compiled by previous governments had a much more extensive section dealing with the promotion of exports than the published plan. The main concern was the balance of payments, and the role of exports in reducing the unfavourable balance, not the stimulus to the economy which exports could provide.

It is not a serious distortion to maintain that the economic benefits of export-led growth in terms of encouraging an economic structure along the lines of comparative advantage were not clearly enunciated until the later 1970s, and throughout the first fifteen years of growth the role of exports was seen in terms of the Chenery thesis of two gaps, domestic savings and foreign exchange to finance the import of capital goods. This will be developed below.

During the 1950s a multiple exchange rate system, with export premiums, export incentives, import licences linked to exporting activities and quantitative restrictions on imports had been in operation. In early 1961 the democratic government devalued the won from 62.5 won to the dollar to 127.5 and instituted a uniform rate of exchange, This was intended to eliminate export premiums, discourage imports and remove the necessity for most quantitative restrictions, while encouraging exports. Unfortunately no provision was made to depreciate the currency during the subsequent rapid inflation under the fiscal policies of the military government. Within two years the real cost of imports was the same as in 1961, while the doubling of the cost of imports used for manufacturing exports after the 1961 devaluation had discouraged immediate expansion.

Early in 1964 the government again devalued from 130 to 214 won to the dollar and adopted a more flexible exchange rate which tended to keep exports competitive in the face of continuing inflation. In evaluating the role of the government, the three most important factors were adjustments in the exchange rate, the supply of credit and the constant pressure of the Ministry of Commerce and Industry through monthly export promotion meetings monitored directly by the President.

Anne Kreuger has singled out the consistency of the government's support of economic growth as a major feature of Korean development (Kreuger, 1979; 82–104). Other countries have tried most of the measures used by Korea, but rarely with the same determination. It would have been easy in 1964 to have retreated from devaluation and resorted to a more import-substitution-oriented policy. The import structure was not seriously modified in 1964, but exporters were given capital loans and more systematic credits for imports required for export manufacture, while a Korea Trade Promotion Corporation (modelled partly on JETRO in Japan) was created.

The temptation to overvalue the won was always present. Prior to 1971 'domestic inflation proceeded much more rapidly than exchange rate depreciation. This appears to have been the result of entrenched business interest in the continuation of special incentives and subsidies, plus weakness in the financial position of some firms with substantial foreign debts' (Brown, 1973: 254). These pressures increased after 1974 when the exchange rate was held until January 1980 despite a 90 per cent increase in prices. As a result whole sections of Korean industry were on the verge of bankruptcy by the end of 1979.

In the Korean context the supply of credit was of vital importance. Recoiling against the corruption of banking institutions in the 1950s the government had taken control of the five major banks in 1961. In order to promote manufactures the government was prepared to supply both fixed and working capital out of all proportion to the equity of individual firms. As long as the economy continued to expand rapidly this high debt-equity ratio did not present any special problem to firms or government. Much of the working capital was provided by 90-day export credits against letters of credit issued by importers. This system assumed that Koreans were not exporting in their own right and probably worked against Koreans trying to export goods themselves.

If entrepreneurs were absent, or if enterprises central to the government's strategy failed, the government was prepared to promote quasi-government corporations, or even joint stock corporations (Jones, 1975). This to a large extent completes the picture of government determination to push forward industrialization as a vital ingredient in the Korean model. In this determination the interlocking of various agencies and the ultimate supervision by the Blue House (Presidential) staff prevented lethargy or inefficiencies which might have occurred in the public sector in other countries.

By 1965 the government had created an economic environment in which exporting was a highly profitable business. The response of entrepreneurs was encouraging. Indeed, before the end of the 1960s the Ministry of Commerce was seriously concerned about 'reckless overcompetition'. The one thing missing was domestic savings which could be channelled into new investment, avoiding both capital imports or increases in the money supply. What was urgently required was an incentive to save in institutional capital markets which the government could use to direct investment.

In 1965 interest rates were lifted from 9 to 20 per cent with dramatic results, far exceeding the expectations of Gurley and Shaw, who framed the reform (Cole and Lyman, 1971: 179–81).[4] Total time and savings deposits increased by 25 per cent in one month, tripled in one year and doubled again the following year. The increase in deposits alone equalled 5 per cent of GNP in 1966 and

6 per cent in 1967 whereas in the three years prior to the reform real savings had not increased at all. Even though the initial increase in savings was largely a transfer from informal to formal capital markets this still shifted savings into the planned from the unplanned sector (Michell, 1979: 130).

In view of the high rate of inflation, rising at over 10 per cent per annum in the second half of the 1960s, the maintenance of a real rate of interest was essential. An important consequence for the development of the economy of the high interest rates was the emphasis it gave to employing the minimum of capital and the maximum amount of labour wherever the two factors were interchangeable. Thus during the 1960s and early 1970s the ICORs remained close to unity and below those forecast in successive economic plans (Hasan and Rao, 1979: 19). This discouragement of capital-intensive investment where labour could be used was undoubtedly in accord with the factor endownments of Korea in the 1960s and encouraged the unanticipated development of 'full' employment by the later 1970s.

To What Degree Was Korea Export-led?

The increase in exports shown in Table 1 is undisputed. How much of Korea's success is attributable to the growth of manufactured exports? To answer this question precisely requires an extensive essay in econometrics. There is no consensus amongst economists as to the correct methodology in evaluating the contribution of exports. Kubo and Lewis concentrated merely on the direct and indirect effects of exports on gross output. Kim and Roemer used several methods based round the methodology evolved by Chenery and Syrquin, which measured the deviance from an assumed 'norm' attributable to export expansion, and by Balassa, which attempted to measure the direct effect attributable to export expansion (Kim and Roemer, 1979; 113–23). Edward Chen (1979: 109–26) has developed a model which also considers the effect of exports on the Chenery two-gap model, which the early Korean planners conceived as central.

As might be expected, all report a significant impact. Unfortunately all existing published calculations stop at 1973 (in the case of Chen in 1970). Thus results for the crucial period 1973–79 are not yet available. Between 1963 and 1970 domestic demand expansion accounted for between 70 and 80 per cent of GNP growth and exports between 20 and 30 per cent, according to the calculations of Kim and Roemer. (Westphal, 1978: 363–66, reports rather higher ratios.) Manipulating their figures for 1970 to 1973 suggests that export growth accounted for more like 40 per cent, and in subsequent years to 1977 the proportion may have been even higher. Chen reports a high correlation coefficient between investment and export performance.

One can anticipate theoretical and empirical advances in the near future. Nevertheless from the existing studies one must draw the conclusion that in the formative period of the transition from low growth to sustained high growth, exports were not the major factor in Korean growth, though doubtless an indispensable one. In particular in the 1960s it was not the employment effect but the ability of exports to stimulate domestic savings and finance capital imports that was important. If this is correct then the explanation of Korea's success lies not in exports, since exports played their smallest part in bridging the import gap in the 1960s, but in other areas of economic activity — most particularly the role of the government in stimulating savings through high interest rates, in promoting an atmosphere in which investment was desirable, and in money-supply policies.

During the early 1970s exports were clearly much more crucial both in terms of employment, savings and foreign exchange. Even so the contribution can be overstated. In 1978 only a quarter of Korean manufacturing output was exported, and on this basis employment was provided for only 6–8 per cent of the labour force (data supplied by Economic Planning Board (EPB)). These figures merely illustrate some of the continuing uncertainties about the Korean experience.

In short, either exports in the 1960s were akin to Rostow's concept of a leading sector of dramatic proportions, with dynamic linkages reaching out far beyond direct employment, or important ingredients in Korea's economic growth are overlooked by the conventional view.

Planning for Rapid Growth

Recent statements of the conventional view have tended to pass over the contribution of economic planning in Korea. Whereas economic planning was the *sine qua non* of development in the early 1960s, by the 1980s planning was in disgrace amongst many academic economists and practising politicians. The unsatisfactory performance in the later years of the Fourth Five Year Plan 1976–81 has undermined the credibility of economic planning in Korea, and although a Fifth Five Year Economic *and Social* Plan is under preparation at the time of writing, there has been much uncertainty about what the plan should and should not attempt.

The problems of planning in the 1980s should not be allowed to detract from the part played by the first three plans. An extremely important preliminary was the reform of government institutions in 1961. Three key ministries were created, the Economic Planning Board, which included both planning and budget functions, the Ministry of Commerce and Industry, playing a part comparable to MITI in Japan, and the Ministry of Construction, with powers similar to the Ministry of Construction in Japan and Taiwan. These reforms were integral to the successful inauguration of economic planning.

The first plan itself was relatively simple, prefacing amended drafts of plans under preparation since 1958 with a condemnation of the economic ills of the country. The major features were the prediction of extremely high GNP figures, and the enunciation of the determination to create an industrial nation. In the absence of exploitable natural resources, the stimulation of manufacturing and building up of the infrastructure were the obvious areas of concentration. The basis of the estimates of GNP were as much guesswork as calculation but on them was built an ambitious plan to build up the infrastructure, notably electricity-generating capacity and transport facilities.

After a faltering start, growth between 1963 and 1966 averaged over 9 per cent, aided by the revival of agriculture. The fact that power and transport facilities were already under construction for this sort of growth meant that planning had eliminated potential bottlenecks which might have retarded development. This remained the fundamental benefit of the general planning process, that in most cases potential bottlenecks were foreseen and provision made before growth could be adversely affected.

The major problems began to emerge when growth proceeded more rapidly than predicted in 1977–78 so that bottlenecks emerged which had not been anticipated, for instance a shortage of skilled labour, undercapacity in manufacturing for the domestic market, a housing shortage and a current account surplus from Middle East construction contracts.

Each five-year plan was intended by its formulators to be indicative. However, with the supply of credit largely in government hands, once the plan was adopted and handed over to the administration, many predictions became virtually centrally directed targets. When for the first time the Economic Planning Board challenged the advisability of attaining the export target in 1979, the proposal created a furore in the Ministry of Commerce and Industry and higher up in the government.

The Korean experience with economic planning has been beneficial. When problems have occurred it has been because the plans did not cover areas where problems developed, or where the wrong policy option was taken, usually for political reasons, or because the world economy behaved contrary to Korean desires. Any country trying to follow a Korean model would require economic planning, but with a more flexible process. During the fourth-plan period planning became more flexible through the use of fixed targets for shorter periods, rather than permitting the market to spell out the optimum option.

Beyond Labour-intensive Manufactures

The rationale of export targets is best explained in terms of the continued preoccupation of the Korean government with the balance of payments. Ever since the 1940s the imbalance of the current account was the overriding preoccupation of the government. This may explain a new course adopted in 1972–3 which is overlooked in the conventional account of Korean development.

In 1972 growth dropped to 5.8 per cent following the 1971 elections which had shown a drastic erosion of support for the government in the rural areas. This was coupled with extraordinary migration into the cities as the terms of trade had turned against rural areas. There were predictions that the Korean miracle was nearly at an end and that growth was slowing permanently. Nothing was further from the truth, the vitality of existing strategies was shown by the fact that in 1973 GNP growth reached 14.9 per cent. Exports grew rapidly, constituting 52 per cent of commodity imports in 1971, 74 per cent in 1972 and 85 per cent in 1973. 1970–73 was *the* period of export-led growth when the policies of the 1960s bore fruit.

However, the government felt a new strategy was required. On the one hand the rural sector must be supported, on the other a further restructuring of the economy away from labour-intensive manufactures was thought to be required. The result was the Saemaul (New Village) Movement and the Heavy and Chemical Industry Plan of 1973. The latter was essentially an attempt to take a short cut to industrial maturity, now the declared goal of the government. It was noted that 'in the process of industrialisation during the 1960s those industries producing raw materials and intermediate goods, such as metal products, machinery and basic chemicals lagged behind other industries'. Accordingly a heavy and chemical industry plan was adopted outside the normal five-year planning process and guided by a 'Heavy and Chemical Industry Committee' located in the Blue House, which would 'remedy these weaknesses and improve the industrial structure' (EPB, 1974 65–8).

Initially the concern was import-substitution. The effect of an investment on the self-sufficiency ratio was conceived as more important than whether Korea had a comparative advantage in a particular industry. It was more important that an item be produced in Korea than that it was cheaper to produce it domestically. Given that the domestic market use was, and still is, highly protected, there was no danger of a product failing to make a profit if there were adequate demand.

To the extent that the products of such industries were used as intermediate goods for exports this helped increase the value-added component in Korean exports which in many cases had been very low. But to the extent that the goods were more expensive, they actually lessened Korea's competitive position. This represented a substantial departure from the concept of export-led growth, only explicable in that most Koreans perceived the value of exporting to lie in solving the balance of payments. Also central to government policy was the awareness that North Korea was increasingly self-sufficient in industries essential for waging war, whereas the type of industry developed in the South had limited strategic value.

Korea was not the only NIC to follow this course. Taiwan, Mexico and Brazil all made similar investments which were clearly outside their comparative advantage. International advisers such as Bela Balassa attempted to get these ambitious industrial plans to reflect some awareness of comparative advantage. Indeed certain industries fulfilled both interests. Shipbuilding is an obvious example. However, here the inadvisability of letting bureaucrats divorced from market forces pick the 'winning' industries became evident. The 1973 plan projected most of the major Korean investments of the 1970s, the Changwon Machinery Industrial Estate (which on completion would produce half the machinery output of Korea) the Kumi Electrical Industrial Estate (located in the home town of President Park), the Yosu Chemical Complex and the Okpo Shipyards.

In the event the plan laid down the conditions under which other industries would be starved of capital, non-tradable goods and social security schemes would be sacrificed and Korea would achieve substantial overcapacity in shipbuilding, colour televisions and motor cars and chronic undercapacity in other directions, such as diesel engines, electric fans and air conditioners. In 1979 it was discovered that 80 per cent of industrial investment was going to heavy and chemical industries, and only 20 per cent to light industries which still provided over 50 per cent of exports by value and probably provided 75 per cent of employment (EPB data).

The government was under pressure to maintain the exchange rate to make imports cheaper, to reduce interest rates and to increase the money supply to compensate for the fact that the period of gestation in such industries was exceptionally long. Indeed, between 1971 and 1978 interest rates on time deposits fell from 22.8 per cent to 14 per cent. Both the increase in the money supply and the lack of funds for domestic-oriented industry increased inflation. Finally, capital-intensive industries employ fewer workers than labour-intensive ones, and those employed are chiefly high-wage earners. Inevitably the income distribution of non-agricultural workers became less even.

Problems of Export-led Growth

Even if Korea had followed investment perfectly suited to her comparative advantage during the 1970s, the economy would still have encountered difficulties in the later 1970s. The most fundamental was the problem of the agricultural sector, which is considered in the next section. The second was the ambivalence of Korean attitudes towards the domestic market. The conventional view of the domestic market is that it is 'small'. By 1978 it consisted of 37 million people, 21 per cent of whom lived in Seoul with an income per head 50 per cent higher than the national average.

The first plan had aimed at reducing domestic consumption. Even though it is argued that wages were held down in Korea by a variety of measures, real purchasing power had increased by a minimum of 180 per cent since the early 1960s (Rosenberg, 1980: 300). Since income distribution was relatively equal it meant that small increments in income would ultimately cross thresholds which would lead to rapid increases in demand for mass-consumption goods or for higher quality foodstuffs.

This was clearly happening between 1976 and 1978 when shortages created panic-buying and hoarding. These were essentially the growing pains of a new maturity in the domestic market. In 1978 the domestic market was clearly the leading force, and in 1979 the volume of exports actually fell, yet the economy still grew by 6 per cent and would have grown more had the government not controlled the money supply to restrict demand.

In the face of mounting trade restrictions and growing competition from other developing countries, Korea could have relied more on domestic demand expansion to continue growth in the 1980s. This would in turn have led to a rather different structure of the economy and a potentially slower growth rate. During the 1970s those industries established for export could easily match increases in domestic demand. Ultimately Korea must face the transition from relying on manufactures established primarily for export to exporting items for which a large percentage of sales were domestic. Curiously the Koreans accepted this argument for only one industry — almost the only industry which would cause critical repercussions in the need for imported energy and social problems in the densely populated cities — the motor car. Relying on foreign experience, Koreans were convinced that 70 per cent of production should be consumed at home. Because of its high taxes Korea currently has a rate of motor-car ownership far below other countries with a similar income per head. In order to achieve economies of scale Korea would need to double the existing stock of motor cars for several years.

Unfortunately motor cars, unlike colour television sets or refrigerators, require additional investment — a virtual restructuring of the nation's major cities to accommodate the car — and increasing oil imports at a time when energy conservation is high amongst the priorities of the government. This example merely illustrates some of the problems of transferring from a strategy which aims at suppressing the domestic market to one of more balanced growth.

A further problem was how to market more sophisticated products abroad through Korean exporters rather than foreigners. This was faced during the recession of 1975 with the creation of General Trading Companies. The GTC formed one dimension of the growth of 'chaebul' or conglomerates similar to those in Japan. In Japan these had created worldwide information networks, financial functions, control over large areas of manufacturing and leadership in foreign investment and pioneering new products. In 1976, Krause and Seguchi queried why trading companies were unique to Japan. They concluded that the success was related to the relative cultural and geographical isolation of Japan, the well-developed entrepreneurial talents and the desire for economic efficiency rather than other social goals (Krause and Sekiguchi, 1976: 389–439).

Reservations about the Korean GTCs fall precisely into the last category. For the most part they are companies already receiving substantial government assistance in connection with the Heavy and Chemical Industry Plan. The Japanese were ready to 'sacrifice other social goals such as income distribution and protection of the natural environment', and 'as long as the major companies that prosper under this policy do not exploit their position of power, society benefits from their activities'. Korean opinion is much more egalitarian, and much more suspicious that any concentration of power will undoubtedly be used to influence other matters. The 1979 World Bank report summarized in the Korean Press even went as far as to echo some of these sentiments (World Bank, 1979).

GTCs were intended to diversify export markets. This was already occurring as a result of market forces, and the GTCs have not achieved the breakthrough which was intended either in the Latin American markets or in Africa. They have, however, taken a commanding position in the traditional markets of Japan and the US and in the Middle East and Europe. By 1977 the twelve Korean GTCs handled 24.6 per cent of Korean exports; by the first three-quarters of 1979 it had risen to 35 per cent. This percentage will rise steadily as large investment projects undertaken by sister companies in the heavy-industry field come on stream. By 1979, the question was not how significant was the control these conglomerates had over the economy, but how much would be left outside their control by the mid-1980s.

Korea had avoided being controlled by multinationals by creating its own. Many would argue this was the only possible option to continue the growth of exports. The effect on income distribution, and even more on the creation of industrial dualism awaits further study.

The final problem was the product of success in a new area, construction contracts in the Middle East. Through adroit diplomacy, contracts bringing in gross earnings of $600 million in 1976 had been completed, growing to earnings of $2.8 billion in 1978 with outstanding contracts worth $15 billion.

Labour exports stand out as one of the most successful achievements of the mid-1970s. By participating in joint ventures with advanced countries, a whole generation of workers and engineers learned construction skills and participated in sophisticated construction techniques, using a large labour force, and the latest technology. These were skills which would have taken a long time to acquire under the circumstances.

However, the success overseas brought two serious consequences. For the first time since independence, Korea ran a small current account surplus. A country with a history of chronic deficits was ill-suited psychologically to recognize the problems of a surplus, particularly a surplus generated on the services account with a closed currency and an underdeveloped financial structure. Since a large percentage of the remittance was in the form of payments to families who could not legally hold foreign exchange, the central bank was forced to print extra money to buy the foreign currency.

For nearly a year planners tried to convince non-economists in the government that some action must be taken. The end result was the 1978 import-liberalization programme. Liberalizing imports was a very acceptable alternative to revaluation. It reduced the increase in the money supply, allowed the import of goods in short supply, and could potentially introduce competition into many sections of manufacturing industry for the domestic market.

Unfortunately, while policy-making may have been in the hands of theorists for whom markets had few imperfections, implementation lay in the hands of cautious bureaucrats highly responsive to pressures from vested interests. On the whole, categories liberalized were either basic materials or those for which there was little domestic demand.

Essentially the overseas construction boom came at the wrong time for Koreans to take full advantage of it. It came just when the economy was experiencing full employment, thus accelerating inflation in the construction industry. A serious evaluation of the costs and benefits of the overseas construction activities has not yet been conducted. It would certainly have been invaluable at an earlier stage of development and may yet help to sustain Korea through the difficult years of the early 1980s when both exports and domestic market are sluggish.

The Agricultural Problem

Since governments live in the real world, not that of economic theory in which all other things are equal, agriculture is bound to be a problem for any rapidly industrializing country. City states such as Singapore and Hongkong can avoid this problem, but the larger the country, the greater the conflict between agrarian and industrial population. With 46 per cent of the labour force in primary occupations in 1975 the conflict was unavoidable.

In economic terms Korea's comparative advantage does not lie in grain cultivation or in livestock. Free trade in food would lower wage demands and give a higher standard of living to the urban population. Such a policy is naturally unthinkable to most Koreans. Basically there are just too many people on the land. After virtual completion of land reform in 1955, 43 per cent of farm households had less than 0.5 of a hectare. The mean farm size in 1978 was 0.99 hectares, with 0.59 of paddy and the rest dry land. Because of the rapid growth of the cities the total area of paddy land has hardly increased since 1967 and total arable land has been falling marginally since 1969. Farming is small-scale mixed farming, so that importing meat in 1978 seriously upset precarious farm household budgets and was suspended in 1979.

There is no developed country that does not protect its farmers to a considerable extent, even though the percentage of the labour force in agriculture may be as low as 3 per cent. No twentieth-century government can permit the working of market forces such as occurred in the UK after the repeal of the corn laws, or in the Netherlands at a similar date. Agriculture therefore presents an intractable problem.

During the 1960s the gap between urban and rural incomes widened. According to official figures, in 1963 a rural household had 116 per cent of the income of a non-farm household (though the fact that rural households were larger more than offset this). By 1968 it had fallen to only 62 per cent, causing a high influx to the cities. In 1971 it had improved slightly to 79 per cent.

In the winter of 1971–2 the Saemaul movement was launched as the Korean government's solution to the agricultural problem. It was described as three things: a social revolution to make people participate voluntarily in activities; a social development movement through which rural people could construct better villages and enjoy 'affluent' lives; and an economic development programme to raise the productivity of rural labour and hence rural incomes (Ministry of Home Affairs, 1975: 8, 86). The Saemaul movement has attracted considerable interest amongst other governments in Asia, and it is important to try to measure its successes and failures (for a critical assessment see Ban *et al.*, 1980: 275–80).

1972 was a good year to start, since the Pusan–Seoul expressway had opened in 1971. This had a major impact on all communities within half-an-hour's drive of the roadway. Since it halved the journey time between Seoul and Pusan from ten hours to five, communities which had never considered sending produce to the major cities now had an opportunity to do so. Subsequent highways of inferior quality were built linking the East Coast and South West between 1973 and 1977 and an ambitious road-paving programme was pushed forward under the first National Land Development Plan 1971–80. Unfortunately a typical inflexibility in the Korean system limited the benefits. The operation of trucks on a commercial basis was rigidly controlled to prevent owner-operators from competing with larger enterprises. Had trucking been deregulated farmers would have benefited greatly (Michell n.d.). As it was it was not until 1979 and 1980 that local village trucks began direct marketing in major cities.

The Saemaul movement was heir to an impressive series of failures to modernize the countryside (Brandt and Lee, 1977). But during the 1970s the infrastructure was in place, including rural electrification which, along with roads, probably represented the biggest benefit to rural dwellers. Also, urban living standards were rising rapidly, leading to a steady increase in demand for both basic and luxury food stuffs.

In view of the circumstances it is questionable whether the priorities were correct. The four main targets were: a general raising of consciousness through a mixture of political and educational measures; the achievement of national self-sufficiency in rice; raising agricultural productivity; rebuilding villages. To the extent that rebuilding villages and raising productivity both required investment by farmers, they were conflicting, and the impression remains that investment in agriculture, particularly motor tillers, was reduced because of the obligation to rebuild villages.

The coercive element was also resented by many farmers. While the enthusiasm of the village might be stimulated temporarily, this enthusiasm faded as the large demands for unpaid labour became obvious, and farmers were required to give up part of their already small holdings for communal roads or village reconstruction. Criticism, even when founded on practical grounds against overhasty plans drawn up by remote officials, was dealt with harshly.

Village rebuilding had virtually eliminated thatched roofs in most areas by 1979, followed by the rebuilding of many settlements with roads, improved drainage, water supplies and electrification. At its best the Saemaul movement was closely co-ordinated with other planning agencies to draw up a local integrated physical plan taking account of local interests. At worst it was a hasty, botched, cosmetic procedure with uncompleted or unnecessary roads leading nowhere.

Agricultural efforts included the rearrangement of paddies to bring modern farming methods within the reach of lowland farmers, and extensive education in new techniques, vegetable cultivation and new strains of rice. Unfortunately, although the goal of self-sufficiency in rice was reached in 1977, yields dropped thereafter as high-yield strains of rice proved prone to common diseases. Since coercive techniques were used to plant these strains, their lack of disease-resistance tended to undermine the farmers' faith in new techniques and the Saemaul movement. At the same time the diversion of fields from vegetables led to severe shortages in the poor harvest of 1978. The rise in vegetable prices was a major factor in the realization of many Koreans that inflation was running at over 30 per cent, which in turn led to the adoption of a stabilization policy in 1979.

Whether Korea should have encouraged self-sufficiency in rice at all is doubtful. Popular sentiment favoured self-sufficiency, but the size of the average Korean farm suggests that a concentration on vegetables and fruit would be more profitable. Imports of rice could then have cross-subsidized the price support under which the government buys grain from farmers at a higher price than it sells to consumers. This led not only to a deficit on the grain account, but also to political pressure from farmers to raise the price further. With the spectre of Japan, where grain-support policies are creating a larger rice surplus every year, in the background, heavy international pressure was brought on Korea to abolish the whole system.

The greatest failure of the Saemaul movement was an inability to increase off-farm incomes. A comparison between household incomes in villages winning Saemaul awards and those not, shows that although in 1978 farm incomes were 31 per cent higher in Saemaul model villages, non-Saemaul villages earned 40 per cent more from non-farm income. When both types of

Table 2 Distribution of Income Estimates

	1965	1970	1976
Bottom 40%	19.34	19.63	16.85
Middle 40%	38.84	38.75	37.81
Top 20%	41.81	41.62	45.34

Source: Based on Choo, Hakchung, *Economic Growth and Income Distribution* (1978). Appendix 1.

income are added, Saemaul village income averaged only 19 per cent more (Whang, 1979: Table 12).

Inevitably, the only solution for a country like Korea is to plan for a steady decrease in the farming population so that land holdings can increase in size to competitive levels and to introduce an element of free trade in agricultural commodities. Steps in this direction taken in 1978 and 1979 were effectively blocked by the agricultural lobby. Even urban dwellers were so close to their rural roots that sympathy for farmers was as strong in the towns as in the countryside. Although the solution is clear, the timing and the mechanism by which it can be achieved are not evident at the present time.

Even if the political will were present, two other preoccupations limit action. Despite the fact that all Korean cities, while high-density, function well by international standards and are largely free of squatter settlements or a large pool of unemployed, Koreans feel that their cities are too large and should be reduced in size. Regional planning is limited to decentralization and other measures designed to reduce the growth of major cities. A policy, such as the run down of the rural sector, which stimulates rapid urban growth is at present unacceptable. Furthermore, if land holdings were permitted to increase in size, rural inequality of income would increase rapidly.

The Distribution of Income

As in any country, advanced or LDC, accurate measurement of distribution of income is extremely difficult. The conventional view acclaims Korea as a model of equal income distribution. In a major study in 1974 Chenery and others concluded that Korea in 1970 fitted into the category of rapid growth with high equality of income (Chenery *et al.*, 1975) Table 2 sets out the best estimates of income.

It can be seen that, in as far as these figures are accurate, between 1965 and 1970 income distribution remained remarkably equal. But between 1970 and 1976 the share of the bottom 40 per cent shrank from 20 per cent to 17 per cent (Choo, 1978). This is a large enough drop to shift Korea from Chenery's high-equality to a medium-equality category. The main criticism of the sources of these figures is that they exclude most households living in small towns (*eups*) and those not practising agriculture but living in rural areas. Secondly, the urban income surveys exclude the very poor and the very rich. Thirdly, these are, as in other countries, pre-tax incomes. Korea has a highly progressive rax rate, with 66 per cent of wage-earners below the tax threshold. On the other hand, the potential for claiming business expenses for the upper-income groups and the highly regressive indirect tax system make the precise effects difficult to evaluate.

On existing information it appears that income distribution deteriorated in the 1970s, precisely during the period when export-led growth became more important, and despite the efforts of the government to support the rural sector. Most Korean academics assume that the deterioration has continued, with the growth of larger business units such as Hyundai and Daewoo and growing evidence for a dualistic structure of industry such as occurred in Japan at an earlier period of development (Ohkawa, 1972: 1–94).

The best that can be said about the Korean experience is that rapid growth has reduced the decrease in income equality. It is clear, however, that if a developing country with an unequal income distribution adopted the Korean strategy the income distribution would be unlikely to improve. Korea's income distribution is a product of her past land reform, the destruction of property during the war and erosion of savings in wartime Korea through hyperinflation, and the colonial heritage. Initially the decrease in (non-farm) unemployment and underemployment from 16 per cent in 1963 to 7 per cent in 1970 had the effect of making distribution more equal, but between 1970 and 1976 unemployment fell only to 6.3 per cent. Rural unemployment was always much lower, 2.9 per cent in 1963 and 1.6 per cent in 1970, falling to 1 per cent in 1976. In 1978 non-farm unemployment fell to 4.7 per cent and, properly speaking, Korea ceased to be a labour-surplus economy.

In the absence of the employment opportunities derived from rapid growth Korea would have faced growing unemployment when the labour force expanded rapidly as the post-Korean war-baby boom entered the labour market. As late as 1977 a World Bank calculation had predicted that if growth fell from 9 per cent per annum to 7 per cent serious unemployment could result (Hasan and Rao, 1979: 86). In the event, growth initially exceeded 10 per cent, leading to a labour shortage. However, in the current recession with negative growth in 1980 there is still the possibility of a growing body of unemployed.

The Future Prospects of Korea

The Korean experience can be assessed in two ways; its relevance to the future development of Korea, and its applicability to other developing nations. As shown in Table 3, Korea underwent a rapid restructuring of the economy in the later 1970s. Many of the problems that emerged were the adjustment pains of rapid growth rather than long-term problems.

Table 3 Structural changes in the Korean economy

Structural characteristics	1964–5	1975	1978	1991 (Projected by KDI)
Per caput income	123.4	243.8	329	1068
(In 1964 constant US dollars)				
(Accumulation process)				
1. Investment as a percentage of GNP				
Investment	14.83	25.8	31.2	37.2
Domestic savings	7.3	19.5	26.4	37.8
Foreign savings	7.6	6.4	3.3	−0.6
2. Government Revenues				
Government revenues	11.9	21.9	21.4	30.0
Tax revenues	8.7	14.6	16.9	27.1
3. Education				
Education expenditures by government	1.8	2.6	2.7	–
Primary and secondary school enrolment ratio	72.0	81.6	85.2	90.0
(Resource allocation process)				
4. Structure of domestic demand				
Private consumption	83.8	67.3	62.1	50.3
Government consumption	9.5	11.9	11.5	15.1
Food consumption	46.5	33.7	26.2	18.0
5. Structure of production				
Primary	46	26.8	24.2	10.5
Manufacturing	13.2	31.6	35.3	40.7

(Including construction)				
Social overhead capital	5.1	7.6	8.7	10.2
Services	30.8	32.1	30.4	38.6
6. Structure of trade				
Exports	8.6	29.4	33.7	40.9
Primary goods	3.1	2.8	2.6	0.5
Manufactured goods	4.7	22.6	25.0	32.3
Services	0.8	4.0	9.1	8.1
Imports	16.15	36.5	36.5	40.0
(Demographic and distributional processes)				
7. Sectoral labour allocation (%)				
Primary sector	53.7	46.0	36.5	22.8
Manufacturing sector	18.3	24.0	29.2	33.8
Service sector	33.1	30.0	34.3	43.4
Unemployment rate (%)	15.0	6.6	3.2	2.8
8. Urbanization				
Urban share of total population	32.9	48.4	54.4	75.0
9. Demographic characteristics (per 1000 persons)				
Birth rate	45.0	24.3	23.7	20.3
Death rate		6.9	6.2	5.2
10. Income distribution (%)				
Share of highest 20%	41.81	45.3	–	41.3
Share of lowest 40%	19.34	16.9	–	19.5

Sources: KDI *Long-Term Prospects* and Korea *Statistical Year Book 1979.* Because of imprecision of certain statistics 1978 figures relating to population have a lower accuracy than those for 1975.

In 1978, the government's most eminent economic research institute, the Korea Development Institute (KDI), published a *Long-Term Prospect for Economic and Social Development 1977–91*. This formed the basis for the assertion at the 1979 Internation Economic Co-operation Organization for Korea (IECOK) meeting that Korea would be the first country to go from LDC to advanced industrial nation in one generation. While it was a bold plan, based on 10 per cent annual GNP growth, the use of a fallacious formula for converting won to dollars led the plan to postulate a 1991 GNP per head of $3893, at 1975 constant prices, higher than most European countries in that year. A strict interpretation would give a figure of $2179, close to the European NICs level in 1975 (KDI, 1978: 12–16, 20). The formula was adapted from Balassa and Shimomura's work on the difference between dollar GNP growth rates and national currency GNP growth rates over time in which both exchange rates and rates of inflation differed. However, for comparison with 1975 advanced countries the historic rate should have been used.

It now seems unlikely that 10 per cent per year will be attainable in the 1980s, due to resource problems and the general economic climate, as well as to underestimates of the amount of investment needed. A compound growth rate of 7 per cent is now being widely used which would give a per head figure of $1512 by 1991 (at 1975 prices).

Korea's continued growth seems hedged by many uncertainties stemming from the contradictions of the 1970s. For instance, social security schemes including pensions, some measure of unemployment pay and comprehensive medical care have been postponed since 1973. (Both free medicare and compulsory medical insurance have been introduced for certain groups since 1977.) Such schemes will undoubtedly lead to slower growth, but appear to be demanded by the majority of the population. Expenditure on housing, sewerage, roads and some areas of education has been postponed while the funds are invested in heavy industry, but many of the industries picked as 'winners' in 1973 now look like 'losers'. Additionally, although economists widely recognize that market forces need more freedom, the whole economic structure is based heavily on central direction which the various ministries will not give up easily. The reason is not only the universal bureaucratic desire of officials to cling to power, but that to the Korean administrator, unconscious heir to 500 years of neo-confucianism, market forces look like anarchy in which no faith should be placed. Although the expansion of domestic demand offers hope of growth, policy-makers still talk of trying to reduce domestic demand to increase private savings and reduce inflation.

Intense concern about inflation has also led to a significant change in financial policy. Throughout the period since 1963 the government has pursued a broadly Keynesian policy, expanding the money supply to stimulate the economy, with inevitable inflation, as illustrated in Figure 1. Inflation has been an integral part of the Korean model. As Gurley and Shaw pointed out in 1967,

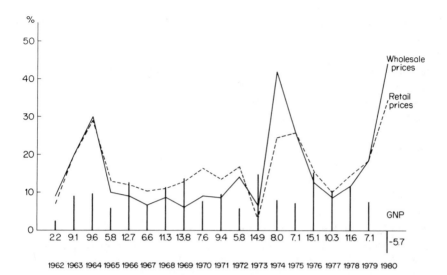

Figure 1   Fluctuations within the Korean economy 1 GNP and price fluctutions

if the result of inflation is 'to depress the wealth position of savers and the debt position of investors below preferred levels a temporary acceleration of saving, investment and debt-asset finance can ensue' (Gurley and Shaw, 1967: 264). Korean growth was achieved with the help of this strategy, but in a world dominated increasingly by Chicago-school economics this becomes anathema.

The slowdown in 1979 was largely the result of a tight money policy in an economy structured to a loose money policy. It was then intensified by the new oil crisis to which the government responded with neo-classical measures, rather than the Keynesian measures which had served so well in 1974–5 (Michell, 1979). The result was stagflation. Korea in 1981 has a substantial overcapacity in many industries. If the world economy recovers, then Korea can recover rapidly — if not, then not.

The Korean Model: The Difficult Transition

The Korean experience described in the preceding pages shows how a densely populated country with little agricultural potential, few natural resources except its well-disciplined population and a close relationship with Japan and the US, grew rapidly in terms of income per head from $241 (1975 prices) in 1961 to $776 (1279 at current prices) in 1978, under the easy circumstances of the international economy prior to 1973 and the less easy circumstances thereafter. It has been suggested that there were other elements at work than those usually stressed and that therefore a model based on Korean experience is less easily applicable to other countries.

In particular, the following questions are suggested by our review of Korean experience. Would a government be prepared to risk a high rate of inflation through the type of financial policies used in Korea? Indeed, was the controllability of this inflation dependent on the underlying stability of international raw material prices during the 1960s? Could a country with a banking system in private hands achieve the sort of investment required in Korea? How could a docile labour force evolve in a society without neo-confucian traditions? Would the labour force accept a generation of sacrifice in order to achieve growth? Given that Koreans only adopted the export of manufactures *faute de mieux* could other countries be persuaded to adapt to the realities of export-led growth? Is not the Korean achievement to have walked the line precisely between the Scylla of autarchy and the Charybdis of multinational domination?

Only gradually has an indigenous concept of an open economy emerged in Korea, and it is doubtful if more than a handful of economists share it inside Korea. Even in June 1979, President Park published a book, *Korea Reborn: A Model for Development*, based round the concept of *chaju* — 'being master in one's own house', to foreigners only a shade different in meaning from *juche*, the doctrine of self-reliance promoted by Kim Il-sung in what is probably the most striking case of virtual autarchic development in the world.

Other countries urged to adopt the Korean style of development may be induced to believe that the Korean economy is much more open than it is. There are certainly mistakes made by Korea which could be avoided in other countries, for instance the overinvestment in heavy and chemical industries in the 1970s. On the other hand, it would be easy to underestimate the role of economic planning in Korean development.

If the successful pursuit of the same policies as Korea could bring a low-income country to middle income, that country would still face the transition Korea faces at the beginning of the 1980s. This is the point where labour-intensive, low-skilled industries have reached their maximum size, either because there is no more surplus labour, so that labour costs rise rapidly, or because the share of world trade in a particular commodity has reached the level where developed countries impose non-tariff barriers, or because other developing countries with lower labour costs begin to erode markets in third countries.

Countries with a markedly smaller population than Korea might pass through this transition relatively smoothly. The share of world trade in any particular commodity might never grow too large, or the small size might permit a rapid absorption of rural labour so that large gains in rural productivity are possible at an early stage. However, for larger countries where this point comes while agriculture still has a large share of the labour force, there is the danger of deceleration or even a medium-development equilibrium trap. The problem becomes one of a rising capital intensity not only in industry, but also in agriculture, services and non-tradable goods. The citizens demand better houses, their cars require better roads, everyone needs better education. Can a medium-level country sustain the levels of investment needed to satisfy all these areas when the ICORs in industry need to rise so fast? A failure to produce this level of investment will inevitably lead to slower growth, and in the period of deceleration investment may fall to almost zero as has happened in Korea. The confrontation with these issues will ensure that developing countries continue to watch the Korean experience very closely during the 1980s.

Notes

1. One of the methodological problems of analysing a country such as Korea with a very rapid rate of inflation is whether current prices or constant prices are an appropriate measure. At 1975 constant prices the growth of exports is even more impressive, from 3.9 per cent in 1962 to 42.6 per cent in 1978. If one is interested in the relationship between exports and GNP at any one time, current prices are more appropriate. The divergence between current and constant prices since 1975 indicates decreasing profitability in export industries, where prices have not risen, compared with domestic industries. Unless otherwise stated, all statistics are drawn from the *Handbook of Korean Economy 1979*, EPB.
2. By contrast, the necessity of keeping pace with South Korean military expenditure, including US military forces, has had a very serious effect on North Korean development. Compared with Taiwan, South Korea has a very low per head expenditure on defence, $21 per head compared with $77 per head in 1977. I am indebted to Richard Luedde-Neurath for this figure.
3. All 1975 constant-price data are taken from the 1978 revision of GNP data since 1953, published by the Bank of Korea, *National Income in Korea* (Seoul, 1978).
4. Rates quoted are for time deposits of over one year; instalment savings deposit rates rose from 10 per cent to 30 per cent.

References

Balassa, Bela (1977). 'A "Stages Approach" to Comparative Advantage', Paper presented to 5th World Congress of the IEA, Tokyo (Macmillan, London).
Ban, Sung-hwan, Moon, Pal-yong and Perkins, Dwight (1980). *Rural Development*, Harvard/KDI, Modernisation of Korea: 1945–1975.
Bergsman, Joel (1980). 'Growth: a tale of two nations — Korea', *News and Views from the World Bank*, May–June.
BOK (1978), *National Income in Korea* (Seoul).
Brandt, V. S. R., and Lee, Man-Gap (1977). 'The Community Development Program in Korea', UNESCO Conference on Community Development, Seoul.
Brown, G. T. (1973). *Korean Pricing Policies and Economic Development in the 1960s* (Johns Hopkins University Press).
Chen, E. K. Y. (1979). *Hyper-Growth in Asian Economies* (Methuen, London).
Chenery, H. B. *et al.* (1975). *Redistribution with Growth* (Oxford University Press).
Chenery, H. B., and Keesing, D. B. (1979). *The Changing Composition of Developing Country Exports, 1978*, World Bank Staff Working Paper No. 314.

Choo, Hak-chung (1978). *Economic Growth and Income Distribution in Korea*, KDI Working Paper 7810.

Cole, D. C., and Lyman, P. N. (1971). *Korean Development: The Interplay of Politics and Economics* (Cambridge, Mass.).

EPB (1974). *Economic Survey of the 1973 Korean Economy* (Seoul).

Gurley, J. G., and Shaw, E. S. (1967). 'Financial development and economic development', *Economic Development and Cultural Change*, **15**.

Hasan, P., and Rao, D. C. (1979). *Korea Policy Issues for Long Term Development* (Johns Hopkins University Press).

Jones, Leroy P. (1975). *Public Enterprise and Economic Development: The Korean Case* (KDI, Seoul, 1971).

KDI (1978). *Long Term Prospect for Economic and Social Development 1977–91* (Seoul).

Keesing, D. B. (1979). *World Trade and Output of Manufactures: Structural Trends and Developing Countries' Exports*, World Bank Staff Working Paper No. 316.

Kim, Kwang-suk, and Roemer, Michael (1979). *Growth and Structural Transformation*, Studies in the Modernisation of Korea: 1945–1975 (Harvard/KDI).

Kojima, Kiyoshi (1979). *Japanese Direct Foreign Investment* (Tokyo).

Krause, L. B., and Sekiguchi, S. (1976). 'Japan and the world economy', in H. Patrick and H. Rosovsky (eds.), *Asia's New Giant* (Brookings, Washington DC).

Kreuger, Anne (1979). *The Development Role of the Foreign sector and Aid*. Studies in the Modernisation of the Republic of Korea: 1945–1975 (Harvard/KDI).

Kubo, Yuji, and Lewis, J. (1978). 'Sources of Industrial Growth in Three Asian Countries', World Bank, September (mimeo).

Lee, Chung. H. (1979). 'United States and Japanese direct investment in Korea: a comparative study', *Journal of Economic Development*, Seoul, pp. 89–113.

McGinn, Noel F., Snodgrass, D. B., Kim, Ung-Bong, Kim, Shin-Bok, Kim, Quee-Young (1980). *Education and Development in Korea*. Studies in the Modernisation of the Republic of Korea: 1945–1975 (Harvard/KDI).

Michell, A. R., *Economic History of South Korea 1945–1980* (forthcoming).

Michell, A. R. (1979). 'Structural Change in a Rapid Growth Economy', unpublished report to EPB.

Michell, A. R. (n.d.). 'Past Transport Policies in Korea', Working Paper XIV, unpublished, RDRI/KIST Comprehensive Transport Project.

Ministry of Home Affairs (1975). *Saemaul Undong* (Seoul).

Ohkawa, Kazushi (1972). *Differential Structure and Agriculture: Essays on Dualistic Growth* (Kinokuniya, Tokyo).

Rosenberg, W. (1980). 'S. Korea: Export-led development — sewered and unsewered', *Journal of Contemporary Asia*, **10**, 300.

Sharpston, M. (1974). 'International Sub-contracting', *Oxford Economic Papers*, pp. 94-135.

Suh, Sang-chul (1979). 'Foreign capital and development strategy in Korea', *Korean Studies*, Hawai, **II**.

UN (1978). *Statistics of International Trade* (Geneva).

Westphal, Larry E. (1978). 'The Republic of Korea's experience with export-led industrial development', *World Review*, **6**.

Whang, In-joung (1979). *Economic Implication of Saemaul Undong and its Future Course of Action* (Korea Rural Economic Institute).

World Bank (1979). *Korea: Rapid Growth and the Search for New Perspectives* (Washington DC).

The Struggle for Development:
National Strategies in an International Context
Edited by M. Bienefeld and M. Godfrey
© 1982 John Wiley & Sons Ltd.

Chapter 8

Costa Rica: How far can Primary Production take a Small Economy?

Ennio Rodríguez

Introduction

Costa Rica exhibits some surprising features for a non-industrial society integrated into the global capitalist system. A democratic form of government has been its prime political characteristic since the formation of the capitalist state around 1870. Education and other means of achieving social consensus have been the main instruments of political domination, repression having remained largely insignificant.

These political and ideological mechanisms for resolving social antagonism have been made viable by the development of productive structures and, hence, social configurations in which the type of polarization that has occurred in other Latin American countries has been avoided. These productive structures have provided possibilities of employment to the working force and of upgrading the productivity of labour in a context in which the concentration of economic power, albeit an existing tendency, has been a slow process and one which has defined many different strata of society in its evolution.

This chapter analyses the global and internal processes which have given birth to these economic and political structures throughout Costa Rican history and discusses likely development alternatives. The final aim is clearly evaluative.

The centrality of the primary export sector in Costa Rica's development justifies discussion, at the theoretical level, of the staple theory of growth as a statement of the possible benefits which can be derived from such development processes, and of the strand within the dependency school that emphasizes the super-exploitation of labour in peripheral societies and, thus, sets limits to the nature of the capitalist development which can be achieved.

The staple approach, stemming from the work of Harold Innis (1954, 1973, 1975) on Canadian history, was later proposed as a theory of economic development. However, its applicability is claimed to be rather limited. The main condition for its relevance is the existence of a favourable man/resource ratio in a country which is not plagued by pre-capitalist institutions and relations of production.

These circumstances provide the possibility of sustained growth on the basis of successive expansions of staples. Economic development is thus the result of diversification from the export base (Watkins, 1963). The dynamism of this export base must be ensured by a capacity to shift resources to the production of the most promising staples. This acceleration in production probably requires the importation of scarce resources.

The nature of the development process is highly dependent on the characteristics of the commodity in question. The production function and the relations of production surrounding the staple are held to leave a definite imprint on the developing society. The 'multiplier accelerator' impact of the expansion of staple production will depend on the network of linkages it establishes with the rest of the economy. Perhaps the most important backward linkage is the construction of a transport system for the collection of the staple which can have widespread effects (Watkins, 1963: 145). Forward linkages are related to the possibilities of increasing the value added embodied in the final export commodity. The final effect, crucially dependent on the nature of the relations of production, is on the size of the internal market. The inducement to invest in other activities is critically related to the distribution of income resulting from the social organization of the production process.

In the long run successful staple growth is subject to many perils. Extension into marginal areas and diminishing returns might curtail the expansion possibilities of a promising staple. Competition from cheaper sources or synthetics and the income elasticity of demand for the commodity may have an adverse impact on price trends. Sustained growth seems thus to rely on flexibility in developing new lines of production and in innovation, which, in turn probably requires the initial conditions of a favourable man/resource ratio and a highly innovative entrepreneurial class (Watkins, 1963: 149).

The possibility remains that a given specialisation can suffer such a negative impact on its terms of trade that immiserizing growth might take place (Bhagwati, 1958). However, if this is avoided by opportune shifting to other commodities and linkage opportunities are full exploited the economy will eventually diversify to the point where 'staple society' becomes a misnomer (Watkins, 1963: 153).

North (1961) has shown the relevance of such an approach for the analysis of the United States in the period 1790–1860, while for Canada, despite continuing discussion (Caves, 1971), it is claimed to be significant throughout its economic history (Bertram, 1963: 184). The fact that these results can be claimed suggests that the theory is weak in explaining the eventual transformation of the staple economy into a fully diversified industrial society. The rate seems to slacken when the United States is undergoing its own process of industrial transformation. The Canadian economy, on the contrary, still relies primarily on staple production for its entry into world markets. Moreover, the capital intensity necessary for competing in the staples in which Canada specializes poses serious doubts as to the dynamic benefits it can derive while relying on foreign technology (Watkins, 1963: 157).

In short, the staple theory of growth places stringent conditions on its applicability and, even if these conditions are initially met, there is virtually no conceptualization of the transformation from staple growth to diversified industrial development. The case of the United States rather suggests that something more than the concept of 'spread effects' is necessary to explain industrialization. The approach seems thus to collapse into the weak proposition that if the initial conditions are continuously met, there is the possibility of successful growth as the export sector expands and injects dynamism into the economy as a whole.

Within the dependency school, on the other hand, Marini (1972, 1975, 1977) develops Frank's conception of a global capitalist system characterized by a drain of surplus from the periphery to the centre (Frank, 1969). Marini further specifies the social conditions for this form of domination and the changes it is subjected to in the history of Latin America. Dependency is thus the relation of subordination between formally independent nation-states. This relationship reproduces or stimulates change in the relations of production in the dominated societies in order to ensure the continuation of dependency (Marini, 1977: 18).

Latin America is integrated into the world market as a producer of primary commodites and thus contributes to the cheapening of the production of industrial goods at the centre. From this process, however, the beneficiaries will be capital and labour at the centre. The industrial centre is capable of resisting a decline in the prices of industrial export commodities relative to prices of primary goods. A transfer of surplus results from this unequal exchange (Marini, 1977: 34–8). Other mechanisms of surplus extraction are foreign investment, financial practices and transactions in technology (Marini, 1975: 7–8; 1977: 69).

The response of capital at the periphery to this drain of surplus from the centre is not to increase productivity, but to exacerbate surplus extraction from labour in the form of super-exploitation (increasing absolute surplus value, in Marxian terms) (Marini, 1977: 37). As production for export develops in Latin America it entails a separation between the spheres of consumption and production. The circulation of primary commodities takes place at the centre and thus is unrelated to the consumption possibilities of the working class. Exploitation can thus be increased without the dangers of overproduction which such an attempt might unleash at the centre. Moreover, Marini argues that even considerations of reproduction of the labour force need not be taken into account, since Latin America has been characterized by large reserves of labour in the Indian populations and as a result of European migratory movements (1977: 52–3).

The process of industrialization only became a significant locus of accumulation during the crisis and the two world wars. But even then the conditions for the super-exploitation of labour were reproduced, although in a modified form. Industrialization expanded to meet existing demand, with its structure divided into two spheres: the low in which industrial goods were virtually non-existent (working classes) and the sophisticated high sphere of the dominant classes and sectors of the middle classes used to the patterns of consumption characteristic of the centre. It is this latter sphere of consumption to which industrialization is geared. Consumption standards of the working classes need not rise as a consequence of the initial industrial expansion. Capital can continue to rely on super-exploitation as a source of surplus. Further expansion is sought by increasing the consumption of the middle sectors and increasing the productivity of labour in order to cheapen industrial goods. The mechanisms to increase the income of the middle sectors are, however, at the expense of the working classes and, hence, continue to reinforce the separation of the structure of demand in its two spheres (Marini, 1977: 56–101). The more advanced dependent economies seek to avoid the conflict between super-exploitation and market opportunities by 'subimperialist' schemes, characterized by increases in state expenditure and attempts to conquer the high spheres of the markets of other dependent economies (Marini, 1972).

In short, small dependent economies end up doomed to having to have highly repressive regimes capable of reproducing the conditions for the super-exploitation of labour if capital is to be accumulated at all. This interpretation, however, assumes the existence of a large reserve army of unemployed in order for domestic capital to be capable of withstanding the drain of surplus via unequal exchange. If, on the contrary, this reserve army is absent, opportunities for capital should be virtually non-existent.

It is reasonable to suggest that the presence of a large reserve of unemployed enables capital to increase the amount of absolute surplus it can extract. But to elevate this feature to a general law of the development of dependent societies is rather implausible. If the possibilities of super-exploitation are so great, this is incompatible with the existence of the possibility of foreign investment. The rates of profit it could command would result in massive inflows of capital from the centre. Another consideration difficult to reconcile with this general law is that virtually any sector subject to capitalist competition is characterized by a periodic process of innovation in which the capitals that do not change to the new technologies succumb to the

more dynamic ones. The periphery has not been isolated fror
competition, regardless of the dimensions of the re
unemployed.

In Marini's view, the conditions for the super-exploitati
self-reproducing and, hence, liberation from unequal exchar
if the economy disengages from the capitalist system and the relations of
production it entails (Marini, 1977: 18). Only such a change can provide the
conditions for full employment and continuous upgrading of labour. Nevertheless, it also follows that in a dependent society lacking a large reserve army
of unemployed the condition for the operation of unequal exchange would be
removed and the reproduction of existing capitals would require improvements in productivity if they were to remain competitive.

The discussion of the peculiarities of the Costa Rican case in the light of
these two approaches demands some detailed reference to the historical
experience of this society. In both interpretations the context of the social
relations of production is a significant explanatory element. For the staple
theory, entrepreneurial capacity and income distribution effects are largely
determined by the technical and social characteristics of the production
function. For Marini, the determination is far more complex: relations of
production define the nature of the extraction of surplus and to some extent,
of the conditions of reproduction of the mechanisms through which this
extraction is effected. But this process of reproduction places the analysis at
the level of the totality; political structures resulting from the changes in the
class composition of society become indispensable for its survival and the
process of class formation is centrally linked to the material developments.

The first section deals with the nature of the relations of production prior to
the moment of opening up to international trade, the level of material
development, class composition and political structures.

Capitalist development takes place simultaneously with the expansion of
foreign trade. Political structures take the form of a capitalist state along with
a modification of the class structure inherited from the colony. The
hypothesis of super-exploitation is discussed in the second section.

Class alliances and antagonisms modify the liberal form of the state and this
is a factor which paves the way for a change in development strategy relying
on the export of staples. The third section discusses the viability of export-led
growth and the alternatives which seem to confront Costa Rica as the limits of
the import-substituting strategy are reached and the late 1970s witness
movements towards different development paths.

Antecedents*

Central America was a marginal area of the Spanish Empire and Costa Rica was

*This section is largely based on Rodriguez (1979)

ts most isolated and depressed province during the colonial period. The absence of precious metals, a small and declining Indian population and the province's lack of strategic military importance offered no incentives to the Spanish Crown. Consequently, the Empire's network of mercantilist policies tended to reproduce this very low level of development by suffocating the settlers' attempts to embark on new economic activities. The strict control of trade by the colonial authorities and the Church and the carefully designed system of grants and monopolies on top of the heavy taxation burden ensured the appropriation of virtually any surplus generated in the province and the absence of competition to economic activities located elsewhere, or to trade routes.

The failure of the various attempts (cattle-raising ranches, cacao and tobacco) to develop surplus-oriented economic activities meant that despite social differences based on the origin of the Spaniards (aristocrats or commoners) an egalitarian society emerged at independence. Although racial stratification did exist, centuries of stagnant subsistence economy provided no material basis for social differentiation.

This *campesino* economy, as Rodríguez has called it, was notable for an almost complete absence of market relations, wage, slave or serf labour and mechanisms of surplus extraction besides the colonial system. With this practically undifferentiated productive structure was associated a unique class configuration, consisting of a vast mass of *campesinos* from whom the colonial system extracted surplus, but otherwise unrelated to each other. It is clear from the reports of the governors to the Crown that the barriers to trade limited the development of the province. More significant, however, were the attempts by a group from the nobility to challenge the colonial authorities with their smuggling activities. This was the fertile soil for the spread of liberal ideas with their emphasis on free trade and economic freedom.

A brief and relatively bloodless civil war tilted the balance in favour of the liberals and away from the conservatives immediately after independence. Pre-capitalist fetters to production inherited from the colony were soon abolished: free trade was declared and the ports were opened and their infrastructure improved; laws regulating money and state finances were issued as well as the General Code concerned with justice and legal procedures; and the burden imposed by the Church on economic activities was partially lifted (Facio, 1972: 35). This was achieved despite an impression of continuity provided by the style of leadership.

Nevertheless, twenty years after independence local rivalries were threatening the weak central government and exploded in another brief civil war. The group headed by President Carrillo won the conflict and this permitted him, as dictator, to lay the basis for a legitimized central authority beyond local disputes, to achieve international recognition of national sovereignty and to deepen the liberal reforms (Rodríguez, 1979: 37).

The success of Carrillo in this historical accomplishment, which entailed periods of virtual anarchy in other Central American countries lasting up to fifty years, is not unrelated to the situation of stalemate between rival groups controlling the important institutions of the *Ayuntamientos* in the principal towns. The context of this conflict was, however, a *campesino* society in which the interests of the majority of the population were related to securing access to their smallholdings and to the possibilities of trade. Thus Carrillo, elevating himself over the immediate interests of the rival groups and apparently representing the interests of the small proprietors by issuing decrees in their favour, created the conditions for the development of a dominant class that was soon to control society and for the expansion of production based on small property, within a superstructural frame that sanctified the process of concentration of landownership that was already occurring.

Staple Growth and Liberal Democracy

In 1832 the first coffee beans were exported to Chile for reshipment to Europe. From then onwards the expansion of production was extraordinary. The total crop was around half a million pounds in 1832 and it had increased to nearly 90 million pounds in 1841.

The more specialized activities of processing and international marketing suffered a rapid process of concentration (Churnside-Harrison, 1979: 239). What little capital and entrepreneurial experience had been accumulated in previous activities during the colonial period proved valuable to some families.

The process of land concentration seems to have been much slower in manifesting itself and its timing is still subject to debate (Churnside-Harrison, 1979; Hall, 1978). Factors which contributed to this process included the financial practices of the coffee processors who had access to British capital and operated as banks for the small producers. In many cases, incapacity to repay debts meant a confiscation of the cultivated plots. Diffusion of new technology in the second half of the nineteenth century did not extend to all the producers and those who found themselves unable to keep pace with the rhythm of rationalization of coffee production were often forced to sell their properties. Also counting against the small producers was the need to buy basic foodstuffs in the market. The instability of the supply of basic grains frequently placed a strain on the financial viability of the new commodity-producing units.

This process of centralization of agricultural capitals was, however, hampered by the nature of the economy in which it developed. The absence of large contingents of free labour on the one hand and of strong capitals on the other, in the face of the intensive but seasonal requirements of labour in the cultivation of coffee, checked the development of the *haciendas* to some extent. A symbiosis between the *haciendas* and the surrounding family plots was encouraged, thus ensuring the survival of small producers who even today represent a significant share of total coffee production. Capital could, nevertheless, appropriate surplus in the processing and export of the commodity without fully bearing the risks of production.

The classes which were formed as the process of social division of labour developed were stamped by the peculiarities of the organization of production. The *peon*, the dispossessed peasant who had to sell his labour to obtain his subsistence, never constituted a large proportion of the population. In addition to the stabilizing impact of coffee production on land tenure a vast agricultural frontier always offered an opportunity to become a landowner once again. The emerging capitalists thus found a situation in which labour had a strong bargaining position and in which their relation to small producers was, to some extent, one of interdependence. These aspects of the relations between classes provided grounds for what Stone has called the paternalistic attitude of the capitalists (1976: 110). They got involved in a complicated system of religious and social duties which ideologically disguised the mechanisms of surplus extraction but which also reflected the potential political strength of the dominated classes. Brute political domination was hardly compatible with this correlation of social forces which, on the contrary, placed the small producers and the labour force in a position in which they could bargain for the liberties and democracy proclaimed in the dominant ideology.

The development of commodity production demanded a transformation of the political structure. Transactions started to require an ever more sophisticated legal frame; in particular land, as it became a commodity, made definitions of property essential. The regulation of the transactions in which all citizens participated with equal rights developed the concepts which sanctioned the basis of class domination: private property. In 1889 the Civil Code was approved, but previously the liberal constitution of 1871 had laid the premises for the legal corpuses.

Relations between propertied classes and labour were thus regulated by an apparent external arbiter. However, the execution of legal sanctions demanded institutions. The construction of a communications infrastructure and of the much needed schooling system were also beyond the activities of private capital. The set of institutions which appeared to meet these social needs took the form of a capitalist state which ensured the preservation of the basis of class domination by arbitrating in the conflicts between all classes on the principle of the inviolability of private property.

These developments reflect the evolution of the dominant classes — coffee producers, exporters, importers and financial capitalists — to the point at which the ideology of their domination had permeated all layers of society. The conditions for the reproduction and expansion of their material base were accepted as the parameters of social organization. These conditions also guaranteed the continuation of the other classes, albeit in a subordinated form.

This period also witnessed the consolidation of the nation-state. A sense of national identity, perhaps formed in the years of isolation, was discovered as the network and other social relations developed. International recognition and a feeling of national pride were outcomes of the successful expulsion of the filibuster W. Walker from Costa Rica and, leading the Central American armies, from Nicaragua in 1856–7. His intention had been to develop a slave entrepôt in the Central American territory.

Political structures during the period prior to 1870 were part of the undifferentiated sphere of activities of private capital. Fernández-Guardia has named these social groupings political merchant oligarchies. The stability of the president and the control over public office depended on the rivalries of these groups (Fernández-Guardia, 1967: 117). After the coup d'état of 1870 Guardia undertook the task of professionalizing the army and, thus, deprived the oligarchies of their military strength. Furthermore, the unprecedented boom in coffee production provided ample room for the activities of the dominant classes. These activities were never threatened by General Guardia, but, on the contrary, were protected for private capital. This bonanza also permitted the formulation of an aggressive fiscal policy which provided a material base for the increasing activities of the state. Finally, the construction of railroads put Guardia in contact with British financial capital, and a liberal policy towards this capital followed (Vega, 1980: 32–42). The absolute control of the political institutions by fractions of the dominant classes was undermined for ever. The state became militarily and economically independent, and foreign capital had its share in the control of the state apparatus.

The form that this state assumed was increasingly democratic. The success of staple growth allowed the benefits to 'trickle down', which at the same time made the class alliance between urban merchants and big and small coffee producers viable. Capital could see its long-term interests of expansion served by a state which regulated social conflict, relying on the legal system and on the socialization of future generations in the ideals of liberalism by an efficient education system.

Generally, most authors agree that the development of Costa Rica during this period was reasonably successful. Although in material terms Costa Rica at independence was the poorest and the most isolated province in the Central American isthmus, indeed in the American continent, it was the first in Central America to have its capital connected by railroad to both the Atlantic and the Pacific Oceans; electricity supplied to the main cities (third in the world); a good education system and an adequate road network (Soley-Güell, 1975: 60).

In fact, the general law that peripheral capitalist accumulation is founded on the super-exploitation of labour finds no confirmation whatsoever in this period of Costa Rican history. The essential condition of an unlimited reserve army of unemployed was not present. On the contrary, reports of the period emphasize labour shortage as a limitation on coffee production (Fernández-Guardia, 1972: 116): the basic problem in railroad construction was the recruitment and organization of labour; labourers were brought from New Orleans, the Caribbean and Europe, but there were always unsatisfied requirements (Churnside-Harrison, 1979; 208–10). The favourable land tenure pattern of coffee production largely reduced the number of displaced peasants and, additionally, the agricultural frontier could absorb any potential reserve army of unemployed. In 1850, only between 2.0 and 4.0 per cent of the territory was legally appropriated by private individuals and in 1927 population density was merely 9.2 persons per square kilometre (Churnside-Harrison, 1979: 154, 440).

Between 1840 and 1880 wages rose steadily. In the late 1850s it was reported that a US journeyman received half of what was paid in Costa Rica to clear an acre of land and prepare it for planting; wages were above $0.50 per day and towards the 1880s they had reached over $1.00 per day (Churnside-Harrison, 1979: 600). In local monetary terms the trend continued. However, in dollars, the trend was reversed after 1890, and real wages may even have decreased. The vulnerable nature of staple growth, due to international fluctuations, emerged during the period and coincided with a spurt in population growth (Churnside-Harrison, 1979: 599). Nevertheless, open unemployment reported in the 1927 census was only 1.0 per cent.

The vulnerability of the accumulation model to the crises of the industrial economies and to fluctuations in coffee markets did not necessarily imply that labour had to suffer all the consequences. An escape route was provided by the colonization of vast and fertile untilled lands. Migration into such areas was not only spontaneous but also promoted by the state: long lists of land grants and homestead acts were approved by the Congress which authorized and encouraged those who wanted land to take it (Soley-Güell, 1975: 167). This possibility of migrating to the subsistence sector not only allowed a situation of full employment in the capitalist sector but also operated as a constraint on the extent to which it could lower wages to increase profits. Super-exploitation could not have been the basis for the expansion of capital and, hence, unequal exchange mechanisms were prevented from operating. It is not accidental that Costa Rica has the highest productivity in the world in the two main export commodities, coffee and bananas. The response of capital to competitive pressures in international markets has been a continuous increase in productivity.

Another productive activity which developed as a result of the construction of the communications system was banana production. Plantations, developed by US capital towards the end of the nineteenth century, expanded employment possibilities. They absorbed labour brought in to build railways and, to a lesser extent, peasants pushed out by the capitalization of coffee. Nevertheless, these developments were vulnerable to changes of location by companies, which could depress whole areas, such as the Atlantic zone in 1934. In terms of class formation, the banana plantations created the first important concentration of proletarians and hence opened up the potential for labour organizations. The unions which developed have gained significant advantages for the banana workers and also had some influence on the historic events of the 1930s and the 1970s.

Limits of Staple Growth: State Interventionism

Some signs of the weaknesses of the dynamic sector of the economy have been present since the late 1880s. The productive structures managed, however, to absorb the external shocks without major social upheavals until the 1930s. This relative success of staple growth was the basis for the unquestioned hegemony of the dominant classes. In the early twentieth century the pattern of state expenditure was modified, and the funds previously destined to meet military and police expenditures were transferred to education (Vega, 1980: 34). This impressive change was also made possible by the homogeneity of interests of the classes and fractions constituting the dominating bloc. The completely open and agricultural economy defined camps of activity which were not antagonistic from the point of view of capital. As a result, political parties reflected differences in personalities and groups rather than in sets of interests. Intellectuals could always invoke the 'Interest of the nation' in their analyses and find social acceptability for their ideas. Today, as society has grown more complex and intellectuals can no longer make such claims without showing party and class allegiances, this has left some social analysts with nostalgic reminiscences of past days; if only the bygone intellectuals of higher stature could return and draw up the agenda of the required reforms!

The situation changed dramatically after 1930. Exports did not recover their 1929 level until the war was over. The economy stagnated throughout this period. The remedy for the rural employment problem was again the colonization of virgin lands. The government issued two Homestead Acts, in 1934 and 1939, with the clear intention of tackling the unemployment problem. Nevertheless, urban unemployment gave rise to a wave of social unrest in the cities and among the banana workers in the plantations; as the strikes spread the newly founded Communist Party gained in strength.

Import-substituting industrialization did not constitute an alternative outlet for idle capital as occurred in other Latin American countries. The size of the internal market was negligible and industrial capacity was virtually non-existent. The political system managed, however, to respond to the articulate demands of the different social groups engendered by the crisis of the process of accumulation without the need to resort to more rigid forms of domination. The structure of property was safeguarded by opportune concessions. Although these concessions guaranteed the reproduction of the social order, they meant a transformation of the form of the state. The new functions undertaken by the state were hardly compatible with a liberal view of society. They intended to regulate social conflict by protecting the weakest classes.

One of the salient features of this erosion of the liberal form of the state is that it took place while the front-line liberal political figures were still in office. This illustrates the more general feature of a tradition of ruling élites with clear diagnoses of the material and political possibilities available to Costa Rica.

The representative form of government allowed the urban movements of protest and social reform to voice their critiques of the liberal order in the Congress. These movements, starting at the turn of the century, saw their efforts begin to materialize in the form of institutions which regulated the relation between capital and urban labour. In 1924 the National Institute of Insurance was created as a state monopoly and the enactment of the workmen's compensation law followed shortly after.

The recession quickened the pace of the reforms. In 1933 minimum wage legislation, including agricultural wages, was approved and the Institute for the Defence of Coffee was created. It regulated the relations between processors, producers and wage labour. The state also assumed more economic functions, besides the insurance monopoly, by reforms of the financial sector in 1937. The state bank was strengthened and a central banking system was adopted. Thus, the significance of small producers in the class configuration, the favourable man/resource ratio and the form of political domination which allowed for some representation of the interests of the dispossessed and small producers seem to explain why Costa Rica, in contrast to her neighbours, survived the worst capitalist crisis so far, without a major upheaval of political and economic structures.

The Second World War had no more impact on the export sector than the First World War had done. A shift from English and German to US markets prevented a serious recession. Nevertheless, the political development of the 1940s led an increasingly interventionist state to adopt the features and functions of a modern welfare state.

The advanced labour legislation and the welfare system for the urban workers could hardly be interpreted as a result of the demands of the working classes. Although there had been singular achievements by the anti-liberal movements during the 1930s, the small dimensions and degree of organization of the working classes (industrial production was negligible) meant they were unable to mount the required pressure against the dominant classes to force such a sizable intervention of the state in their favour (Schifter, 1979: 62).

In 1917, President González Flores had attempted to deal with the fiscal crisis, largely created by the speculative activities of coffee exporters, mainly by setting controls on the convertibility of the currency, establishing a progressive income tax and cutting civil servants' salaries. He was quickly overthrown and the state returned to liberal parameters. The dominant classes apparently limited the state's room for manoeuvre according to their perception of their long-term interests. In 1942, after the labour legislation was issued, the government, previously backed by the dominant classes, found itself increasingly isolated and in danger of a coup d'état.

The Communist Party, which had been hostile up to this point, was drawn into an alliance with the government as the social reforms came under threat from the dominant classes. The progressive church leadership blessed the alliance and settled the theological issues involved. The international background was the alliance with the USSR against Hitler.

After the victory of the allied forces, the context of the cold war placed Costa Rica in the unsympathetic US sphere of influence. Internally, the social reforms, corruption and inefficient management and an increasingly mobilized and militant Communist party fed the furnaces of the discontent of the dominant classes. It was expressed and diffused to the rest of society, especially to the middle sectors, through their absolute control over the media. The attempt to continue in office by a reputed electoral fraud in 1948 enabled the previously minute Social Democratic Party successfully to lead the mounting opposition to the regime in a military confrontation. This eruption of the social democratic intelligentsia had profound implications. The return to the liberal order, as had occurred in 1917, was never accomplished. Although the new constitution of 1949 came closer to the liberal constitution of 1871 than to the project drafted by the Social Democratic Party, sufficient changes were introduced in the months of *de facto* government to enable the state to be transformed within this legal framework.

The social democratic intellectuals had been critical of the vulnerability of the staple development pattern throughout the 1940s and, hence, of the role played by the traditionally dominant classes and foreign capital (Facio, 1972). The policies implemented by the Junta and later by the newly founded National Liberation Party (PLN) further modified the integration of the hegemonic bloc by increasing the economic functions of the state on the one hand and dismantling the army on the other. Among the measures taken were the nationalization of the banking system; the creation of state institutions and public enterprises in the fields of education, price control and electricity (completely nationalized as well); the strengthening of labour legislation and the welfare system; and, finally, a tax reform which provided new sources of revenue for this highly interventionist state.

The highly polarized nature of the class antagonisms following the civil war, in which the organized workers still backing the government had been militarily defeated, was the context for the attempt of the PLN to rally all classes in harmony around a *desarrollista* project. Workers found the social reforms they had fought for not only untouched but strengthened. The traditionally dominant classes found that these reforms were there to stay, but, at least, the communist threat was over and the political stability and the post-war boom provided numerous investment opportunities. But perhaps the main beneficiaries were the middle sectors and a new entrepreneurial nucleus both inside and outside the public sector. The expansion of these two social groupings was encouraged by the successive PLN governments as the basis for political stability and economic dynamism.

During the late 1940s and the early years of the following decade the expansion in global demand as a consequence of the fast growth of the export sector made investments in the industrial sector profitable. Domestic capital was thus carrying out the diversification of the productive structure following the pattern of staple growth. This strategy of development was, however, unconsciously abandoned shortly after. The monetary measures of 1950 and the tariff of 1951, issued for fiscal and balance of payments purposes, operated as protectionist barriers which made industrial investments more profitable. The advantages of protectionism were readily perceived by the rising entrepreneurs; hence they started lobbying for more explicit industrial protection. The modernizing ideology of the PLN leadership, now under the influence of the UN Economic Commission for Latin America (ECLA), saw in an import-substituting strategy the possibility of developing a significant entrepreneurial nucleus and an industrial base. In 1954 a moderate tariff for industrial protection was issued which in 1959 was replaced by the Law of Protection and Industrial Development.

The political economy of this drastic change in development strategy is still largely undocumented. The difficulty is partly due to the unexplored and difficult issue of the relationship between class, PLN and the state. In the background, however. the behaviour of the export sector must have had some effect on the conduct of the traditionally dominant classes. The upward trend in coffee prices, which more than trebled from 1945 to 1954, was reversed after its 1954 peak. Consequently, the barter terms of trade deteriorated by 40 per cent between 1954 and 1962 (OFIPLAN, 1965: 91). The profit squeeze which resulted in the export sector was partially offset by increases in productivity. In balance of payments terms inflows of capital also ameliorated the effects of the terms of trade. The colón, however, had to be devalued in 1961. The predictions of ECLA had been fulfilled, at least for this export basket and during this period. The exporters and merchants could also see the impressive dynamism of the industrial sector. Protected markets offered investment opportunities in which handsome profit margins were not subject to erosion from downward trends in the terms of trade. Super-exploitation of labour and the concomitant forms of authoritarian domination were an unlikely alternative given the employment situation and the class stratification, with its wide urban and rural middle sectors from which the PLN could draw immediate support.

The limits to staple growth were thus reached. Expansion alongside the traditional export sector was limited geographically in the case of coffee and by the policies of the multinationals in the case of bananas. In addition, the negative effect of the trend in the terms of trade could not have been completely offset either by increases in productivity or by the intensity of the labour process.

Possible shifts to other staples could hardly inject sufficient dynamism into the economy to raise the living standards of a population growing at a rate of 3.5 per cent per annum. The agricultural frontier was about to be reached and therefore new export commodities would have to be the result of changes in the pattern of land utilization. Prevailing techniques also entailed capital-intensive processes if the new commodities were to be internationally competitive, especially for an economy with comparatively high labour costs. The condition of a favourable man/resource ratio had been removed before the economy could provide sufficient employment opportunities in the secondary and tertiary sectors as a result of a diversification of the export base.

Staple growth actually became a misnomer for the Costa Rican economy towards the end of the 1950s because, fortunately, the political conditions for a change in the strategy of development were present. Although favourable conditions for staple growth had been found for more than a century the spread effects thus generated had been insufficient to set in motion a significant process of industrialization.

Import-substituting Industrialization

ECLA's prescription to tackle the limitations imposed by the small size of internal markets was regional integration. For the Central American case the need was more acute and a careful project was devised. However, this formulation on the one hand, largely ignored the changes in the behaviour of US capital and its interest in the industrializing processes of Latin America; whilst, on the other, the absence of political analysis omitted a characterization of the classes undertaking industrialization and the changes in their behaviour as the links with the central economies were renewed with unprecedented vigour after the Second World War.

The aims of balanced growth, development of Central American MNCs and co-ordination of agricultural and industrial policies were severely undermined by the US (Bodenheimer, 1974). The propositions of the US, including free play of market forces, unrestricted conditions for foreign capital and promises of aid, were readily accepted by the Central American entrepreneurs and the project was turned into action. Costa Rica, however, did not join the Common Market (CACM) until a few years later, after the party controlled by the traditionally dominant classes lost the elections to the PLN.

Industrial production was boosted, increasing its share of GDP from 25 per cent in 1962 to 29 per cent in 1973; industrial employment (widely defined) increased its share of total employment from 22 to 25 per cent and industrial exports, which represented 4 per cent of total exports, increased to 27 per cent in 1974. The overall rate of growth of the economy was 7.1 per cent per annum for the period 1962–74. This dynamism of the economy and of the export sector in particular is only partially explained by industrialization. Sugar and cattle beef exports rose significantly as well as banana production, now in the hands of national producers. Income from coffee also increased, although prices remained low until 1969: productivity increases explain this result. The context of these impressive rates of growth was the overall expansion of the capitalist system and, especially, the price stability of the Costa Rican exports until the 1973–75 recession.

Centralization of existing capital and further expansion in the industrial sector led by foreign capital proceeded rapidly (Garnier-Rimolo and Herrero-Acosta, 1977: 107–16). The lack of co-ordination of industrial policies in the region enabled foreign capital to play the Central American states against each other to obtain privileged treatment in terms of tax incentives, cheap inputs from the state sector (including credit) and communications infrastructure. Competition to attract foreign capital resulted in an even stronger position for the national-international industrial interests in the array of forces demanding services from the state.

The expansion of the state sector to provide services and commodities, not only to the private sector but to the population at large, was continuous throughout this period, regardless of the times the opposition to the PLN was in office. To dismantle the welfare programmes would obviously have been very unpopular, but the situation was further complicated in Costa Rica by the legal determinants of the budget. Specific sources of income are attached to well-defined uses by laws and regulations which are difficult to modify, especially given the fact that the PLN controlled the Congress from 1951 to 1978. The effect has been a very strong public sector with possibilities of expanding its activities, given both the inertia or the bureaucratic processes and the directions and emphases the PLN has dictated. In this way further independence of the state apparatus from the coffee constellation of interests has been achieved, and this has been used by the PLN to foster the development of the entrepreneurial and middle sectors and to cater for its wide electoral clientele. The overall constraint has been, however, the chronic tendency to fiscal crises.

Politically, this development of the public sector has given rise to at least two well-defined sectors within the bureaucracy. These are a well-organized majority that has managed significantly to improve its standard of living and an élite of 'state entrepreneurs' who command an important share of the decisions on allocation of resources in the economy, for example, the financial sector and key industrial inputs as well as in the private enterprises which some have managed to develop. These 'state entrepreneurs' constitute a significant political force within the PLN.

Costa Rica again seems not to fit in with Marini's characterization of Latin American industrialization subject to the law of super-exploitation. The main condition of a large contingent of unemployed was absent to start with.

Although active population was growing at a rate of 3.5 per cent per annum and the share of the agricultural sector in total employment figures was steadily falling, open unemployment did not rise beyond 7.0 per cent. The dynamism of the economy enabled the services sector, in particular the state, to absorb an increasing share of total employment. Consequently, the effect of real wages and the trend they followed also contradicts Marini's hypotheses. Real wages in Costa Rica have been the highest in the CACM throughout this period; moreover, the impressive rates of growth in real wages suggest that labour has managed to appropriate part of the increases in productivity (Reynolds and Leiva, 1978: 223).

The proposition that markets in Latin America are subdivided into two spheres, difficult to operationalize in any case, can hardly describe the dynamic internal market industrial expansion in Costa Rica. Workers in sectors of industry of high productivity enjoy higher than average real wages in the economy (OFIPLAN, 1973: 71). It would be difficult to argue that they do not constitute part of the industrial internal market.

In Marini's view, as might be the case in Brazil (Marini, 1975: 113–19), expansion of the internal market can only take place at the expense of the working classes via concentration of income in the middle sectors. In Costa Rica, the middle-income sector of the population increased its share of the national income from 1961 to 1971: the lowest income bracket, however, kept its share. Public-sector workers, in particular, have always managed to enjoy higher than average real wages (OFIPLAN, 1973: 71).

Marini's contention that full employment and upgrading of the labour force are incompatible with peripheral capitalism is thus undermined, as also is his case for self-reliance. Moreover, the small size of the Costa Rican economy, indeed of the CACM, simply leaves autarchic self-reliance out of the question. This immediately implies a need to integrate to a larger unit. The Soviet bloc being an implausible assumption, the need to remain within the capitalist camp seriously undermines the capacity to change the internal relations of production. The imperial reaction to the attempt at transition would necessarily imply self-reliance whether voluntary or involuntary. Thus, the proposition that socialism is a better setting for a small, peripheral, rather successful economy seems to stand on thin ice.

Import-substituting industrialization has been assessed from a different standpoint. The claim is that a route à la Singapore exists and it is only a matter of eliminating 'market distortions' and an internationally competitive industry would be generated which was consistent with factor endowments. This proposition has, however, been shown to be theoretically unsound:

> One can certainly now see that the view that with 'flexible' money wages there could be no unemployment has no convincing argument to recommend it ... Even in a pure tatonnement in traditional models convergence to an equilibrium cannot be generally

proved. In a more satisfactory model matters are more doubtful still. (Hahn, 1977: 37)

Capital movements do not take place in the full-employment equilibrium of pure trade models. If this were the world we lived in, the price mechanism would be sufficient for achieving efficient allocations of resources. But, on the contrary, disequilibria in resources and commodity markets, unemployment and uncertainty about the future are the norm in market economies. Most propositions in current textbooks of economics illustrate what actual economies are incapable of achieving.

Studies in the location of economic activities indicate that capital movements tend to be guided by considerations of maximization of economies of agglomeration which describe more accurately the current picture of the centripetal forces prevailing over the centrifugal tendencies within the capitalist system, unemployment being concomitant with weak development poles (Murray, 1972). The movements of capital towards certain peripheral locations since the late 1960s need thus to be at least briefly explained. These centrifugal flows from the central economies became significant only after competitive pressures rose as a result of overinvestment in the major industrial sectors, especially after the rise of Japan to an industrial power. Full employment has aggravated the profit squeeze in these economies and it is then that capital has started reallocating labour-intensive processes elsewhere.

The first wave of these movements consisted mainly of US capital, which more strongly felt the profit squeeze as a result of its lower rates of productivity increase as compared with Japan and Germany after the Second World War. The latter capitals, however, responded in the same way and the new industrial centres received a further boost. Nevertheless, the dimensions of this tendency should not be overestimated. It can be argued, moreover, that the current trends in automation as well as the recession and unemployment at the centre might eventually end up reasserting the centripetal forces.

Undoubtedly, certain peripheral economies have benefited enormously, but competition is fierce and the long-term viability of these industrial structures might be limited to a handful of economies. In this context, to argue that Costa Rica could have industrialized following this strategy demands further consideration than the elimination of 'market distortions', such as advantages of location (geographical and military importance) and of labour costs. Costa Rica is certainly unfavourably located compared with the Mexican border and Puerto Rico. Moreover, this strategy has succeeded when the state has been highly 'interventionist' in the labour market, to the extent that labour organizations have been suppressed, enabling wages to reach internationally competitive levels. Thus, the chances of success if Costa Rica adopted this strategy seem slim and the social costs far too great.

The Limits of Import Substitution: the Alternatives

The CACM as a whole saw a decline in the rate of industrial investment in the 1970s compared with the 1960s. The rapid exhaustion of the 'easy phase' of import substitution has been associated with the highly skewed income distribution of the region (excluding Costa Rica it is comparable to Mexico and Brazil) and its political instability (Reynolds and Leiva, 1978: 253). Costa Rica, nevertheless, witnessed high rates of investment, and the early 1970s in particular showed a marked increase in the rate of investment. The expansion of the internal market which has postponed the appearance of the demand constraint on the growth of light industry can partly be explained by the overall dynamism of the economy. The boom in consumer durables, especially, could also be the result of the credit expansion after the financial reforms of 1972 which allowed private financial intermediaries to tap savings and lend for consumption purposes and enabled the fast growth of shop credit (Salazar-Xirinachs, 1980: 60). This later exhaustion of the import-substituting possibilities of Costa Rica as compared with the other members of the CACM may also be explained by the different patterns of specialization of their productive structures. Costa Rica has specialized in consumer durables (metal goods and electrical equipment), her neighbours in the traditional manufacturing sectors (textiles/clothing and leather/shoes) (Bulmer-Thomas, 1978). To the extent that income elasticity of demand is higher for durables than for traditional manufactured goods it is to be expected that Costa Rican industry shows dynamism while her partners might have already exhausted the possibilities of the regional market.

The overall rate of capital formation remained high for the period 1970–77. Significant changes appeared, however, in the statistics of the period: first, agriculture stagnated; secondly, the private sector invested more in real estate and housing to the detriment of industry and especially agriculture; and, finally, the share of the public sector in accumulation increased (Salazar-Xirinachs, 1980: 35). The implications of the lagging agricultural sector cannot be overemphasized; balance of payments and fiscal crises are immediately entailed. These conditions were further aggravated by the 1973–75 recessionary and inflationary pressures.

In spite of the dynamism of the economy, which was already faltering in its export sector and eventually also in the industrial sector, employment problems began to accumulate, albeit hidden from the employment statistics. 'Informal sector' activities began to emerge in certain cities and rural employment took the form of the largest peasant invasions of private land ever recorded.

Urban mobilization also resulted from the attempts by university students to secure state financing of higher education and from the opposition to the concessionary rights granted to Aluminium Company of America (ALCOA) to exploit bauxite. New radical political parties emerged which articulated the demands of the popular sectors.

The response from the state was to modernize the police. A tendency to undermine the democratic form of domination was apparent, repression was taking the place of concession. The right wing of the PLN was in office.

In 1974 a different faction of the PLN won the elections. The weight of the sector of 'state entrepreneurs' was unprecedented. A new political project was very quickly implemented for the length of the presidential period (four years) and the role of the state was substantially modified. If private investment was sluggish for various reasons, it was felt that the state should undertake investment projects, especially those involving high risk and only long-term profitability. In the dealings with MNCs, the state was seen as better equipped for the negotiations leading to the formation of joint ventures. The state, in the words of the President, was to become an 'entrepreneur' and indeed it did. Public gross fixed capital formation which represented 5.8 per cent of GDP in 1970–73 increased to 11.3 per cent in 1975–78, being highest in the last two years (Salazar-Xirinachs, 1980: 35, 45). The state went into new fields of capital accumulation such as agroindustry, cement, aluminium and tourism.

But this modification of the role of the state was only part of a larger project involving a change in development strategy and in the social agents conducting it. It was a project which entailed the transformation of the hegemonic bloc. The state entrepreneurs, by controlling their indispensable instrument of the state, attempted to arrange a new pact of domination in which the traditionally dominant classes would play a subordinated role. The involvement of the state in the process of accumulation was to provide the material basis for the hegemony of the state entrepreneurial class; public enterprises and the state-fostered private concerns were eventually to become the most dynamic sectors of the economy as they were the only ones capable of overcoming the limits of staple growth and import-substituting industrialization. Politically, alliance with the popular classes was sought through a policy of redistribution of land to landless peasants, squatting was halted and the demands for land were channelled institutionally. Also instrumental to this purpose was the impressive improvement in the welfare services: social security coverage was extended to previously excluded sectors of the population and a programme of direct transfers of income to lower income groups both in the urban and rural areas was started. In 1976 this had already raised funds equivalent to 1.7 per cent of GDP (ILO-PREALC, 1979: 34). Nor was the ideological front left unprotected: a short-lived but very ambitious newspaper broke the monopoly held by the traditional sectors. State radio and television channels were also set up.

Short-term inflationary and recessionary pressures largely due to the world recession were met by an unorthodox stabilization programme which dealt with inflationary pressures while protecting employment levels and consumption standards of the low-income strata. Central to the strategy was an incomes policy which transferred income from the high and middle towards the low-income groups; as a result there was some shift of the demand pattern from imported to locally produced commodities, easing the balance of payments difficulties and avoiding the import of external inflation. Production of basic foodstuffs was successfully stimulated as well as production for export through a system of incentives which avoided having to affect the nominal exchange rate. The expansionary character of the programme, however, placed added pressures on the balance of payments, given the high import component of total demand; increased state intervention could only increase the fiscal deficit and debt burden. Although the overall economic strategy included the nationaliza-tion of the oil companies (refinery and distribution) as an important source of surplus to finance state activities, the spectre of the IMF could sound the death-knell of the stabilization programme and thus of the entire political project.

A lucky element, without which the possibilities of success of the expansion-ary stabilization programme would have been open to question, was that of the commodity booms which followed the world recession, in particular the extraordinary rise in the price of coffee in 1977. The balance of payments and fiscal financing constraints were immediately relaxed.

Inflation was brought under control and open unemployment never rose. The effect of the programme was, nevertheless, a reduction in the average real wage, especially of the high and middle wage sectors (ILO-PREALC, 1979: 15).

The traditional oligarchy, perceiving the nature of the political project, was growing restless. 'Animal spirits' were not only channelling investment into unproductive activities (real estate and housing), but also guiding a systematic campaign to end the project in the next electoral confrontation. The share in the new pact of domination was never accepted; competition from the state was feared, in spite of the fact that the aim of state intervention was to reactivate the process of accumulation in which private capital could have opportunities of expansion, perhaps the only ones compatible with a democratic society.

The critique of the 'state entrepreneur' fell on the fertile soil of the urban middle sectors that had suffered from the incomes policy. The alternative strategy proposed was the need to 'get factor prices right' and to dismantle 'excess' state intervention in the economy.

The government which came into office in 1978 was, nevertheless, not fully committed to the liberalization strategy. The steps advanced by the 'liberal' hawks in the administration have been undermined by several others (e.g. the structure of interest rates). In any case the political viability of a process of de-industrialization is doubtful. The confrontation it would unleash with the industrial bourgeoisie and labour interests and with the state entrepreneurs and, hence, with a large section of the PLN, could hardly be won by democratic means.

At present, the recessionary and inflationary world pressures, added to a situation of excess liquidity in the economy, have led the government to an orthodox stabilization programme with the IMF since March 1980. Meanwhile the discussion on the nature of the future development strategy is present not only in academic and political circles but in the daily newspapers as a matter of growing social concern. There is an increasing awareness that significant changes are required if the economy is to return to 'normal' post-war growth rates, the direction of which will be elucidated by the political forces of the country. But it is also clear that, at any rate, if such changes are not attempted the special features of the Costa Rica of today will certainly be lost.

References

Bertram, G. W. (1963). 'Economic growth in Canadian industry, 1870–1915: the staple model and the take-off hypothesis; *Canadian Journal of Economic and Political Science*, **29**, no. 2.

Bhagwati, J. N. (1958). 'Immiserizing growth: a geometrical note', *Review of Economic Studies*, **25**, no. 6.

Bodenheimer, S. J. (1974). 'El Mercomún y la ayuda norteamericana', in Bodenheimer, S. J. *et al.*, *La inversión extranjera en Centro América* (EDUCA, San José).

Bulmer-Thomas, V. (1978). 'Trade, structure and linkages in Costa Rica. An input-output approach', *Journal of Development Economics*. no. 5, 73–86.

Cardoso, F. H. (1976). 'Current theses on Latin American development and dependency: a critique', paper presented to the Third Scandinavian Research Conference on Latin America, Bergen, 17–19 June.

Caves, R. D. (1971). 'Export-led growth and the new economic history' in *Trade, Balance of Payments and Growth* (North-Holland, Amsterdam).

Churnside-Harrison, E. R. (1979). 'The development of the labour force in Costa Rica', University of Sussex, unpublished DPhil thesis.

Facio, R. (1972). *Estudios sobre economía costarricense*, (Editorial Costa Rica, San José).

Fernandez, L. (1886). *Colección de documentos para la historia de Costa Rica* (Pablo Dupont, Paris).

Fernandez-Guardia, R. (1967). *Cartilla histórica de Costa Rica* (Lehman, San José).

Fernandez-Guardia, R. (1972). *Costa Rica en el siglo XIX* (EDUCA, San José).

Frank, A. G. (1969). *Capitalism and Underdevelopment in Latin America* (Monthly Review, New York).

Garnier, Rimolo, L. and Herrero-Acosta, F. (1977). 'El desarrollo de la industria en Costa Rica. Elementos para su interpretación, University of Costa Rica, unpublished Licenciatura dissertation.

Hahn, F. H. (1977). 'Keynesian economics and general equilibrium theory: reflections on some current debates', in Harcourt, G. C., *The Microeconomic Foundations of Macroeconomics* (Macmillan, London).

Hall, C. (1978). *El café y el desarrollo histórico-geográfico de Costa Rica* (Editorial Costa Rica, San José).

ILO-PREALC (International Labour Office-Programa Regional del Empleo para América Latina y el Caribe) (1979). *Investigaciones sobre empleo 16. Salarios, precios y empleo en coyuntura de crisis externa. Costa Rica 1973–1975* (Santiago).

Innis, H. A. (1954). *The Cod Fisheries: The history of an international economy* (Toronto University Press).

Innis, H. A. (1973). *Essays in Canadian Economic History* (Toronto University Press).

Innis, H. A. (1975). *The Fur Trade in Canada* (Toronto University Press).

Marini, R. M. (1972). 'Brazilian sub-imperialism', *Monthly Review*, **23**, no. 9.

Marini, R. M. (1975). *Subdesarrollo y revolución* (Siglo XXI, Mexico).

Marini, R. M. (1977). *Dialéctica de la dependencia* (Era, México).

Murray, R. (1972). 'Underdevelopment, international firms and the international division of labour', in *Towards a New World Economy,* (Rotterdam University Press).

North, D. C. (1961). *The Economic Growth of the United States 1790 to 1860* (Prentice-Hall, Englewood Cliffs).

OFIPLAN (Oficinade Planeamiento) (1965). 'Características de la economía de Costa Rica 1950–1962' (San José).

OFIPLAN (Ofic012n de Planeamiento) (1973). *Plan Nacional de Desarrollo 1974–1978* (San José).

Reynolds, C. W. and Leiva, G. (1978). 'Employment problems of export economies in a common market: the case of Central America', in Cline, W. R. and Delgado E. *Economic Integration in Central America* (The Brookings Institution, Washington DC).

Rodriguez, G. M. (1979). 'Economic development during the colonial period and political implications after independence: the case of Costa Rica', University of Sussex, unpublished MA dissertation.

Salazar-Xirinachs, J. M. (1980). 'The state and economic development in Costa Rica', University of Cambridge, unpublished MPhil dissertation.

Schifter, J. (1979). *La fase oculta de la guerra civil en Costa Rica* (Editorial Costa Rica, San José).

Soley-Guell, T. (1975). *Compendio de historia económica y hacendaria de Costa Rica* (Editorial Costa Rica, San José).

Stone, S. (1976). *La dinastía de los conquistadores* (Editorial Costa Rica, San José).

Vega, J. L. (1980). 'Estado nacional y sociedad en Costa Rica (1821–1930)', University of Costa Rica (mimeo).

Watkins, M. H. (1963). 'A staple theory of economic growth', *The Canadian Journal of Economics and Political Science,* **29**, no. 2.

The Struggle for Development:
National Strategies in an International Context
Edited by M. Bienefeld and M. Godfrey
© 1982 John Wiley & Sons Ltd.

Chapter 9

Ireland: Sustained Growth through Foreign Capital and Manufactured Exports?

ANTHONY COUGHLAN

No country is dependent in exactly the same way as another, or underdeveloped for the same reasons. Indeed it may seem paradoxical to regard the Republic of Ireland as underdeveloped in anything like the sense of some of the other economies examined in this book. In terms of income per head the Republic, a member of the EEC, is one of the top 25 of the 150 or so members of the UN. Average calorie consumption is among the highest in the world. The population is predominantly urbanized. Ownership of cars, televisions and telephones puts it among the richer countries. Literacy is universal. There is compulsory schooling to fifteen years and high school participation rates for sixteen- and seventeen-year-olds. Two-thirds of dwellings are owner-occupied. Infant mortality is very low and life expectancy at birth is over 70 years for both sexes. The public health and social security system is reasonably comprehensive. Two thirds of the labour force are wage and salaried workers, over half of them in trade unions.

A Non-poor Underdeveloped Country

The paradox may be expressed by calling Ireland a non-poor underdeveloped country, although the indicators of underdevelopment are not always superficially obvious. In observing the relatively affluent inhabitants of modern Ireland one needs to recall that there move among them, as it were, the ghosts of the country's emigrants, who were born there but forced abroad by economic circumstances. For the island of Ireland — comprising the Republic and Northern Ireland — is unique in the world in having a population today which is not much more than half what it was in the 1840s. During most of the period since that time the rate of emigration has been greater than the rate of natural population increase. Today there are nearly 1 million Irish-born people living in Britain compared with around 4¾ million at home. Net emigration has ceased since the early 1960s, in large part because of the rapid development of the Irish economy since that time, and in recent years there has been some net immigration, although this seems to be the result of two flows — single people in their teens and early twenties mainly emigrating, and retired persons and breadwinners with dependent spouses and young children returning from abroad, which tends to increase the ratio of dependants to producers. The population and labour force is now growing rapidly, half the population being under the age of 25.

A second indicator of underdevelopment is chronically high unemployment in both parts of Ireland, at rates well above West European norms. Currently one-eighth of the Irish labour force is workless. A crucial test of the development strategies used in Ireland over the past two decades is whether they can provide enough jobs at acceptable incomes for the growing population and labour force. If they cannot, unemployment rates must soar further or heavy net emigration resume. At the start of the 1980s the portents look gloomy.

The Republic is also differentiated from the other countries examined in this book in that for a long period it was politically incorporated within a metropolitan state, as Northern Ireland still is. Indeed as England's first and oldest colony, Ireland has formed, with Scotland and Wales, the local Celtic periphery to an industrialized English core. One legacy of this is a highly developed banking, communications, civil service and education system. In the nineteenth century when the whole of Ireland formed part of the United Kingdom and was directly represented in the Westminster Parliament these institutions were in fact disfunctional to Irish economic development (O Tuathaigh, 1972; Lee, 1973) so that when the Irish state was established in 1921 it inherited some institutional features more characteristic of a metropolitan than a dependent economy.

Nineteenth-century Ireland was a classic case of peripheralization. Its rural proletariat was victim of the conflict between population and the institution of private property in pastureland (Crotty, 1966, 1974). Marx, in Volume 1 of *Capital,* treated Ireland as a special case of capital accumulation in which capital in the form of cattle was increased by appropriating the subsistence of the labourer, who was moved off the land which had previously maintained him so that it could be turned into pasture. Most of the country became a supplier of cheap labour and of cattle to Britain. Its industries declined in the face of competing British imports as its population and internal market fell and, apart from the industrialized areas of the North-East, the rest of the country, which had undergone considerable industrial development in the eighteenth century, was 'deindustrialized'.

The Republic and Northern Ireland

The partition of Ireland by the Westminster Government of Ireland Act 1920 in part reflected a division of interest between the petty bourgeoisie of the north and south. The industries of Northern Ireland — shipbuilding, textiles and engineering — were export-oriented and dependent on access to British and imperial markets and on British naval contracts. The unionism of their owners was a political expression of their hostility to the tariffs, higher taxes and state interventionist policies which a government bent on industrializing the rest of the country would be pressed to adopt. The employers were supported by the skilled workers in the Belfast mills and shipyards, a classical labour aristocracy, who were separated from the predominantly Catholic labourers by religion as well as by degree of skill. Outside the North-East the population was overwhelmingly nationalist and all classes saw political separation from Britain and the establishment of an independent state as essential for development. Such expectations have been a common motif in the many anti-colonial revolutions which have taken place around the world this century and of which the Irish were pioneers.

The new Irish state — the Free State, later the republic — was faced with acute difficulties. Despite its relatively advanced infrastructure there was little manufacturing industry apart from some food processing. Nine-tenths of foreign trade was with the UK and the export of live cattle predominated. Partition also limited its development potential. It derived the new government of control over one-third of the population and nearly half the taxable capacity of the whole country. Northern Ireland, dominated by a handful of export industries, needed diversification. The rest of the country needed a programme of industrialization. Ideally the impulse for diversifying the industry of the North could have come from the development of the remainder of the island, but the absence of one government ruled this out. Partition thus helped to foster two local economies within Ireland, each with an inherent imbalance within itself. Forbidden to support one another under a common government in a unitary state they each leaned separately, as it were, upon Britain.

Despite these handicaps the progress of the Republic has nonetheless been remarkable, especially in the past two decades. It is no longer Northern Ireland's poor relation. During the 1960s the Republic's growth rate in manufacturing was higher than Northern Ireland's and it continued at a high level during the 1970s, whereas Northern manufacturing output declined in consequence of the political troubles and the effects of recession on its traditional shipbuilding and textile industries. Average income per head in the Republic is now the same as in Northern Ireland, although it was two-thirds of Northern levels two decades ago. Average earnings per employee in the Republic are higher. The gap in standards of public social services has significantly narrowed. The Republic's industrial structure is now more diversified than Northern Ireland's. These differences are in large part due to the existence of a politically independent state in the south. As a class capable of creative development the Northern manufacturing bourgeoisie has shown none of the élan of its southern counterpart. Although both parts of Ireland rely heavily on attracting foreign development capital, the influence of southern business on the policy-making of an independent state offers it opportunities for political and economic advance which are unavailable in the North, where business interests must look for support to the UK government — which must of course attend as well to the demands of the 97 per cent of its population living in Britain. Separate statehood gives the Republic greater flexibility in dealing with foreign industry and transnational firms (Moore *et al.*, 1978).

State and Economy

There are indeed few capitalist countries where the state plays a more active role in economic life today. Investments by the state and state-sponsored firms account for one-half of total fixed investment. The latter in turn has amounted to between 25 and 30 per cent of the Republic's GNP during the 1970s, one of the highest rates in the world. In addition, the government's capital programme influences a further quarter of fixed investment by subsidizing capital formation by home and foreign companies through grants and loans. One-third of all employees work in the public sector, which is a higher proportion than in any other EEC country.

This economic importance of the state is not evidence of socialist influence, any more than it is in Portugal, Brazil or Japan. The ideological climate is in general hostile to socialism. Although trade unions are numerically strong social democracy is weak, mainly due to the failure of the political labour movement to play a leading role in the country's national independence struggle, which was led by the political representatives of the bourgeoisie and petty bourgeoisie. There is a high level of religious practice and communist influence is slight, being mostly confined to some trade unions. Proposals for nationalization have never caused party contention. There has in fact never been any nationalization of private profit-making companies. Criticism of state intervention on ideological grounds has consequently tended to be mute in Ireland. The extensive state economic involvement is accepted as an essential support for private enterprise, including the local branches of the transnational firms which in recent years have been the most dynamic element in the Republic's industrial structure.

The Republic of Ireland is a good example of the truth of the proposition that when the bourgeoisie of an underdeveloped capitalist country is economically weak, its political hegemony over the state and machinery of government is all the more crucial for its development. The state is under bourgeois hegemony in the sense that policy-makers, politicians and bureaucracy accept that the profitability and accumulation of private capital is the prime determinant of

growth, development and employment. State intervention, however extensive, is seen as complementary to and not as substituting for private
investment and the proper role of the state is regarded as being to provide the
most fruitful political and economic framework for 'free enterprise'. The
economic policies and modes of political legitimation adopted by Irish
governments since the foundation of the state are all consistent with these
assumptions. Owners of capital of course are not a uniform entity, in Ireland
any more than elsewhere, and may be divided into manufacturing, financial,
commercial and agricultural fractions. Business in turn may be categorized
into large or small, domestically-oriented or export-oriented, wholly native-
owned, partly foreign-owned and wholly foreign-owned companies — all of
them variously affected politically by the development strategy adopted. Irish
economic policy has gone through two main phases over the past half-
century, a period of protectionism from the 1930s to the 1950s, followed by a
period of reliance on growth through foreign capital and manufactured
exports which has lasted up to the present. In both phases the political
hegemony of the Irish bourgeoisie over the state has remained important —
all the more so because of the economic weakness of Irish capital vis-à-vis its
competitors in other countries. This continuity is symbolized in the career of
Mr Sean Lemass, who as minister responsible for industry and commerce for
most of the first period was architect of the protectionist policy and who
presided, as industry minister and later as prime minister, from 1957 to 1966
over the initial phase of the second. In both periods the development strategy
adopted was profoundly influenced by the situation of the international
capitalist system as a whole.

The Protectionist Period: The 1930s to the 1950s

The first period entailed a policy of import substitution behind high tariff
barriers, accompanied by laws to keep the ownership of new enterprises in
Irish hands. Protectionist policies were widespread during the 1930s, during
which Irish exports fell by half. For some years there was a trade war, known
in Ireland as 'the economic war', between Ireland and Britain. Irish protectionism was approved at the time by Keynes, although he posed the question
'whether Ireland is a large enough unit geographically for more than a very
modest measure of national self-sufficiency to be feasible ...' (Keynes, 1933).
Tariffs were accompanied by the establishment of a number of state companies in areas of the economy where private capital was either too weak or
unenterprising. By the 1950s these existed in air transport, shipping, tourist
promotion, industrial research and the production of steel, fertilizers, sugar
and turf. In the 1930s protectionism led to a marked expansion of industrial
output and employment. During the 1940s public policy was concerned with
surviving in face of the shortages of the Second World War, during which the

Irish State remained neutral, and with post-war reconstruction, but by the 1950s the impetus behind the protectionist phase of development was faltering.

The crucial problem was lack of demand in the small domestic market due to the falling population and the low incomes of the agricultural sector. Radical land reform might have stimulated agricultural output and incomes, as in various LDCs today, but this would have adversely affected the cattle trade, which remained the principal export commodity and source of finance for imports throughout this early period (Crotty, 1966). From the late 1940s on mechanization of agriculture caused a rapid decline in the rural population and a rise in emigration. Tariffs subsidized industry at the expense of higher prices for consumers, which added to the pressures to emigrate. The protectionist policy has often been criticized for featherbedding inefficient firms and causing a bias against manufactured exports. The domestic market remained too small to enable many firms to reach technologically optimum size. In reality there was little opportunity to build up export markets in manufactures during the 1930s and the war years, even if the will had been there. The currency also showed signs of being overvalued — the exchange rate of the Irish pound having been tied by law to sterling since 1927. Nonetheless by the 1950s a healthy export trade in manufactures had begun, whose importance was overshadowed by severe balance of payments crises in 1950 and 1955. These were due to temporary factors but governments of the day reacted to them with conservative deflationary policies which cut home demand even further (Kennedy and Dowling, 1975; Walsh, 1979). Emigration reached massive proportions in the 1950s, and in 1958 a new Fianna Fail government under Mr Lemass pointed the country towards free trade, repealed the legislation inhibiting the foreign ownership of industry and set out to attract foreign capital to Ireland

Free Trade and Foreign Investment: The 1960s and 1970s

The new departure was not adopted without misgivings. Several speeches he made throughout the 1950s show Lemass vacillating between a policy of economic nationalism and dependence on outside development. The immediate impulse behind the new policy was the need to do something about high emigration and unemployment. Foreign investment was seen as pragmatically justified if it would add to jobs. More fundamental was Lemass's recognition of the need to accommodate Ireland to the liberalization of trade and capital movements then occurring throughout the capitalist world. The EEC had just been formed and EFTA was being established. In 1959 Macmillan oriented British government policy towards membership of the EEC. Lemass personally decided that Ireland should seek full EEC membership rather than associate status and Ireland applied for full membership simultaneously with Britain in 1961 (Whitaker, 1973). A negative reason for this step was the desire to prevent the EEC adding a new dimension to the partition boundary across Ireland by imposing tariffs on Irish goods and interfering with the tariff-free access to the UK which Ireland had had since 1938. A positive one was the desire to get the benefit of free market access and high EEC prices for Irish agricultural goods, which at the time still constituted about three-fifths of total visible exports. Currency devaluation was ruled out as a stimulus to exports, so that the strategy adopted was one of supplementing the expected EEC boost to agriculture by subventing manufactured exports through subsidies financed by the taxpayer.

The politically important farming interest was enthusiastically in favour of the new 'outward-looking' policies, but there was surprisingly little opposition to the prospect of free trade from those Irish firms hitherto oriented towards the domestic market. One reason was that the most efficient of these had already begun to export and could be expected to welcome the widening of export markets in the EEC. Moreover, full free trade was a long time in coming because of the delay until 1973 in joining the EEC, followed by the final dismantling of all tariffs five years later. The Republic's initially high levels of protection meant that free trade only began to bite seriously at the domestic market towards the end of this long period. This gave the more progressive firms time to adapt, in which they were helped by generous government grants and advice. The strong political lead given by the government to the whole process overbore what qualms there might have been among particular business sections.

The commitment to free trade and the attraction of foreign investment was accompanied by more active and sophisticated modes of state intervention than hitherto, geared to preparing the economy for the EEC. The public capital programme was used more consciously as an instrument of economic policy. New research institutes improved the quality of economic and technical advice. During the 1960s the government committed itself to a series of economic development programmes. This was 'programming' rather than planning (Katsiaouni, 1978). Its political impact was probably more important than its economic, in that the complex of advisory and consultative bodies set up as part of the exercise encouraged a consensus among civil servants, academic economists, businessmen and trade union leaders on the main lines of the new departure. Opposition had little coherent focus. Finally, the Government created in the Industrial Development Authority (IDA) a new arm of the state with sufficient resources and flexibility to act effectively in attracting foreign capital and supervise the radical restructuring of the Irish manufacturing sector in the following two decades.

Ireland was lucky to be embarking on its export-led growth strategy at a time when the world capitalist economy was set on a long period of expansion, export markets were booming and foreign investment by transnational firms was accelerating. Only a small proportion of international investment capital needed to come to Ireland to make a big impact on an economy with a population of 3.2 million, a total employed labour force of 1,048,000, (22 per cent in agriculture, 30 per cent in industry and 48 per cent in services), an employee labour force of about 750,000 and an employee labour force in manufacturing of 212,000 (CSO, 1979a). While the competitive bidding for foreign investment which many countries now engage in tends to shift resources from labour to capital on a global scale and probably has small effect on its total amount, it doubtless does affect its distribution. The Republic's incentives package to attract such investment is one of the most generous that there is.

Investment Incentives: The Industrial Development Authority

For most of the period since 1950 this incentive package has included fifteen years complete tax exemption on export profits, cash grants of from 35 to 50 per cent of fixed capital costs depending on location, possible state equity participation, grants towards re-equipment, the training of workers and managers, the employment of consultants and company research, guarantees and subsidization of loans, the provision of advance factories in industrial estates, industrial training centres and special housing programmes, as well as general supportive infrastructure where necessary. In addition there is complete freedom to expatriate profits, no restrictions on employment of foreign personnel, duty-free import of capital goods and raw materials for export production and free depreciation for new investment, which may be entirely set off against tax in any one year. Firms for whom the latter offers no advantage because they pay no tax on their export profits anyway, may pass on this advantage to the banks in return for cheaper finance through preferential share and equipment leasing arrangements. The incentives are tailored to the needs of individual firms by the IDA, which markets Ireland's advantages as a location for foreign investment from a network of local offices in the advanced capitalist countries. The operation is highly sophisticated. The IDA does not wait passively for enquiries. Nowadays it deliberately seeks out foreign firms whose prospective investment plans might complement the existing Irish industrial structure. In the later 1970s it has made successful efforts to attract pharmaceutical, health-care, petrochemical and electronics firms and aims to make the Republic a West European centre for manufacturing micro-chips and electronic components during the 1980s.

Although in effect an arm of the state, the IDA has a large element of discretion in negotiating with foreign firms. Only projects entailing state grants of £1¼ million or upwards have, in 1980, to be directly approved by the government. In 1969 the IDA was reorganized on lines recommended by an American consultancy firm and made responsible for giving grants to existing industry as well as to new foreign firms. Its board, nominated by the government, includes businessmen from foreign and domestic firms as well as civil servants but does not include trade unionists. It appoints its own staff and IDA personnel can and do move easily on to the management staff of the firms it introduces to Ireland. It is undoubtedly an advantage for the IDA, as an autonomous state-sponsored body, to be separate from the Republic's highly centralized, traditionalist and rather inflexible civil service. This has enabled it to develop an acute political and public relations consciousness of its own. The IDA campaigned actively in support of Irish membership of the EEC in the 1972 referendum, giving detailed local and regional projections of the numbers of extra jobs which could accrue from foreign firms once, it was implied, Ireland joined the EEC. 'Markets in Europe, Jobs at Home' was a persuasive slogan for many at the time.

The tax relief on export profits is the most important single incentive, for as all the new firms are geared primarily towards export, most in effect pay no tax at all, so that corporate taxation in Ireland is very low. The Accession Treaty which the Republic signed with the EEC includes a protocol committing the latter to take account of Ireland's development needs, which implicitly refers to these incentives. From 1981 a corporation tax rate of 10 per cent will apply on all profits, as the Government considers that in free trade conditions it no longer makes sense to distinguish between profits made on sales on home and export markets; recently established foreign firms will still retain their totally tax-free status until 1991. The generosity of government-provided incentives is of course only one attraction of Ireland to foreign capital. During the 1960s and 1970s unit labour costs in the Republic were significantly lower than in the advanced capitalist countries, especially when social security, training and control costs were taken into account (Stanton, 1979). For American and British investors there is the advantage of a common language, English being the predominant language in a country heavily penetrated by the Anglo-American media and culture. There is political stability and a welcoming attitude to foreign investment. As the American Ambassador to Dublin stated in 1979: 'In other countries 30 per cent of the population is voting communist. All the leading parties in this country are sympathetic to the private investor, so that an American industrialist does not have to fear that his operations might be nationalised.' Finally, even though Ireland is an island on the European periphery, it is not far from the rich markets of the EEC to which as a member it has full duty-free access.

Growth and Diversification

Over 800 overseas projects have been established in the Republic since the programme to attract foreign investment began. In the 1960s Britain was the largest single source of grant-assisted investment, but in the 1970s she was surpassed by America and followed by German, Japanese and other foreign firms. There is some evidence that foreign companies in Ireland tend to belong to relatively small transnational firms who do not have a large number of branch plants worldwide and who are concerned about minimizing the risk and uncertainty associated with foreign direct investment. TNCs of this kind seem particularly responsive to the individual package approach and after-care services of the IDA (O'Loughlin and O'Farrell, 1980). Since the Republic joined the EEC there has been a number of large projects requiring continuous flow manufacturing and using extensive fixed assets, oriented towards European markets. These are in petrochemicals, pharmaceuticals, electronics manufacture and synthetic textiles and are mostly from America, which in the late 1970s accounted for nearly half of total foreign direct investment in manufacturing. The return on US capital in Ireland averaged 28 per cent in the late 1970s according to US Department of Commerce figures advertised by the IDA in the foreign press. The chairman of one US firm, Documation Ltd., was quoted at this time as paying pleased tribute to 'the purely capitalistic approach of the IDA', contrasting it with 'the creeping socialism of other countries, where people wanted more employment and a share of the profits even before they had been created', whereas the IDA's attitude was different. 'Let's have a big pie and split it', he said. 'That attitude is prevalent here. You hold on to it. It's beautiful!' (Halbert, 1979).

The average growth rate of the Irish economy, which had been just less than 2 per cent per annum in the 1950s, doubled to 4 per cent per annum during the 1960s. This growth rate was maintained throughout the following decade, the downturn in 1974 and 1975 being counterbalanced by above average growth in 1977 and 1978. It produced rising living standards, a decline in and eventual cessation of net emigration and a rapidly growing population. A less favourable picture is given when one looks at growth in income per head, taking into account the doubling in the rate of population increase during the 1970s, together with the deterioration in Ireland's terms of trade since 1973 because of oil price rises. Real GDP per caput, terms of trade adjusted, is now at the same level as at the time of EEC entry in 1973. Real income per worker has grown by 2.7 per cent a year on average between 1973 and 1980, but only because employment rose much less than population (Kennedy, 1980). The contribution of the various economic sectors at the beginning and towards the end of these two decades is shown in Tables 1 and 2, which indicate a rise in industry's share of output matching a decline in agriculture's, as well as a rise in employment in both industry and services, though a fall in total employment.

The ratio of visible exports to GDP at current factor cost increased from 20 per cent in 1950 to 28 per cent in 1961, 31 per cent in 1968 and 52 per cent in 1977. The share of manufactures in visible exports at current values, excluding food and drink, increased from 6 per cent in 1950 to 18 per cent in 1961, 33 per cent in 1968 and 55 per cent by 1977. The share of total manufacturing output which was exported grew from about 5 per cent in 1950 to 19 per cent in 1961,

Table 1 Sectoral share in gross domestic product at current factor cost

	1961 %	1968 %	1977 %
Agriculture	24	19	19
Industry	31	36	35
Services	45	45	46
	100	100	100
G.D.P.	£599m	£1076m	£4862m

Source: CSO (1979b)

Table 2 Sectoral distribution of employment

	1961		1968 (thousands)		1977	
Agriculture	379	(36%)	313	(29%)	236	(23%)
Industry	259	(25%)	305	(29%)	310	(30%)
(of which in manufacturing)	(178)	(17%)	(204)	(19%)	(210)	(18%)
Services	415	(39%)	449	(42%)	490	47%)
Total at work	1053	(100%)	1067	(100%)	1036	(100%)
Unemployed	56		61			108
Total labour force	1109		1128		1144	
Population	2818		2913		3200	(est.)

Source: Annual Review and Outlook, various years: Keating (1977).

one-third in the early 1970s and nearly one-half by 1979 (Kennedy, 1971; Kennedy and Dowling, 1975; Prl. 8547, 1979; CTT, 1979). A breakdown of the contribution to manufactured exports of foreign-owned and domestically-owned indsutry is not available, as the IDA gives grants not only to incoming enterprises but also to established industry, foreign or native, undertaking export-oriented expansion. A survey in 1974 showed that new industry, so defined, accounted for almost two-thirds of manufactured exports at the time (McAleese, 1977). The export/gross output ratio of new industry was then 72 per cent compared with 19 per cent for the rest of Irish manufacturing. The survey made clear that the leading force behind the diversification of Irish exports during the previous decade had been newly arrived firms from the USA and continental Europe. It also showed that at the time three out of every four overseas firms traded with affiliates, such sales accounting for 55 per cent of the exports of overseas new industry. The weight of foreign-owned firms in the Irish industrial structure, whether due to the advent of more overseas firms or reinvestment by existing ones, has further increased since then. In 1978 buoyant exports in manufactures, as well as in food and live animals, gave the Republic the highest export value and volume growth rates in the EEC. Diversification of exports has also lessened the Republic's dependence on the British market, the share of exports going to the UK declining from 84 per cent in 1950 to 80 per cent in 1961, 69 per cent in 1968, 61 per cent in 1972 and 46 per cent in 1979.

An Industrial Success Story?

The conventional wisdom in the Republic is to regard these developments as a case of export-led growth on the basis of manufacturing industry; but that is to exaggerate one aspect of the story. Important as well has been the fact that exports of live animal and food and drink, which have traditionally formed a large if declining share of Irish exports, have faced a buoyant foreign demand throughout the past two decades. In the 1960s invisible exports, in particular tourism, were also a significant contributor to growth. In their study of the modern Irish economy Kennedy and Dowling show that the crucial difference between the 1950s and 1960s was not the expansion of exports in the 1960s, important though that was, but the fact that home demand was buoyant as well, encouraged by expansionary public policy, in contrast to the deflationary policy pursued in the 1950s. They stress the continuities as well as dicontinuities in Irish manufacturing in the two periods; for example, the average annual growth rate of manufactured exports was the same in 1950–61 as in 1961–68, the difference being that in the former period manufactured exports started from a very low base, so that their continued expansion led to their becoming proportionately more important in the economy as time went on (Kennedy and Dowling, 1975, Chapters 2 and 5).

   Moreover, as can be deduced from Table 1, between 1961 and 1977 just less than one-third of the rise in GDP was derived from the growth of industry. Agriculture, whose low import content makes it a proportionately greater contributor to net exports than manufacturing, grew markedly also, as did services, much of whose growth was underpinned by rapidly rising public spending. E. T. Nevin has commented (1978) that in the period 1961–73 only about 11 per cent of the increase in gross output of manufacturing was attributable to the growth of net exports outside the traditional food and drink industries, which were largely unaffected by the 'outward-looking policies' adopted in the 1960s, and some of this growth would presumably have occurred in any event.

Input-output tables for 1976 show the high import content of production in the industrial sectors to which foreign capital has been particularly attracted: import coefficients per unit of final demand in that year were 0.45 for chemicals and plastics, 0.43 for metals and engineering, 0.44 for textiles and 0.43 for 'other manufacturing' (Henry, 1980). Of course the effect of manufactured exports on the balance of trade and payments is positive nonetheless. In 1976 the net effect of IDA supported new industry on the balance of trade was estimated to be £792 million, equivalent to 43 per cent of visible exports that year, as against a net credit for the rest of industry of £282 million. The net capital flows associated with investment operations in Ireland would have to be added to these figures to arrive at the total net effect of new industry on the balance of payments (IDA, 1980).

Political criticisms of aspects of foreign investment which have caused concern elsewhere have been muted in the Republic. One writer comments sardonically that resentment at dependence on a rich metropolitan neighbour has been obviated by the varied sources of the foreign investment; resentment at tax evasion through transfer pricing schemes and the like has been avoided by exempting foreign firms from tax altogether, and resentment at the high profits of such firms has been avoided by not requiring the disclosure of such information¡ (Jacobsen, 1978). Data are not available on the repatriation of profits by foreign firms, but the impression is that many of them tend to plough back their profits, avoiding repatriation because of tax liability in their country of origin. But there seems little doubt that the outflow of profits on existing capital will rise as compared to new investment capital in the 1980s.

Some Criticisms

A common criticism of foreign investment in LDCs is that it gives rise to a dualism between the export-oriented sector and the domestic sector, with differences between the two in relation to productivity, wage rates and density of local linkages through purchases and sales. In a study of the Limerick-Shannon area of the West of Ireland, where many foreign firms have been attracted to the Shannon customs free industrial zone, Steward (1976a, b) found some evidence of this. He concluded that foreign industry had fewer backward and forward linkages than native-owned industry and suggested that the tax exemption for export profits might discourage forward linkages. Other possible influences might be the desire of transnational corporations to maximize value added within their operations as a whole rather than in a particular country, and the fact that foreign firms tend to be concentrated in such sectors as metal and engineering, chemicals and plastics and textiles, with few sources of local raw materials, whereas Irish-owned industry tended to concentrate in natural-resource-endowed sectors such as food processing, wood and leather. He also found that American and German firms were

inclined to pay higher wages, spend more on training and be more personnel-
and labour-relations-oriented than Irish, or even British, firms and warned that
this could lead to foreign investment having a virtual monopoly of management
and skilled labour, especially in an area with a large rural hinterland like
Limerick-Shannon, which would tend to raise the general wage level and make
conditions more difficult for unskilled employment and labour-intensive firms.
These criticisms were based on one region. McAleese, in his 1974 statistical
profile of enterprises receiving IDA 'new industry' grants, found that around
two-thirds of their current expenditure was on goods and services of Irish
origin. There were substantial interindustry differences in import content, with
food processing occupying an exceptional place; excluding that, the Irish
content of current expenditure was slightly less than half. However, he pointed
to evidence that new enterprises buy more goods and services locally with the
passage of time, as they become more familiar with the availability and quality
of domestic suppliers and concluded that they were no more inclined to
concentrate on low-value-added activities than the national average. With
regard to closures his survey showed that about one-fifth of the projects
receiving grants had closed by 1974, most of them smaller firms, accounting for
12 per cent of total IDA capital grants to new industry. Four-fifths of managers
employed in 'new industry' firms were Irish nationals (McAleese, 1977).

Cooper and Whelan (1973) also made the point that the high import content of
much export manufacturing meant that the gains to the Republic's balance of
payments were much less than appeared from the export data alone,
impressive though they were. They urged the need to encourage high-value-
added projects based on Irish natural resources, in particular food and minerals
processing, and pointed out that diverting large resources to foreign companies
meant fewer grants and less credit to encourage Irish business. They made the
case for a more selective approach in state support for industry, so that 'foreign
investment should be used so as to complement not substitute for native
technology and resources', and commented that most foreign firms outside the
food sector did not come to Ireland because of any natural comparative
advantage the country had.

Capital-intensive Investment?

Attracting investment by means of capital grants and free depreciation has
been criticized as encouraging labour-saving rather than labour-using investment, whereas the purported aim of the investment programme is to help meet
national employment targets in a state whose registered jobless rates have been
the highest in Western Europe. The imposition on employers of compulsory
insurance contributions in respect of employees acts as a further disincentive to
employing labour. Official policies in Ireland have raised the cost of labour

relative to capital (Geary and McDonnell, 1979). This point has been made particularly in recent years since it has become evident that, in Ireland as elsewhere, a more competitive environment has tended to shift the Verdoorn relationship between output, employment and productivity. A higher proportion of growth is now due to accelerated productivity rather than increased employment (Kennedy and Foley, 1978; Katsiaouni, 1979). A comparison of the experience of Irish output and employment in two recessionary periods, 1956–62 and 1974–78, showed how much more slowly employment recovered in the second period by comparison with output. Labour has become relatively more expensive than capital, in part because of public policy and in part because of continuous pressure from rising real wage rates during the 1970s (OECD, 1979). This makes the attainment of official employment targets more difficult.

The IDA denies that there is any overall bias towards capital intensity in its incentive scheme. While the grants lower the cost of capital to firms, the actual grant rate, which averages around one-third of fixed investment, varies in accordance with the IDA's estimate of a project's benefit to the national economy. In negotiating with clients the IDA claims in recent years to favour projects with a high potential for growth on international markets, with low investment per job created and with high value added in Ireland. It assesses highly capital-intensive projects by reference to their potential for linkages with existing firms or for providing jobs for educated and highly skilled labour.

Only projects which the IDA estimates are commercially viable are approved for grants. McKeon (1980) describes a cost-benefit exercise which is now used to guide the decision on grant levels. While the grants are based on 'cost per job' criteria which take into account the level of investment incentives in competitor countries, he states that in 95 per cent of projects the IDA manages to keep them below a fiscal threshold which measures the direct fiscal returns to the Exchequer from creating the jobs. The latter is based on the discounted present value of the tax yield and social security contributions per worker employed over fifteen years, together with the exchequer savings on unemployment benefit. For large-scale projects, or where the grant level required approaches this fiscal threshold, the IDA makes an assessment on the basis of net domestic value added, taking into account the difference between the market and shadow prices for labour, capital and foreign exchange and comparing this with the discounted value of the costs to the state of aiding the project. In calculating shadow prices for the labour of school-leavers, housewives or the unemployed, who constitute half the recruits to new grant-aided industry, the opportunity cost of labour is treated as zero. Not surprisingly the subsidization of jobs in this way is thereby shown to yield a substantial net gain to the Exchequer. The fiscal threshold is nearly three times the average grant per job approved, so that the fiscal returns from the labour employed directly in operating projects are estimated to cover the grant cost per job, which was £5000 in 1979, in less than three years. In the case of large projects the grants offered are maintained at less than one quarter of the estimated benefits in net domestic value added. Ruane (1980) also suggests that, on the assumption that IDA capital grants do actually operate as labour subsidies, they fall well within a range of optimal labour subsidies which she estimates for Ireland.

Of course the labour subsidies claimed to be implicit in the Republic's capital grants could be said to be higher still if account were taken of other government incentives to manufacturing, such as the tax relief scheme on export profits or free depreciation of capital, which can also be assumed to incorporate implicit subsidies. However, the demonstration by these exercises that employment creation brought about in this way yields a net gain to the Irish exchequer and in net domestic value added, does not prove that capital grants and tax-free profit schemes are necessarily the most effective way of increasing the number of jobs — which is the principal official justification given for them — however effective they have been in stimulating exports. Other possibilities are direct labour subsidies instead of the indirect ones used at present, the subsidization of exports through output or value added subsidies and a shift of resources towards defensive or replacement investment to save existing jobs threatened by competition from imports, with less emphasis on attracting brand-new industry. The Irish government has in fact introduced a number of direct labour subsidies for some industries hit by free trade in recent years and it has started some direct labour employment schemes in the services sector at a cost per job lower than IDA grant levels, but these schemes have not aimed to generate exports. The Irish trade union movement and the political left have advocated a more direct and adventurous approach by state enterprise towards job creation. They claim with some plausibility that the solicitude for private enterprise and the transnational firms which is required by the IDA prog-ramme and which characterizes Irish public policy in general, inhibits state enterprise from launching new profitable projects which could add to output, exports and employment.

The Unemployment Problem

Job creation is at the heart of the Irish economic problem: how to provide employment at acceptable living standards for the fastest growing population and labour force in Western Europe, to reduce the high unemployment rate of 10 per cent plus and prevent a resumption of the heavy net emigration of the 1980s. Put another way, it is the problem of how to attain a level of output which would require the employment at prevailing levels of productivity of all those seeking work. The consensus of a number of projections is that a net increase of from 10,000 to 15,000 jobs in manufacturing would be needed per year in the late 1970s and 1980s. The gross number of new jobs required would consist of this figure plus a figure for replacement of jobs lost. The rate of job increase this implies is well above the best performance of any OECD country in the past two decades and seems incapable of attainment in Ireland on the basis of present policies.

During the 1970s, as Table 2 indicated, the picture has been one of new manufacturing jobs, created at heavy cost in public subsidy, just about balancing the number of jobs destroyed, without any overall increase in manufacturing employment. From the point of view of its impact on overall employment the IDA has been running fast, as it were, only to stay in the same place. Of course, the jobs lost have tended to be mainly, though not exclusively, in the more traditional labour-intensive firms which have been especially hard hit by the advent of free trade, the general capitalist recession, rising labour costs and the more rapid replacement of labour by capital in recent years. The jobs created have tended to be in the new, capital intensive, high-technology and export-oriented firms. What has taken place has been a remarkable restructuring of the Republic's manufacturing industry, which contributed significantly to a high growth rate in national output and income in the later 1970s. The Republic now possesses a specialized, sophisticated and modern manufacturing sector which is much more internationally competitive than it was, but its heavy unemployment problem seems no nearer solution. The decline of jobs in agriculture over the past two decades has been counterbalanced by the increase in employment in services and to a lesser extent in industry, but total employment is virtually unchanged since 1961, although total population has grown rapidly.

Shifts in Policy Emphasis

It looks very much as if economic development in Ireland has now entered a new phase in which the policy of basing industrial growth on attracting foreign capital will be more critically assessed. In part this reflects a necessary adaptation by the Republic to the impact of international recession. Competition for international investment capital becomes ever tougher and more expensive. Even if the governemnt were willing to raise markedly the grants to foreign industry, this would put further heavy strains on an exchequer which has been running large deficits for years, financed by heavy borrowing, much of which has been used to cover current spending (Bruton, 1978).

Moreover, capital-intensive industry tends to be energy-intensive. The Republic depends for three-quarters of its energy consumption on imported oil. This puts a question mark over some types of project formerly considered acceptable.

In part a change of emphasis is also due because the potential of those firms attracted in the past and now established as part of the industrial structure is obviously considerable. It makes sense to build on what has been achieved and to be more selective in relation to new firms from outside. The criticism about the lack of local linkages and low value added of some foreign firms has been taken note of by the IDA. It is now actively encouraging the development of such linkages and when seeking out individual new foreign projects it is being much more discriminating in assessing how new arrivals will fit in with the existing industrial structure. The IDA is seeking to develop 'downstream' industries based on the Republic's natural resources of food and minerals. It is encouraging indigenous Irish entrepreneurs and small industries catering for the domestic market or making components for foreign firms and substitutes for imports. It provides grants and helps negotiate finance for domestic Irish projects which otherwise would never get started because of lack of capital. Since the Republic joined the EEC the IDA has doubled the rate of grants to existing industry to re-equip and modernize. The IDA's programme to attract computer and electronics firms seeks to establish in the Republic companies with a high value added which would employ highly educated and skilled workers. In 1979 there occurred the paradox of a shortage of certain kinds of skilled workers, whom the IDA sought to attract from Britain, at the same time as there was an unemployment rate of over 10 per cent among the unskilled. In recent years the IDA has set up a project identification unit to decide on new investment opportunities for Irish industry. It has sponsored export-oriented service industries who employ consultants, engineers and technologists. As part of this 'new approach' the IDA has redefined established foreign industry together with native-owned industry as 'domestic', which it now compares in its reports with new foreign industry. 'Domestic' industry so defined contributed nearly half the new jobs created in the 1970s (IDA, 1980).

These shifts of emphasis, though desirable, will hardly meet the Republic's unemployment problem or enable the manufacturing sector to make the contribution necessary if the 'solution' is not once again to be a return to heavy emigration. Over the past two decades the policy of encouraging export-oriented manufacture, bolstered by healthy agricultural exports and 'invisible' exports like tourism, has helped finance a level of imports which supported higher output and incomes for those in employment within Ireland. The goods and services supplied to meet a buoyant external and internal demand have been based on one of the highest rates of investment in the world. Gross domestic fixed capital formation averaged 20 per cent per annum in the early 1960s, 24 per cent in the early 1970s and nearly 30 per cent in the late 1970s. Not surprisingly, the Republic's growth has been among the highest in the OECD; yet it is surely remarkable that despite the investment of thousands of millions in manufacturing, agriculture and services, total employment has remained virtually static.

How Open an Economy?

This can only be because the vast bulk of Irish investment, whether by government or private business, has been in capital-intensive methods of production. The tendency of foreign firms, encouraged by public policy, to import into a labour-surplus economy like Ireland technology appropriate to economies which have an abundance of capital and a shortage of labour has already been referred to. The Irish public sector's own investments and purchasing policy show no evidence of being systematically guided by the aim of maximizing job creation and minimizing imports. But more important than either of these factors, as Tussing points out (1976), is that the price structure in Ireland, the relative prices of goods, labour, capital and so forth, reflects the price structure of the dominant British economy rather than its own endowment of resources. This arises from the high degree of openness of the Republic's economy — exports being the equivalent of 52 per cent of GNP, imports of 63 per cent in 1978 — and its relatively small size, which make it like a region of the British economy in some respects. Accession to the EEC, with its rules on free movement of goods, capital and labour, aggravates this openness, as the EEC's resource endowment differs even more from Ireland's than does Britain's and because Ireland becomes an even smaller part of the larger economy.

Openness is relative and the position of even the most open economies is not immutable. The limitations of existing Irish policies are evident when one sees their failure to expand employment. The classical development path of the old industrialized countries entailed rapid employment growth on the basis of an expanding home market as well as exports. In Ireland's case the present growth of its population entails a growth in demand for housing, furniture, food, clothes, entertainment and all the other appurtenances of modern life. Meeting these demands with goods and services produced at home can generate employment for those making them, although in a country with such a high propensity to import this will not happen automatically. It requires government intervention and a conscious effort to minimize the economy's openness.

Buy Irish campaigns already exist. There have been calls for more imagination in devising non-tariff barriers to trade with other EEC countries. Public procurement policy could be more deliberately used as an employment generator. The assumption that agricultural policy entails a continual decline in agricultural employment needs to be questioned, especially now that energy-intensive modes of agricultural production become relatively more expensive. The Irish break with sterling after 150 years on joining the European Monetary System (EMS) offers the possibility of greater freedom in exchange rate policy; the Republic was lucky not to be tied to sterling when that currency soared at the end of the 1970s. There have been demands, especially from within the trade union movement, for the reimposition of tariff protection for vulnerable industries or for new infant industries with growth potential and prospects of moving in time into export markets. Such steps would entail a confrontation at political level between the Irish state and the EEC which is unlikely to happen as long as the common agricultural policy maintains high guaranteed prices for the Republic's agricultural exports. This could well change during the early 1980s. The spread of protectionist trade policies in consequence of an early 1980s recession could change things also. A rupture between Britain and the EEc and the imposition of import tariffs by Britain would of course create a quite new situation for the Republic, which still does half its trade with the neighbouring island.

Political Consequences of Open-door Policies

Over the past twenty years the Republic of Ireland has been integrated more closely into the economic and political structures of West European capitalism. Here is a case of dependent, if moderately successful, industrialization showing similarities with Portugal, Spain and Greece as well as other areas of the Celtic periphery — Northern Ireland, Wales and Scotland. Reliance on foreign capital for development, and associated policies such as commitment to free trade and the EEC, have had important political consequences for the Republic and affected its internal class structure.

At one level penetration by foreign capital has lessened the independence of the Irish bourgeoisie, but at another it has given it new confidence, strengthening the capitalist system in the country and increasing the political weight of the business interest in the Irish scene in partnership with foreign capital. In the political sphere, at the level of state sovereignty, the Republic must now conform to EEC policies and obey directives from Brussels; the Irish state no longer has the legislative freedom it had before joining the Common Market. On the other hand it does have some influence on EEC policy-making, even if this is marginal in most cases and even if on major issues the interests of the larger powers ultimately prevail. Membership of the EEC, which was a political corollary of the policy of reliance on development capital from outside, has aligned the Irish state much more closely with the foreign policy positions of the West European powers. Although the Republic is formally neutral and is not in NATO, she now plays a less independent role in international affairs than in the 1950s or early 1960s. Her neutrality is less positive than that of Austria or Sweden for instance; an example is the Republic's decision in 1980 to join in common EEC sanctions against Iran over the US hostages. In the Republic's conflict with Britain over Northern Ireland the Irish Government hopes that a more compliant attitude on international affairs will lessen any strategic or military objections Britain or her NATO allies may have to a policy of working towards Irish reunification.

In the business sphere proper the ownership of Irish firms has been strikingly affected by the inflow of foreign capital, of which direct investment in manufacturing is only one element. Since the early 1960s foreign capital has taken over numbers of previously Irish-owned firms and has moved strongly into banking, insurance, the property market, distribution, services and the hotel trade. Only approximate estimates are available of the composition of capital ownership; one assessment is that as much as one-half of the assets of Irish industrial and service companies are owned externally (Sweeney, 1973). Another method of estimation is to note that the 800 or so overseas projects established in the Republic since the programme to attract foreign investment began were due to employ around 100,000 persons when at full capacity. Taking into account foreign investment in Irish manufacturing before 1960, together with foreign purchases of shares in Irish public companies, it seems plausible to conclude that the amount of manufacturing employment accounted for by foreign investment should be from two-fifths to a half. As foreign firms tend to have higher productivity on average than native-owned ones, the proportion of manufacturing assets owned or controlled from outside is probably higher still. In Northern Ireland, incidentally, it is estimated that three-quarters of the manufacturing workforce are employed in companies controlled from outside the area (HMSO, 1974).

At the same time the growth and development accompanying the foreign capital inflow have opened new avenues of expansion for native-born business-men — in subsidiary production for foreign firms, in construction, services and distribution and in meeting the expanded domestic demand consequent on higher incomes. The various financial professions have also got extra business. There is little doubt that Irish entrepreneurs are more numerous, confident and sophisticated today than at any time in the past of the Irish state, even though they no longer dominate the larger manufacturing firms outside the state sector (Fogarty, 1973; Rothery, 1977). Ireland's financial bourgeoisie has also grown in strength in the past two decades. The commercial banks have been reduced in number from eight to four and the two largest bank groupings are Irish-owned. As already mentioned, the banks play an important role in financing foreign investment and have begun to take equity participation in industry. There are close ties between the Republic's industrial and financial bourgeoisie, native and foreign, and the senior public service, running state agencies like the IDA. One indicator of the self-confidence of the Irish bourgeoisie in partnership with foreign capital is the emergence of Irish-based companies with branches outside the country. Over a dozen Irish-based public companies now have foreign subsidiaries, mostly in Britain, so have the two major banking groups, as well as state companies like the national airline and the Milk Board.

Conclusion

The Republic of Ireland is of interest to the student of development policy because it shows some familiar features of underdevelopment although forming part of the developed world. Its experience illustrates both advantages and disadvantages of relying on foreign capital and manufactured exports as an economic motor and perhaps offers lessons for some of the more advanced LDCs. In recent years in fact the Republic's Industrial Development Authority has organized courses for civil servants and development planners from various LDCs, in which the IDA's experience has been laid before them — though not without warnings locally about the unwisdom of giving tips to potential competitors: The IDA's work is also an interesting example of a link between an organ of a state which is committed to national development, if withal in strongly capitalist terms, and foreign capital. It is unlikely that the climate of the 1980s will be as encouraging to the kind of strategy the IDA is geared to as was that of the 1960s and 1970s; but the confidence gained in the past two decades should enable the Irish state to make the necessary adaptation. Evidence that a more discriminating attitude is already being adopted towards foreign capital has been cited above. The Irish experience also shows some of the political as well as economic implications of an 'outward-looking' strategy. Both its economy and its politics have been more deeply marked than most by the legacy of its relations with a former colonial power, Great Britain, whose first colony indeed Ireland was. As Britain's relations with continental Europe have been altered by EEC membership, Ireland's traditional dependence upon Britain has been broadened into a more general dependence on the EEC as a whole. EEC membership in turn has made Britain herself in some ways part of a new periphery, dependent on the EEC's more economically developed core, with Ireland thus on a further periphery still. But such relations are not immutable. The tensions they give rise to are likely to form the framework of the next phase of Ireland's development story.

References

Bruton, R. (1978). *Irish Public Debt* (Economic and Social Research Institute, Dublin).

Cooper, C. and Whelan, N. (1913). *Science, Technology and Industry in Ireland* (National Science Council, Dublin).

Crotty, R. (1966). *Irish Agricultural Production* (Cork University Press, Cork).

Crotty, R. (1974). *The Cattle Crisis and the Small Farmer* (National Land League, Mullingar).

Crotty, R. (1980). *Cattle, Economics and Development* (Commonwealth Agricultural Fund, Oxford).

CSO (1979a). *The Trend of Employment and Unemployment in 1978* (Central Statistics Office, Dublin).

CSO (1979b). *National Income and Expenditure, 1977* (Central Statistics Office, Dublin).

CTT (1979). *Annual Report 1978* (Coras Trachtala, Dublin).

Fogarty, M. (1973). *Irish Entrepreneurs Speak for Themselves* (Economic and Social Research Institute, Dublin).

Geary, P. T. and Mcdonnell, E. (1979). 'The cost of capital to Irish industry', *Economic and Social Review*, Dublin, **10**, No. 4.

Halbert, R. (1979). Chairman of Documation Ltd., *Sunday Press*, Dublin, 18 February; *Irish Times*, Dublin, 15 February.

Henry, E. W. (1980). *Irish Input-Output Structures 1976* (Economic and Social Research Institute, Dublin).

HMSO (1974). *Northern Ireland Discussion Paper: Finance and the Economy* (Northern Ireland Office, Belfast).

IDA (1980). *Annual Report 1979* (Dublin).

Jacobsen, K. (1978). 'Changing utterly? — Irish development and the problem of dependence', *Studies*, No. 268, Dublin.

Katsiaouni, O. (1978). 'Planning in a small economy: the Republic of Ireland', *Journal of the Statistical and Social Inquiry Society of Ireland*, **23**, Part 5, Dublin.

Katsiaouni, O. (1979). *Manufacturing Output, Productivity Trends and Employment Planning in Ireland* (Institute of Public Administration, Dublin).

Keating, W. (1977). 'Recent demographic trends with population projections for 1981 and 1986', *Journal of the Statistical and Social Inquiry Society of Ireland*, **23**, Part 4, Dublin.

Kennedy, K. (1971). *Productivity and Industrial Growth, The Irish Experience* (Clarendon Press, Oxford).

Kennedy, K. (1980). 'Employment and unemployment prospects in Ireland', *Irish Banking Review*, September 1980, Dublin.

Kennedy, K. and Dowling, B. (1975). *Economic Growth in Ireland, The Experience Since 1947* (Economic and Social Research Institute with Gill and Macmillan, Dublin).

Kennedy, K. and Foley, A. (1978). 'Industrial development', in Dowling, B. and Durkan, J., *Irish Economic Policy, A Review of Major Issues* (Economic and Social Research Institute, Dublin).

Keynes, J. M. (1933). 'National Self-Sufficiency', *Studies*, June.

Lee, J. (1973). *The Modernisation of Modern Ireland 1948–1918* (Gill and Macmillan, Dublin).

McAleese, D. (1977). *A Profile of Grant-Aided Industry in Ireland* (Industrial Development Authority, Dublin).

McKeon, J. (1980). 'Economic appraisal of industrial projects in Ireland', *Journal of the Statistical and Social Inquiry Society of Ireland*, Dublin, 1980/81 issue.

Moore, B., Rhodes, Joy and Tarling, R. (1978). 'Industrial policy and economic development: the experience of Northern Ireland and the Republic of Ireland', *Cambridge Journal of Economics*, **2**, No. 1, March.

Nevin, E. (1978). Comment on paper by McAleese, D., 'Outward-looking policies, manufactured exports and economic growth: The irish experience' in Artis, M. and Nobay, A. (eds.), *Contemporary Economic Analysis* (Croom Helm, London).

OECD (1979). *Economic Surveys: Ireland* (Paris).

O'Loughlin, B. and O'Farrell, P. (1980). 'Foreign direct investment in Ireland', *Economic and Social Review*, Dublin, **11**, No. 3.

O Tuathaigh, G. (1972). *Ireland Before the Famine 1798–1848* (Gill and Macmillan, Dublin).

Prl. 8547 (1979). *Investment and National Development 1979–1983* (Stationary Office, Dublin).

Rothery, B. (1977). *Men of Enterprise* (Institute for Industrial Research and Standards, Dublin).

Ruane, F. (1980). 'Optimal labour subsidies and industrial development in Ireland', *Economic and Social Review*, Dublin, **11**, No. 2.

Stanton, R. (1979). 'Foreign investment and host country politics, the Irish case' in

Seers, D. et al., *Underdeveloped Europe, Studies in Core-Periphery Relations* (Harvester Press, Sussex).

Stewart, J. (1976a). 'Linkages and foreign direct investment', *Regional Studies*, **10**, 245–58 (Pergamon Press, Oxford).

Stewart, J. (1976b). 'Foreign direct investment and the emergence of a dual economy', *Economic and Social Review*, Dublin, 7, No. 2.

Sweeney, J. (1973). 'Foreign companies in Ireland', *Studies*, Autumn/Winter Dublin.

Tussing, D. (1976). 'Investment and its control' in *The Irish Economy, What Has To Be Done* (Association of Scientific, Technical and Managerial Staffs, Dublin).

Walsh, B. (1979). 'Economic growth and development 1945–1970' in J. Lee, *Ireland 1945–1970* (Gill and Macmillan, Dublin)

Whitaker, K. (1973). 'From protection to free trade, the Irish experience', *Administration*, Dublin, **24**, No. 4.

The Struggle for Development:
National Strategies in an International Context
Edited by M. Bienefeld and M. Godfrey
© 1982 John Wiley & Sons Ltd.

Chapter 10

Kenya: African Capitalism or Simple Dependency?

MARTIN GODFREY*

Kenya is one of a select number of African countries with a fully-fledged and fairly longstanding controversy about the nature and trajectory of its political economy. Is Kenya to be characterized as a successful capitalist economy, with an emerging and increasingly vigorous national bourgeoisie, or as a classic case of dependent peripheral capitalism, with all that implies in terms of a distorted development process and limited industrialization prospects?

Leys (1975)

Research of relevance to the debate† had been going on for several years, but the debate itself only began to get into its stride in the mid-1970s, with the publication of some of the results of that research. Particularly important was Leys' book *Underdevelopment in Kenya* (Leys, 1975), based on research carried out in the late 1960s and early 1970s.

Leys identifies two threads in policy since independence in December 1963. The first is the adaptation of 'peasant' modes of production to the capitalist mode in new ways. The second is the establishment of new African petty-bourgeois strata within sectors of the economy formerly reserved for foreign capital. Foreign capital was not much affected by these developments. It simply

---

* Thanks, with the usual disclaimer, are due for helpful comments from Michael Cowen, Diana Hunt, Raphie Kaplinsky and Nicola Swainson.
† See Campbell (1979) for a review of the controversy from the point of view of an underdevelopment theorist.

moved into growth sectors, such as manufacturing and tourism, which remained almost wholly foreign-owned.

The new class of African businessmen thrown up by this process, according to Leys, were mainly 'small retail traders, bar owners, small-scale transporters, builders' and so on. They owed their position to the exclusion of competition from Asians and access to credit on favourable terms. These embryo African capitalists had, he recognizes, gained some political power by the end of the 1960s but the share of the surplus appropriated by them was still 'very modest'.

These petty-bourgeois strata gradually gave rise to what Leys characterizes as an ' "auxiliary bourgeoisie" tightly linked to foreign capital':

> These processes constituted Kenya's experience of underdevelopment under neo-colonialism. The economy was far from static; during these years, although the poor remained poor, it is doubtful if they became, in aggregate, absolutely poorer. What the mass of people experienced was, rather, a consolidation of their subjection to the power of capital. This was still overwhelmingly an alien power, though increasingly linked to the political power of domestic capital. It meant a continuation of the structure of exploitation and domination established by colonial rule, which for the vast majority of the population meant a continuing prospect of hard unproductive labour, mainly for the benefit of others, accompanied by growing inequality, insecurity, social inferiority and the virtually complete absence of political rights. (Leys, 1975: 257)

Leys quotes with approval, and draws a parallel with, Samir Amin's description of dependent African capitalists in Senegal:

> It is not so much that the positions held by the Senegal private sector are quantitatively modest as the fact that they are qualitatively dependent on foreign import houses and foreign owned local manufacturers, still more largely dependent on state support. (Amin, 1969: 183)

In Kenya the use of their political power by this new stratum of African capitalists brought them several rewards, according to Leys. These included: partnerships with foreign capital, in which political protection was traded for a share in the profits; contracts to supply foreign companies with goods and services; and contracts to become part of a foreign company's distributive network. Looking forward, he sees as likely the consolidation of a firm alliance between foreign capital and the new African 'auxiliary bourgeoisie, operating under more and more heavily protected conditions'. As for the state, he describes it as an 'imitation bourgeois' state. 'The neo-colonial state does not represent the interests of a dominant national bourgeoisie.'

---

* See also Stewart (1976).

Several other researchers* share Leys' pessimism about the prospects for Kenyan capitalism, while differing from him in the details of their analysis. For instance, Weeks, largely responsible for the 'dependency' flavour of the International Labour Office (ILO) employment report (ILO, 1972), has published a background paper which he wrote for the mission (Weeks, 1975). He argues against 'the possibility of averting underdevelopment and stagnation in Kenya' and suggests that the 'redistribution-from-growth' solution put forward by the ILO mission is both politically unlikely and practically absurd. Langdon, whose contribution is based on a comprehensive survey of multinational corporations in Kenya (Langdon, 1974, 1975a,b, 1977, 1980a,b), differs from Leys (1975) in seeing the state as playing a central mediating role in shaping 'a relatively stable symbiosis by which an emerging domestic bourgeoisie is integrated intimately into the transnational capitalist economy' (Langdon, 1977: 97). In his most recent paper he concedes that 'a powerful class of African industrialists is emerging in Kenya, but they seem most unlikely to lead a dynamic transformation of social relations in the country' (Langdon, 1980b: 56).

Cowen and Swainson

Leys emphasizes that there is nothing permanent or inescapable in the structure he describes. Indeed his book was hardly published before he began to have doubts about it. He began to read papers coming out of Nairobi University, particularly those by Cowen (1972, 1976, 1979a,b, 1980a,b, 1981; Cowen and Kinyanjui, 1977), who, on the basis of a long period of painstaking research in Central province in the late 1960s and early 1970s, argues that indigenous capital accumulation, particularly among the Kikuyu bourgeoisie, is substantial and growing fast and has its roots in pre-colonial Kenya, in spite of obstacles to African accumulation erected by the colonial state. Cowen also argues that the political base of the post-colonial state is founded on the interests of the indigenous bourgeoisie. The clearest statement of his views on these issues is contained in one of his more recent papers. He maintains that:

> an indigenous class of capital in Kenya's Central Province was formed long before the agrarian reforms of the 1950s. By the early 1920s, an exclusive class had come to establish forms of commodity production [in the wattle industry] which were based upon the direct employment of wage labour ... At the end of the 1940s individuals of the class had entered into competition with Asian and European merchant capitalists, adopted aggressive strategies towards the acquisition of land and other instruments of production and commanded forms of political organisation (particularly the Kikuyu Central Association and Kenya African Union) which were directed towards removing the racial constraints over property ownership. (Cowen, 1980a: 20)

In the subsequent growth of the indigenous class which he describes as a 'bourgeoisie-in-formation' Cowen places a lot of emphasis on the phenomenon of 'straddling' — 'a specific historical form of accumulation in which the position of [managerial] employment provides a base from which sources can be created for the expanded reproduction of capital' — and on state corporations, 'manned by individuals of the indigenous class of capital and subject to their control as a class'. By 1980 he suggests that

> there can be no more serious questioning of the fact that estate agriculture is now predominantly under the ownership of individuals of the indigenous class. Any disputation over the degree of ownership centres upon non-agricultural sectors and, even then, mainly upon the manufacturing sector. (Cowen, 1980a; 26)

He points out that the question of ownership and control is difficult to settle by recourse to simple statistical indices but claims that, even

> in the case of manufacturing, it is becoming clear that the subsidiaries of international firms, as much as those of the ... public corporations, have provided a base from which managing directors are able to create their own sources of local accumulation. (Cowen, 1980a: 26)

Leys was also influenced at this time by draft chapters of a thesis by Swainson, since published as a book (Swainson, 1980). She disputes Leys' view of the indigenous bourgeoisie as 'auxiliary' and sees it as mounting a challenge to foreign firms. She cites such evidence as: the expansion in the number of African joint-stock companies; the Africanization of management and directorships; state equity participation in foreign firms; state regulatory mechanisms vis-à-vis foreign firms; the entry of indigenous capital into sectors previously monopolized by foreign firms and the participation of indigenous capital in the equity of foreign firms. She concludes that:

> in comparison with large multinational firms in Kenya, indigenous capital is small and insignificant. Nevertheless, at the *present stage* of accumulation in Kenya it is still the case that value formation if *nationally* based and the state is able to support the interests of the internal bourgeoisie. During the independence period, within the limits set by Kenya's position in the global economy, the indigenous bourgeoisie have extended their control over the means of production. (Swainson, 1980: 289)

Another influence on Leys' thought at this time was a thesis by Njonjo (1977) in which he argues that a landed bourgeoisie has emerged and established itself on the basis of its takeover of former settler estates in the 'White Highlands' and that this landed class is wielding political power on the basis of its occupation of positions in the state apparatus. *

* Swainson, Njonjo and Leys emphasize the emergence of the landed bourgeoisie, to the detriment of the peasantry, whereas Cowen argues that at least in the areas of Central province which he has studied the middle peasantry has entrenched itself under the hegemony of international capital from the 1950s onwards.

Leys (1978)

So by 1978, when, after a return visit to Kenya, Leys wrote a paper for *Socialist Register* on 'capital accumulation, class formation and dependency — the significance of the Kenyan case', he was taking a quite different view from his earlier self. Now he emphasizes the 'relatively high and sustained level of capital accumulation' and the 'extension of capitalist relations of production', which are not to be explained by large flows of official capital or technical assistance, nor by exceptional growth of primary commodity exports as a whole nor by exceptional growth in one or two 'enclave' sectors.

> A more plausible explanation of Kenyan economic growth since the 1940s lies, rather, in the specific social relations of production developed before, during and since the colonial period, and particularly ... in the *key role of the class formed out of the process of indigenous capital accumulation.* (Leys, 1978: 247)

Taking over Cowen's view of the process of accumulation during the colonial period, Leys now states that, 'when negotiations for independence were begun in 1960, the economic and political weight of the indigenous owners of capital was already decisive'. And from 1966 onwards 'the state superintended a series of measures which rapidly enlarged the sphere and rate of indigenous capital accumulation'. In noting the 'important role of the state in facilitating this movement of African capital out of circulation and into production', Leys continues, 'we must avoid the mistake of attributing to it an independent role. Its initiatives reflected the existing class power of the indigenous bourgeoisie, based on the accumulation of capital they had already achieved'.

Leys frankly admits his errors of three years earlier and analyses the reasons for them:

> Instead of seeing the strength of the historical tendency lying behind the emergence of the African bourgeoisie I tended to see only the relatively small size and technical weakness of African capital in the face of international capital, and to envisage the state as little more than a register of this general imbalance; rather than seeing the barriers of capital, scale and technology as relative, and the state as the register of the leading edge of indigenous capital in its assault on those barriers. (Leys, 1978: 251)

He concludes that 'Kenya appears, from this analysis, as a modest example of a "systematical combination of moments" conducive to the transition to the capitalist mode of production'. What this implies is that

> capitalist production relations may be considerably extended within and through them, for reasons having primarily to do with the configuration of class forces preceding and during the colonial period: and that the limits of such development cannot be determined from the sort of general considerations advanced by underdevelopment and dependency theory. (Leys, 1978: 261)

Kaplinsky

This sudden and dramatic change of view must have left many readers of Leys' 1975 book feeling uneasy, among them Kaplinsky, whose recent re-examination of the Kenyan case (Kaplinsky, 1980) is essentially a message to Leys that he was right the first time.

Kaplinsky tries to reduce Leys' 1978 paper to five hypotheses: (i) the Kenyan economy has seen a successful period of growth since independence; (ii) an independent indigenous industrial bourgeoisie now exists; (iii) there has been a significant increase in ownership and control of industry by this indigenous bourgeoisie which has moved to supplant foreign capital holdings; (iv) the state has moved from a mediating position to become an instrument for increased indigenous control over foreign capital; (v) the Kenyan economy will see continued successful capitalist accumulation. Kaplinsky then reviews the evidence relevant to each of these hypotheses.

On (i) he agrees that capitalist relations of production have probably been extended, but argues that changes in economic structure have been limited and that the outflow of surplus from Kenya has exceeded the inflow of investment. Economic growth, in his view, was indeed fast from 1964 to 1973 but (the 1977 coffee boom aside) has since tailed off. And further agricultural growth is limited by the shortage of good land (in relation to a total population of around 15 million).

On (ii) Kaplinsky reviews evidence to show that the indigenous industrial bourgeoisie is small and weak; it would like to supplant foreign capital but is incapable of doing so.

On (iii) he tries to show that there has been little overall change in ownership and even less in control of industry, although there is a trend towards the establishment of new Kenyan-owned and -controlled enterprises and an advance in parastatal participation.

On (iv) he cites many examples of state actions since 1975 in favour of foreign rather than local capital and maintains that the Kenyan state remains a 'soft touch' as a joint-venture partner.

On (v) he argues that, barring windfalls, continued capital accumulation is only possible if there is rapid growth in manufacturing exports, and that Leys is too optimistic about this possibility.

Kaplinsky summarizes his position as follows:

> I believe that the evidence shows that, although an indigenous capitalist class has managed to carve out a slice of the benefits arising from accumulation in large scale industry, this has arisen from an alliance between this class and foreign capital. Not only does little prospect emerge for indigenous capital to squeeze out foreign capital but the inbuilt contradictions of economies of this type make it difficult to foresee that such a pattern of accumulation — with or without foreign capital — can proceed in a viable form. (Kaplinsky, 1980: 1104)

Leys (1980)

Leys exercises his right of reply to this onslaught in vigorous style (Leys, 1980). He describes Kaplinsky as an 'empiricist' and an 'a-historical' dependency theorist, who

> does not grasp conceptually the historical process of capital accumulation and class formation. His view of Kenya starts and finishes with *appearances*, as they present themselves at a more or less fixed point in time. (Leys, 1980: 108)

Kaplinsky is accused of observing that foreign capital is strong and indigenous capital relatively weak and inferring from this observation that indigenous capital is therefore 'dependent', 'auxiliary', 'petty', etc. and 'as such incapable of playing a significant role in expanding the forces of production'.

> Yet the history of the sixteen years since independence in Kenya [claims Leys] shows one thing unambiguously: a massive retreat by non-indigenous capital *out of* one sphere of accumulation after another *into* — in particular — manufacturing and large-scale tourism and at the same time there has been a significant increase in income per head. (Leys, 1980: 109)

Leys disputes whether Kaplinsky's five hypotheses accurately represent his views. For instance, he is not intending to claim that an indigenous industrial bourgeoisie exists, but merely to point to 'the fact of African entry into manufacturing'. He suggests, moreover, that figures on ownership and control of industry at a single point in time are irrelevant to the question of the *trajectory* of the political economy. Figures on the growth in the proportion of state capital invested in African controlled manufacturing companies and on the rate, scope and conditions of growth in African shareholdings in manufacturing are of more interest for this purpose than are Kaplinsky's figures.

On the role of the state Leys suggest that the inspection of individual decisions out of context is an inadequate methodology. He goes on:

> What Kaplinsky, I suspect, thinks is that the state must either be *neutral*, or it must be the *instrument* of one or other of these contending fractions of capital. But what has to be grasped is that the fundamental interests of capital coincide; that the general form of this coincidence in Kenya is the general need of all fractions and strata of the bourgeoisie for further investments of foreign capital; and that what are in conflict are the interests of different elements of the bourgeoisie differentially affected by the specific forms this takes. Among these are the interests of particular African capitalists vis-à-vis those of particular foreign capitals. The state's resolutions of these conflicts register a complex interaction of economic, political and ideological forces, which it would be difficult to say has not, over time, advanced and hence also expressed the *growing* strength of indigenous capital. (Leys, 1980: 110)

On economic growth Leys would not dispute that the share of manufacturing has not increased much but would emphasize the fact of growth *within capitalist production relations* as being more important. The key questions, as he sees them, are (a) whether Kenyan growth represents a real expansion of the productive forces and (b) 'whether an alternative pattern is historically possible which would expand them faster, with lesser ... costs in terms of the current living standards of the masses'.

On (a) Leys maintains that real growth in this sense *has* occurred. On (b) he suggests that the most likely alternative strategy is one

> *labelled* 'socialist', put forward by the petty-bourgeoisie, involving 'state socialism' in industry and trade along lines already broadly charted in Ghana, Uganda and Tanzania. It is very difficult to believe that this alternative holds out the possibility of more rapid expansion of production at lower social cost than the historical path so far actually pursued in Kenya. (Leys, 1980: 112)

Common Ground?

It is presumptuous to try to mediate in this lively dispute, but convincing points are being made on both sides and there may be an element of cross-purpose argument.

To begin with, we should recognize that the domestic bourgeoisie does have roots in the pre-colonial past and has developed a momentum of its own. The case put by Cowen, Swainson and the latter-day Leys, based on careful research, is surely unanswerable on this point.* The number of Kenyan capitalists is increasing and they are continually moving into new sectors of activity. Nor does there seem to be much mileage in disputing that this process has gone along with fairly rapid economic growth. One can dispute, as does Kaplinsky, the welfare gains of protected import substitution, and be inclined to qualify Hazlewood's statement that 'great advances were made in the welfare of ordinary people during the first fifteen years of independence' (Hazlewood, 1979: ix). But the fact of Kenyan growth, at least up to 1973, can hardly be denied.

It would be a much more dubious procedure to label the small but growing group of Kenyan capitalists a 'national bourgeoisie', actually or potentially posing in the market and through the state a strong 'nationalist' challenge to international capital. Certainly there is a growing local bourgeoisie, which, at least until 1978, was in control of the state and used this control in its own interests. But we should beware of characterizing the retreats of foreign capital as 'defeats' in the face of fierce challenge rather than as flexibility in order to take best advantage of a situation that is recognized to be changing. The

---

* And Kaplinsky, for one, accepts this (personal communication).

ascendancy of some of Kenya's emerging capitalists has proved to be distinctly ephemeral.

For instance, Swainson draws attention to the fact that

> the chairmen of both Lonrho and Mackenzie Dalgety by 1974 were Kenyans. These appointments represented a strategic alliance between the foreign firm and prominent members of the indigenous bourgeoisie. The two chairmen of foreign companies are examples of the 'younger generation' of businessmen who have had long periods of higher education abroad and at a young age were appointed to the boards of these major foreign firms in the early 1970s. They are typical of a pattern of indigenous managers using the foreign firms to acquire their *own* capital for investment. (Swainson, 1980: 202)

They are also unfortunately typical of a pattern of appointments to foreign companies of people with good connections with the 'royal family'; the Lonrho chairman was the President's son-in-law, the Mackenzie Dalgety chairman his nephew. And since the President's death in August 1978, both have been eased out of some of their positions of influence, as part of what has been described as 'a clean sweep of the Kenyatta family and its acolytes'. *

In this context, as Cardoso points out (Cardoso, 1976: 12), the growth of a local bourgeoisie within an internationalized system of production does not amount to the emergence of a national bourgeoisie in the sense of a class that will lead 'a drive towards economic and social progress'. It may be that Leys and Swainson would agree with Cardoso on this point. At any rate they both quite carefully qualify their view of the trajectory of this local bourgeoisie.†

Leys emphasizes that his analysis does not

> imply that the indigenous bourgeoisie is 'progressive' in the anti-imperialist sense ascribed to it by the theorists of the Comintern, still less that it is preparing a bourgeois-democratic revolution, in the 19th century sense of *that* term. Nor ... does it imply a 'menshevik' political position of support for capitalism in Kenya as the necessary preliminary to communism. (Leys, 1978: 261)

And Swainson says that her 'argument does not support the thesis of "independent" industrialisation put forward by Bill Warren' (Swainson, 1980: 286).

---

* 'How Lonrho dropped the Kenyatta clan', *African Business*, December **1979**, 13.

†In an early contribution that has tended to be overlooked in the subsequent debate Van Zwanenberg similarly insists on a dynamic but non-revolutionary Kenyan bourgeoisie: 'The new bourgeoisie of Africa cannot be expected to be revolutionary in the classical Marxist sense ... The historic mission of Kenya's new national bourgeoisie has been to open up the forces of production at all levels, to remove the old restrictions on the productive forces based on race, and to introduce commodity relations in every part of their territory' (Van Zwanenberg, 1974: 171). He concludes, however (p. 182), that 'it seems most doubtful that this process can continue into an industrial revolution'.

If the local bourgeoisie is not seen as 'progressive' in any of these senses then it seems likely that common ground between both sides in the controversy could quite easily be found in an agreement that their number is growing and that they captured state power during the 1970s. In which case the argument about the *nationality* of the bourgeoisie (which passports do they hold?) might be seen as important but secondary to the real political question for the 1980s, which is *exactly* the question posed by Leys (1978): 'Is an alternative pattern historically possible which would expand Kenyan productive forces faster, with lesser costs in terms of the current living standards of the masses?'

As we have seen Leys sees a 'Tanzanian' strategy as the likely alternative and compares the likely results of this unfavourably with what he expects Kenyan capitalism to continue to deliver during the 1980s. So the question reduces to one partly of the prospects for Kenyan capitalism and partly of the nature of the alternative.

Prospects for Kenyan Capitalism — agriculture, tourism and ISI

Kaplinsky (1980) paints a gloomy view of Kenya's economic prospects with which it is difficult to disagree. The 'Kenyan miracle', based on the 'easy options' (as they are now called by the Minister for Finance) of import-substituting industrialization and Africanization of land-ownership, cash-cropping and commerce, had already largely burned itself out by the early 1970s. A chronic underlying tendency towards trade and balance of payments deficit reflects the import-intensiveness of the 'import substitution' process (with big increases in the import bill for capital goods and transport equipment and, since 1973, for fuel) and the fact that the end of the easy stage of that process had virtually been reached as early as 1971–72, The 1977 coffee and tea boom, when extremely high export prices coincided with record crops due to good weather conditions, disguised this for a time, but since early 1979 the tendency has reimposed itself with a vengeance. This has meant resort to IMF standby arrangements on three occasions between the end of 1978 and October 1980 and an ominous first step into the Eurodollar market in July 1979 when $200m was borrowed from a thirteen-bank syndicate at a high interest rate.

The key to any possible revival in accumulation and growth in Kenya clearly lies in agriculture, which still accounts directly for 36 per cent of gross domestic product (GDP) and provides the markets, raw materials, wage goods, foreign exchange and capital on which the prosperity of the rest of the economy is largely based. The question-mark over agricultural prospects comes from the very high rate of population growth; at almost 4 per cent on some current estimates, this is the highest rate in the world due to purely natural increase. Even on optimistic assumptions about possible deceleration this implies a doubling of the population of 15 million (as provisionally estimated in the 1979 census) by the end of the century. No one would suggest that Kenya has reached its ultimate land frontier, but pressure on land in some areas of the country is undoubtedly heavy. Only 13 per cent of the total land area of 570,000 square kilometres is officially described as 'high potential' (with an average rainfall of 900 mm or more per year) — and 75 per cent of the total population are crowded into this area. What are the chances of escaping the consequences for agricultural productivity of a rising labour-land ratio?

Both the 1979–83 *Development Plan* and the more recent *Sessional Paper No. 4 of 1980 on Economic Prospects and Policies* emphasize the possibility of expanding the supply of agricultural land through irrigation, drainage or the conversion of forests and pastures. However, scepticism seems to be growing about the cost-effectiveness of large-scale irrigation as an escape route from the land constraint. For example, Mwangi (1980) points out that, while irrigation potential is estimated at 600,000 hectares (equivalent to some 6 per cent of the existing high- and medium-potential* land area), the cost per hectare, including additional infrastructure costs but excluding much of the cost of dam construction, would range between K£3000 and K£6000, implying a total cost of between K£1,800m and K£3,600m! At the same time, results of such schemes have so far been somewhat dubious. Drainage, which also could add an estimated 600,000 hectares to the land area, is cheaper (at around K£400 per hectare) but, as Mwangi points out, Kenya has little experience in this area. All in all, while there is certainly some cultivable land at present lying uncultivated, particularly in Coast province, converting it to productive use would not be a simple matter, and neither irrigation nor drainage appears to offer highly promising immediate possibilities of extending the cultivable land area.

More hopeful, perhaps, are the chances of increasing yields per existing hectare through increased inputs of improved fertilizers, seeds, herbicides and pesticides. One should beware, however, of assuming that yields obtained in other countries or in research institutes under test conditions can easily be approached by smallholders. To a larger extent than is generally realized Kenya's agricultural growth of the 1960s and 1970s was a reflection of increased area under cultivation and of transfer from large-farm to small-farm use and from low-value to high-value crops rather than of increased yield per hectare. This means that there is certainly scope for the use of more fertilizers and of improved seeds, etc. but it also points to possible problems in achieving this.

A shift within the existing land area from lower-value to higher-value crops would be another way of increasing yield per acre. Purely from this point of view coffee, tea and pyrethrum are more effective at existing world prices than are most food crops. However, in 1979 and 1980 Kenya has had its first traumatic experience of food shortages, affecting maize, wheat, rice and milk. Given, also, that food is now at the centre of international politics, it is understandable that food self-sufficiency is emerging as an overriding policy

---

* 'Medium-potential' land is defined as land with an annual average rainfall of between 600 and 900 mn.

aim. This will diminish the risk of localized famine and of food queues but will also reduce the productivity gains to be expected from changes in cropping patterns.

The effect of redistribution of land on output is more controversial. The subdivision of large farms of good quality would certainly increase the carrying capacity of the land and would probably increase output also; at least output per hectare would be unlikely to fall as a result. A process of creeping subdivision of larger farms is already going on but it appears to be more than offset by concentration of ownership in other areas. Although the 1980 sessional paper reiterates the promise to review land policies and to change them 'in order to encourage more intensive cultivation where appropriate', we argue below (page 288) that the nature of the support for the Moi regime makes it unlikely that a programme of drastic redistribution of land will be initiated, such as would be necessary for a significant impact on output and carrying capacity.

Finally, what scope is there for increasing *marketed* yield per acre by improving the efficiency of marketing, particularly of food? A few years ago Heyer suggested that 'Kenya's food distribution system functions quite effectively, despite its shortcomings' (Heyer, 1976: 337). However, she also pointed out that the experience with co-operatives and statutory trading authorities had been less satisfactory than with food distribution through private channels, and recommended that the dismantling of the system of control inherited from the colonial period should be speeded up. 'The detailed examination of individual food marketing systems highlights the incidence of pricing problems, of the lack of competition leading to relatively high costs and a relatively poor range and quality of services, and it suggests that there is considerable room for improvement in all these respects' (Heyer, 1976: 337). Since then there has been the fiasco of the disappearing maize. In early 1979 the problem in maize distribution was the acute lack of storage space. Foreign markets were being sought for surplus maize. The internal producer price had been cut by 19 per cent in February 1979 to help this process. Between February 1978 and July 1979 180,000 tons of maize were exported, subsidized by the Kenyan taxpayer because of the continuing difference between the world and the local price, bringing strategic reserves to their minimum level. Incredibly, selling continued and by May 1980 the reserves were exhausted. Thus did extraordinarily inept management compound problems caused by bad weather, hoarding and smuggling. The experience has revived support for the decontrol of food marketing, particularly maize, and for allowing the producer price to find its own level. Given shortages in neighbouring countries, however, such a move might have disruptive transitional effects and is unlikely to be contemplated for this reason, among others (such controls also yield rents and surpluses for individuals); indeed the tendency during the food shortage is to tighten rather than to relax controls on movement of maize.

In short, as far as agriculture is concerned, there appears to be only limited scope for expanding the cultivable area, for increasing yields, for changing cropping patterns towards higher-value crops, for redistributing land and for making spectacular gains from improved marketing efficiency. Thus, apart from one-off increases in productivity due to improvements in weather, it appears that agriculture is unlikely to be the source of dynamism for the Kenyan economy that it has been for the past few decades. Moreover, slow growth in physical productivity is unlikely to be offset by significant improvements in world prices. World coffee output will be swollen in the early 1980s by the response to the price boom of 1977–78. China is entering the international tea market in a big way, at a time of moderately increasing demand. In spite of producers' efforts to regulate world markets, unless Brazil is hit by another frost, the most that might be expected is for Kenya's primary product prices to keep pace with international inflation rates.

Tourism, too, is a poorly performing primary product from the price point of view. In spite of a 68 per cent increase over the 1972 figure in the number of bednights spent by foreign visitors to over 3 million in 1979, foreign exchange receipts in 1979 were only K£62m ($155m), lower than seven years earlier at constant prices. The number of visitors may continue to increase but the trend towards the increasingly competitive packaged beach tourism means that this will be reflected in a much lower rate of growth of expenditure.

Meanwhile, in manufacturing import-substitution opportunities are becoming increasingly difficult to find. For example, Hazlewood has calculated the proportion of total supply of manufactures accounted for by imports in 1964 and 1975 (with total supply defined as output of large firms + imports). The results of his calculations are shown in Table 1. The table suggests that the easy options in the manufacture of consumer goods (particularly food, drink and tobacco) have already been taken up. With further expansion in output of textiles and paper products and with the establishment of three vehicle-assembly plants since 1975, import-substitution opportunities are now mainly in industries such as capital goods which face particular problems because of the small size of the domestic market. So the growth in manufacturing production for the home market can be expected to be considerably slower than in the 1960s and early 1970s.

Prospects for Kenyan Capitalism — Porter (1974)

As import substitution becomes increasingly difficult and as Africanization opportunities in land ownership, cash-crop-growing and commerce are exhausted and the shortage of land begins to bite, the tendency is to look outwards for sources of dynamism. In particular, as Kaplinsky emphasizes, rapid growth in manufactured exports becomes the necessary condition for a continued high rate of capital accumulation and growth.

Table 1: Imports as proportion of total supply of manufactures by economic class and
of particular manufactures

	1964	1975
Manufactures by economic class		
Consumer goods	26.8	15.9
Intermediate goods	40.5	27.8
Capital goods	63.6	55.6
All manufactures	40.8	31.0
Particular manufactures		
Food, drink and tobacco	65.4	6.2
Textiles and clothing	73.6	40.6
Paper and printing	49.0	34.4
Chemicals, rubber and petroleum products	39.6	24.3
Metals	59.4	43.8
Machinery	83.8	78.6
Transport equipment	58.9	60.4

Source: Hazlewood (1979) Tables 5.16 and 5.17.

In a careful study of 'Kenya's future as an exporter of manufactures' published in 1974, Porter spells out some of the problems of relying on export-led growth as the next stage of Kenya's industrialization. He points out that half of Kenya's exports of manufactures (including only slightly processed goods) in 1971 went to the markets of Tanzania and Uganda, at that time protected by the external tariff of the East African Community. These markets had always been extremely volatile and Kenyan manufactures had only maintained their exports to them by keeping 'one step ahead' of industrialization in Tanzania and Uganda. Thus Kenyan exports had once included beer, soap, paint, bicycle tyres, footwear and matches but, as its neighbours set up their own manufacturing facilities, it had become necessary to switch to such products as batteries, insulated wire, gramophone records and plastic products. At the time Porter was writing in 1973 it was becoming more and more difficult for Kenya to rely, for export growth in these markets, on keeping one step ahead. The markets were growing more slowly; Tanzania and Uganda were accelerating their own import substitution; and the cost of Kenya's new products relative to imports from elsewhere was increasing.

Porter describes exports of manufactures to the rest of Africa and to the Middle East as mainly 'the marginal disposal in neighbouring countries of goods essentially produced for the domestic and East African Community market' and does not regard them as much of a foundation for an export-led growth strategy. There is competition in these markets from Tanzania and Uganda, from other industrializing neighbours and from the import-substituting industries of the countries themselves. As far as distant markets are concerned, Porter identifies some sectors which might, *given a change towards an export-oriented policy*, have a comparative advantage (on the basis of lower than average earnings per employee, value-added, labour cost and non-wage value added per worker). These include canning of fruit and vegetables, furniture and wood products, textiles and clothing, footwear, sugar, confectionery and cordage. Significantly all of these are based on processing local raw materials. Porter's calculations imply that there is little prospect of Kenya inserting itself into world trade in manufactures purely on the basis of cheap labour.

Exports of Manufactures 1973—79

Since Porter's paper was published in 1974 there have been enormous changes affecting Kenya's export-manufacturing prospects, almost all of them for the worse. To begin with, even Porter's limited list of possibilities is based on the assumption that 'the rapid growth in the world trade in manufactures and in the LDC share of this trade over the past two decades will continue'. This in turn is based on an assumption of continued growth in industrialized countries. Such countries, however, have suffered since 1973 from slow growth and massive unemployment, and such growth as is likely to occur is expected to be relatively jobless. This means not only that markets for coffee, tea, tourism and other primary products are going to be growing relatively slowly, but also that the protectionist mood in industrialized countries is likely to be reinforced and competition in third markets for manufactured goods to be increased. In addition, the collapse of the East African Community and the closure of the Tanzanian border (cutting off the markets of Zambia, Rwanda and Burundi as well as that of Tanzania), the war and its aftermath in Uganda (which has been the third largest market for Kenyan exports in recent years) and poor relations with Somalia have hampered the traditional policy of keeping one step ahead of import substitution in neighbouring markets. A dangerous new competitor in these markets (and in the Kenyan home market) has emerged in the form of independent Zimbabwe; members of an export-promotion mission in September 1980 ominously reported great potential in the Kenyan market for a wide range of goods from Zimbabwe, including steel, agricultural equipment, footwear, vegetable seeds and higher quality clothing. Markets for manufactured goods have expanded in oil-producing countries, particularly in the Arab region, but infrequent, unreliable and costly shipping schedules make it difficult for Kenya to gain a foothold in these. And cut-throat competition between cheap-labour producers has made it even more difficult for Kenya to penetrate markets for labour-intensive products.

All this has been reflected in a slow growth of manufactured exports since 1973. As Table 2 shows, the annual rate of growth in earnings at current prices

Table 2. Kenya's exports of manufactured goods
(K£000)

	1973	1977	1978	1979
Processed food and beverages	15,071	25,9443	19,350	30,394
Processed industrial supplies	28,021	36,879	35,792	42,515
Processed fuel and lubricants	21,585	82,978	68,771	77,158
Machinery and other capital equipment	3,272	1,228	1,489	1,509
Transport equipment	4,026	999	965	1,079
Other consumer goods	13,657	14,627	14,615	15,060
Total manufactured goods	85,632	162,654	140,982	167,715
Total excluding fuel and lubricants	64,047	79,676	72,211	90,557

Source: Republic of Kenya, Central Bureau of Statisticss, *Economic Survey,* 1977 and 1980.

of such exports (including even slightly processed products but excluding the special case of fuel and lubricants, based on entirely imported crude oil) was only 5.9 per cent between 1973 and 1979.

Since price inflation has been high in this period this implies a fall in the volume of Kenya's manufactured exports between 1973 and 1979 in spite of vigorous promotional efforts. Indeed the volume of exports of chemicals fell by 47 per cent in this period, that of manufactured goods classified by material by 46 per cent, that of machinery and transport equipment by 64 per cent and that of miscellaneous manufactured articles by 54 per cent, while the volume of total exports fell by only 14 per cent. Kenya has been notably unsuccessful in breaking into markets outside Africa. The World Bank has recently pointed out that 86 per cent of Kenya's manufactured exports go to markets in developing countries (mainly Africa), compared with only 11 per cent to industrialized market economies, 1 per cent to centrally planned economies and a negligible amount to petrodollar markets.* The Bank's warning about the dangers of such a trade pattern is borne out by the figures: total exports to other African countries, at current prices, were worth K£99m in 1979, only 37 per cent higher than in 1973 and implying an annual average rate of increase of only 5.4 per cent. Since the vast majority of such exports consists of processed fuel and lubricants, which increased more than three-and-a-half-fold in this period, this implies a drastic fall in other manufactured exports to these markets.

In a recent paper Langdon (1980b) points out that, given the ownership structure of Kenyan industry, one condition for building up new manufactured exports to Western Europe is that European multinationals must be interested in

* Reported in *Weekly Review*, Nairobi, 15 August 1980, 31.

this option. He takes the example of textiles and clothing which has signally failed to live up to its early promise in export markets. Fabric production, at 98 million square metres, was five and a half times greater in 1978 than ten years earlier, but exports were negligible. Langdon draws a contrast between the Ivory Coast's textile industry, in which Western European capital has been heavily involved since the 1960s and the Kenyan industry in which the foreign capital involved in early import substitution was Japanese and Indian rather than European. This meant that the restructuring of the European textile industry during the 1970s opened up exporting opportunities for the Ivory Coast industry through its (mainly French-owned) transnationals. These opportunities may turn out to be short-lived, but they were not even open to the Kenyan industry because of its different ownership structure. As far as the European market is concerned, the only Kenyan industry which is favourably placed in this respect is food-processing.

In official and business circles the great hope for the growth of manufactured exports lies in the reopening of the border with Tanzania (and hence of access to the markets of Zambia, Rwanda and Burundi as well as that of Tanzania) and the revival of the Ugandan market. The Tanzanian market for Kenyan manufactured goods reached its peak in 1975 (when it was worth K£11.3m) and was already beginning to decline before the closure of the border in 1977. The peak for the Ugandan market was the coffee-boom year of 1977, when it reached K£12.6m.

The Tanzanian market is undoubtedly attractive but there are several problems in pushing manufactured exports back to 1975 levels. To begin with there is uncertainty about the reopening of the border. Strong rumours of its imminence have circulated since 1977. And the longer the reopening is delayed the more difficult it will be for Kenyan industry to win back the market; in particular, quite apart from existing suppliers the competition from newly independent Zimbabwe is being given time to establish itself in Tanzania and in Zambia, Rwanda and Burundi.

The Ugandan market is less open to competition from the South but it may not offer the bonanza that some appear to expect. For one thing, for all the recent troubles of the Ugandan economy, it has never collapsed completely. 1977 was a wholly exceptional year which, in the absence of another frost in Brazil, will not repeat itself. In comparison with the mid-1970s, Kenyan manufactured exports to Uganda since the end of the coffee boom have been quite high. The deindustrialization of Uganda, presided over by Idi Amin, has worked to Kenya's benefit to some extent, offsetting the effect on market growth of the disruption of cash-crop production and distribution. Thus the rehabilitation of the Ugandan economy, which will in any case take time, will have two effects as far as Kenyan manufactured exports are concerned. The restoration of its agricultural foreign-exchange-earning capacity will increase the total size of the market; but the reconstruction of its manufacturing industry will reduce the proportion of that market available to foreign suppliers. And the rehabilitation process itself, in so far as it involves aid agencies and transnational corporations, may generate more imports from their countries of origin than from neighbouring countries like Kenya.

In short Kenya has failed to capitalize fully during the 1970s on its position as a 'peripheral centre' in relation to neighbouring countries. This position was developed during the colonial period, when Kenya (and particularly Nairobi) offered a wide range of transport, banking, insurance and other services to neighbouring territories and exerted a strong 'backwash' effect on their development. Nairobi still enjoys substantial benefits of this kind, particularly as a regional base for head offices of multinational corporations and international organizations. But the vision of Nairobi and Kenya as an industrial centre for the region, expressed in the following submission to a 1971 salaries commission by a senior civil servant, quoted by Leys (1975: 196), is far from having been achieved:

> The City of Nairobi has now achieved the status of an international centre and its future planned development must be approached in that light ... We must not spare our efforts, in keeping Nairobi facilities, etc, well above those of Johannesburg, our only competitor in this part of the world.... By provision of suitable facilities we can force ourselves into the circuit ... Nairobi offers all necessary advantages for industry, we can at a stroke convert it into a major industrial centre in the East and Central African region.

As far as export manufacturing is concerned Nairobi has not yet succeeded in 'forcing itself into the circuit', largely due to the resistance of neighbouring countries for the reasons outlined by Porter. Thus not only have efforts to break into more distant markets met with little success, but also the 'Brazilian' or 'subimperialist' route to post-import-substitution industrialization has so far eluded Kenya.

The New Industrialization Policy

Of course, one condition for any success as an export manufacturer, insisted on by Porter, was a change towards an export-oriented policy. Some may feel that such a change has been slow in coming and that it will yield its benefits in the future. Certainly there have been recent moves in this direction. They were foreshadowed in the 1979–83 *Development Plan*, which announced that 'in manufacturing, our emphasis will shift from producing goods for our domestic use to the more difficult challenge of increasing our exports in highly competitive world markets' (page iv). Specifically, the plan proposes the phasing out of all non-tariff protection to existing industries within five years and the limiting of any concessions to new, genuinely infant industries to a maximum period of five years. Tariff protection will be standardized and extended to all types of imports, including industrial equipment, raw materials and agricultural products will gradually be reduced to between 20 and 30 per cent, except in those cases where high tariffs have a revenue-raising purpose.

The new industrialization policy has been spelled out in more detail in *Sessional Paper No. 4 of 1980 on Economic Prospects and Policies*. The emphasis on the substitution of tariffs for quantitative restrictions will initially be on 'imported consumer items, especially those in the luxury goods category'. At the same time, three new measures are intended to encourage industrial exports: an export credit and guarantee scheme will be established; the administration of the existing export compensation scheme, under which local manufacturers who export their products are entitled to claim a refund of import duty provided their exports have at least 30 per cent local content, will be simplified; and the scheme will be reviewed to ensure that the rate of compensation is sufficient 'to make efficient exports at least as rewarding as local market sales'. The 1980–81 budget has given the first concrete expression to these policy intentions, banning the imposition of new quantitative import restrictions, raising the level of customs duty on some specific items, adding a 10 per cent 'surcharge' duty on all dutiable goods and raising the rate of export compensation from 10 to 20 per cent of the FOB value of goods declared for export. This amounts to a partial devaluation of the shilling, at least as far as manufacturers are concerned. This was taken a stage further during 1981, when the Kenyan shilling was devalued by about 20 per cent in relation to the special drawing right (SDR), the International Monetary Fund (IMF) unit based on a basket of international currencies.

The new package, with its strong IMF/World Bank flavour, is a source of some worries for Kenyan manufacturers. They are worried about the increased rates of duty on raw materials and are seriously confused about the new export-compensation arrangements which had still not been clarified several months after the budget. More generally they are uneasy about the removal of protection by quantitative controls. The Kenya National Chamber of Commerce and Industry (which includes a large number of smaller firms among its membership) has asked that such protection should be continued on a more specific and precisely defined basis and that its removal should be implemented only gradually. In particular it feels that protection should be continued for small firms, firms that are being threatened by competition from imported products and new industries established for import-substitution purposes.

The view of the Kenyan Association of Manufacturers (KAM) (with a higher proportion of larger firms in its membership) is that the shift towards export manufacturing is potentially feasible but that the government needs to take 'more constructive action to boost industry, investment and exports'. By this it means primarily the abolition of price controls on all manufactured goods (except basic consumption items) on the grounds that by killing profitability at home they are removing the base on which exports can be built. The replacement of quantitative restrictions by tariffs, also, in their view, needs to be carefully planned, with the new tariffs set high enough to avoid complete destruction of infant industries.

This might be dismissed as the kind of special pleading that is only to be expected. But, for all the reasons already discussed, there must be serious doubts as to whether Kenyan industry is ready yet for the removal of quantitative protection (unless it is replaced by fully equivalent tariffs), let alone for the conquest of world markets that seems to be expected of it. For a wide range of consumer and producer goods the prices of locally-produced items are between two and eight times as high as the border prices of imported equivalents. This is at once a strong argument for reducing protection and an indication of the long transition period that will be necessary — unless a decimation of Kenyan industry is regarded as acceptable. And it is difficult to see how Kenyan planners can reconcile their expectation of an annual rate of increase in manufactured exports, in real terms, of between 10 and 15 per cent (compared with a fall in such exports in real terms over the past six years) with their own sober statement in the Sessional Paper of the changed external circumstances facing the economy in the 1980s:

In the 1979/83 Development Plan we advised the nation that 'the era of soft options is over'. This admonition was with reference to the difficult domestic economic policy decisions then pending. It was implicitly assumed at that time that the four-fold increase in the price of crude oil which had occurred in the world market since 1973 was not likely to go on, and that the industrialised countries would somehow break free of the inflation-cum-recession pattern into which they had fallen. In short, it was thought that implementation of the 1979/83 plan could be carried out within an international economic environment similar to the pre-1973 setting. It is now clear that this will not be the case — and instead that the 1980s will be a time of perpetual crisis in the world economy. We must temper our optimism — and prepare our defences accordingly. (page 30)

It is ironical to see a country as poor as Kenya, under pressure from international agencies and doctrinaire economic advisers, prematurely dismantling its industrial protective system 'at a time of perpetual crisis in the world economy', when industrialized countries are busily increasing their own protection. It is ironical, also, that one beneficiary may be Zimbabwean manufacturing industry which built up its strength behind just such a protective wall as Kenya is proposing to abolish. The main point, however, is that there are few grounds for optimism about the impact of the new measures on export-manufacturing prospects. To return, then, to Leys' question ('is an alternative pattern historically possible which would expand Kenyan productive forces faster, with lesser costs in terms of the current living standards of the masses?'), it seems that the *existing* pattern is no longer

Table 3 Indices of real income per head

Per cent of population	1974 urban (1969 = 100)	1974 smallholder Central province (1963 = 100)	1974 smallholder Nyanza province (1970 = 100)
Poorest 40	115	96	81
Middle 30	137	141	97
Richest 30	195	138	119

Source: Collier (1978).

likely to expand productive forces particularly fast over the next few years. An alternative pattern would not have to be particularly dynamic to be preferable on growth grounds alone.

The Costs of Growth

What, then, of 'costs in terms of the current living standards of the masses'? One aspect of the existing pattern which is easier to observe than to document statistically is its tendency to generate increasing inequality, and to reproduce poverty. As in most countries it is very difficult to produce conclusive evidence on this. Because of the poor quality of the data, comparisons of grandiose overall income-distribution estimates and Gini coefficients are a waste of time. Table 3, based on a careful comparison by Collier (1978) of three sets of surveys, is probably the best we can do. Interpretation of these data is complicated by the fact that 1974 was a bad year for Kenyan agriculture but, to judge from this table, intraurban income distribution deteriorated between 1969 and 1974, as did distribution between smallholders in Nyanza province between 1970 and 1974. Within Central province the middle peasants improved their relative position between 1963 and 1974, and a widening of rural-urban differentials can be confidently inferred for the 1969–74 period. As Collier comments, since smallholder/wage-earner and skilled/unskilled wage-earner differentials narrowed over this period, this suggests a very fast increase in urban non-wage incomes.

Underlying the unequal distribution of income is an unequal distribution of assets, particularly land. Collier has calculated that the 40 per cent of the smallholder population of Central province with the smallest holdings (excluding the landless) owned 18 per cent of the smallholder land area in 1974; moreover, this proportion had fallen from 26 per cent in 1963. A similar increase in the degree of concentration of landownership among smallholders seems to have taken place in Nyanza province between 1970 and 1974. In large farm areas the distribution of land ownership is even more unequal; indeed, the main authority on the situation in these areas (Njonjo, 1979) describes it as 'one of the most concentrated patterns of land ownership existing in the world today'.

As far as poverty is concerned, also, the fact that 1974 was a bad agricultural year complicates interpretation of the data in Table 3. On the face of it they imply a deterioration in the absolute standard of living of the poorest smallholders in the Central and Nyanza provinces over the periods shown. In urban areas the table implies a slight improvement in the absolute standard of living of the poorest 40 per cent between 1969 and 1974. More recent evidence suggests that wage-earners have been unable to protect themselves against inflation since 1973 so that the incidence of poverty among this group has increased.

As for the pattern of poverty, in addition to the most impoverished smallholders (in the 39 per cent of smallholder households below a nutritionally derived 'poverty line'*) and urban unskilled wage-earners and members of the informal sector (whose average incomes are below a similarly derived poverty line), there are several categories not covered by Table 3. Preliminary estimates from the second integrated rural survey* put the number of landless households in 1976 at 237,000 (containing 890,000 people) or about 12 per cent of the households in the six provinces surveyed. The geographical incidence of landlessness reflects the process of rural 'marginalization', whereby the poor sell land to finance schooling costs, to repay loans or to survive. Landlessness in the overcrowded high-rainfall areas, such as Central province, would be even higher were it not for rural-rural migration to less crowded areas of lower agricultural potential. Nutritional data suggest that extreme poverty may be more common among the landless than among smallholders, underlining Collier's point (1978) that Kenya's 'rural poverty is an intra-regional rather than an inter-regional problem'.

Another group which suffers from intermittently acute poverty is the pastoralists, perhaps 1.4 million in all, spread over five provinces, extremely vulnerable to the vagaries of the weather and confined by encroaching agriculture, wildlife and environmental destruction to an ever-decreasing area. Finally, a disproportionate number of the poorest rural households will be among those (almost a quarter of the total) headed by women. In general women are responsible for a disproportionate amount of work on the farm, producing much of the food that their families consume as well as for fetching water and firewood, housekeeping, preparation of meals and childcare. Women have a low rate of participation in the modern sector. And the large size of families means, in the words of a recent official monograph (Central Bureau of Statistics, *Women in Kenya*, July 1978), that 'most women spend much of their lives in a continuing cycle of pregnancy, birth and child dependency'.

* See Crawford and Thorbecke (1978).

In spite of the poor quality of the data they suffice to suggest that the 'costs in terms of the current living standards of the masses' of the existing pattern of Kenyan development have not been negligible. Slower growth in the 1980s would mean a slower rise in average living standards; paradoxically it might mean a relative improvement in the lot of the poorest, but it would hardly be likely to make them absolutely much better off.

The 'Historically Possible Alternative'?

It is relatively easy to establish what the existing pattern is, much more difficult to establish what the historically possible alternative pattern is likely to be. As has been seen, Leys (1980) suggests that the likely alternative is a strategy '*labelled* socialist, put forward by the petty-bourgeoisie, involving "state socialism" in industry and trade along lines already broadly charted in Ghana, Uganda and Tanzania'. In fact the question of alternatives has hardly been explored in the Kenyan context. How relevant is the comparison with Tanzania? Is it really as much in Kenya's favour (in terms of growth with less cost to the masses) as Leys *et al.* (and the World Bank) would have us believe? Bienefeld in Chapter 11 of this book suggests that Tanzanian growth record is better than is often assumed, but a comprehensive and objective comparison of the records of the two economies has not yet been made.

Is it, in any case, the only possible alternative? What would Kenyan 'populist nationalism' look like? Its economic programme would presumably be some form of 'redistribution with growth', widening the internal mass market (and thereby restoring dynamism) by investment and other policies which benefit those at the bottom of the income scale rather than (and perhaps at the expense of) those at the top. Is President Moi's government, in power since the death of Jomo Kenyatta in August 1978, already on that route?

The new regime certainly has a populist flavour. In a flood of directives in his early months of office, under the slogan 'fuata nyayo' ('follow the steps'), President Moi gave the impression of wanting to differentiate himself sharply from the previous regime. One of his first actions as acting president was to suspend the allocation of plots of land in September 1978 on the grounds that 'too many people with too much land are still trying to get more while most Kenyans have none'. At the same time he has launched a drive against corruption, smuggling, inefficiency and drunkenness, purging the police, military and diplomatic services and drastically reducing the number of beer halls. He has also released all detainees.

He has abolished all fees for primary schooling, attempted to ban school levies of all kinds, such as building fund contributions, equipment levies, etc., and initiated a programme of free milk for primary-school children. Soon to be implemented is a scheme for all secondary-school form-six leavers to do compulsory practical work of national importance in hospitals, agricultural training centres, secondary schools and adult literacy centres, before they go on to the university, to another institution of higher learning, or to direct employment.

Finally, employers were directed in 1979 to increase their employment by 10 per cent, in return for wage restraint on the part of the trade unions; companies are being urged to sell their shares to small inverstors and have begun to do so; 'measures to liberalise all sectors where monopolies exist' (including tyre manufacture) have been set in motion; tribal organizations have been ordered to wind themselves up; the university staff union and the civil servants union have been banned; measures to increase the rate of Kenyanization of jobs and distributorships have been taken; and presidential speeches have acquired an increasingly hectoring tone.

All in all, the new regime seems quite distinct from the old in its explicitly populist appeal. However, while its appeal is certainly to the poor — the least progressive smallholder, the landless, the pastoralist, the slumdweller, the unemployed — its political strength depends on its retaining the support of the petty bourgeoisie — the ambitious smallholder with several acres under cash crops and/or some livestock, the small businessman on his way up, the middle-level civil servant or schoolteacher, the small urban landlord. This may limit the extent of what can be expected from it.

Measures such as free milk for schools, which benefit the poor *and* the dairy farmers, are certainly on the cards, as are moves against large businessmen to clean up Kenyan capitalism and to prevent the unfair use of political power for economic ends. But measures which go further and actually challenge the basis of the market system and/or the benefits which the petty bourgeoisie, the new regime's constituency, is able to extract from that system, look unlikely. For instance, in the most important case of land allocation, those who are found by current enquiries to have acquired land improperly will no doubt be relieved of it; some form of land tax may be a possibility; but any more drastic redistribution of land can hardly be expected.

This, then, seems to be the limit of Moi's 'nyayo' populism. But does it represent the limit of what is 'historically possible' as an alternative to the existing pattern? Such crucial political questions have hardly been touched on in the Kenyan development debate so far.

Summary and Conclusions

To return then, finally, to the question posed at the beginning of this chapter: Is Kenya to be characterized as a successful capitalist economy, with an emerging and increasingly vigorous national bourgeoisie, or as a classic case of dependent peripheral capitalism, with all that implies in terms of a distorted development process and limited industrialization prospects?

We should be grateful to those researchers, particularly Cowen and Swainson, who have drawn our attention to the historical roots and the growing strength of the local bourgeoisie. The number of Kenyan capitalists is increasing and they are continually moving into new sectors of activity. And the fact of Kenyan economic growth at least up to 1973, can hardly be denied. However, we would regard this phenomenon *not* as the emergence of a national bourgeoisie in the sense of a class that will lead a drive towards economic and social progress but as the growth of a local bourgeoisie within an international system of production. In which case the argument about the nationality of the bourgeoisie (which passports do they hold?) might be seen as relatively unimportant. As Kaplinsky points out, local capitalists already tend to shift their surplus abroad and are more guilty of transfer pricing than are foreign subsidiaries. If the 1980s see Kenyan dynamism running out of steam, against a background of international recession and labour-saving technical change, this tendency will become even stronger.

For this reason we have devoted most of our attention to the real political question for the 1980s, posed by Leys (1978): 'Is an alternative pattern historically possible which would expand Kenyan productive forces faster, with lesser costs in terms of the current living standards of the masses?' Our starting point in discussing this question was Leys' own answer to it: that the most likely alternative strategy for Kenya is one *'labelled* "socialist", put forward by the petty-bourgeoisie, involving "state socialism" in industry and trade along lines already broadly charted in Ghana, Uganda and Tanzania. It is very difficult to believe that this alternative holds out the possibility of more rapid expansion of production at lower social cost than the historical path so far actually pursued in Kenya' (Leys, 1980: 112).

Our review of prospects in agriculture, tourism and manufacturing (both for the home market and for export) led us to suggest that the existing pattern is no longer likely to expand productive forces particularly fast — so that an alternative pattern would not have to be particularly dynamic to be preferable on growth grounds alone. As for 'costs in terms of the current living standards of the masses', data are poor but they suggest that these costs have not been negligible. Everything rests, then, on the nature of the 'historically possible alternative'. In view of its importance, this question has been amazingly little explored. The most that we have attempted in this respect is to mark out the limits of the 'nyayo' populism of the current regime of President Moi. This is a start, but it leaves a lot of political questions unanswered.

References

Amin, Samir (1969). *Le Monde des Affaire Sénégalais* (Minuit, Paris).
Campbell, Horace (1979). 'The So-called National Bourgeoisie in Kenya', *Ufahamu*, Winter.

Cardoso, F. H. (1976). 'Current Theses on Latin American Development and Dependency: a Critique', *Occasional Paper No. 20*, May, New York University, Ibero-American Language and Area Centre.

Collier, Paul (1978). 'Notes on the Problem of Poverty in Kenya', mimeo, Oxford University Institute of Economics and Statistics.

Cowen, M. P. (1972). 'Differentiation in a Kenyan Location', East African Universities Social Sciences Council Conference, Nairobi.

Cowen, M. P. (1976). 'Capital and Peasant Households', mimeo, CDS Swansea.

Cowen, M. P. (1979a). *Capital and Household Production: the Case of Wattle in Kenya's Central Province, 1903–1964*, PhD Thesis, University of Cambridge.

Cowen, M. P. (1979b). 'Notes on the Nairobi Discussion of the Agrarian Problem', CDS Swansea.

Cowen, M. P. (1980a). 'The British State and Agrarian Accumulation in Kenya after 1945', mimeo, CDS Swansea.

Cowen, M. P. (1980b). 'Commodity production in Kenya's Central Province', in J. Heyer and G. Williams (eds.), *Rural Development in Tropical Africa* (Macmillan, London).

Cowen, M. P. (1981). 'The British State, State Enterprise and an Indigenous Bourgeoisie in Kenya after 1945', mimeo, CDS, Swansea.

Cowen, M. P. and K. Kinyanjui (1977). 'Some Problems of Class and Capital in Kenya', *Occasional Paper No. 26*, IDS, Nairobi.

Crawford, E. and Thorbecke, E. (1978). 'Employment, Income Distribution and Basic Needs in Kenya', Report of an ILO Consulting Mission, mimeo, Cornell University.

Godfrey, Martin and Langdon, Steven (1976). 'Partners in underdevelopment? The transnationalisation thesis in a Kenyan context', *The Journal of Commonwealth and Comparative Politics*, **XIV**, 1, March.

Hazlewood, Arthur (1979). *The Economy of Kenya: the Kenyatta Era* (OUP, Oxford).

Heyer, Judith (1976). 'The marketing system', Ch. 10 in Judith Heyer, J. K. Maitha and W. M. Senga (eds.), *Agricultural Development in Kenya:; an Economic Assessment* (OUP, Nairobi).

International Labour Office (1972). *Employment, Incomes and Equality: a Strategy for Increasing Productive Employment in Kenya* (ILO, Geneva).

Kaplinsky, R. (1980). 'Capitalist accumulation in the periphery — the Kenyan case re-examined', *Review of African Political Economy*, No. 16.

Langdon, Steven (1974). 'The political economy of dependence: note towards analysis of multinational corporations in Kenya', *Journal of Eastern African Research and Development*, **4**, 2.

Langdon, Steven (1975a). *Multinational Corporations in the Political Economy of Kenya*, DPhil thesis, University of Sussex.

Langdon, Steven (1975b). 'Multinational corporations, taste transfer and underdevelopment: a case study from Kenya', *Review of African Political Economy*, No. 2.

Langdon, Steven (1977). 'The state and capitalism in Kenya', *Review of African Political Economy*, No. 8.

Langdon, Steven (1980a). *Multinational Corporations in the Political Economy of Kenya* (Macmillan, London).

Langdon, Steven (1980b). 'Industry and Capitalism in Kenya: Contributions to a Debate', mimeo, Department of Economics, Carleton University.

Leys, Colin (1975). *Underdevelopment in Kenya: the Political Economy of Neo-Colonialism* (Heinmann, London).

Leys, Colin (1978). 'Capital accumulation, class formation and dependency — the significance of the Kenyan case', *Socialist Register 1978*.

Leys, Colin (1980). 'Kenya: What does dependency explain?', Review of African Political Economy, No. 16.

Leys, Colin, with Jane Borges and Hyam Gold (1980). 'State capital in Kenya: a research note', Canadian Journal of African Studies, 14, No. 2.

Mwangi, W, M. (1980). 'Implications of the Predictions of "Agriculture Towards 2000" to Present Planning', mimeo, Dept of Agricultural Economics, University of Nairobi.

Njonjo, Apollo (1977). The Africanisation of the White Highlands: a Study in Agrarian Class Struggles in Kenya, 1950–1974, PhD Thesis, Princeton University.

Njonjo, Apollo (1979). 'The Kenyan Peasantry: a Reassessment', Paper No. 2, University of Nairobi, Department of Government, Staff Seminar, 1978/9.

Porter, Richard C. (1974). 'Kenya's future as an exporter of manufactures', Eastern Africa Economic Review, 6.1, June.

Stewart, Frances (1976). 'Kenya: strategies for development', in U. Damachi et al. (eds.), Development Patterns in Africa and China (Macmillan, London).

Swainson, Nicola (1977). 'The rise of a national bourgeoisie in Kenya', Review of African Political Economy, No. 8.

Swainson, Nicola (1980). The Development of Corporate Capitalism in Kenya, 1918–1977 (Heinemann, London).

Van Zwanenberg, Roger (1974). 'Neocolonialism and the origin of the national bourgeoisie in Kenya between 1940 and 1973', Journal of Eastern African Research and Development, 4.2.

Weeks, John (1975). 'Imbalance between the centre and the periphery and the "employment crisis" in Kenya', Chapter 5 in Ivar Oxaal, Tony Barnett, and David Booth, Beyond the Sociology of Development: Economy and Society in Latin America and Africa (Routledge & Kegan Paul, London).

Chapter 11

Tanzania: Model or Anti-model?

MANFRED BIENEFELD

Tanzania[1] is a tiny economy occupying an area larger than England, France and West Germany combined, but with a population less than 10 per cent and an economic output less than one-half of 1 per cent of theirs. Before it obtained independence in 1961 it was at the periphery of the periphery, being administered under the shadow of the British colonial presence in Kenya. Few newly independent nations have embarked upon the rocky road of independence less well-prepared. It was desperately poor in skills, resources and infrastructure; its sparse population was scattered across a land where malaria and bilharzia were endemic, and large parts of which were dry or tse-tse infested, or both; its known or suspected mineral wealth was pitiful; and its people belonged to hundreds of tribal groupings, the largest of which constituted only 13 per cent of the population.

Against this combination of problems one could set only: that the broadly-based nationalist movement which came to power enjoyed a high level of political support throughout the country; that Kiswahili was a *lingua franca* for most of the population; and that exports were relatively diversified, comprising three major primary products: coffee, cotton and sisal.

Twenty years later Tanzania is still one of the UN's twenty-five least developed countries. It remains extremely poor and very vulnerable to international economic pressures. Indeed by the end of the 1970s its painfully won social and economic advances were being reversed, and the relative social and political stability which it had maintained since independence was under severe stress.

Undoubtedly more surprising is the attention which this small and remote country has received in the international development debate. Unfortunately this concern has often generated more heat than light as protagonists seek to enlist Tanzania's experience to buttress their conclusions with an enthusiasm which often impedes understanding. The intensity of the debate stems from the fact that Tanzania moved towards a more self-reliant development strategy without a socialist revolution and at a time when in many developing countries the crisis associated with the end of the easy phase of import substitution was creating contradictions which had to be resolved either through greater self-reliance, implying a radicalization of import substitution, or through an economic reorientation towards the international market, involving an emphasis on export promotion and diversification.

In this context the debate about Tanzania has often recalled Nyerere's[2] proverb: 'When elephants fight it's the grass that suffers'. Unfortunately for Tanzania's more idealistic supporters, disillusion set in early, as the ambiguity and intransigence of a painful and stubborn reality asserted itself. After 1973, when the combined effects of the international oil crisis, drought and war destroyed Tanzania's already precarious balance of external payments and wreaked havoc in the economy, the ranks of supporters dwindled and many disillusioned radicals joined a growing chorus of rightists and leftists announcing the failure of Tanzania's policy of self-reliance, or of self-reliance policies in general (Lofchie, 1976, 1979; Boesen, 1976; Raikes, 1980; von Freyhold, 1979; see also Leys, 1981).

This paper will examine that conclusion, and suggest that Tanzania's experience cannot simply be summarized as a failure, nor can it be used to confirm one's faith in either of the competing panaceas of the market or of comprehensive planning. Instead it calls for a realistic consideration of the problems involved in a move towards greater self-reliance and socialism, especially because it cannot be argued that there has been no serious attempt to effect such a move in Tanzania.

In fact, Tanzania's experience illustrates the contradictions inherent in any technologically backward society's efforts to achieve economic growth with a degree of social justice, within the existing international context. It illustrates both the urgent need for a significant degree of self-reliance and the enormous obstacles standing in the way of its realization. It emphasizes the importance of achieving greater scope for formulating national policies in response to international competitive pressures, but also indicates the narrowness and the variability of the constraints within which such room for manoeuvre is won, and the difficulty of creating political structures which will ensure that it is utilized effectively.

Tanzania's experience does not provide general answers to the debate about alternative strategies because there are no general answers. Indeed there are insurmountable obstacles even to giving a clear answer to the specific question of whether Tanzania's particular development strategy will eventually prove to have been in the interests of the mass of its population. The difficulty is that to answer even such a specific question one must: assess future developments in the national and international spheres; consider the counter-factual case of what would have happened if ...; and attach weights to the various social and economic consequences of existing policies.

While it may be difficult to answer such questions it is nonetheless necessary, and even though for Tanzania's peasants and workers times are desperately hard, with food shortages appearing for the second time in seven years, this paper will argue that Tanzania's strategy still deserves their support.

The discussion divides Tanzania's experience since independence into three distinct phases: the first, from independence to 1967, was the period of market-oriented development; the second, from 1967 to 1973, was the period during which the new 'self-reliance strategy' began to be implemented; the third, from 1973 to the present (1981), was a period dominated by efforts to absorb a series of exogenous disturbances, without abandoning the new strategy.

1961–1967: Phase One: Seeking the Acceptable Face of Capitalism

Tanzania's independent government came to power in a world where the capitalist industrial nations displayed a supreme confidence based on the reality of full employment, low inflation, and rapid growth associated with rising standards of living and political stability. From this vantage point the difficulties confronting the developing countries were easily forgotten, or, when remembered, were deemed amenable to infusions of assistance from the prosperous west. It was the era of aid, epitomized by the American Alliance for Progress and enshrined in the Pearson Report.

Unfortunately aid did not live up to its promise for recipients or donors. The transfers involved were always small and the consequences inevitably ambiguous. It soon became clear that not only could aid never rectify significant foreign exchange imbalances for any length of time, or for any significant number of countries, it could even contribute to the creation of such imbalances by supporting the establishment of structures of production and of consumption not sustainable in the longer run.

The situation which was to emerge in the mid-1960s in many developing economies would provide a powerful reminder of this fact. By then, efforts to grow faster than primary exports by raising GDP/Export ratios through import substitution had brought many countries to meet their foreign exchange constraint again, but this time with exports lower than they would otherwise have been, with the foreign exchange constraint more binding than previously, with skewed and politically problematic patterns of consumption now materialized in equivalent patterns of production, and with the dream of rapid technological advance based on dynamic externalities largely unfulfilled.

Such results would eventually polarize alternatives between a more radical form of import substitution, or a fully market-oriented strategy designed to expand and diversify exports. However, when Tanzania embarked on its independence these developments were still in the future and the dominant view saw aid and import substitution as effective bases for policy, especially when a strategy aiming at competitive manufactured exports was clearly not a feasible alternative.

The 'facts of economic life' confronting Tanzania's new government in 1961 were harsh and intransigent. The country's ability to produce internationally competitive products was effectively confined to a few traditional primary exports, most of which were threatened with global overproduction. Moreover, only a few bulky or perishable products destined for domestic consumption could be locally produced on a competitive basis so that the abolition of colonial restrictions led only to a short burst of investment which exploited the most obvious opportunities. Furthermore, a significant increase in the number of locally competitive activities would have required such a large reduction in production costs, and effectively in wages, that their enforcement would have imposed heavy and indeterminate social and political costs in the short run, in return for hypothetical and highly uncertain benefits in the long run.

That conclusion was not drawn on the basis of *a priori* reasoning, but on the basis of a serious attempt to implement a market-oriented strategy between 1961 and 1966. That attempt was made by a Party (TANU)[3] whose leadership was aware of the existence of certain 'facts of economic life', and of the need to respect these in the formulation of policy, but which was nevertheless determined to maintain control over the social and political limits within which that market-oriented strategy was to be pursued. However, like many others before and since, it was soon induced to redefine those limits, as it discovered just how relatively unattractive Tanzania was to the private investor, although eventually growing resistance to further concessions led to the abandonment of the market-oriented strategy. The following discussion will briefly consider: the route by which this point was reached; the balance of political forces which led to this particular response; and the nature of the 'solution' which was espoused.

The initial strategy relied upon foreign capital to generate rapid economic growth which it was hoped, rather unrealistically, would help to bring about a narrowing of the extreme social and economic gap between the African population and the tiny European and Asian minorities, controlling private capital in commerce, industry and plantation agriculture (namely sisal and a large part of coffee). The bridging of this gap was thought essential for the political viability of the new nation (Nyerere, 1959), and no doubt the fervent desire to see it eliminated had been one of the foundations of the nationalist struggle.

It was accepted from the outset that certain conditions would have to be met if foreign capital was to be attracted and if its presence was to lead to the desired results. Hence, there was no shortage of exhortations to hard work, denunciations of the 'mango tree mentality' and gestures such as Ministerial salary reductions. It was also recognized that success would require 'fiscal responsibility' and security for investors, so that there were balanced and austerity budgets, state guaranteed development finance institutions, legal guarantees and financial incentives for foreign investors. Finally, since private investment funds woiuld be more difficult to mobilize for infrastructural investment there were intensive efforts to mobilize official aid funds.[4]

At the same time the government was fiercely protective of its right to determine Tanzania's foreign and social policies, and it gave an early indication of the limits to its willingness to make concessions by militantly resisting strong external pressures on a number of occasions.[5] This conflict became critical when it came to providing the private capital operating in Tanzania with labour on terms acceptable to it. Here it soon proved impossible to define limits to the competitive process which were acceptable to employers, government and workers.

The new government began by legislating limits with respect to the conditions of labour. It established these with respect to pay, through minimum wage legislation; with respect to disciplinary matters, by providing for severance pay and for disciplinary procedures involving workers' representatives; and with respect to social security, through the establishen of a National Provident Fund. Having embarked on this road, it would, however, eventually discover that if the market was not to determine the conditions of labour, then some comprehensive, systematic and defensible mechanism had to take its place.

Once it had established these limits, including a relatively high minimum wage, the government soon came into conflict with some of the stronger trade unions seeking further wage increases. But such sectoral demands could not be reconciled with the government's strategy since they were bound to raise difficulties concerning differentials between sectors, and especially between industry and agriculture.[6] In this context the government moved one step further towards a centralized incomes policy, by restricting the right to strike and introducing all but compulsory arbitration. However, the conflict intensified and in 1964, in the wake of an abortive military coup with apparent trade union connections, it disbanded the country's trade union federation and replaced it by a central federation (NUTA) affiliated to the Party.[7]

Although these changes have been denounced as a simple repression of labour on behalf of capital (Shivji, 1975), this is not an adequate description. Indeed an influential representative of international capital in London urged all possible opposition to the proposed move on the grounds that 'the end of free labour represents the beginning of the end of free capital' (Bienefeld, 1979), and thereby captured the essence of the contradiction which was unfolding. In effect, the government was pursuing a strategy whose social and political implication it could not accept. It would eventually reject the strategy, when it realized that it ultimately demanded an open-ended willingness to compromise. In the meantime, the take-over of the trade unions represented a final attempt to reconcile the market-oriented strategy with the maintenance of some effective control over the social limits within which the market should operate. By 1967 the attempt was abandoned, and with it the market-oriented strategy.

Why did the government eventually respond in this way to these developments? The answer lies in the objective, material weakness of the country; the patterns of capital and trade flow then prevailing internationally; the structure of political power within the country; and the particular Party leadership which had emerged in the course of the nationalist struggle.

The country's objective, material weakness needs little elaboration. It lacked the physical or locational assets which might have made it attractive to foreign capital, and its extreme poverty of infrastructure and skill provided little scope for overcoming that handicap. The prevailing international capital and trade flows provided for little flexibility in any event. Capital did not flow freely to the developing world, and when it did, it tended to be closely linked to the exploitation of primary resources. Apart from special cases like Hongkong or Puerto Rico, manufacturing production in the developing world was expanding exclusively in the context of import-substitution strategies, which were themselves closely linked to each economy's export potential, because for international capital the needs of people in such countries were transformed into effective demand and hence attractive 'internal markets', only in so far as their economy earned foreign exchange. Without that, those needs would no more stimulate investment than would the needs of the poor in their home economies.

Our knowledge of the balance of political power must be largely inductively derived from an interpretation of the government's and the Party's actions and reactions, because there is relatively little understanding to be gained by the *ex ante* constitution of classes or of class fractions, assumed to be acting 'for themselves' in the political sphere. Such attempts at an *ex ante* definition of political actors invariably result in tautologies of the sort which claim to explain X, by the hegemony of class (fraction) Y, while basing the assertion that Y is hegemonic on the fact that X occurred. Without resort to such sleight of hand one may suggest that in Tanzania, the balance of political forces was clearly affected by the low level of private capital's political influence. The relative weakness of private capital, combined with its close identification with tiny ethnic minorities politically compromised by their association with the colonial past, substantially weakened support for the idea that the market was in effect the only justifiable and feasible determinant of the social conditions of production.

Of course this did not mean private capital had no political influence. The preceding account has indicated that as long as the government pursued its market-oriented strategy, it was private capital which, by its reaction, judged the acceptability or adequacy of its policies. In fact, private capital had found the conditions offered so unattractive, that there was evidence of a substantial net outflow of capital (Yaffey, 1970; A. v.d. Laar, 1973; Mittelman, 1978).

Naturally, capitalist interests had been attempting to increase their representation at the political level. However, formal efforts in this direction failed utterly when soon after independence the UTP (United Tanganyika Party) was crushed at the polls, and its representatives within TANU were equally heavily defeated. Eventually, in the 1962 elections, their rival candidate to Nyerere received a mere 2 per cent of the popular vote.[8]

Even so, the possibility that in future these interests could use their wealth to acquire direct political influence was considered a sufficient threat, that in 1965 Nyerere, once widely regarded as the great liberal and moderate hope of independent Africa, introduced legislation to establish a single-party state. The legislation was designed to inhibit the degree to which wealth could be translated into direct political power through a competitive political process, pitting 'independent' parties against one another. The considerable dangers of this move were recognized and the new political structure provided for regular opportunities for the expression of popular opinion through elections in which rival Party candidates would stand against each other (Cliffe et al., 1965). Unfortunately, in spite of these safeguards, there is no doubt that this attempt to deal with one problem laid the basis for new contradictions, but for the moment at least, the change achieved its specific purpose of further inhibiting the political influence of private capital.

Naturally, private capital's political views would also find expression within TANU, and with the change to a one-party state this channel assumed central importance. Since the Party had embarked on its market-oriented strategy, it was already learning, though with some reluctance, to adjust its aspirations and principles to the messages conveyed by the market. Furthermore, the willingness of Party leaders to follow that logic to the point where social and political conditions are essentially left to be determined by the market, will increase markedly if they can be personally protected from any adverse material consequences resulting from such a willingness to compromise. Indeed they may find this logic totally compelling once they are so directly associated with private capital that they materially benefit whenever they agree to approve the imposition of more onerous social conditions for the direct producers.

Within TANU such a process of co-option was clearly at work. However, the Party's leadership, in alliance with the popular base of the Party, strongly resisted that trend, even though its personal interests would certainly have been better served had it allowed itself to drift with the tide, to use its influence to gain control over assets and then to 'allow itself' to employ these for its private benefit. Instead, the issue was identified as a major problem threatening the populist objectives of the Party, and was squarely attacked in the context of a reversal of the market-oriented strategy itself.

That reversal was enshrined in the Arusha Declaration, which in February 1967 committed the country to a 'socialist' strategy based on greater self-reliance (TANU, 1967).

1967–1973: Phase Two: Discovering Some New and Some Old Facts of Life

The Arusha Declaration nationalized the commanding heights of the economy in industry and finance. It set out to give greater priority to agriculture and to the efforts of the Tanzanian people. It established a leadership code making it illegal for party and government officials (from middle-level civil servants upwards) to receive any income other than their official salary. And finally, it restricted TANU membership to those who supported its new 'socialist' strategy.

The Declaration did not increase the resources of the country nor the incomes of its people. It did not even reduce the contribution which foreign capital and technology could objectively make to development, nor the need for hard work, nor the need to make wages and incomes commensurate with production and effort.

What it did do, was to give the Tanzanian state greater control over the investible surplus being produced in the country. It also further reduced private capital's direct influence within the Party, and its indirect influence through its command over resources. As a result, it achieved greater freedom for determining a wide range of economic, social and political policies, including the country's foreign policy. Of course, there could be no guarantee that this change would produce long-run benefits for Tanzania's people. That would depend on the actual use made of these possibilities and, no doubt, these too would fall short of the ideal.

The primary objective of the new strategy was to permit a less uncertain, a more domestic needs-oriented and a more socially responsive utilization of investible resources. It was thought that it could elicit greater effort and commitment from those engaged in production, and that it could eventually capture dynamic external economies,[9] through a greater freedom to direct investment towards nationally defined, long-term objectives.

It was always likely that these changes would inhibit the inflow of private capital in the short run, but then that flow had been so limited and its future prospects had been so poor, that if steadier growth could be achieved through this alternative strategy, more foreign capital might actually be attracted and it was made clear that it would be welcome as long as it accepted the government's conditions. This merely emphasizes that no self-reliance strategy sets out to reduce the inflow of capital as an objective in itself (Biersteker, 1980) so that it is quite wrong to suggest that such a strategy's success can be measured by the reduction in capital flow which it brings about (Schubert, 1978; Coulson, 1973). Instead a self-reliance strategy must be justified on the basis that certain changes in a country's material and political circumstances (control over investment, trade, production) can reduce the (direct and indirect) influence exerted by international interests, and that this is important *because these conflict with certain domestically defined social or economic objectives*. Such strategies bear some affinity to 'socialist strategies' because the influence they inhibit is generally that of international capital. In Tanzania that connection was even closer, because its self-reliance strategy also further reduced the influence of domestic private capital.

This also means that self-reliance strategies cannot be extolled, or defined, in general. The degree of change in a country's structure required to open up certain policy options, and the likelihood that such options will subsequently be utilized effectively must be established in each particular case, and always in the knowledge that the protection from external influences afforded by such a policy could end up protecting an inefficient, corrupt and oppressive regime, especially if there was no broad and effective political base for the policy or the government.

Tanzania's experience from 1967 to 1973 illustrates both the strengths and the weaknesses of such a strategy. Many objectives were not fulfilled, and some were revealed as idealistic fantasies. But the economy performed well over all, especially when compared to other sub-Saharan African economies. There was political stability. Policies to benefit the mass of the population were formulated and introduced in health, education, income distribution, water and rural development (van der Hoeven, 1979; ILO/JASPA, 1978). Significant amounts of foreign resources were attracted on favourable terms with the frame of the government's new policies and priorities. There was significant structural change, towards a reasonably efficient industrial sector (Bienefeld, 1981), internal linkages in the economy increased (Schubert, 1978), the GDP/Export ratio increased (Bienefeld, 1975a), the savings ratio rose and remained high (Green *et al.*, 1980), and the country's financial institutions were reorganized and placed under effective national control (Loxley, 1973; Caselli, 1975; Mittelman, 1978). Towards the end of the period a long-term industrial strategy began to be formulated to provide a firmer basis for the generation of those dynamic external economies which are a central long-term economic objective of the strategy (Roemer *et al.*, 1973).

At the same time, certain major contradictions emerged. In the economic sphere a set of interrelated problems manifested itself in a growing balance of trade deficit, bearing the hallmarks of a classic import-substitution crisis. Typically the deficit reflected a sluggish growth of exports, due in part to a worsening of their internal terms of trade, and a relatively rapid growth of intermediate and capital goods imports. The significance of the increase in the GDP/Export ratio[10] was reduced by the poor export performance, and by the import intensity of the newly established manufacturing activities (Rwegasira, 1976; Clark, 1978). There was thus a real danger that eventually the economy

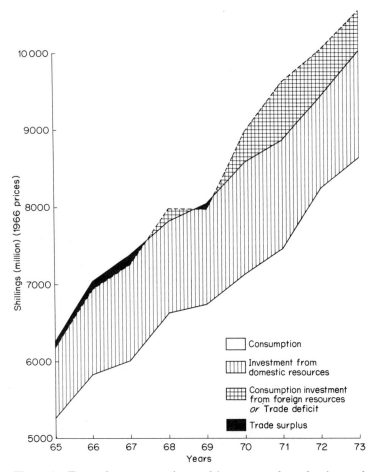

Figure 1   Tanzania: consumption and investment from foreign and
domestic sources, 1965–73

might meet its foreign exchange constraint at a relatively lower level of GDP, because the effect of fewer exports (than otherwise attainable) would more than offset the gains obtained through structural change.

For the moment the problem was resolved by capital inflows, largely in the form of concessional aid facilitated by the new strategy.[11] Until 1973 this meant that total investment could exceed domestic savings by a substantial margin (Figure 1) without the consequent trade deficits creating a balance of payments problem and without the foreign borrowing leading to a debt service problem. Indeed in 1973 there was concern that foreign exchange reserves exceeded those required by normal produce (Green *et al.*, 1980) while the proportion of exports, required for debt service, remained at below 5 per cent. However, even though wisdom with hindsight is a cheap commodity, it seems that the

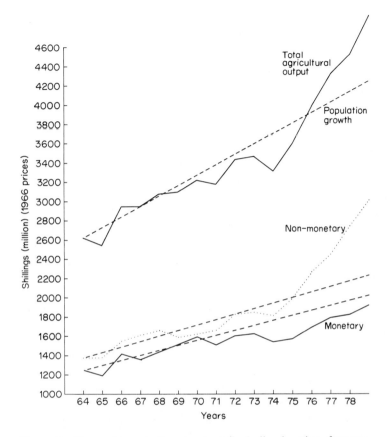

Figure 2 Tanzania: agricultural output (including hunting, forestry, fishing) at 1966 prices: 1964–78

underlying tendencies should even then have given cause for concern, since it was always unlikely that the widening import-export gap could be permanently bridged in this way.

Exports were almost wholly dependent on agriculture, and its performance had been extremely uneven. There were some grounds for optimism. Between 1970 and 1973 food grain imports were negligible; for the whole period to 1973 cashew nut production had climbed steeply and there had been significant increases in minor cash crops like tea and tobacco. Overall, marketed production had exceeded the long-term rate of population growth (3.3 per cent p.a.) between 1967 and 1970, but had fallen fractionally short for the whole of the period 1967 to 1973 (Figure 2) While this compares favourably with most other sub-Saharan African economies (FAO, 1977:1.5 and 1.9), the growth of export crops was insufficient to meet the longer term foreign exchange requirements of the government's ambitious development programme, especially since over time an increasing proportion of these export crops were having to be diverted to internal industrial users.[12]

By the early 1970s, agricultural growth was clearly emerging as a critical problem for the new self-reliance strategy, which in effect sought to 'multiply' the agricultural surplus by using it to employ labour productively in a widening range of domestic non-agricultural activities. Inevitably, in the early stages, when that multiplier was still small, and when efficiency in the non-agricultural sectors was bound to be relatively low, changes in the size of the agricultural surplus dominated other factors, so that one could say the relationship between agriculture and non-agriculture was highly geared, in that a small decline in the performance of agriculture required a very large increase in non-agricultural efficiency to offset it.

Furthermore, since a large proportion of the agricultural surplus was required to earn the foreign exchange needed for inputs to non-agricultural production, changes in the external terms of trade would also tend to dominate changes in the relationship between agricultural and non-agricultural efficiency. Although this would work positively when the terms of trade improved, in fact, between 1967 and 1980, Tanzania's terms of trade reached their 1966 levels in only two years, and in no year did they ever return to their 1964 level. Between 1967 and 1973, they drifted steadily downwards, interrupted only by a brief recovery in 1972.[13]

Given these trends in agriculture and in the terms of trade in the context of this economic structure; given the major changes effected in the organization of financial and industrial enterprises; and given the relative emphasis on non-directly productive investment in social and economic infrastructure, it is creditable that the economy grew at a real 5 per cent per annum and that the Party retained widespread popular support for its policies over this period. This was achieved through a reasonably good performance in finance and industry,[14] an increase in the domestic rate of savings and a sustained, high level of domestic investment, while a careful husbanding of foreign exchange kept the volume of imports unchanged between 1966 and 1969 and transformed an average deficit on net service transfers[15] of Shs. 70 million for 1965–67, into an average net surplus of Shs. 230 million (equivalent to 12 per cent of average merchandise exports).[16] Even so, after 1970 momentum was sustained through an increased inflow of foreign capital and it began to become clear that a number of the earlier gains had come from 'once for all' type changes. In a poor economy one could not keep increasing the savings ratio, or improving net foreign exchange earnings by a reorganization of external services, or further restricting consumer goods imports, while reliance on concessional international finance had to be treated with care because it was uncertain, conditional and ultimately limited. There was thus no way to avoid dealing with the underlying trends in agriculture re exports and in industry re imports.

While the central importance of agriculture could be reduced if non-agricultural efficiency were further improved, or if structural change reduced the economy's dependence on agriculture and primary exports, in the short and medium term these possibilities depended on the agricultural surplus. The problem thus lay in achieving the right balance between the urgent need for increased agricultural output, and the equally urgent need to effect structural changes. Unfortunately that balance is always difficult to strike because peasant agriculture is dispersed and hard to influence, while infrastructural and industrial projects are concentrated and amenable to central direction, so that there is a universal tendency for an interventionist state to neglect the former in favour of the latter. In Tanzania, even though the Arusha Declaration had shown a clear awareness of this danger, this problem was clearly emerging by the early 1970s.

To meet this challenge the government decentralized its administrative and planning structure[17] and transformed its efforts to encourage the spontaneous formation of communal ('ujamaa') villages into a massive drive to establish villages (i.e. nuclear settlements) as a means of making agriculture more receptive to technical improvement and change, of increasing the rural weight in the political process, and of controlling rural private capital accumulation and differentiation.[18]

Unfortunately, by this time the political base of the strategy had developed its own contradiction as concern over the nature of the Party became more acute, more general and almost certainly more justified. The Party's own 'TANU Guidelines' of 1971 (TANU, 1971) acknowledged these problems in its encouragement of grassroots activism, which did elicit a significant response (Mapolu, 1972; Bienefeld, 1975b) but certainly did not reverse the Party's tendency to becoming more bureaucratized and insulated from popular pressures.[19] This was creating a dangerous situation, in which the government's basic strategy became increasingly dependent on a Party leadership being isolated within a Party whose roots in the mass of the population were withering away.

1973–1981: The Struggle for Survival

How these contradictions would have evolved after 1973, if the external world had not changed dramatically, is now impossible to tell. There was little indication of impending disaster, but a clear need for political initiatives and some policy changes. In the event it is possible only to analyse how this situation responded to a series of extreme and devastating changes in the international environment.

Some of those changes were global and are well-known. The oil price increases of 1973–74 and 1979–80, the accelerating inflation of industrial goods prices, and the explosion of grain prices in 1974 resulted in a sharp deterioration in Tanzania's terms of trade. By 1980 a given volume of exports would buy only between one-half and two-thirds the volume of imports it would have purchased in 1966 (Green *et al.*, 1980).

Between 1972 and 1975 it is estimated that the terms of trade deteriorated by 23 per cent (Green *et al.*, 1980, Table A-5). For a trade-intensive economy which had already achieved a high savings ratio despite a very low *per capita* income, cut out non-essential imports and assumed substantial control of its foreign exchange flows, the impact of such a deterioration is difficult to exaggerate. If the circumstances of early 1973 had already signalled the need for accelerated agricultural growth, more rapid structural change, a reduction in the import content of domestic non-agricultural production, and greater efficiency in resource use generally, by the end of 1973, the situation called for literally miraculous change on all of these fronts at once.

But the worst was yet to come. In 1974–75 two consecutive harvest failures shattered the previous trade balance on food. The quantum index for food imports rose from 100 in 1973 to 369 in 1974, so that even at 1973 prices, food imports would have added 22 per cent to the total 1973 import bill. Now even the oil-inflated 1974 import bill saw the share of food in total imports rise from 8 to 20 per cent, remaining at 18 per cent in 1975.

The initial impact of these changes was absorbed by a fall in reserves, and by the mobilization of balance of payments supports, covering roughly 16 per cent of the merchandise trade deficit over the two years. In addition, the domestic savings ratio was allowed to slip back sharply, while real Gross Fixed Capital Formation stabilized in 1974, and fell in 1975. The Government recurrent budget registered a small deficit in 1974–5, while a substantial increase in bank borrowing was used to finance a still growing level of development expenditure (Green *et al.*, 1980, Tables A-9, A-2). The consequent inflationary pressure was eased by a fall in most real incomes,[20] and by real GDP growth of 2.5 per cent (1973–74) and 5.9 per cent (1974–75).

However, the costs to Tanzania's political economy were much greater than this might suggest. The sudden scarcity of foreign exchange led to a 10 per cent decline in manufacturing production in 1975, and the general shortages encouraged corruption and demoralized and overtaxed an already strained and partially disaffected bureaucracy. Their behaviour, especially in the villagiza-tion drive, together with the general economic difficulties, reduced popular support for, and confidence in, the government's politics. Mistrust of the bureaucracy grew, and this, as well as the sharp reduction in their real incomes (Valentine, 1980), in turn further increased their alienation and their tendency to authoritarian behaviour. In the process, the possibility of a more efficient or accountable bureaucracy receded, and the solid base of popular support which had been a major strength of the policy began to erode. Meanwhile, inefficiency in many particular areas increased, and where it did not, existing levels of resource underutilization became more unacceptable. Unit costs rose as levels of capacity utilization fell (Wangwe, 1976), while maintenance on many major infrastructural projects and in many industries was neglected in a desperate effort to sustain production, creating serious problems for future levels of efficiency.

In agriculture the effects of drought, of disruption of the distribution networks due to foreign exchange shortages, and of villagization were difficult to disentangle. All three certainly bore some responsibility for the reduction in output, although in the short run drought was undoubtedly the major problem. The government responded on all three fronts.

To the drought it responded with an effective famine relief programme, and with a radio-based campaign, organized through its adult education prog-ramme, which produced a vitally important and widespread late planting of emergency crops. To the problems of distribution it responded by establishing widespread price controls and by creating a nationalized transport corporation. To the more general problems of agriculture and villagization, it responded by raising the relative prices of agricultural products, and especially those of food (Ellis, 1980) and by accepting that the establishment of communal production had to be made a long-term objective, in deference to the evident impossibility of achieving it in the short run through the sorts of bureaucratic structure at its disposal (Raikes, 1979).

Apart from the emergency famine relief measures, which did avert starvation, the effectiveness of the government's other responses would only become apparent in the following period.

The years from 1976 to 1978 brought normal weather and a stabilization of the terms of trade, thus providing an opportunity to re-establish various vital economic balances. Over 1976 and 1977 total agricultural output increased by 20 per cent in constant prices, while real GDP grew by a healthy 13.3 per cent. The domestic savings rate was again pushed up, and reserves were rebuilt in spite of the fact that the balance on merchandise trade continued to show substantial (though much reduced) deficits in both years. The Government recurrent budget returned to a healthy surplus, enough in 1976–77 to finance almost half of its development expenditure (Green et al., 1980, Tables A-2 and A-9). Even export growth was encouraging. Although this was partly due to the high coffee price of 1977, the production of export crops seemed to have returned to its pre-1974 pattern, with cotton and coffee continuing along the plateaux they had reached in the late 1960s/early 1970s, cashews embarking on a vigorous recovery from the collapse of 1974 and 1975, tobacco and tea continuing their steady growth, while sisal continued on its headlong decline (Figure 3). While this situation appeared quite favourable when compared to 1974–75, its longer term failure as an adequate source of foreign exchange for a vigorous 'self-reliance' policy should still have been evident.

The government's hope was of course that villagization had laid the basis for a long-term acceleration of agricultural growth, and if 1974–75 had been largely

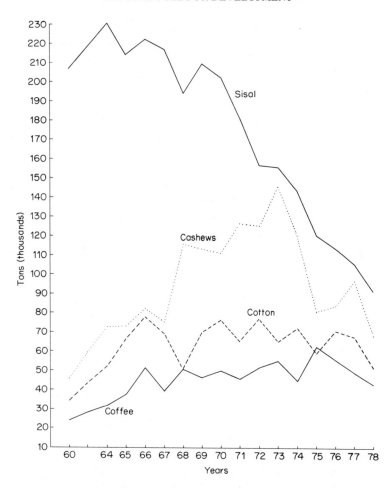

Figure 3   Tanzania: marketed production of major export crops, 1960–78

due to drought and to the initial establishment of the villages, it was conceivable that 1976 and 1977 might represent the beginning of such an acceleration. Unfortunately 1978 dashed those hopes. While total agricultural production continued to expand (by a healthy 4.6 per cent), the production of export crops took an ominous turn. In spite of reasonable weather, the volume of output of each of the four major crops declined for the first time since independence — coffee and sisal each fell by 12 per cent, cotton by 23 per cent, and cashews by no less than 29 per cent. When combined with the collapse of coffee prices, the effect was to reduce *nominal* export earnings by 20 per cent.

Meanwhile the nominal import bill rose by 43 per cent partly as a result of international inflation, but also because of a sharp increase in the import of machinery and transport equipment (only 5 per cent in the form of saloon cars), which recorded nominal increases of 61 and 80 per cent respectively. In part this reflected a catching up on the maintenance and replacement neglected in the previous years, but in part it also indicated an unwise decision to maintain, or rather to restore, the economy's dynamism by pushing ahead with projects involving foreign exchange commitments exceeding any reasonable estimate of the economy's short-term earning capacity. As a result the 1978 trade deficit exploded. Merchandise exports covered only 41 per cent of merchandise imports, which was the lowest 'cover' ever, even worse than the 48 per cent experienced in 1975. In fact, even if the previous year's value of exports had been maintained, exports would still only have covered 51 per cent of imports.

By this time, there is no doubt that economic and political strains had weakened the country's administrative capacity, so that decisions were now taken, which either ignored foreign exchange implications, or considered them on the basis of absurdly favourable assumptions about export crop production, terms of trade and international capital flows. It seems clear, at least in retrospect, that this should have been a period for consolidation, for improvement in the efficiency of established operations, for an emphasis on agriculture, and for support of the encouraging development of small-scale industry which had followed from the foreign exchange crisis of 1974–75 (ILO/ JASPA 1978).

In the event the government's implicit foreign exchange optimism was not borne out. Indeed the next two years produced a repetition of the 1974–75 crisis, with a sharp deterioration in the terms of trade, and disastrous harvests, impaired by flood and drought in successive years. Worse still, Idi Amin's destruction of the Kagera district unleashed a war which Tanzania could neither afford nor avoid, and while there were many international expressions of sympathy, there was virtually no material support and no relief from the Commonwealth forces requested by Tanzania after Amin's fall.

Obviously the position was now more difficult than ever. The international situation had deteriorated. By 1980–81 concessional finance was more difficult to obtain, and the prospects for primary product prices were decidedly gloomy, given slow growth in global demand and widespread global balance of payments pressures inducing most developing countries to redouble their export efforts. Internally the situation was also more difficult. The real incomes of most groups had already fallen in the mid-1970s; maintenance had been neglected and replacement postponed; the distance between Party and people had already grown wide; the administrative structure had been dramatically weakened; and the possibilities of effective collaboration with neighbouring states were curtailed by the collapse of the East African Community and by the fact that they all suffered from similar, or even more severe foreign exchange problems.

By 1980 foreign exchange shortage was once again choking off the country's industrial production. Only this time, with the 1981 harvest again impaired by failure of the early rains, the economy was being trapped in a vicious circle in which a growing shortage of industrial goods defeats attempts at price control, encourages corruption, shifts the real terms of trade against rural producers, reduces their incentive to produce marketed crops, and thus further inhibits the production of export crops, which in turn further reduces foreign exchange and industrial output. In such a situation the demand for relative price increases for agricultural products (Ellis, 1980) may simply be a demand for inflation.

The agricultural situation was by now complicated by the fact that total agricultural production was growing much faster than officially marketed output, while food crops were expanding more rapidly than export crops. The first trend indicated a peasant withdrawal from official marketing channels, which threatened the agricultural surplus on which the non-agricultural economy depended for its food and foreign exchange. The second trend determined that the impact of the first would be mainly concentrated on foreign exchange earnings, although the urban food situation also remained difficult because the new price incentives of 1975 had led to the explosive growth of a number of minor food crops, some of which eventually proved difficult to market (Ellis, 1980). In addition, inadequate storage meant that the substantial food surpluses of 1978 either deteriorated or had to be exported (often below cost) before they were needed to make up the shortfalls of 1979–80 and 1980–81.

In general the overall increase in agricultural output since 1976, as well as the longer run trends, suggests that the underlying situation is not disastrous, while the extraordinary post-1975 increases in the production of various food crops once again confirms the price-responsiveness of peasant producers, in terms of their output mix. The real problem lies in the peasant withdrawal from official markets, which illustrates the real power over material production still exercised by the peasantry (Hyden, 1980), as well as a substantial breakdown in the mechanisms linking the urban and rural economies. Undoubtedly this represents the key problem in Tanzania's economy today.

This problem is of long standing (Kriesel, 1970) and its complexity arises from the fact that it combines problems of transport, with problems of prices, crop purchase, distribution of agricultural inputs and distribution of industrial products. After the spectacular failure of the National Transport Corporation which was dissolved when it became clear that a centralized solution to such a decentralized, fragmented task was not feasible, it is now the centralized crop authorities which are under review.

These replaced the co-operative societies, dissolved in 1976 partly because these also suffered from major problems (Presidential Committee, 1966; Cliffe et al., 1975; Hyden, 1976; Widstrand, 1970) but largely in order to reduce the political influence of the big co-ops, based as they were on the richer, more highly differentiated areas of export crop production. The centralized agencies which assumed their tasks of crop collection, payment and input distribution have performed very unevenly and the government is currently considering changes which would devolve more responsibilities back on to the villages. While this will undoubtedly generate new problems, especially in the less advanced areas, it appears a pragmatic and sensible response to an urgent problem. Certainly it is necessary to change the present situation in which villagers are placed in a passive position, so that the delayed collection of crops leads to progressive alienation and discouragement, rather than to an urgent search for some solution to their specific problem.

For the moment the peasant withdrawal from the cash economy has insulated them partially from the current crisis, and has shifted the burden of that crisis squarely on to the urban areas. Of course, in the longer run, peasant welfare depends on a transformation of their methods of production, and this will require increasing access to non-agricultural goods, both for consumption and for use as inputs to agriculture. What remains to be seen, is whether in Tanzania that integration can be accelerated in a context other than one of rural capitalism. The maintenance of 'ujamaa' as a long-term objective, current efforts to bring villages more directly into the planning process and the proposed shift back to a more decentralized, village-based marketing structure, reflect a continuing search for a path to achieve this vital transformation of rural production, without re-establishing in the process a political base for private capital. For Tanzania's strategy everything depends on this and the possibility of long-term success will critically depend on whether the necessarily centralized, and often heavy-handed, push given to the social and political structure of the rural areas in the mid-1970s can eventually become the basis for creating more vocal, more independent and more influential political and economic units in rural Tanzania (Ellman, 1975).

Conclusions

Fourteen years after adopting its self-reliance strategy, Tanzania depends once more on external balance of payments support to escape from a vicious deflationary circle. It is confronted by a major political and economic crisis which has developed because contradictions inherent in its self-reliance strategy have been dramatically worsened by a devastating combination of climatic, military and international economic developments. With hindsight it is all too easy to suggest these should have been foreseen, but before the event, the short-term costs of planning on such pessimistic assumptions would probably have appeared indefensible.

The real test of Tanzania's self-reliance strategy lies in whether it has strengthened the possibility of formulating and implementing policies reflecting nationally determined priorities. This requires the consolidation of a political structure capable of such a task, and the development of an economic base, technically and structurally equipped to respond more flexibly to exogenous disturbances.

There is no question that the policies pursued since 1967 have increased national control of the Tanzanian economy and that this has made possible the implementation of policies which could not otherwise have survived, because they would have been undermined by the private investors' loss of confidence. These include policies concerning: the provision of social services, the setting of minimum wages, the restriction of managerial and other higher level salaries, the support of liberation movements in Mozambique, Zimbabwe and southern Africa generally, the restriction of speculation in distribution, housing and foreign exchange and the emergence of a pro-food bias in agriculture, triggered by the crisis of the mid-1970s.

In this context the country has been able to mobilize its resources reasonably effectively over an extended period. During times of difficulty and uncertainty, it has been able to contain the impact of disruptive shifts of finance, internationally and domestically between sectors. Its overall growth perform-ance has been reasonably good. Savings ratios have been over 20 per cent of GDP. Investment has been maintained at a high level, the generation of investible surplus from directly productive non-agricultural investment has been consistently high, while the extent of social and political polarization was long contained. However, the crisis of the 1970s has progressively restricted the state's 'room for manoeuvre', until today its virtual exhaustion has called into question the strategy's survival, and the erosion of its political base has undermined its very foundations.

While external shocks have dominated the past eight years, it is important to recognize the contradictions already emerging before that time. While these were summarized in the deteriorating balance, that deterioration stemmed from the slow pace at which technological capacities were developing, due to the low initial level of skills and the heavy reliance on foreign technology (Barker et al., 1975; Mitschke-Collande and Wangwe, 1977); the effect which foreign capital, even in its changed form of concessional, state-negotiated flows, still had on patterns of investment and the organization and structure of production (Coulson, 1977; Loxley and Saul, 1975; Clark, 1978; Barker et al., 1975); the continued difficulties encountered in efforts to stimulate agricultural production through a bureaucratic mechanism; and finally, the growing gap between people, Party and bureaucracy which was undermining the political foundation on which the strategy depended (Saul, 1973b; Pratt and Mwansasu, 1979). These underlying contradictions already existed in 1973, and most were strongly reinforced by the developments after that date.

One possible conclusion is that Tanzania's current problems are insurmount-able, and that its self-reliance strategy has been a failure. However, the implication that it should therefore be abandoned in favour of a strategy centrally based on international integration and on private capital rests on the plausibility of the counter-factual case that this would produce significantly better results and prospects for the nation in general, or for its workers and peasants in particular. At present, the force of this argument is by no means compelling. It is not supported by Tanzania's experience before 1967, nor by comparisons with other similar sub-Saharan African countries, nor indeed by Ghana's post-Nkrumah experience, once hailed as the beginning in that country's transformation. Indeed, given current international economic prospects; given a realistic assessment of how private capital would operate in Tanzania today; and given the current situation in many other sub-Saharan African countries also confronted by a deepening foreign exchange crisis, it is possible to draw the opposite conclusion, namely that these countries will have to move towards more self-reliant strategies if they are to avoid literally explosive levels of social and political polarization.

To date Tanzania's strategy has, under difficult circumstances, produced a pattern of economic and social development which compares favourably with most other African economies, and which is in many respects better placed to meet the challenges of the 1980s, so that there is a clear case for continued critical but constructive support of that strategy, in spite of its many difficulties. This conclusion rests on a belief that more self-reliant strategies will be a necessary feature of sub-Saharan Africa in the 1980s, and on the argument presented in this paper, namely that an assessment of Tanzania's experience since independence suggests that the Party under its current leadership has created a political and an economic structure which makes the future pursuit of such a strategy more feasible.

One may challenge this conclusion by arguing that some class fraction is in 'hegemonic' control of the state and will inevitably use that state primarily to serve its own particular interests. The 'class fraction' (interest group?) said to occupy this position in Tanzania, is either that of international capital (Shivji, 1975) or that of a bureaucratic bourgeoisie (von Freyhold, 1977), though neither of these arguments is compatible with Tanzania's general experience. The notion that the Tanzanian state is primarily an agent of international capital is impossible to reconcile with: Tanzania's foreign policy in southern Africa; its treatment of management (especially foreign management) in disputes with workers over managerial practices (Nyalali, 1975); its excessive neglect of exports and foreign exchange (necessarily a primary objective of international capital); its treatment of transfer pricing, external services and capital flows; or its treatment of firms like Barclays Bank, Lonrho and others, which have over the years come into direct conflict with its domestic or foreign policy objectives.

The argument that the state is primarily a vehicle for a bureaucratic bourgeoisie's self-aggrandizement is equally untenable. While Tanzania's strategy does put substantial power into the hands of the state, that does not define the way that power will be used. Furthermore the argument that it is primarily used to serve the interests of bureaucrats is not compatible with the extraordinary material and political restrictions which have been imposed on that group: from the Arusha declaration's leadership code, to the partial nationalization of high-cost rental housing, to the extension of civil service salary scales to parastatals (rather than vice versa), or to the ways in which the burden of the later 1970s were shared (Green, 1974; Valentine, 1980). In any case, these facts merely highlight the point that unquestionably the best way for those with state power in a poor economy to serve their own interests is to use that power to gain access to the economy's more valuable assets and then to legitimize their private use of these, alone or in partnership with foreign capital.

In fact the actual situation is almost diametrically opposed to that suggested by this argument. In reality, significant parts of the bureaucracy, in government and parastatals, are deeply alienated from the basic strategy because of the restrictions it imposes on them. They constitute a politically dangerous, and a technically and administratively highly debilitating problem. Many of them would not only welcome a change, but the more senior and influential of them would also stand to gain greatly by it.

There is, however, a more serious argument, which also reaches the conclusion that Tanzania's strategy cannot ultimately succeed. This accepts that TANU did set out to curb the power of private capital in an attempt to est4ablish a more viable and more equitable alternative pattern of national development, but argues that the difficulties and shortcomings of its actual experience are the inevitable result of the contradictions inherent in any such attempt (Bahro, 1978).

This argument points out, correctly, that any attempt to replace the allocative function of the market by some other mechanism will necessarily generate new contradictions, which are not random but systematic. They arise fundamentally from the need to establish explicitly and consciously a macroeconomically coherent pattern of economic activity, which is sufficiently stable and politically acceptable to permit accumulation over time. This implies an inevitable conflict between participation and local autonomy on one hand, and efficiency on the other. Furthermore, in underdeveloped countries, with low levels of available skills, a weak administrative apparatus, a high degree of involvement with external markets, and frequently a low degree of internal social or economic integration, this contradiction will be politically and economically so debilitating that one must conclude (however reluctantly), that a more self-reliant or a socialist strategy is an idealist illusion for countries like Tanzania. Hence, the Tanzanian experience not only represents a failure, but cannot be expected to improve significantly. Although this is a powerful argument, its conclusion is not ultimately persuasive, because it defines failure in relation to an unspecified hypothetical ideal, rather than to some feasible, and preferable alternative. The conclusion that should be drawn from it, is rather to stress the need for a pragmatic and realistic view of the problems which such alternative strategies must face in developing countries so that totally unrealistic expectations do not lead to rapid and premature disillusionment.

This paper's conclusion is that Tanzania's self-reliance strategy cannot be described as a failure to serve as a warning to others who might be tempted to follow its example. Indeed the strategy has produced in Tanzania a long-term pattern of social, political and economic development which compares favourably with most similar African economies. At the same time the strategy's problems cannot be simply dismissed as aberrations, since many of them represent basic contradictions which any similar strategy would confront. The lesson to emerge most clearly from Tanzania's experience is that these inherent contradictions represent a perpetual threat to the economic and the political viability of such strategies, and that the chance of containing that threat depends on the ability to sustain and involve a mass political base in the policy. Furthermore, if the links which a government pursuing such a strategy maintains with the international economy are not treated with the greatest care, mistaken judgements about future international developments may lead to major foreign exchange problems which will generate economic and political pressures to deepen these basic contradictions, potentially beyond the strategy's endurance. Since this risk cannot realistically be avoided by cutting all links with the outside world, it must necessarily remain a central feature of such strategies.

In the context of just such a situation of external imbalance the political forces in Tanzania seeking a fundamental policy change have now grown very strong. With large sections of the bureaucracy disillusioned and antagonized; with much of the population no longer mobilized, either politically within the Party, or ideologically; with substantial sections of the left vying with the right as to who can paint a starker picture of internally generated unmitigated failure; and with the real material conditions of most groups declining, the stage is set for the emergence of one further fundamental problem common to strategies which entrust (or burden) the state with a wide range of explicit responsibilities. These create a situation in which that state readily becomes a focus of discontent, and especially when economic problems arise, the fact that the state apparatus inevitably has many real shortcomings in its day-to-day operations, encourages its identification as the ultimate scapegoat. That process is now at work in Tanzania, and once unleashed it is most difficult to reverse. It is also little affected by the fact that many of the people who now consider a basic policy reversal desirable, might soon have cause to regret their decision.

However, if there is to be any chance of the present policy's consolidation and further development, then it will be possible only if the gap between Party and people can be narrowed, and the political base of the policy rebuilt. This will be no easy task under existing material conditions. Unfortunately, as so often, the same conditions which make this task more difficult, also make it more important that it should succeed.

Notes

1. The United Republic of Tanzania was constituted in 1964 through a fusion of Tanganyika and Zanzibar. Throughout this paper I shall refer simply to Tanzania, unless specifically referring to the colonial period before 1961. Until the mid-1970s the discussion of this paper relates in essence to mainland Tanzania (i.e. the former Tanganyika).It is only in the latter half of the 1970s that the political and economic structures of the two founding members of the Union have been drawing closer together.

2. Dr Julius Nyerere was the leader of Tanzania's nationalist struggle, and has been head of TANU and President of the Republic since its independence in 1961. His writings provide an important background for the study of Tanzania's early years of independence (Nyerere, 1966a,b, 1968, 1973).

3. TANU is the Tanganyika African National Union, which led the independence struggle and which has been in power ever since. In 1977 it was merged with the Afro Shirazi Party of Zanzibar to form the CCM (Chama Cha Mapinduzi).

4. A more detailed discussion of these early policies can be found in Pratt (1976), in various articles in Cliffe and Saul (1973) and in Bienefeld (1979).

5. A variety of issues concerning Tanzania's policy in southern Africa; Tanzania's relations with certain socialist bloc countries; and Tanzania's internal policies vis-à-vis private capital have led to repeated breaks in its relations with various major industrial countries. Some of the earlier instances are recounted in Nyerere (1966b).

6. This was a very real problem in view of the 'high minimum wage policy' which the government had adopted (Chesworth, 1962), which had raised the wage of unskilled workers substantially (ILO, 1967 — 'Turner Report'). The Government had adopted this policy in spite of the fact that it realized that it would involve a reduction in the number of jobs available (Bienefeld, 1973).

7. There is a heated debate over the meaning of these changes on the labour front. The issues are fully discussed in Friedland (1969), Shivji (1975) and Bienefeld (1975b and 1979).

8. Discussion of these attempts will be found in Pratt (1976) and in Cliffe (1967).

9. Essentially economic advantages not derived from the application of least-cost solutions based on existing prices and technical conditions, but rather from a pattern of resource allocation which incurs short-term, statically defined costs in the expectation that thereby improvements in the factors or the structure of production can be attained which would lead to longer term benefits for the economy.

10. This is a central objective of import-substitution strategies. The argument is simply that if the capacity to export is constrained, the only way in which the growth of GDP can exceed that of exports is by a change in the amount of GDP related to a unit of exports.

11. Aid flows increased in some cases undoubtedly because Tanzania's new strategy was deemed genuinely desirable by donors. In others equally certainly because aid was deemed better than sanctions or an economic blockade (as in Cuba or Chile) for preventing the emergence of a fully-fledged socialist alternative.

12. The share of GDP which stemmed from manufacturing production had risen from 8 per cent in 1967 to 10 per cent by 1973, due to a growth in output from the large scale (over 10 employees) manufacturing sector, of 12.5 per cent per annum. The programme and policy are fully discussed in Rweyemamu (1973), Roemer et al. (1973), Kim (1978) ILO/JASPA (1978) and Bienefeld (1981).

12. Although there is inevitable disagreement over the precise magnitude of the changes, given the difficulty of constructing a reliable index for imports, there is general agreement about the nature of the trend, Green et al. (1980), IBRD (1981).

14. This was particularly remarkable in finance, where the abrupt withdrawal of Barclay's Bank after a failure to reach agreement over an orderly transfer had led to predictions of chaos (Loxely, 1973). In industry there were obvious problems, with little success in introducing greater workers' participation (Mapolu, 1972; Bienefeld, 1975b) but with a general maintenance of efficiency (Silver and Kmietowicz, 1977; Bienefeld 1981), although industrial growth was very much at the expense of small-scale producers during this period (Phillips, 1976).

15. Travel, Insurance, Freight, Investment Income and other services.

16. A good summary of the statistics for this period can be found in Green et al. (1980), in the reports of the IBRD for 1977 and 1980 (although these have not been officially published), and in ILO/JASPA (1978), McHenry (1979) and Clark (1978).

17. The decentralization of Government was clearly intended to give a greater weight to rural and regional questions in the planning process (Nyerere, 1972). As always the results were ambiguous, with a certain loss of efficiency at the centre, and the development of a not always desirable regional differentiation.

18. These events brought together two strands of thought about rural development. The first was concerned with overcoming the problem of dispersed settlements, a concern which sketched far back into the colonial era (Georgulas, 1967; Cliffe and Cunningham, 1973; Ruthenberg, 1968; Ellman, 1972; Raikes, 1980). The second was concerned to establish socio-economic structures which would contain rural differentiation and establish communal production units based on the traditional communality of the family or clan, with the Kiswahili name Ujamaa. This objective went back to the first year of independence (Nyerere, 1962).
    Both objectives were to be attained by the policy of Ujamaa Vijijini ('Ujamaa villagization') and by the very definition of ugamaa villages this had to occur as a result of the spontaneous actions of peasants recognizing the potential benefits of such a structure (Nyerere, 1967). This, however, proved a vain hope, so that by the early 1970s differentiation was proceeding (Cliffe and Saul, 1969; Raikes, 1975: see Gottlieb (1973) for a contrary view) and ujamaa was confined to a few villages located in the poorer areas of the country. Furthermore, the difficulty of effecting such a radical transformation of rural society under then existing circumstances was becoming abundantly clear (Awiti, 1972; Boesen, 1972; Cliffe, 1973; Dore, 1971; Feldman, 1969; v. Freyhold et al. 1972; Sender, 1974; v. Velzen, 1970, 1973, for a more positive assessment see Cliffe et al., 1969; Ellman, 1970).
    At this point the Party chose to abandon the 'spontaneous' aspect of ujamaa and decided to implement a large-scale resettlement necessarily implemented through its bureaucratic machinery. The result was an 'operation' which raised serious political and agronomic problems: because of inadequate planning, which led to poor sites being selected, and a frequently inadequate concern with the ecological rationale which occasionally lay behind the dispersed settlement patterns; and also because of the authoritarian nature of the bureaucratic structure and function, which led in certain regions to the excessive use of force and to consequent political

problems (Raikes, 1980; v. Freyhold, 1979; Boesen, 1976; Coulson, 1975; Mwapachu, 1976). Arguments that the consequent problems of production reflected the shortcomings of communal agriculture (Lofchie, 1978) cannot be taken too seriously since the move to communal agriculture was abandoned as an immediate objective relatively early in the exercise (Raikes, 1979). In the eyes of many of the above critics the long-term consequences of villagization are likely to be disastrous, but the experience between 1976 and 1978 would suggest that this is not obvious. A few analyses (Ellman, 1976; ILO/JASPA, 1978), including a recent sample survey of villages done by a Nordic team for the Vice President's Office, suggest that this is not at all clear. Work on various poor regions like Kijama or Rukwa, as well as unpublished results from the Household Budget Survey also suggest a reasonably encouraging (though very uneven) picture in many areas. While this does not necessarily justify the measures of the mid-1970s it is an important factor for assessing the long-term implications of these events

19.   The nature of the Party, and its change over time, has been extensively discussed. The general conclusion that the Party has become increasingly bureaucratized is shared by virtually all such studies Saul (1973b), Pratt and Mwansasu (1979). Others have argued that it is the 'colonial structure' of the state which lies at the root of the problem (Othman, 1974).

20.   This has been widely documented although there is much dispute concerning the precise impact of these changes (Ellis, 1980; ILO/JASPA, 1978; Valentine, 1980). In spite of the controversy there is little doubt that the higher urban income groups bore an unusually large share of the resulting burden.

References

Awiti, A. (1972). 'The development of ujamaa in Ismani' in Cliffe *et al.* (eds) (1975).

Bahro, R. (1978). *The Alternative in Eastern Europe* (New Left Books, London).

Barker, C. E., Bhagavan, M. R., von Mitschke-Collande, P. M., and Wield, D. V. (1975). 'Industrial Production and Transfer of Technology in Tanzania: The Political Economy of Tanzanian Industrial Enterprises', Institute of Development Studies, University of Dar Es Salaam, 1974–5 (mimeo).

Bienefeld, M. A. (1973). 'Planning people', *Development and Change*, **IV**, No. 1.

Bienefeld, M. A. (1975a). 'Special gains from trade with socialist countries, the case of Tanzania', *World Development*, **3**, No. 5m May.

Bienefeld, M. A. (1975b). 'Socialist development and the workers in Tanzania', in R. Cohen and R. Sandbrook (eds), *Towards an African Workings Class* (Longman, London).

Bienefeld, M. A. (1979). 'Trade unions, the labour process, and the Tanzanian state', *Journal of Modern African Studies*, **17**, No. 4, 553–594.

Bienefeld, M. A. (1981). 'Evaluating Tanzanian industrial development between 1961 and 1978', in M. Fransman (ed), *Industry and Accumulation in Africa* (Heinemann, London).

Biersteker, T. J. (1980). 'The Logic of Disengagement and National Self-Reliance', IDS, Sussex (mimeo), May.

Blue, R. N. and Weaver, J. H. (1977). 'A Critical Assessment of the Tanzanian Model of Development', *USAID Development Studies Program, Occasional Paper No. 1*, Washington, June.

Boesen, J. (1972). *Development and Class Structure in a Smallholder Society and the Potential for Ujamaa* (Institute for Development Research, Copenhagen).

Boesen, J. (1976). *Tanzania: From Ujamaa to Villagisation* (Institute for Development Research, Paper A76.7, Copenhagen).

Caselli, C. (1975). *The Banking System of Tanzania* (Cassa di Rirparmio delle Provincio Lombarde, Milan).

Chesworth, D. (1962). *Report of the Territorial Minimum Wages Board* (Government Printer, Dar es Salaam).

Clark, W. E. (1978). *Socialist Development and Public Investment in Tanzania 1964–1973* (University of Toronto Press).

Cliffe, L. (ed) (1967). *One Party Democracy: the 1965 Tanzania General Elections* (East Africa Publishing House, Nairobi).

Cliffe, L. (1973). 'The policy of ujamaa vigigini and the class struggle in Tanzania', in Cliffe and Saul (1973).

Cliffe, L., Luttrell, W. and Moore, J. E. (1969). 'Socialist Transformation in Rural Tanzania, a strategy for the Western Usambaras' *Rural Development Paper No. 6*, University of Dar es Salaam, December.

Cliffe, L. and Saul, J. S. (1969). 'The District Development Front in Tanzania', in Cliffe and Saul (1973).

Cliffe, L. and Cunningham, G. (1973). 'Ideology, organisation and the settlement experience in Tanzania', in Cliffe and Saul (1973).

Cliffe, L. and Saul, J. S. (eds) (1973). *Socialism in Tanzania*, 2 vols (East African Publishing House, Nairobi).

Cliffe, L. *et al.* (eds) (1975). See RDRC (1975).

Coulson, A. C. (1973). 'A Simplified Political Economy of Tanzania', paper presented to the University of East Africa Social Science Conference, Dar es Salaam.

Coulson, A. C. (1975). 'Peasants and bureaucrats', *Review of African Political Economy*, No. 3.

Coulson, A. C. (1977). 'The fertilizer factory: A Tanzanian case study', *Journal of Modern African Studies*, **15**.1, March.

Desfosses, H. and Levesque J. (eds) (1975). *Socialism in the Third World* (Praeger, New York).

Dore, R. P. (1971). 'Modern cooperatives in traditional communities', in Worsley (1971).

Ellis, F. (1980). 'Agricultural Pricing Policy in Tanzania 1970–1979: Implications for Agricultural Output, Rural Incomes, and Crop Marketing Costs', in ILO/JASPA (1980).

Ellman, A. O. (1970). 'Progress, problems and prospects in ujamaa development in Tanzania', in v. Freyhold *et al.* (1972).

Ellman, A. O. (1972). 'Introduction', in v. Freyhold *et al.* (1972).

Ellman, A. O. (1975). 'Group Farming Experiences in Tanzania', paper presented to the Group Farming Conference, Land Tenure Center, University of Wisconsin-Madison, 10–12 June.

FAO (1977). *The State of Food and Africulture* (Rome).

Feldman, D. (1969). 'The economics of ideology: some problems of achieving rural socialism in Tanzania', in Leys (1969).

Freyhold, M. V. *et al.* (1972). *Rural Development through Ujamaa Vijijini; Some considerations based on experience in Tanga*, University of Dar es Salaam (mimeo).

Freyhold, M. V. (1977). 'The post-colonial state', *Review of African Political Economy*, No. 8, January–April.

Freyhold, M. V. (1979). *Ujamaa Villages in Tanzania, Analysis of a Social Experiment* (Heinemann, London).

Friedland, W. H. (1969). *Vuta Kamba: the development of trade unions in Tanganyika* (Hoover Institute Press, Stanford).

Georgulas, N. (1967). 'Settlement patterns and rural development in Tanganyika', *Ekistics*, No. 24.

Gottlieb, M. (1973). The extent and characterisation of differentiation in Tanzanian agricultural and rural society 1967–69', *African Review*, **III**, 2.

Green, R. H. (1974). 'Toward Ujamaa and Kujitegemea: Income Distribution and Absolute Poverty Eradication Aspects of the Tanzanian Transition to Socialism', *Discussion Paper*, No. 66, Institute of Development Studies, University of Sussex.

Green, R. H., Rwegasira, D., and van Arkadie, B. (1980). *Economic Shocks and National Policy Making: Tanzania in the 1970s*, Institute of Social Studies, Research Report Series, No. 8, The Hague.

Hill, F. (1975). 'Ujamaa: African socialist production in Tanzania', in H. Defosses and J. Levesque (1975).

Hyden, G. (1976). *Co-operatives in Tanzania*, Studies in Political Science No. 4 (Tanzania Publishing House, Dar es Salaam).

Hyden, G. (1980). *Beyond Ujamaa in Tanzania: Underdevelopment and an Uncaptured Peasantry* (Heinemann, London).

IBRD (1974). *Tanzania: Agricultural and Rural Development Sector Study*, 3 vols (Washington).

IBRD (1977). 'Basic Economic Report on Tanzania' (unpublished mimeo).

IBRD (1980). *Economic Memoranda on Tanzania* (Washington).

ILO (1967). 'Report to the Government of the United Republic of Tanzania on Wages, Incomes and Prices Policy' (The Turner Report), *Government Paper No. 3 of 1967* (Government Printer, Dar es Salaam).

ILO/JASPA (1978). *Towards Self-Reliance* (Addis Ababa).

ILO/JASPA (1980). *Development, Employment and Equity Issues in Tanzania.* Report of a National Seminar held 21–25 July 1980 by the Government of Tanzania in collaboration with the University of Dar es Salaam and ILO/JASPA, Addis Ababa.

Katabaruki, D. L. (1976). 'Marketing Arrangements in Tanzania' (mimeo).

Kriesel, H. C. (1970). *Agricutural Marketing in Tanzania*, USAID, Dar es Salaam and Department of Agricultural Economics, Michigan State University.

Kim, K. S. (1978). 'Industrialisation strategies in a developing socialist economy. An evaluation of the Tanzanian case', *The Developing Economies* (Tokyo), **XVI**, No. 3, September.

Laar, A. v. d. (1973). 'Foreign business and capital exports', in L. Cliffe and J. S. Saul (1973).

Leys, C. (ed) (1969). *Politics and Change in Developing Countries* (Cambridge University Press).

Leys, C. (1981). 'What does dependency explain?', *Review of African Political Economy*, No. 17, January-April.

Lofchie, M. F. (1976). 'Agrarian socialism in the Third World', *Comparative Politics*, April.

Lofchie, M. F. (1978). 'Economic liberalisation in Tanzania', *Journal of Modern African Studies*, **16**.3, September.

Loxley, J. (1973). 'Structural changes in the monetary system of Tanzania', in L. Cliffe and J. S. Saul (1973).

Loxley, J. and Saul, J. S. (1975). 'Nationalising the multinationals in Tanzania', *Review of African Political Economy*, No. 2, January–April.

McHenry, D. (1979). *Tanzania's Ujamaa Villages* (University of California, Berkeley).

Mapolu, H. A. (1972), 'The Organisation and Participation of Workers in Tanzania', *ERB Paper No. 72.1*, University of Dar es Salaam.

Mighot-Adholla, S. E. (1975). 'The politics of a growers' cooperative society', in RDRC (1975).

Mitschke-Collande, P. v. and Wangwe, S. M. (1977). 'Structure and Development of the Engineering Sector in Tanzania', *ERB Paper 77.11*, University of Dar es Salaam.

Mittelman, J. H. (1978). 'Underdevelopment and nationalisation: banking in Tanzania', *Journal of Modern African Studies*, **16**.4, December.
Mtei, E. (1973). 'Exchange control', in *Bank of Tanzania Economic and Operation Report*, June.
Mwapachu, J. (1976). 'Operation planned villages in rural Tanzania: a revolutionary strategy for development', *African Review*, **VI**, 1.
Nyalali, F. L. (1975). *Aspects of Industrial Conflicts* (East African Literature Bureau, Dar es Salaam).
Nyerere, J. K. (1959). 'We cannot afford to fail', *African Special Report*, December (reprinted in J. K. Nyerere (1966a).
Nyerere, J. K. (1966a), *Freedom and Unity* (Oxford University Press).
Nyerere, J. K. (1966b). 'Principles and development', in Nyerere (1968).
Nyerere, J. K. (1967). 'Socialism and rural development', reprinted in Nyerere (1968).
Nyerere, J. K. (1968). *Freedom and Socialism* (Oxford University Press).
Nyerere, J. K. (1972). *Decentralisation* (Government Printer, Dar es Salaam).
Nyerere, J. K. (1973). *Freedom and Development* (Oxford University Press).
Nyerere, J. K. (1977). *The Arusha Declaration: Ten Years After* (United Republic of Tanzania, Dar es Salaam).
Othman, H. (1974). 'The Tanzanian State — Who Controls it and who does it serve?', *Monthly Review*, No. 7.
Othman, H. (1979). *The State in Tanzania: A Collection of Articles*, IDSm University of Dar es Salaam.
Phillips, D. (1976). 'Industrialisation in Tanzania Small Scale Production Decentralisation and a Multi-technology Program for Industrial Development', *ERB Paper 76.5*, University of Dar es Salaam.
Pratt, C. (1976). *The Critical Phase in Tanzania — 1945–68* (Oxford University Press).
Pratt, C. and Mwansasu B. V. (eds) (1979). *Towards Socialism in Tanzania* (University of Toronto Press).
Presidential Committee (1966). *Report of the Presidential Special Committee of Enquiry into the Cooperative Movement and Marketing Boards* (Government Printer, Dar es Salaam).
Raikes, P. (1975). 'Wheat production and the development of capitalism in North Iraqw', in Cliffe *et al.* (1975).
Raikes, P. (1979). 'Agrarian crisis and economic liberalisation in Tanzania: a comment', *Journal of Modern African Studies*, **17**.2, June.
Raikes, P. (1980). *State and Agriculture in Tanzania* (Harvester Press, Brighton).
Roemer, M., Tidrick, G. M., and Williams, D. (1973). 'The Range of Strategic Choice in Tanzanian Industry', paper presented to University of Toronto Conference on 'Development in Tanzania since 1967', 22–24 April.
RDRC (Rural Development Research Council) (1975), *Rural Cooperation in Tanzania* (University of Dar es Salaam) (Tanzania Publishing House, Dar es Salaam).
Ruthenberg, H. (ed) (1968). *Small-holder farming and small-holder Development in Tanzania* IFO Afrika Studien No. 24 (Weltforum Verlag, München).
Rwegasira, D. (1976). 'Inflation and Monetary Expansion: The 1966–73 Tanzania Experience', *Economic Research Bureau Paper*, University of Dar es Salaam.
Rweyemamu, J. (1973). *Underdevelopment and Industrialisation in Tanzania* (Oxford University Press).
Samoff, J. (1976). 'Education in Tanzania: Class Formation and Reproduction', paper presented to the Annual Meeting of the American Political Science Association, 2—5 September.
Saul, J. S. (1973a). 'Marketing cooperatives in Tanzania', in Cliffe and Saul (1973).

Saul, J. S. (1973b). 'Tanzania: African socialism in one country', G. Arrighi and J. S. Saul (eds), *Essays in the Political Economy of Africa* (Monthly Review Press, New York).

Schubert, J. (1978). *DFG Projekt: Entwicklungsstrategien in Afrika: Elfenbeinküste, Maalawi, Sambia, Tansania*, Kapitel 4: Ökonomische Entwicklung und Abhängigkeit, Berlin (mimeo, draft).

Sender, J. (1974), 'Some Preliminary Notes on the Political Economy of Rural Development in Tanzania', *Economic Research Bureau Paper 74.5*, University of Dar es Salaam.

Shivji, I. G. (1975). *Class Struggles in Tanzania* (Heinemann, London).

Silver, M. S. and Kmietowicz, Z. M. (1977). 'An Index of Industrial Production for Tanzania: 1965 to 1972', *University of Aston Management Centre Working Paper, No. 83*, December.

TANU (1967). *The Arusha Declaration*, reprinted in Nyerere (1968).

TANU (1971). 'The TANU Guidelines', Dar es Salaam.

Valentine, T. (1980). 'Wage Policy in Tanzania Since Independence: Trends and Perceptions', ILO/JASPA (1980).

van der Hoeven, R. (1979). 'Meeting Basic Needs in a Socialist Framework: The Example of Tanzania', *ILO-World Employment Programme Research, WEP2-32/WP20*, July.

van Velzen, H. T. (1970). *Some Social Ostacles to Ujamaa, A Case Study from Rungwe* (Afrika Studiecentrum, Leiden, Holland).

van Velzen, H. T. (1973). 'Staff, kulaks and peasants', in Cliffe and Saul (1973).

Wangwe, S. M. (1976). 'Excess Capacity in Manufacturing Industry: A case study of selected firms in Tanzania', *ERB Paper 76.2*, University of Dar es Salaam (reprinted in K. S. Kim *et al.* 1979).

Widstrand, G. G. (ed) (1970). *Cooperatives and Rural Development in East Africa* (Scandinavian Institute of African Studies, Uppsala).

Worsley, P. (ed) (1971). *Two Blades of Grass* (Manchester University Press).

Yaffey, M. (1970). *Balance of Payments Problems of a Developing Country: Tanzania* (Weltforum Verlag, München).

The Struggle for Development:
National Strategies in an International Context
Edited by M. Bienefeld and M. Godfrey
© 1982 John Wiley & Sons Ltd.

Chapter 12

North Korean Juche:
The Political Economy of Self-reliance

GORDON WHITE*

Though a great deal has been written about the theory and reality of national dependence or 'dependency' in the Third World, much less is known about the political economy of independence — the potential for, problems in and limits to 'self-reliance' or 'autocentrism' as a viable mode of development for smaller Third World nations. (For notable exceptions to this generalization, see Amin, 1977: 1–21; Thomas, 1974; Senghaas, 1979.) In this chapter I intend to explore this question through a case study of North Korea or, to be precise, the Democratic People's Republic of Korea (DPRK). The leadership of the DPRK has made the concept of politico-economic self-reliance embodied in the idea of *juche* (also spelt *chuch'e*), the cornerstone of its domestic and foreign policies. I shall first examine the origins and content of *juche* and then describe how it has been put into practice in North Korea's economic development strategy. (Useful studies of North Korean self-reliance include Brun and Hersh, 1976; Foster- Carter, 1977; Halliday, 1981.)

   This case study should prove relevant to the themes raised in this volume for several reasons. First, the DPRK, with a population of 18 million (in 1978) is a medium-sized nation and thus, unlike a country such as China, more comparable with smaller and medium-sized nations in the Third World. It also shares a similar historical heritage of poverty and colonial occupation — Korea was a Japanese colony from 1910–45. Moreover, the country has achieved a high rate of socio-economic growth and development over the past three decades through a conscious strategy of politico-economic self-reliance, eschewing a high degree of economic integration with either capitalist or socialist international economies. In illustrating the mechanics and impact of

* The author would like to thank Meriel Price, Janet Penny and Magdalene Reid for their assistance.

'de-linking' or 'dissociation', North Korea is very relevant to the problems both of Third World countries faced with the constraints and opportunities of the international capitalist economy and of those countries, such as Cuba, Ethiopia, Afghanistan and Angola, which have become closely integrated with the USSR in recent years. Moreover, the Koreans themselves promote *juche* as a model for other Third World countries to emulate, and use it as an important component in the strategy to win international support both for their broad anti-imperialist struggle and their campaign for Korean unification.

The task of describing and assessing Korea's self-reliant development is far from easy given the paucity of reliable information, the secretiveness of the Korean regime and its tendency to present an overly rosy account of its developmental experience. In consequence, some of the conclusions of this study will necessarily remain tentative to some degree.

The Origin and Development of *Juche* as an Ideological Concept

According to the North Korean leader Kim Il-song, speaking in 1972, 'all policies and lines of our Party [the Korean Workers Party of KWP] emanate from the *juche* idea and they embody this idea' (Kim Il-song, 1972: 14–15). But the concept did not emerge fullgrown with the foundation of the DPRK in September 1948. It has deeper roots in the history of modern Korean anti-imperialist thought and, specifically, in the experiences of Kim Il-song and his guerrilla band in Manchuria during the struggle against the Japanese in the 1930s. It developed into its present form, moreover, in response to a succession of political circumstances after the establishment of the DPRK, achieving primacy in the late 1950s and the 1960s. Scholars in the United States, notably Chung, Scalapino and Lee, tend to present *juche* as merely a political defence-mechanism against the unreliability of the Soviet Union as an ally or aid-giver, or as a cynical tool used by Kim Il-song to discredit opposition factions within the KWP (Sang-hoon Chung, 1974: 92–3; Scalapino and Chong-sik Lee, 1972, Part I: 499–504). These 'virtue out of necessity' or Machiavellian approaches capture part of the truth but tend to ignore the more fundamental cultural, historical and political aspects of the idea.

In the broader perspective of modern Korean history, *juche* can be seen as a response to the traditional practices of *sadae* ('rely on the great') and *mohwa* ('emulate China'), characterized by political reliance on and cultural deference to imperial China. (For discussions of these ideas, see Nahm, 1971: 141–62; Walker, 1971: 1–14.) These ideas had a major influence on the foreign policy of the imperial Korean élite and resulted in a conscious effort to model Korean institutions on those of a 'superior' foreign society. In the late nineteenth century, however, *sadae* came to be used disparagingly by Korean nationalists to attack those members of the élite who collaborated with foreign powers bent on dominating Korea. In the words of two Korean historians, in their study of

Korea's response to western and Japanese imperialism in the late nineteenth and early twentieth century, '*sadae* had become a mental fixation that discouraged self-reliance' (Eugene Kim and Han-kyo Kim, 1967: 221).

Viewed as a reaction against this political and cultural tradition, *juche* is an important component of modern Korean nationalist ideology, shared by communists and non-communists alike. It was an important theme in the anti-colonial struggle before 1945 and, more recently, in the successive mass movements in South Korea over the past three decades demanding national reunification and independence from the United States and Japan. (For a discussion of the concept by a South Korean theorist, see Cho Kah-kyung, 1965.)

The origins of *juche* can also be traced back to the early political experiences of its chief exponent, Kim Il-song. Born into a rural family active in the opposition to Japanese rule, he became involved in communist politics in the late 1920s. He fought against the Japanese in Manchuria as a partisan leader between 1930 and the early 1940s, withdrawing to the Soviet Union's Far East, probably in early 1941, when the pressures of Japanese counter-insurgency became too great. Thus, although his rise to power in northern Korea after the end of the Second World War was clearly aided by Soviet political support, he had a solid record of over a decade of anti-imperialist activities and had considerable prestige as a guerrilla leader. (For the official biography of Kim Il-song see Baik Bong, 1973. For western accounts of Kim's career see Scalapino and Chong-sik Lee, 1972; Breidenstein, 1973; Halliday, 1970.)

Juche also reflects a desire to reassert the distinctiveness of Korean culture after systematic Japanese attempts during the colonial period to subordinate it to Japanese culture. The assimilation policies of the colonial authorities extended to Korean language, religion, education, dress and nomenclature. In 1938, for example, Korean-language instruction was prohibited in primary and secondary schools; an attempt was made to indoctrinate pupils in Shintoism; schoolchildren were pressured to speak Japanese both in and out of school; and Koreans were forced to take Japanese names (Lee, 1963: 265). The North Korean communist leadership has emphasized the need to efface the legacy of this period of humiliation by developing Korean culture and protecting it from further foreign depredation. (For a fascinating example of Kim's attitude to this problem see Kim Il-song, 1971, Vol. IV: 7–13.) More recently, the 'American way of life' has been seen as a cultural threat. Though some American influence has apparently reached the North as a re-export from Eastern Europe, the North Koreans are clearly reacting to the displacement of Korean cultural values by the process of 'coca-colaization' in South Korea. (Kim Il-song, 1971, Vol. III: 328; for an example of North Korean critiques of American and other western philosophical ideas, see An Tong-yang, 1967.)

Juche is also prescribed as an antidote to a feeling of inferiority vis-à-vis foreign, notably European, ideas and institutions. Kim-Il-song has criticized, for example, the 'tendency of unconditionally regarding everything in European countries as advanced and blindly idolizing it' and the idea that Korea can never catch up with the 'advanced' European societies (Kim Il-song, 1971, Vol. II: 241–2).

Seen in this cultural context, therefore, *juche* is a form of psychological decolonization, an attempt to rid the consciousness of the Korean people of the stunting influences of the Japanese period and to prepare them for the task of transforming Korea into an advanced and independent nation. At the same time as it strengthens the cultural identity of the North, moreover, it strengthens common bonds with the South and thus eases the transition towards eventual reunification.

Let us now turn to the evolution of *juche* as a political theme in North Korean politics after the country was liberated in 1945. Hagiography aside, it cannot be argued that Kim Il-song originated the concept since other communists and leftists were arguing for self-reliance in the immediate post-war period. Kim did succeed, however, in elaborating the theme and developing its full political potential. Although he did not introduce *juche* by name until 1955, a survey of his writings and speeches in the early post-war period shows clear signs of the idea in an embryonic form. It is also reflected in the policies of the early period. For example, the educational system was reorganized to lay more stress on Korean language, culture and history, and the communist government announced its determination to establish an eventually self-sufficient economy.

In general, however, policies were ambiguous in this early phase. On the one hand, the new organs of representative power, the land reform and the united front policies adopted by the new government combined institutional innovation with selective borrowing from both Soviet and Chinese models. On the other hand, as in China in the early 1950s, the Soviet imprint on the new institutional structure was quite marked. Official statements contained frequent references to 'the great Soviet people, the Red Army and Comrade Stalin' and the fledgling DPRK, established in 1948, was heavily dependent on the Soviet Union economically, politically and militarily. At the same time that Korean culture was being revived, moreover, large doses of 'advanced Soviet culture' were prescribed for Korean consumption and study of the Russian language was given high priority. These two sets of themes — Korean nationalism and the Soviet model — were to coexist in official statements and in practice, the latter gradually losing ground after the Korean War until the concept of *juche* was institutionalized in the early 1960s.

Kim Il-song first specifically introduced the idea of *juche* in a December 1955 speech (Kim Il-song, 1971, Vol. I: 582–606). Judging from the political context of this speech, it is clear that Kim was reacting to several political trends which he regarded as harmful to Korea's future: continued heavy reliance on the Soviet Union in spite of proven Soviet unreliability as an ally in the Korean War; the preference shown for Soviet or Chinese institutional models and political practices by certain leadership elements in the KWP; and the consequent danger of North Ko.ea being 'deKoreanized' and losing control over its own political destiny, thus threatening the goal of reunification with the South.

The idea of political self-reliance became an issue in the disagreements between KWP leaders during 1955 and 1956. Kim criticized the head of the KWP Propaganda Department, Soviet-born Pak Chang-ok, for giving Soviet and other foreign literatuie, history and art precedence over Korean. He cited examples of disregard for indigenous culture:

> I noticed in a primary school that all the portraits hanging on the walls were of foreigners such as Mayakovsky, Pushkin, etc., and there were none of Koreans. If children are educated in this way, how can they be expected to have national pride? (Kim Il-song, 1971, Vol I: 587).

Kim criticized mechanical imitation of Soviet or Chinese forms, from ideological theory to mundane matters such as the phrasing of newspaper headlines, paintings on hostel walls and national dress and cited an incident from the Korean War to illustrate his point:

> During the war, [several comrades] once quarrelled stupidly among themselves over the problem of how to carry on political work in the army. Those from the Soviet Union insisted upon the Soviet method and those from China stuck to the Chinese method. It is important in our work to grasp revolutionary truth, Marxist–Leninist truth, and apply it correctly to the actual conditions of our country. There can be no set principle that we must follow the Soviet pattern. Some advocate the Soviet way and others the Chinese, but is it not high time to work out our own? (Kim Il-song, 1971, Vol I: 591)

The resemblances between the arguments in Kim's 1955 speech and statements by Chinese leader Mao Tse-tung on the need to 'sinify' Marxism – Leninism and break free from institutional imitation are striking. Compare, for example, Mao's critique of Soviet and other foreign-influenced Chinese Communists in May 1941:

> [Too many comrades] are not ashamed but proud, when they understand very little or nothing about their own history ... For the past few decades, many returned students have been making this mistake. They return from Europe, America or Japan, and all they know how to do is to recite a stock of undigested foreign phrases. They function as phonographs but forget their own responsibility to create something new. (Mao Tse-tung, 1966: 62–3)

Both Mao in 1941 and Kim in 1955 were engaged in factional struggle and their words were weapons. But they were both grappling with a deeper cultural and political problem — how to reshape foreign ideas and institutions to fit a particular society and tradition. Thus the purpose of Kim's 1955 speech was similar to Mao's Rectification Campaign of 1942–44 — to bring about 'koreanization' or 'sinification' of Marxist ideology. In his 1955 attack on the adoption of inappropriate Soviet *institutional* models, moreover, Kim paralleled a similar process of re-evaluation taking place in China in the mid-1950s.

The mid to late 1950s and early 1960s saw several major institutional innovations which were specifically Korean solutions to Korean problems: a distinctive rich-peasant policy during agricultural collectivization, the Chol-lima movement for rapid economic development, the Taean Work System for industrial management. (For a useful discussion of the distinctive aspects of Korean communism, see Cumings, 1974: 27–41.) Political education increas-ingly focused on the theme of learning from the 'revolutionary tradition' of Kim's anti-Japanese Korean partisans in Manchuria. The Soviet and Chinese experience was thus replaced by an indigenous political tradition as an object of emulation. By the Fourth Party Congress in September 1961, *juche* was established as the major principle underlying Party policy.

The policy implications of *juche* were expanded further in the early 1950s. Economic self-sufficiency was one of the major goals of the Seven Year Plan (originally scheduled for 1961—67). With the deterioration of relations with the Soviet Union during 1962–63, moreover, the principle was extended to the realm of defence policy, resulting in large increases in budgetary outlays for military purposes. By 1965, the concept had crystallized into a comprehensive political theory which Kim expounded at length in two important addresses: a lecture at the Ali Archam Academy of Social Sciences in Indonesia on 14 April and his report to the Celebration of the 20th Anniversary of the KWP on 10 October. In the former, Kim stated the concept in its comprehensive form:

> Our Party has made every effort to establish *Juche* in opposition to dogmatism and flunkeyism towards great powers. *Juche* in ideology, independence in politics, self-sustenance in the economy and self-defence in national defence — this is the stand our Party has consistently adhered to. (Kim Il-song, 1971, Vol IV: 229—30)

This basic formulation of the concept, including ideology, politics, economics and defence, has remained consistent from 1965 to the present. Kim has used it as a political weapon against government in the South, pointing to the contrast between North Korea's independent stance vis-à-vis its great power neigh-bours and South Korea's economic, political and military dependence on the United States and Japan.

Juche and the DPRK's Economic Development Strategy

I shall now discuss the evolution of *juche* as a programme of self-reliant economic development. This is a complex problem involving a wide range of political and economic considerations: disagreement within the Korean leadership over the correct economic strategy; relations between the Korean economy and other socialist economies, notably those of the COMECON group; trade relations between socialist and non-socialist countries; the comparative importance of economic and political criteria in framing economic programmes; and the political and social costs of different sets of economic choices.

In 1946, Korea was an agriculture-dominant economy, even in the North where most of the Japanese-sponsored industrialization on the peninsula had taken place. (See US Government, 1969: 286–9, 295, 368; Sang-hoon Chung, 1974; Scalapino and Lee, 1972.) In 1946, agriculture comprised 59 per cent of the GNP and industry 23 per cent. During the colonial period, the emphasis in industrial policy was mainly on the production of raw materials and processed goods for export to Japan — mineral ores, metals, marine and timber products. Though a chemical industry existed (10 per cent of industrial output in 1944), it was oriented towards the production of war-related chemicals and explosives for the Japanese military effort. The foreign trade of Korea as a whole was almost exclusively geared to Japan (until the Second World War, Japan and its empire took over 93 per cent of Korean exports and provided 94 per cent of its imports) and imports were mainly manufactured goods such as machinery and textiles. In agriculture, land use was highly fragmented and land ownership very unequal. Industry was overwhelmingly Japanese-owned and managed and, at the end of the Second World War, was depleted by lack of maintenance and Japanese sabotage and in sore need of skilled workers and trained managers.

The economy of northern Korea in 1945 clearly conformed to the classic model of dependence: a poorly integrated industrial structure linked to external needs; emphasis in investment on extractive and initial processing industries; export of primary products in return for manufactured goods imported from the metropole; dependence on the metropole for managerial talent, capital and technology. From the point of view of potential heavy industrialization, however, the northern sector was a more favourable base than the South. In 1940, for example, 86 per cent of Korea's heavy industry was situated in the North and by 1944 the North produced 88 per cent of Korea's fuel, 78 per cent of its minerals, 98 per cent of its metals, 92 per cent of its electricity and 82 per cent of its chemicals. In the field of light industry, the South was dominant, producing 74 per cent of Korea's total output value in 1940. But the location of industries was distorted by the logic of colonial relations with Japan and the railway network skewed by the priority of communications between Japan and the puppet state of Manchukuo (rails ran from north to south and east-west lines were lacking).

Unlike the experience of many later ex-colonial countries, the removal of the colonial power was decisive and comprehensive and the Japanese defeat was not followed by western economic penetration. Indeed, given the Soviet presence and the strategic realities of the emerging cold war and ensuing hot war in Korea, the most imminent threat to North Korean economic independence was posed by the USSR, not the resurgent global capitalist economy.

In the early years, in fact, the North relied heavily on Soviet advice, techniques, institutional models and aid. But Kim's aim from the beginning seems to have been to reorient a dependent and lopsided economy producing raw materials and semi-finished goods to a balanced and comprehensive economy producing manufactured goods. As industry expanded, it was envisaged that the primary nature of the economy would change from agro-forestry to industry. Quantitative questions of growth were seen as inextricable from qualitative questions of structure, the latter being the key to economic independence. In a talk on state industry in 1948, Kim described his goals as follows:

> [We] have become more firmly confident that it is quite possible for us to develop the national industry independently ... [We] should not send out to foreign countries the raw materials which we extract from the abundant domestic sources, as in the bygone days of Japanese imperialist rule, but should proceed in the direction of processing all of them at home to produce finished goods. (1971, Vol I: 188–9)

After the North's industrial capacity was bombed to rubble during the Korean War, reconstruction plans continued to emphasize the qualitative reorientation and geographical redistribution of industry required for economic decolonization. In a major speech on post-war rehabilitation, Kim diagnosed the situation as follows:

> Out of sheer necessity the Japanese imperialists built a deformed colonial type industry in our country in the closing years of their colonial rule ... They built industrial establishments in places convenient and easy to ship materials from Korea to their own country ... This is apparent above all in the fact that they set up all major plants on the east and west coasts of our country ... In the rehabilitation and construction of industry, therefore, we should not follow the course of mechanically restoring the destroyed factories on their former sites, but should redistribute industry. (Kim Il-song, 1971, Vol I: 421)

Technical aid was to be accepted from abroad, but the underlying aim was self-reliance:

> We have invited a large number of technicians from the Soviet Union for postwar rehabilitation. Our task in this connection is to learn technique from them sincerely and quickly ... Our technical personnel must strive to study the necessary advanced technique at the earliest possible date and thus become trustworthy technical cadres capable of tackling all technical problems independently. This is one of the most important tasks facing the management workers and technical personnel at present. (Kim Il-song, 1971, Vol I: 449)

In the Three Year Plan (1954–56) for reconstruction after the Korean War, state investment policy gave priority to industrial sectors such as machine-building, electricity, mining and metallurgy. Heavy industry was given precedence over light industry and agriculture, and a similar weighting was built into the Five Year Plan (1957–61). The nationalization of industry was completed and agricultural collectivization carried out between 1953 and 1958. Consumption for the short term, it was argued, had to be restricted to allow investment in the capital good necessary for laying the basis for comprehensive industrialization, national self-reliance, rapid growth-potential and expanded levels of consumption in the future. (For an argument supporting the idea of initial emphasis on capital goods industries, see Dobb, 1963: 45–59; 1967: 107–24. On the role of the machine industry in industrialization strategy, see Raj, 1967: 216–26. For a Korean discussion of the importance of the machine industry see Sin Tong-sop, 1969. For a retrospective discussion of the debate over economic priorities in both industry and agriculture and an assessment of achievements, see Yun Nae-gil, 1967 and Chong Kwan-yong, 1967: 2–4.) At the same time, however, investment priorities in the first two plans were not skewed as heavily towards heavy industry as in other cases of socialist development. As Motohashi has pointed out (1967: 78), they contained a better balance between heavy industry, light industry and agriculture than the Chinese First Five Year Plan (1953–57).

Although the initial Three Year Plan after the Korean War was clearly successful, certain sections of the leadership had reservations about the wisdom of maintaining such a scale of priorities. Opposition figures such as Pak Ch'ang-ok called for greater emphasis on light industry to meet the consumer needs of the population. There is evidence to suggest, moreover, that the new leadership in the Soviet Union gave indirect support to a change in economic policies. Apparently annoyed at not being adequately consulted in the process of framing the new Korean plan, they expressed their reservations in the speech made to the Third Congress of the KWP by the Soviet representative, Leonid Brezhnev (Kim, 1970). He alluded to 'difficulties' which the Koreans would meet in their Five Year Plan and argued indirectly for a greater degree of attention to consumer needs and the agricultural sector. In later speeches, Kim Il-song was to allude to this domestic and foreign opposition to the priorities of the Five Year Plan. In his speech at the Ali Archam Academy in 1965, he referred to the disagreements of the mid-1950s in the following terms:

> The anti-Party elements lurking in the Party, and the revisionists and dogmatists at home and abroad were very critical of the line of guaranteeing the priority growth of heavy industry simultaneously with the development of light industry and agriculture. They cast slurs on our Party line, alleging that 'too much stress is being put on the building of heavy industry while the people are leading a hard life,' 'machines do not provide food' and the like. Their argument was that everything had to be applied to immediate consumption without being the least concerned about the future. It was, in the final analysis, aimed at preventing our country from building its own economic foundations. (Kim Il-song, 1965: 206)

In his speech at the DPRK's twentieth anniversary celebration in October 1965, moreover, Kim said there had also been opposition from 'revisionists' abroad to the Korean priority on economic self-reliance. It was this issue which became one of the major causes of friction between Korea and the Soviet Union in the early 1960s.

In the socialist camp as a whole, the late 1950s saw greater stress placed on the idea of international economic integration and national specialization. (For a discussion of the evolution of the theory and practice of international economic integration in the socialist bloc, see Köhler, 1965: 79–157.) The early post-war years of autarkic national economic planning gave way to attempts, in the period 1949–54, to co-ordinate foreign trade plans between the Soviet Union and the Eastern European socialist countries. From 1954 onward, the principle of co-ordination was extended to include national production and investment plans, with the process gaining momentum after 1958. Greater co-ordination led to resistance from a number of states: the Czechs protested about the development of an automobile industry in Poland; the GDR refused to abandon the production of heavy caterpillar tractors; and Romania stood firm over the building of the Galati steel complex.

The DPRK acquired observer status in COMECON in 1957 and in 1958 it seemed that the Koreans would be willing to associate themselves more closely with the Community. But the rising pressure for integration in the late 1950s came into conflict with the Korean desire for economic self-reliance. The Koreans clearly saw trade as an important part of their development strategy; they needed to import both machinery and raw materials such as coking coal, synthetic rubber, oil, wool, sugar and cotton. But they were unwilling to pay the costs of tighter integration which would, in their eyes, have led to economic and therefore political dependence on the Soviet Union. (For a discussion of the clash between the Soviet Union and North Korea over the issue of economic integration, see Freedman, 1970: 141–9.)

Korean resentment surfaced in early April 1963. President Ch'oe Yong-gon delivered a speech to the Supreme People's Congress praising China's economic progress and rapid recovered from the economic results of Soviet pressures. Ch'oe noted that China 'has succeeded in replacing most imported raw materials with home materials and producing with its own techniques many kinds of machines that could not be manufactured until recently' (Schwartz, 1963). Shortly afterwards, (on 12 June 1963), a long editorial in the KWP paper *Nodong Sinmun* provided a full analysis of the policy of economic self-reliance. It argued that economic independence was a precondition for political independence and for the construction of an integrated economy, particularly in ex-colonial nations where industry was weak:

[Each] country must develop its economy in a many-sided way; each country must grow into an independent economic unit which is run with its own technique, natural resources, raw and other materials and by its own efforts and personnel.

The Soviet Union was criticized on several counts, not by name but by the cryptic tag 'some people'!

Economic enslavement, exploitation and plundering of the backward agricultural countries by the industrially developed countries and, on this basis, political domination of the former by the latter — this typifies the mutual relations between countries in the capitalist world. But it is both impossible and impermissible for such phenomena to exist between socialist countries ... Some people, who while talking about independence, equality and non-interference in internal affairs, disapprove of independent national construction, are in fact denying the sovereignty and equality of other countries.

While the editorial welcomed the idea of international co-operation, it rejected some of the (Soviet) arguments for closer international economic co-ordination:

What will happen if attention is directed only to 'traditional production,' to 'natural economic advantages,' to the 'gains' [i.e. profitability] and thus to the development of a few limited departments of production? The national economy of the country in question will become lopsided and, moreover, be paralyzed without economic aid from other countries. If only the traditional productive departments are developed, formerly industrially underdeveloped countries in particular will remain forever in a backward state without modern industry.

On 30 October 1963, the same ideas were expressed even more forcefully:

[Certain] persons doggedly oppose and obstruct the line of self-reliance and of building an independent economy in the socialist countries. They brand the construction of an independent national economy as a 'nationalistic tendency' or a 'closed economy' and accuse it of being a 'politically dangerous and economically harmful' line ... [They] allege that a comprehensive economy developed in a many-sided way can be built only in big countries. This means in the final analysis that the other countries should develop only a few limited branches of economy and always have a one-sided economy.

International inequality and dependence were seen as inherent in the COMECON ideal of integration and division of labour:

Those who oppose the building of an independent economy advocate, instead, the establishment of an 'integrated economy' of the socialist countries ... The enforcement of an 'integrated economy' will reduce in the long run the economy of each socialist country to an appendage of the economy of one or two countries, and subordinate it to the interests of the development of the economy of one or two countries ... Then the differences in the level of development of the socialist countries will not be eliminated, but rather widened, and the dependency of a backward country on the developed will remain unchanged.

When the Soviet Union replied by mentioning their previous aid to the DPRK, the Koreans retorted by accusing the Russians of exploitation:

In rendering aid after World War II, you furnished us with equipment, stainless steel plate and other materials at prices much higher than world market prices and took away from us scores of tons of gold, quantities of valuable non-ferrous metals and raw materials at prices much lower than world market prices. (cited in Freedman, 1970: 148)

The Korean rejection of Soviet plans for integration was not without cost: it was one of the factors, for example, which led to the postponement of the completion of the Seven Year Plan from 1967 to 1970. Soviet manipulation of aid and possibly trade arrangements hampered the achievement of the Plan's original targets. Moreover, after the credibility of the Soviet military guarantee embodied in the 1961 Korea-Soviet treaty declined and military aid was shut off for several years, a greater percentage of state expenditure had to be devoted to defence. But relations with COMECON were not discontinued. Though Korea did not become a full member, like Mongolia, it did assume an associate status which enabled it to reap some of the benefits offered by COMECON (notably the possibility of barter trade and avoidance of the need for hard currency) without compromising any significant degree of political or economic autonomy.* No doubt some of this policy leeway was obtained by North Korea's ambiguous or 'neutral' stance in the Sino-Soviet dispute.

The concept of economic self-reliance has remained basic to North Korean economic strategy since the mid-1960s. The principle was written into the DPRK Constitution, adopted in December 1972: Article 2 includes 'an independent national economy' as one of the three foundations of society (FLPH, 1972: 1–2). (For a discussion of the economic aspects of the Constitution, see Chung, 1973: 28–34.) Economic self-reliance has also been elaborated theoretically and practically, both by Kim Il-song himself and in general political economy texts. (For two informative accounts, see FLPH, 1975 and 1977.) The main components of the theory are as follows:

(i) As mentioned earlier, economic self-reliance is to be seen as one part of a more general self-reliant posture, affecting politics, culture, ideology and military affairs — these aspects are interdependent.

(ii) Economic development is primarily achieved by *states* within *national* frameworks:

* I am indebted to Jon Halliday for this point.

[As] long as boundaries remain between states while communism has not been realized on a world-wide scale, the material and technical foundations of socialism should be built by each national state as a unit ... Only if the material and technical foundations of socialism are established within the bounds of each national state as a comprehensive, independent economic unit, can the country's national resources be tapped and utilized to the fullest. (FLPH, 1975: 7–8 c; FLPH, 1977: 19–20)

This principle implicity invokes the arguments voiced against tighter-integration within COMECON.

(iii) A nation should aim, where feasible, for a high degree of self sufficiency (the Koreans reject the term 'autarky' though this surely applies here, in a scalar rather than a dichotomous sense). Self-sufficiency has three basic aspects. First, the sources of accumulation should in the main be generated internally. This principle allows for foreign aid (and credits) but assigns it only an auxiliary role; it does not allow for direct foreign investment in the Korean economy (FLPH, 1977: Ch. 8). Secondly, it requires the establishment of a comprehensive, diversified and 'organically inter-related economy:

Developing a comprehensive national economy means equipping it with every production branch and securing organic inter-relations between them so that it can meet on its own the domestic needs for heavy and light industrial products and farm produce ... An independent national economy forms a perfect system in which every process of production from extraction of raw materials to making of finished goods is in organic combination; it is an economy which produces the means of production and consumer goods on its own and connects production and consumption mainly through home markets. (FLPH, 1977: 7–8, 20–21; cf. Ch. 4)

Thirdly, there should be reliance on domestic raw materials and fuels. The *locus classicus* here is Kim Il-song:

For industry to become a sound, independent one, more than 70 per cent of raw materials must be secured on one's own ... Industry dependent on the raw materials of other countries is a subordinate industry. (FLPH, 1977: 158; cf. Ch. 5)

(iv) Complete autarky is neither feasible nor advisable for two reasons. First, no nation is totally self-sufficient, so there is need for specialization and trade. This essential exchange, however, must be founded on self-reliance:

Natural and economic conditions and the levels of the productive forces and science and technology differ from country to country and so the variety and quantity of goods they produce differ from one another. It is therefore necessary for each country to produce essential goods needed in large quantities, while procuring such goods as are needed in a small quantity or are in short supply or are not produced by it, through trade with other countries on the principles of equality and mutual benefit. (FLPH, 1975: 10)

Any static conception of comparative advantage is explicitly rejected on the grounds that the existing international division of labour, especially but not exclusively in the capitalist world, is oppressive and unequal. Structural change through politico-economic self-reliance is necessary for reducing this inequality and making trade mutually advantageous. Decisions about investment in particular sectors should be governed by both long and short term, micro and macro considerations. (FLPH, 1977: 102–6). Secondly, the establishment of a modern, diversified economy (and a credible military force) requires the 'latest, up-to-date science and technology'. Though it is crucial to develop the capacity to generate advanced technology internally, much of it must be absorbed from abroad by a variety of means: information flows, overseas training, technical assistance and imports of blueprint or embodied technology. Similarly, foreign technicians may play an ancillary role in this process, though the main emphasis is on 'our own national cadres' (FLPH, 1977, Chs. 6 and 7).

(v) Though international economic ties of various kinds are necessary, they must be arranged in such a way as to maximize the nation's autonomous power of politico-economic decision (what one could call *autarchy*) — excessive dependence on one or a few sources of aid or trade should be avoided, though relations with other socialist countries are potentially less threatening than those with capitalist countries.

(vi) The viability of *juche* as an economic strategy is *generalizable* given certain political preconditions:

> Every country has more or less its own natural wealth and raw material resources. If only there is the revolutionary spirit of self-reliance, it is fully possible to tap them by one's own labour ... and turn one's own potentialities into a material force guaranteeing economic independence (FLPH, 1977: 34).

At the theoretical level, the concept of *juche* is similar to theories of self-reliance developed by Third World spokesmen such as Amin and Thomas. It has been embodied in Korean development practice over the past three decades. In the next section we shall look at the historical record to assess the specific content and impact of the strategy.

Self-reliance in Economics: An Evaluation of Policy Effectiveness

The Causes and Achievements of North Korean Economic Development

Although quantitative economic growth is an important aspect of Korean plans for economic self-reliance, primary attention must be paid to qualitative structural factors. In his report to the Fifth Congress of the KWP in 1970, Kim Il-song made the following claim:

Table 1 North Korea: Aggregate economic indicators, 1946–65

Year	Index: 1953 = 100		Industrial production
	Agricultural production		
	total[a]	grains	
1946	87	81	46
1949	131	114	156
1953	100	100	100
1956	139	123	285
1960	195	163	972
1963	233	223	n.a.
1965	n.a.	193	1900

[a]Gross value
Source: Chung, J. (1974). *The North Korean Economy, Structure and Development* (Stanford University, California).

[The] historic task of socialist industrialization has been carried out successfully in our country and ... a once colonial agrarian land far removed from modern technical civilization has now been turned into a socialist industrial state with modern industry and highly developed agriculture.... Our people, never again to suffer all those insults and contempts because of their backward economy, can now proudly enter the international arena as a mighty and advanced nation on an equal basis with all the other nations of the world, large and small.

This statement is clearly seasoned with rhetoric and exaggeration (and seems to contradict North Korea's claim to be a member of the Third World), but the basic message — successful industrialization and agricultural modernization — is valid. *New York Times* correspondent Harrison Salisbury, who visited the North in 1972, spoke of 'a tremendous technical and industrial achievement' and described it as 'on a *per capita* basis ... the most intensively industrialised country in Asia, with the exception of Japan' (Salisbury, 1973: 199–200). The regime has been able to maintain a consistently high level of savings, estimated to be 25–35 per cent of GNP. Industrial growth has been rapid though uneven and improvements in agricultural performance have also been creditable — the US CIA estimates that grain output rose by an average of 5.4 per cent per year between 1965–77. (Central Intelligence Agency, 1978: 4. Other statistics in this section are taken from Shinn *et al.*, 1969, and J. S-h Chung 1973.) The following tables (1–3) contain the basic statistics on aggregate and sectoral growth performance. Aggregate growth in GNP faltered in the mid-1970s with the emergence of problems in North Korea's foreign trade and the impact of the international recession and rise in oil prices (see below). However, it appears to have picked up in the late 1970s and official confidence in the country's ability to maintain high rates of industrial growth remains high: the

Table 2 North Korea: Aggregate economic indicators, 1960–78

	GNP (billion 1978 US$)	GNP per head (US$)	Index: 1970 = 100 Agric. prod[a]	Ind. prod[b]
1960	2.9	270	n.a.	30
1965	4.6	380	90	59
1970	6.1	430	100	100
1973	8.3	540	107	160
1974	9.3	580	140	188
1975	10.0	610	154	225
1976	9.7	570	160	248
1977	9.7	550	170	276
1978	10.4	570	170	323

[a]Based on official grain claims.
[b]Official statistics (gross value).
Source: US CIA *Handbook of Economic Statistics 1979*, (Washington DC, August 1979).

Table 3 North Korea: Annual average economic growth by sectors

Period	GNP	Grain prod.	Ind. prod.
1947–49	—	12	50
1950–53	—	−3	−11
1954–56	—	7	42
1957–60	—	7	36
1961–65	10	3	14
1966–70	6	2	11
1971–73	11	2	17
1974	12	31	18
1975	8	10	20
1976	−3	4	10
1977	negl.	6	11
1978	7	negl.	17
1947–65	7	5	22
1966–78	6	5	14

Notes and Sources: Cols 2 & 3, 1966–78 and col. 1: Table 2: cols 2 & 3, 1947–65: see Table 1.

projected annual average growth rate for the current Seven Year Plan (1978–84) is 12.1 per cent.

Growth has been accompanied by important structural changes in the economy. Industry (91.2 per cent state-owned by 1963) had become the dominant economic sector by the mid-1950s and had risen from 23.2 per cent of GNP in 1946 to 63.2 per cent in 1963 (agriculture declined from 59.1 per cent to 19.3 per cent). The percentage of the labour force in industry rose from 12 per cent in 1946 to about 42 per cent in 1963 (the proportion in agriculture, forestry and fisheries decreased from 75 per cent in 1946 to 42.8 per cent in 1963). The geographical distribution of population has shifted accordingly, the urban proportion rising from 17.7 per cent in 1953 to 47.5 per cent in 1965 to c. 65–70 per cent in 1975.

Though the overall balance between industrial departments I and II appears to have changed little (59:41 of GIP in 1949; 62:38 in 1970), the relative prominence of specific industrial sectors has changed markedly. Sectors which were important in 1945 — notably minerals, timber and timber products and marine products — declined dramatically as a proportion of industry, while the combined share of the crucial metal-working and machine-building industries rose from 1.6 per cent in 1944, to 21.3 per cent in 1960, to 31.4 per cent in 1967. As for light industry, textiles increased their share of total industrial product from 6 per cent in 1944 to 18.6 per cent in 1963. Other industries which were fairly well developed in the Japanese period have been restructured to serve the wider priorities of the economy. Chemicals, for example, was reoriented away from production for the Japanese war machine to the manufacture of synthetic import substitutes to reduce dependence on imported raw materials and chemical fertilizers to raise agricultural productivity and promote self-sufficiency in food grain.

These changes are also reflected in the product composition of foreign trade. At the end of the 1950s, the main export commodities continued to be raw materials, primarily mineral ores. During the 1960s, however, there was a trend towards the export of ores already processed into pig iron or rolled steel and finished goods such as electric motors, transformers and machine tools. According to Chung's figures, minerals decreased from 81.7 per cent of exports in 1953 to 7.2 per cent in 1969, while metals increased in the same period from 9 to 40 per cent (Chung, 1974: 106). The nature of imports also changed from a predominance of machinery, factory equipment and consumer items to raw materials, fuels (notably petroleum and coking coal) and sophisticated machinery which could not be produced at home.

Thus North Korea has made considerable progress towards an economic structure characteristic of an industrial state: rapidly rising income per head (from about $375 in 1965 to $590 in 1975 — in constant dollars — according to CIA estimates) and industrial output per head, industrial predominance in the GNP, a shift away from primary to secondary industries (notably sophisticated and strategic industries such as machine tools) and a capital-intensive, highly productive agricultural system.

In North Korea, a great deal of the credit for these successes is attributed to political factors: the new institutions and social relations created by socialist transformation, the nature of the state and party and the 'correct' policy lines adopted by its leadership (virtually equated with Kim Il-song), and the strategy of mass mobilization. In view of these claims, it is important to assess the extent to which the industrialization of North Korea has been the result of political choice and consciously directed institutional change and economic management, or the product of various environmental or external factors, such as the availability of abundant natural resources, a pre-existing industrial base, or foreign aid.

Though the northern part of Korea did have the beginnings of an industrial base in 1945, Koreans lacked technical and managerial skills because of overwhelmingly Japanese ownership, management and technical co-ordination. Moreover, most of this industrial base was destroyed in the Korean War. Thus, though it was an advantage in comparison with South Korea, this base cannot be viewed as the decisive factor in the modern industrialization of North Korea.

The fact that North Korea is rich in minerals and other industrially relevant resources is an important precondition for self-reliance. (For information on North Korea's natural resources, see Shinn et al., 1969, Ch. 1; FLPH, 1958, Ch. 1.) The North has 300 different kinds of minerals of which about 200 are of economic utility. North Korea ranks among the top ten countries in the world in both available deposits and production of such crucial minerals as gold, tungsten, magnesite, molybdenum and fluorite. It also has substantial deposits of asbestos, aluminium, chromium, copper, lead, silver, zinc, nickel, iron ore and coal. Being a mountainous region, the potential for electricity generation is good. For a relatively small country, therefore, North Korea's resource base was favourable for a strategy of industrialization which stressed heavy industry, the major lacunae being oil and bituminous coal for coking. In this respect, North Korea enjoys an advantage over many Third World countries of comparable size and population.

Yet one should not overestimate the influence of these two factors of historical industrialization and natural factor endowments. Simon Kuznets makes the following important point in his study of the economic growth of small nations:

> The existence of a valuable natural resource represents a permissive condition, facilitates — if properly exploited — the transition from the pre-industrial to industrial phases of growth. But unless the nation shows a capacity for modifying its social institutions in time to take advantage of the opportunity, it will have only a transient effect. (Kuznets, 1960: 28)

In other words, institutional, cultural, social and political factors — not merely technology or natural resources — are key determinants of modern industrial development. Korea's homogeneous population and long history of cultural continuity and national identity have contributed to the stronger sense of community and greater social coherence which, Kuznets argues, are advantageous for a small society's economic development. To these factors must be added the crucial impact of politics. The role of the strong Korean state and the Party leadership has been crucial. At three major junctures — after the Korean War, during the formulation of the Five Year Plan in 1956, and at the time of disagreement with the Soviet Union over international economic integration — political choices have been made among competing options to achieve the goal of comprehensive industrialization and economic self-reliance. If different decisions had been taken at any of these junctures, then the structure of the North Korean economy and its relationship to the Soviet Union might have been very different today.

The KWP leadership has also been extraordinarily successful in mobilizing the support and commitment of the general population to the national goals of independence and economic development. It is important to note the unprecedented degree of mass involvement in political organizations (an estimated 11–12 per cent of the total population, or 25 per cent of the adult population, are members of the KWP); the ideological appeal of *juche* as an expression of both national and individual aspirations; 'mass line' leadership theory and practice; and the distinctive role of Kim Il-song as the supreme leader and national symbol. (For an excellent discussion of 'mass line' theory in North Korea, see Cumings, 1974: 29–34.) The Party has also contributed to rapid economic development by raising the level of skills and human welfare among the general population through the use of the Korean Han'gul writing system instead of Chinese characters to improve literacy, the provision of a free and well-equipped medical system, the popularization of compulsory technical education up to and including senior high school, a rapid increase in the number of technicians and other specialists with tertiary qualifications, and a stress on education as a lifetime task for the individual, not merely as a transient stage of one's youth.

To what extent was North Korean economic development the product of foreign aid? (see Chung, 1974: 92—3, 118–24). The primary stress since the foundation of the DPRK has been on development through the mobilization of domestic resources. After the ravages of the Korean War, however, there was substantial aid from socialist nations in the form of grants and loans, the Soviet Union being the chief donor. Immediately after the Korean War, the Soviet Union provided a grant of $250m and China $200m, supplemented by a credit of $265m from Eastern Europe. At the beginning of the Five Year Plan in 1956, the Soviet Union provided another grant of $75m and a credit of $125m. China provided a credit of $25m in 1958 and a long-term loan of $105m in 1960. In the same year, the Russians cancelled a North Korean debt of $190m. Where possible, these initially large amounts of external aid were used to minimize future reliance on aid, i.e. to finance imports of capital goods intended to create the material basis for an autarkic industrial complex rather than consumer goods to raise living standards in the short run. Thus the Chinese credit of $25m in 1958, for example, was used to finance the import of a power station and a textile mill.

In general, the importance of aid declined over the decade after the Korean War. Foreign aid was important during the period of reconstruction, but its role had declined by the Five Year Plan (1957–61), which was overwhelmingly financed by domestic savings. The major source of finance for the 1957–61 industrialization programme was the agricultural tax in kind, but this was abolished *de facto* in 1965(*de jure* in 1966) as industry developed the capacity to generate the necessary capital. US sources estimate that the proportion of budget revenues coming from aid declined from about 40–50 per cent during 1950–55 to 4.5 per cent in 1958 and 1.9 per cent in 1961.

After the deterioration of relations with the Soviet Union in 1962, aid levels dropped and became unreliable, but it is likely that Soviet and Chinese aid, in grant or credit form, continued to be significant during the 1970s in partially making up for North Korea's trade deficits with these two countries, notably between 1971 and 1974. In general, it is likely that the total amount of aid received from fellow socialist countries far exceeds the official Korean tally of US $550m by the mid-1970s. Foreign estimates vary widely and there is little data on which to base a firm conclusion. One can argue, however, that though aid has played a larger role in Korean development than the Koreans themselves admit, it had ceased to be a crucial component of national development by the late 1950s and, though it continued as a significant adjunct to the Korean economy during the next two decades, donors have been unable to convert this into pressure capable of deflecting the economic or political priorities of the Korean regime.

Specific Policies for Economic Self-Reliance

The North Korean leadership has thus played a key role in successfully restructuring and developing the economy without prolonged or excessive reliance on foreign aid. The basic question remains: how self-reliant is the Korean economy at this higher stage of development? The North Korean leaders have succeeded in creating an economy which is not dependent on foreign aid, but how successful have they been in dealing with other forms of economic dependence?

The development of a more balanced and comprehensive industrial system has alleviated the problem of lopsidedness, and industrialization has moved the country away from the status of a mere primary producer dependent on more advanced economies for manufactured goods and technical knowhow. But these trends *per se* have not necessarily solved the problem of dependence. It can be argued, for example, that as a small nation becomes more advanced, it becomes *more* dependent on external sources of raw materials and technology because of the expanded needs created by increased economic capacity and sophistication. Changing the composition of exports from primary to manufactured products, moreover, does not necessarily solve the problem of inadequate and unstable markets, though it may ease the problem to some extent when markets for manufactured goods are more stable than markets for primary products. Even then, however, if the markets remain heavily concentrated the problem of dependence remains. The problem of agricultural self-sufficiency is also significant. Has the reorientation of the economic structure away from agriculture created a reliance on external sources of food, thus diverting foreign currency away from the import of capital goods necessary for continued industrialization?

The North Korean leaders have been aware of these problems and, basic domestic economic strategy aside, have responded in two ways. They have attempted to increase the degree of *autarky* of the economy by expanding the available supplies of domestic natural raw materials through exploration, by encouraging import substitute industries, and by increasing the production of synthetic raw materials. Secondly, they have taken steps to increase their degree of *autarchy* in economic decision-making by diversifying foreign economic ties — between China and the Soviet Union on the one hand and between socialist and non-socialist trade partners on the other.

Beginning in the mid- and late 1950s, the DPRK has mounted a determined effort to become as self-sufficient as possible in raw materials. The Seven Year Plan, announced in 1961, included a series of measures designed to establish a 'stable raw material base' (FLPH, 1961: 57). This involved the stepping up of exploration work to discover fresh sources of minerals and energy; the expansion of extractive industries (Son Kyon-jun, 1967: 46—50), an emphasis on the economical use of available resources, notably iron, timber and electricity; the use of resources available in abundance to substitute for those in short supply (for example, investigating methods of using anthracite instead of coking coal in the smelting of iron); the design of industrial processes and communications equipment to suit available resources (for example, the electrification of railways and urban transport); the use of chemical processes to produce synthetic substitutes for imports (notably synthetic fibres such as vinalon, synthetic ammonia, urea made from anthracite, artificial leather to replace rubber in consumer goods such as shoes, synthetic rubber and resins and the chemicals necessary to make aluminium from domestic bauxite). Scientific research has been directed towards the solution of these problems (Tong-uk, 1968). The aim of 60–70 per cent self-sufficiency was included in the current Six Year Plan (1971–76).

The major resource deficiencies are coking coal and oil, for which Korea still depends heavily on China and the Soviet Union. Kim noted in his report to the Fifth Party Congress in 1970 that the country could not afford to import the coking coal necessary for projected industrial growth, implying that satisfactory substitutes had still to be found (Kim Il-song, 1972: 442). On the problem of petroleum, though no major oil finds have yet been made, exploration continues and Korean officials remain optimistic. In the meantime, there has been a concerted effort to reduce dependence on oil by developing alternative sources of energy. It is estimated that in 1976 oil was a mere 5 per cent of primary energy consumption; coal was 77 per cent and hydroelectric power 18 per cent. The comparable figures for South Korea were 63 per cent, 35 per cent and 2 per cent (CIA, 1978: 12). Given the potential financial drain of oil imports and the political implications of heavy reliance on Soviet or Chinese oil, this achievement is a basic underpinning of the entire *juche* strategy. Measures have also been taken to reduce the cost of necessary oil imports, notably by building two oil refineries with Soviet assistance to reduce dependence on Soviet refined as opposed to crude oil.

The desire for self-sufficiency in food-grains was a major motive behind the greater priority assigned to state investment in agriculture in the late 1960s and 1970s. The DPRK was a net importer of food-grains throughout the 1960s. Part of this deficit can be explained by the policy of exporting rice and importing wheat products because of the favourable price ratio between the two commodities and the consequent increase in nutritional value from the exchange. Part of the problem resulted from previous underinvestment in agriculture and the unfavourable ecological conditions of the North, notably the lack of arable land. Thus one of the major goals of the extended Seven Year Plan (1961–70) and the Six Year Plan (1971–76) was to raise agricultural productivity through increased inputs of machinery, electric power and chemical products. A programme of tideland reclamation was also launched. By the mid-1970s agriculture was highly mechanized, with a high level of fertilizer usage and a nationwide irrigation system; yields appear to be high by international standards. In 1969, a surplus was registered in the import and export of food-grains and good agricultural performance in the 1970s suggests a continued capacity to maintain self-sufficiency — grain production rose from 5m tons in 1970, to 6m in 1973, to 9m in 1979. Given the difficult climate and the shortage of arable land, this is no mean achievement.

In the field of light industry, import substitution has been systematically applied and the role of local industry has been stepped up to meet consumer needs. As any visitor to North Korea can attest, most consumer goods, from talc to TVs, are made domestically. There are continuing problems, however, in terms of quality (too low), variety (too little) and prices (too high). Many of these problems, of course, were the inevitable result of placing early emphasis on defence and heavy industry and, by the early 1970s, as the economy matured and the level of defence spending declined, consumer spending was stimulated by price cuts and wage rises.

In the field of heavy industry, production has been geared to the needs of the domestic market for machines and plant equipment, and a systematic programme of import substitution was adopted. In his report to the Fourth Congress of the KWP in 1961, Kim Il-song claimed that Korea was already producing medium- and small-size machines for domestic use as well as metallurgical and power-generating equipment, vehicles, rolling stock, tractors, locomotives, excavators and other types of heavy machinery (Kim Il-song, 1961: 21–2). Self-sufficiency in tractors and trucks was claimed by 1963. The brand name of the trucks was, significantly enough, *Charyok Kaengsaeng* or 'Self Reliance'. Imported electric locomotives were too expensive, Kim told foreign journalistss in 1969 (Kim Il-song, 1970: 77), so Korea decided to build its own and by the early 1970s, a surplus was being exported to the Soviet Union and Eastern Europe.

By the Fifth KWP Congress in 1970, Kim was able to report on the production of a large range of heavy equipment (such as large power presses, heavy trucks, large tractors, bulldozers, electric and diesel locomotives, 5000-ton ships and precision machines) and complete sets of plant equipment for power stations, metallurgical and chemical factories (Kim Il-song, 1972: 413). Harrison Salisbury, who visited North Korea in 1972, reported that the country was 98 per cent autarkic in machine tools and that the quality of the equipment was comparable to the Soviet equivalent and superior to the Chinese (Salisbury, 1973: 198–200). A Soviet source in 1973 described the production of metal-cutting lathes, large refrigerator ships, hydraulic turbines, electromotors and transformers, tractors and trucks, electric locomotives and freight cars (Sinitsyn, 1974: 41). The country also produces much of the modern military equipment it requires: submarines, destroyers and gunboats, armoured cars, tanks and sophisticated artillery. But it still remains dependent on outside sources, notably the USSR, for advanced equipment such as fighter planes.

But *juche* does not entail absolute autarky and the North Korean leadership has been faced with the general issue of what level and structure of foreign trade are compatible with a strategy of self-reliance. The problem has grown more pressing and complex with the very success of Korean industrialization. During the 1950s, foreign trade was conducted overwhelmingly with other members of the socialist world. Up to the early 1960s, trade was in deficit and the balance was made up by aid and long-term credits. During the 1960s, however, surpluses were registered in 1962, 1966 and 1967, but deficits returned in the late 1960s and early 1970s. Foreign trade expanded rapidly during the 1960s, rising faster than the growth in national income between 1961 and 1967 (11.9 per cent compared to 8.9 per cent). Throughout this decade, trade was still heavily oriented towards other socialist countries. In 1967, for example, out of a total trade volume of $500m (the GNP was $2.78), 87 per cent ($434.2m) was with other socialist countries, of which $387m was with the Soviet Union ($218m) and China ($169m). At this stage, the Korean leadership seemed reluctant to move away from this pattern. Kim Il-song, in a speech in late 1967, emphasized the 'primacy' of the 'world socialist market',

declaring that trade ties with capitalist countries were of 'secondary importance'.

> [The] socialist market enables the newly independent states to realize their surplus
> industrial goods and farm produce and purchase foreign industrial equipment, raw
> materials ... on the principle of complete equality and mutual benefit. (Kim Il-song,
> 1971, Vol I: 599)

Here Kim implicitly recognized the advantages which Korea might lose by
too radical a reorientation of trade ties away from the socialist economies. The
greater potential for barter trade with these countries allows for the payment
for imports through exports rather than foreign exchange (see Freedman,
1970: 3–17). Moreover, trade agreements with the Soviet Union and China
tend to be relatively long-term and would thus insulate Korea from fluctuations
in price and demand in the international capitalist market. Another important
advantage, notably in the export of manufactured goods, is that, for political
reasons, Korea's socialist neighbours are willing to take 'soft goods', i.e. goods
which are difficult to sell on the non-communist international market because
of poor quality, tough competition or lack of demand.

Thus China and the Soviet Union provide the major outlets for Korean
finished and intermediate items such as machine tools, electric motors,
transformers and steel products (Soviet Union) and machine tools, industrial
chemicals, tractors and cement (China). Korea has striven to avoid dependence on either of these neighbouring giants as a market or source of supply. In
the crucial area of oil imports, for example, Korea imported most of its oil from
the Soviet Union until the mid-1970s when a 'friendship pipeline' was opened
from north-east China. In the late 1970s, oil has also been imported from
Indonesia and the Middle East. The early 1970s, moreover, saw a gradual
decrease in trade with the Soviet Union and an accompanying increase in trade
with China — by 1976 they were nearly equal (US $401m and $386m total
value). However, Korea has continued to run a deficit with its socialist
partners, particularly the USSR, and the shortfall has presumably been made
up, at least partially, through aid and long-term credits as in the 1950s. Tables 4
and 5 provide the basic picture of trade with the socialist countries up to 1976.
Korea's balanced foreign policy seems to have prevented either of the two
great powers from translating those financial obligations into political influence.

Though earlier attempts to diversify trade relations to the capitalist world
were impeded by the US-sponsored embargo, in the late 1960s and early 1970s
the DPRK mounted a considerable effort to increase trade with western
Europe and Japan. The motives behind this effort seem to have been threefold:
first, the economy needed an infusion of advanced technologies in strategic
industries which could only or optimally be acquired from western or Japanese
sources; secondly, this technical infusion and a general effort to force the pace

Table 4 North Korea, trade with socialist countries 1949–76
(% of total trade)

	Exports	Imports	Total
1949	n.a.	n.a.	83
1955	n.a.	n.a.	95
1959	n.a.	n.a.	98
1960	96	96	96
1961	96	91	94
1962	97	95	96
1963	94	94	94
1964	88	90	89
1965	89	84	87
1966	86	86	86
1967	856	88	86
1968	n.a.	n.a.	n.a.
1969	72	74	73
1970	81	85	83
1971–74	n.a.	n.a.	n.a.
1975	63	53	57
1976	57	60	59

Sources: 1949–69: Chung, J. S. *The North Korean Economy* (Stanford, Cal., 1974). 1970, 75–76: US CIA, *Korea: The Economic Race between the North and the South* Washington, DC, January 1978). 1977–78: Halliday, J., 'The North Korean Model — Gaps and Questions', in Lein (ed.), *Tradition and Change in the PPRK*, (Saabrucken, 1981).

of industrialization were thought necessary in response to South Korea's economic success of the late 1960s and early 1970s; thirdly, in the context of Sino-American rapprochement and growing contacts between East and West, the international context seemed more favourable for potentially beneficial relations with capitalist economies (notably the offer of credit on attractive terms), particularly given optimistic assessments of international market demand for and price of Korean exports, especially non-ferrous metals. The estimated increase was from $65.8m in 1967, to about $90–100m in 1969, to around $200m in 1972. Trade with Japan showed particularly rapid growth, rising from $36m in 1967, $57.7m in 1970, to $131.2m in 1972. By the mid-1970s, trade with non-socialist countries had increased to nearly one-half of total trade.

With the dramatic rise in oil prices and the onset of the world recession, this vigorous drive ran into trouble. The planners' calculations went awry: demand for Korean exports declined alarmingly, the cost of imports rose (for example, the Soviet Union raised the price of its oil by 130 per cent in 1975) and Korean trade, mainly conducted in sterling, was affected by the decline of the pound. Korea ran large trade deficits between 1974 and 1977 and by 1976 faced a foreign debt estimated by some sources to be as high as $1800m (including about $700m to the Soviet Union). Most of this was normal liability for credit

Table 5 North Korea, trade balance with the USSR, Eastern Europe and the PRC, 1946–76
(million US$)

	Two)way trade			Trade balance		
	USSR	E. Europe	PRC	USSR	E. Europe	PRC
1946	19	n.a.	n.a.	n.a.	n.a.	n.a.
1949	85	n.a.	n.a.	n.a.	n.a.	n.a.
1955	85	12	10	−3	−8	n.a.
1957	123	n.a.	59	3	−21	n.a.
1962	169	41	92	9	−2	n.a.
1968	293	65	100	−51	−3	±0
1969	328	79	110	−75	±0	±0
1970	373	93	100	−87	n.a.	±0
1971	502	95	135	−231	n.a.	−5
1972	458	119	200	−149	n.a.	−10
1973	485	128	250	−123	n.a.	−20
1974	453	166	300	−60	n.a.	−60
1975	468	183	369	−49	n.a.	16
1976	401	170	386	−84	n.a.	−6

Sources: Youn-Soo Kim (ed), *The Economy of the KDPR 1945–77* (German Korea-Studies Group, Kiel, 1979). Chung, J. S-h., 'Noth Korea's economic system and the new Constitution', *Journal of Korean Affairs,* **III**. 1, April 1973.

repayments but, by mid-1977, the country owed about $400m in *overdue* principal and interest. (For a discussion of this and other aspects of the debt problem, see Halliday, 1981; Brun and Hersh, 1978: 19–28; Foster-Carter, 1977: 97–102.)

The Korean response was typically feisty. Although under considerable pressure to repay the defaults and though given a bad name in international financial circles for several years, the government stood firm and got western banks to agree to deferment or rescheduling (though with added interest). Available statistics suggest, moreover, that the government refused to adjust internally by lowering growth targets or reducing social spending, though it did take a year for economic 'readjustment' in 1977 before launching the next plan. Steps were also taken to bring foreign trade back into balance, as Table 6 shows, and by the end of the decade moves were under way to normalize and expand trade with the OECD countries once again.

North Korean spokesmen have tended to play down or ignore the impact of these problems, but they do point to a serious miscalculation on the part of the Korean planners who launched a buying binge between 1972 and 1975 — compare the similar Chinese miscalculations of 1978–9. This was partly the result of their own lack of experience and partly of fluctuations in the world economy. The incident illustrates the Hobson's choice posed by the prospect of 'relinking' with the world capitalist market: on the one hand, the logic of

Table 6 Balance of trade 1946–78 (million US$)

	Exports	Imports	Total	Balance
1946	n.a.	n.a.	23	n.a.
1949	76	106	182	−30
1953	31	42	73	−11
1954	n.a.	n.a.	68	n.a.
1955	45	60	105	−15
1956	66	74	140	−9
1957	100	115	215	−15
1958	135	155	290	−20
1959	113	235	348	−122
1960	154	166	320	−12
1961	160	166	326	−6
1962	124	129	353	+96
1963	191	230	421	−39
1964	193	222	416	−29
1965	208	233	441	−25
1966	244	219	463	+25
1967	260	240	500	+30
1968	665	434	699	−169
1969	307	402	696	−83
1970	315	395	710	−80
1971–74	n.a.	n.a.	n.a.	n.a.
1975	755	1075	1835	−320
1976	555	825	1380	−270
1977	550	800	1300	−250
1978	900	900	1800	±0

Sources: 1946–69: Chung, J. S. *The North Korean Economy* (Stanford, Cal. 1974). 1970, 75–76: US, CIA, *Korea: The Economic Race between the North and the South* (Washington, DC, January 1978). 1977–78: Halliday, J. 'The North Korean Model — Gaps and Questions' in Lein (ed.), *Tradition and Change in the OPRK* (Saarbrucken, 1981).

successful industrialization calls for greater integration; on the other, the process of relinking is booby-trapped and requires caution and skill. One must assume that the Koreans learned a sharp lesson. But the incident also demonstrates Korea's capacity, through a combination of internal politico-economic strength and uncompromising external policies, to react effectively, restore balance and minimize external interference.

Clearly the commitment to increased trade with the capitalist world has not been abandoned. In the late 1970s, Korean leaders have been showing greater awareness of the deficiencies in the domestic economy which obstruct commercial expansion, notably the need to increase the quality of existing exports and develop new 'hard' products which can enter western (and increasingly sophisticated Soviet and East European) markets. In fact, Kim Il-song, in his 1979 New Year's speech, stated that from then on 'precedence' would be given to export sectors in the economy (cited in Halliday, 1980: 19).

No doubt much attention will be devoted to shifting the pattern of exchange in foreign trade, but this will not be easy. Though Korea has been successful in exporting more advanced manufactured products to some markets (COMecon and the Third World), trade in general and with the advanced capitalist countries in particular is still mainly an exchange of raw materials and primary products, processed and unprocessed, for manufactured articles. This pattern differs from the previous colonial trade relationship with Japan in so far as a higher proportion of Korean primary products are now processed (pig iron, metal alloys, rolled steel, etc.) and most of the manufactured imports are being used to strengthen the self-reliant capacity of the Korean economy. In view of the DPRK's special political relationship with the Third World, opportunities to expand exports of manufactured goods to the developing countries of Asia and Africa seem good. However, a large increase in the export of manufactured goods to non-socialist industrialized countries such as Japan and Canada, and the countries of Australasia and western Europe) must await further modernization of the Korean economy, the introduction of advanced technology from abroad and improvement in the range and quality of goods. This is a formidable task for the 1980s, but it must be achieved as an important precondition for further development.

If one were to ignore the political realities of the Korean peninsula for a moment, the most reasonable expectation for the future would be that, as the North Korean economy becomes more advanced and as the quality of its manufactured items increases, the DPRK would become a small industrial country on the model of Austria, East Germany, Sweden or Switzerland, with a relatively large foreign trade sector importing technology and raw materials and exporting finished and intermediate products. If the expansion of foreign trade were accompanied by a diversification of outlets, this would not necessarily pose a threat to North Korea's economic autarky though the goal of substantial autarky would go by the board.

Setting the problem in political context, however, the policy of economic self-sufficiency must be viewed in relation to the overriding goal of Korean reunification. Economic *juche* has two major political goals: to reduce the possibility of political pressure by economic means from unreliable large allies, and secondly, to prepare the North Korean economy for eventual integration with the South, unencumbered by a heavy degree of economic interdependence with the large socialist powers. Given these goals, the policy has been very successful. Given the continuing priority of reunification, moreover, one may expect continued emphasis on economic autarky and a willingness to bear the costs which such a strategy may entail over the longer run. As tensions on the peninsula ease, however, the extra costs imposed by the need to allocate an inordinately large percentage of the state budget to military-related expenditures to maintain *juche* in the military field can be reduced, allowing the reallocation of funds for productive purposes. There were major cuts in defence spending reported in the 1970s. With the eventual reunification of Korea, moreover, many of the economic problems of *juche* would decrease: the domestic market would expand, creating significant economies of scale; consumer goods production could be expanded and diversified, thus lowering social and political costs by increasing consumer satisfaction; the agricultural base would be strengthened and the range of export commodities and markets would be diversified, given the differences between the economies of the North and South.

Conclusion

The DPRK has done a creditable job in developing a fairly sophisticated and balanced industrial economy with a relatively small foreign trade sector (17.8 per cent in 1967, rising to about 30 per cent in 1974) and a relatively high degree of self-sufficiency in food-grains, industrial raw materials, basic consumer goods and industrial machines and equipment. It has combined rapid quantitative and qualitative development with a high degree of national autonomy, in both economics and politics. It has avoided being tied to the international political economies of either socialism or capitalism while trying, with varying success, to use the political and economic opportunities offered by each. These are quite remarkable achievements for a small country confronted by a hostile or suspicious West and a divided East.

But implementation of the *juche* strategy has not been as unproblematic as the Koreans themselves claim. It has been a difficult process with many costs which must be considered in a realistic assessment. (The best critical assessment of both positive and negative aspects is Halliday, 1981.) Some of the problems and costs can be attributed to the conflict with the South, but others seem to be part and parcel of the *juche* strategy. The high degree of political mobilization has a negative side: the stultifying cult of Kim Il-song, suppression of political dissent and socio-cultural regimentation; uninformative propaganda and an atmosphere of all-pervasive secrecy cloaking the processes of politburo politics and macroeconomic planning; the tendency for nationalism to degenerate into chauvinism, self-reliance into irrational exclusionism. In the economy, moreover, the familiar problems of centralized state socialist economies have remained evident and have been reinforced by the strategy of self-reliance: rigid and inaccurate planning practices, inefficiencies in the utilization of capital equipment, waste of raw materials, insufficient attention to quality, ineffective incentive systems and inadequate provision for growing consumer demands. The 1970s was a testing decade for 'models' of all kinds with the demise of the 'Chinese model' in 1976 and the faltering of both South Korean and West German 'economic miracles' at the end of the decade. North Korea's foreign debt problems in the mid- and late 1970s threw many of its economic deficiencies into sharp relief. To relink successfully with the capitalist world market requires considerable economic readjustment; this in turn implies *political* changes. Indeed, the pressures of the 1980s may well undermine the 'Kim Il-songist' system itself, bring the ideological legitimacy of *juche* into question and precipitate a succession crisis comparable to the Soviet Union in the mid-1950s and China in the late 1970s.

The drawing of general lessions for other Third World countries is a complex task. The main positive lessons come through clearly: the importance of a strong state, a determined party, a united nation and a mobilized population; the principle of basing economic strategy on domestic demand (for food and basic consumer products) and dynamic comparative advantage in foreign trade, and the attempt to integrate emerging economic sectors as far as possible; the need to use aid to strengthen the nation's economic capacity for self-reliance and to maintain politico-economic autonomy through skilful foreign policy which avoids overdependence on any one large power. There are negative lessons too, the most notable being the contradiction between the need to 'relink' as the economy develops and the dangers involved in doing so, and the apparent need to sacrifice basic goals, liberal or socialist, to maintain the unity and commitment (what the North Koreans call 'monolithism') necessary for self-reliant mobilization. In assessing the viability of the North Korean experience as a general model, moreover, it is important to consider its specific features: a divided nation, its strategic geographical position between East and West and between the two warring protagonists of the East, its abundant natural resources and unified culture. These qualifications aside, however, there is still much to learn from North Korea and it is to be hoped that further research will be devoted to this aim.

Bibliography

Amin, Samir (1977). 'Self-reliance and the new international economic order', *Monthly Review*, July–August.
An Tong-yang (1967). 'The trend of modern bourgeois philosophy', *Kulloja* (Worker) 30 August (translated in *Joint Publications Research Service: Translations on North Korea* (JPRS:NK) no 64).
Baik Bong (1973). *Kim Il-Song: Biography* (3 vols) (Dar Al-talia, Beirut).
Breidenstein, Gerhard (1973). 'The Communist movement and socialism in Korea', *Journal of Contemporary Asia*, **III**, no 3.
Brun, Ellen and Hersh, Jacques (1976). *Socialist Korea: A Case Study in the Strategy of Economic Development* (Monthly Review Press, New York).
Brun, Ellen and Hersh, Jacques (1978). 'North Korea: default of a model or a model in default?', *Monthly Review*, February.
Central Intelligence Agency, National Foreign Assessment Center (1978). *Korea: The Economic Race Between the North and the South*.
Cho Kah-kyung (1965). 'Philosophical aspects of modernization of the modern consciousness and the problems of subjectivity', in *Report: International Conference on the Problems of Modernization in Asia* (Asiatic Research Centre, Seoul), cited in Cumings (1974).

Chong Kwan-yong (1967). 'The glorious victory of the Party's economic line', *Nodong Sinmun* (Labor News), 5 August, in JPRS:NK, no 59.

Chung, J. S-h. (1973). 'North Korea's economic system and the new Constitution', *Journal of Korean Affairs*, **III**:1(April).

Chung, J. S-h. (1974). *The North Korean Economy* (Stanford University Press).

Cummings, Bruce G. (1974). 'Kim's Korean Communism', *Problems of Communism*, **XXIII**, no 2 (March–April).

Dobb, Maurice (1963). *Economic Growth in Underdeveloped Countries* (International Publishers, New York).

Dobb, Maurice (1967). 'The question of "Investment priority for heavy industry"', in his *Papers on Capitalism, Development and Planning* (Routledge and Kegan Paul, London).

FLPH (Foreign Languages Publishing House) (1958). *Democratic People's Republic of Korea* (Pyongyang).

FLPH (1961). *Documents of the Fourth Congress of the Workers Party of Korea* (Pyongyang).

FLPH (1972). *Socialist Constitution of the DPRK*, 27 December (Pyongyang).

FLPH (1975). *Our Party's Policy for the Building of an Independent National Economy* (Pyongyang).

FLPH (1977). *The Building of an Independent National Economy in Korea* (Pyongyang).

Foster-Carter, Aidan (1977). 'North Korea, Development and Self-Reliance: A Critical Appraisal', in Gavan McCormack and John Gittings (eds) *Crisis in Korea* (Spokesman Books, London).

Freedman, R. O. (1970). *Economic Warfare in the Communist Bloc* (Praeger, New York).

Halliday, Jon (1970). 'The Korean communist Movement', *Bulletin of Concerned Asian Scholars*, **II**, no 4, Fall.

Halliday, Jon (1980). 'Capitalism and socialism in East Asia', *New Left Review*, no 124 (November–December).

Halliday, Jon (1981). 'The North Korean model: gaps and questions', in Albrecht Lein (ed), *Tradition and Change in the DPRK* (Saarbrucken).

Lee, Chong-sik (1963). *The Politics of Korean Nationalism* (University of California Press, Berkeley).

Kim, C. I. Eugene and Kim, Han-kyo (1967). *Korea and the Politics of Imperialism 1876–1910* (University of California Press, Berkeley and Los Angeles).

Kim, J-W. A. (1970). 'Soviet policy in North Korea', *World Politics*, **XXII**, no 2 (January).

Kim, Il-song (1961). 'Report of the Central Committee of the WPK to the Fourth Congress', in *Documents of the Fourth Congress of the WPK*.

Kim, Il-song (1970). *Answers to the Questions Raised by Foreign Journalists*, 1 July 1969 (FLPH, Pyongyang).

Kim, Il-song (1971). *Selected Works*, Vols. I–IV (FLPH, Pyongyang).

Kim, Il-song (1972). *Selected Works*, Vol. V (FLPH, Pyongyang).

Kim, Il-song (1972). *On Some Problems of Our Party's Juche Idea and the Government of the Republic's Internal and External Policies*. (Answers to the Questions Raised by Journalists of the Japanese Newspaper *Mainichi Shimbun*, 17 September 1972) (FLPH, Pyongyang).

Köhler, Heinz (1965). *Economic Integration in the Soviet Bloc* (Praeger, New York).

Kuznets, S. (1960). 'Economic growth of small nations', in E. A. G. Robinson (ed), *Economic Consequences of the Size of Nations* (Macmillan, London).

Mao Tse-tung (1966). 'The reconstruction of our studies' (1 February, 1942) translated in Boyd Compton (ed.), *Mao's China: Party Reform Documents, 1942–1944* (University of Washington Press, Seattle).

Motohashi, Atsushi (1967). 'Comparison of the socialist economies in China and Korea', *Developing Economies*, Tokyo, **5**:1.

Nahm, A. C. (1971). 'Reaction and response to the opening of Korea, 1876–1884', in Yung-hwan Jo (ed.), *Korea's Response to the West* (The Korea Research and Publications Inc., Kalamazoo, Michigan).

Raj, K. N. (1967). 'Role of the "Machine-tools sector" in economic growth', in C. H. Feinstein (ed.), *Socialism, Capitalism and Economic Growth: Essays presented to Maurice Dobb* (Cambridge University Press).

Salisbury, H. E. (1973). *To Peking and Beyond: A Report on the New Asia* (Quadrangle, New York).

Sang-hoon Chung, Joseph (1974), *The North Korean Economy: Structure and Development* (Hoover Institution Publications 132, Stanford).

Scalapino, Robert A. and Lee, Chong-sik (1972). *Communism in Korea* (University of California Press, Berkeley).

Schwartz, Harry (1963). 'North Korean reports Chinese are prospering', *New York Times*, 8 April.

Senghaas, Dieter (1979). 'Dissociation and Autocentric Development: Concepts, Evidence and Implications', *Forschungs-bericht* no 3 (Universität Bremen).

Shinn, R-s, *et al.* (1969). *Area Handbook for North Korea* (Washington).

Sing Tong-sop (1969). 'Further development of the machine industry is urgent', *Kulloja* (Worker), 15 March in *JPRS:NK*, no 115.

Sinitsyn, B. (1974). Cited by B. C. Koh, 'North Korea: Old goals and new realities', *Asian Survey*, **XIV**, no 1, January.

Son Kyon-jun (1967). 'The central problem in granting priority to extracting industries', *Kulloja*, 20 June, in *JPRS:NK*, no 57.

Song Pok-ki (1967). 'The central problem in chemicalizing the national economy', *Kulloja*, 30 November, in *JPRS:NK*, no 79.

Thomas, Clive (1974). *Dependence and Transformation* (Monthly Review Press, London).

Tong-uk, O. (1968). 'The concept of self-identity and our scientific and technological development', *Kulloja*, 30 July, in *JPRS:NK*, no 94.

US Government (1969). *Area Handbook for North Korea* (Washington).

Walker, H. D. (1971). 'The weight of tradition: preliminary observations on Korea's intellectual response', in Yung-hwan Jo (ed.), *Korea's Response to the West* (The Korea Research and Publications Inc., Kalamazoo, Michigan).

Yun Nae-gil (1967). 'Our country has emerged as a strong, socialist industrial-agricultural state', *Minju Choson* (Democratic Korea), 21 November 1967, in *JPRS:NK*, no 71.

Appendix: Comparative Data on Countries Covered by Chapters 5 to 12

Chapters 5 to 12 contain, to a varying extent, data on the countries covered by them. This appendix aims to ease the comparison between the cases by bringing together data on them from a single source, the World Bank's *World Development Report, 1980*. Because of differences in definitions etc., the data in this appendix may not in all cases be exactly consistent with data in the chapters drawn directly from national sources.

Table 1 Basic indicators

	Year	Brazil	Costa Rica	India	Ireland	Kenya	Korea, N.	Korea, S.	Tanzania
Population (millions)	Mid-1978	119.5	2.1	643.9	3.2	14.7	17.1	36.6	16.9
Area (Thousands of square kilometres)		8512	51	3288	70	583	121	99	945
GNP per capita Dollars	1978	1570	1540	180	3470	330	730	1160	230
Average annual growth (per cent)	1960–78	4.9	3.3	1.4	3.3	2.2	4.5	6.9	2.7
Average annual rate of inflation (per cent) 1960–70		46.1	1.9	7.1	5.2	1.5	..	17.5	1.8
1970–78		30.3	15.7	8.2	14.7	12.0	..	19.3	12.3[b]
Adult literacy rate (per cent)	1975	76[a]	90	36	98[a]	40[a]	..	93	66[a]
Life expectancy at birth (years)	1978	62	70	51	73	53	63	63	51
Average index of food production per capita (1969–71 = 100)	1976–78	117	114	100	128	91	130	116	93

[a] For a year other than 1975 but generally not more than two years of divergence.
[b] Figure refers to 1970–77 not 1970–78.
Key to all tables: .. Not available; (.) Less than half the unit shown; All growth rates in real terms.

Table 2 Growth of production

Average annual growth
rate (per cent)

	Year	Brazil	Costa Rica	India	Ireland	Kenya	Korea, N.	Korea, S.	Tanzania
GDP	1960–70	5.3	6.5	3.6	4.2	6.0	7.8	8.5	6.0
	1970–78	9.2	6.0^a	3.7	3.4^a	6.7	7.2	9.7	5.0
Agriculture	1960–70	..	5.7	1.9	0.9	..	..	4.5	..
	1970–78	5.3	2.5^a	2.6	..	5.5	..	4.0	4.5
Industry	1960–70	..	9.4	5.5	6.1	..	..	17.2	..
	1970–78	10.1	9.1^a	4.5	..	10.4	..	16.5	2.3
Manufacturing	1960–70	..	10.6	4.8	..	..	..	17.2	..
	1970–78	9.5	8.8^a	4.6	..	11.7	..	183	4.5
Services	1960–70	..	5.7	5.2	4.3	..	..	8.4	..
	1970–78	9.2	5.7^a	4.6	..	6.0	..	8.7	6.4

^{a} Refers to 1970–77 not 1970–78.

Table 3 Structure of production

Distribution of Gross Domestic Product (per cent)	Year	Brazil	Costa Rica	India	Ireland	Kenya	Korea, N.	Korea, S.	Tanzania
Agriculture	1960	16	26	50	22	38	..	40	57
	1978	11	22[b]	40	..	41[b]	..	24	51
Industry	1960	35	20	20	26	18	..	19	11
	1978	37	27[b]	26	..	19[b]	..	36	13
(Manufacturing)[a]	(1960)	26	14	14	..	9	..	12	5
	(1978)	28	20[b]	17	..	12[b]	..	24	9
Services	1960	49	54	30	52	44	..	41	32
	1978	52	51[b]	34	..	40[b]	40	36	

[a]Manufacturing is a part of the Industrial sector, but its share in GDP is shown separately because it typically is the most dynamic part of the industrial sector.
[b]Figures refer to 1977, not 1978.

Table 4 Growth of consumption and investment

Average annual growth rate (per cent)	Year	Brazil	Costa Rica	India	Ireland	Kenya	Korea, N.	Korea, S.	Tanzania
Public consumption	1960–70	3.5	8.0	-1.7	3.9	10.0	..	5.5	[b]
	1970–78	8.6	7.4	4.2	6.3[a]	8.7	..	8.7	[b]
Private consumption	1960–70	5.1	6.0	4.2	3.7	4.6	..	7.0	5.2
	1970–78	9.0	4.9	3.0	2.7[a]	6.2	..	7.5	5.8
Gross domestic investment	1960–70	7.0	7.1	5.6	8.8	7.0	..	23.6	9.8
	1970–78	10.7	9.3	6.1	1.7[a]	2.3	..	13.7	1.9

[a]Figures refer to 1970–77 not 1970–78.
[b]Separate figures are not available for public consumption, which is therefore included in private consumption.

Table 5 Structure of demand

Distribution of Gross Domestic Product (per cent)	Year	Brazil	Costa Rica	India	Ireland	Kenya	Korea, N.	Korea, S.	Tanzania
Public consumption	1960	12	10	7	12	11	..	15	9
	1978	10	a	10	19	19	..	12	14
Private consumption	1960	67	77	79	77	72	..	84	72
	1978	69	85	70	64	63	..	60	79
Gross domestic investment	1960	22	18	17	16	20	..	11	14
	1978	23	25	24	27	28..	32	20	
Gross domestic saving	1960	21	13	14	11	17	..	1	19
	1978	21	15	20	17	18	..	28	7
Exports of goods and non-factor services	1960	5	21	5	31	31	..	3	31
	1978	7	29	..	54	27	..	34	15
Resource balance	1960	-1	-5	-3	-5	-3	..	-10	5
	1978	-2	-10	-4	-10	-10	..	-4	-13

aSeparate figures were not available for public consumption which is therefore included in private consumption.

Table 6 Industrialization

	Year	Brazil	Costa Rica	India	Ireland	Kenya	Korea, N.	Korea, S.	Tanzania
Distribution of value added (per cent)									
Food and agriculture	1976	15	42[a]	15	31	18[a]	..	15	..
Textiles and clothing	1976	10	12[a]	29	16	13[a]	..	25	..
Machinery and transport equipment	1976	30	6[a]	13	12	19[a]	..	24	..
Chemicals	1976	12	10[a]	12	11	8[a]	..	8	..
Other manufacturing	1976	33	30[a]	31	30	42[a]	..	28	..
Value added in manufacturing (millions of 1970 1970 dollars)	1970	9972	180	7093	1186	174	..	1431	116
	1976	19147	292	8973	..	357	..	3934	156
Gross manufacturing output per capita (1970 dollars)	1970	229	..	51	..	55	..	111	27
	1976	..	..	62	..	116	..	320	..

[a]Figures refer to 1975.

Table 7 Energy

	Year	Brazil	Costa Rica	India	Ireland	Kenya	Korea, N.	Korea, S.	Tanzania
Average annual growth rate (per cent)									
Energy production	1960–74	8.1	9.5	4.4	0.1	9.3	9.1	6.3	10.6
	1974–78	5.6	4.7	5.5	3.8	10.5	4.3	3.2	13.4
Energy consumption	1960–74	8.6	10.4	4.9	4.7	4.2	9.1	13.2	10.4
	1974–78	7.0	5.6	5.1	2.6	−0.6	4.3	9.6	0.5
Energy consumption per capita (kilograms of coal equivalent)	1960	332	233	108	1838	143	989	258	41
	1978	794	564	176	3292	139	2702	1359	65
Energy consumption per dollar of GDP (kilograms of coal equivalent)	1960	0.6	0.4	1.0	1.2	0.8	3.8	1.2	0.3
	1978	0.6	0.5	1.2	1.1	0.5	4.4	1.8	0.4
Energy imports as percentage of merchandise exports	1960	21	7	11	17	18	..	70	..
	1977	37	13	26	15	24	..	22	22[a]

[a]Figure refers to 1976 not 1977.

Table 8 Growth of merchandise trade

	Year	Brazil	Costa Rica	India	Ireland	Kenya	Korea, N.	Korea, S.	Tanzania
Merchandise trade (millions									
Exports	1978	12527	816	6614	5678	1022	..	12711	457
Imports	1978	14538	1184	7954	7097	1709	950	14971	1117
Average annual growth rate[a] (per cent)									
Exports	1960–70	5.0	9.4	3.1	7.2	7.2	..	35.2	3.5
	1970–78	6.0	5.9	6.0	8.4	0.8	..	28.8	–6.0
Imports	1960–70	4.9	10.0	–0.9	8.2	6.3	..	20.1	6.0
	1970–78	6.6	4.7	3.2	6.3	(.)	..	13.5	–1.0
Terms of trade (1970 = 100)									
	1960	88	103	104	94	112	..	78	96
	1978	90	81	80	108	104	..	81	104

[a]In real terms; calculated from quantum (volume) indices of exports and imports.

Table 9 Structure of merchandise exports

Percentage share of merchandise exports	Year	Brazil	Costa Rica	India	Ireland	Kenya	Korea, N.	Korea, S.	Tanzania
Fuels, minerals and metals	1960	8	0	10	5	1[a]	..	30	(.)
	1977	10	(.)	9	3	18	51	2	4
Other primary commodities	1960	89	95	45	67	87[a]	..	56	87
	1977	64	76	35	42	72	31	13	90
Textiles and clothing	1960	0	0	35	6	0[a]	6	32	1
	1977	4	3	20	9	(.)	6	32	1
Machinery and transport equipment	1960	(.)	0	1	4	0[a]	..	(.)	0
	1977	11	3	6	15	1	1	17	(.)
Other manufactures	1960	3	5	9	18	12[a]	..	6	13
	1977	11	18	30	31	9	11	36	5

[a]Figure relates to 1961 not 1960.

Table 10 Structure of merchandise imports

Percentage share of merchandise imports	Year	Brazil	Costa Rica	India	Ireland	Kenya	Korea, N.	Korea, S.	Tanzania
Food	1960	14	13	21	18	12[a]	..	10	..
	1977	7	8	16	13	6	..	8	10[b]
Fuels	1960	19	6	6	12	11[a]	..	7	..
	1977	34	10	26	13	22	..	20	18[b]
Other primary commodities	1960	13	6	28	11	8[a]	..	25	..
	1977	7	3	15	5	4	..	19	5[b]
Machinery and transport equipment	1960	36	26	30	21	27[a]	..	12	..
	1977	26	30	19	27	34	..	27	35[b]
Other manufactures	1960	18	49	15	38	42[a]	..	46	..
	1977	26	49	24	42	34	..	26	32[b]

[a]Figure refers to 1961, not 1960.
[b]Figure refers to 1976 not 1977.

Table 11 Destination of merchandise exports

Destination of merchandise exports (percentage of total)	Year	Brazil	Costa Rica	India	Ireland	Kenya	Korea, N.	Korea, S.	Tanzania
Industrialized countries	1960	81	93	66	96	77	..	89	74
	1978	64	68	55	90	62	..	73	65
Developing countries	1960	13	7	23	4	22	..	11	25
	1978	26	28	20	7	35	..	17	28
Centrally planned economies	1960	6	(.)	8	(.)	1	..	0	1
	1978	7	3	13	1	2	..	(.)	6
Capital surplus oil exporters	1960	(.)	(.)	3	(.)	(.)	..	0	0
	1978	3	1	12	3	1	..	10	1

Table 12 Trade in manufactured goods

Origin → ↓ Destination of Manufactured exports (percentage of total)	Year	Brazil	Costa Rica	India	Ireland	Kenya	Korea, N.	Korea, S.	Tanzania
Industrialized countries	1963	59	::	56	94	::	::	57	::
	1977	53	12	52	92	11	5	74	85
Developing countries	1963	40	::	35	6	::	::	43	::
	1977	43	88	24	6	86	13	14	15
Centrally planned economies	1963	1	::	7	(.)		::	0	::
	1977	2	(.)	12	1	1	73	(.)	0
Capital surplus oil exporters	1963	(.)	::	2	(.)	::	::	0	::
	1977	2	0	12	1	2	9	12	0
Value of manufactured exports (millions of dollars)	1963	45	5	677	133	12	::	39	16
	1977	3141	203	3356	2420	116	197	8480	35

Table 13 Balance of payments and debt service ratios

	Year	Brazil	Costa Rica	India	Ireland	Kenya	Korea, N.	Korea, S.	Tanzania
Current account balance before interest payments on external public debt (millions of dollars)	1970	−701	−67	−205	−189	−38	..	−553	−29
	1978	−5310	−309	915	−178	−474	..	−455	−442
Interest payments on external public debt (millions of dollars)	1970	136	7	189		11		70	6
	1978	1725	63	342		45		653	18
Debt service as percentage of GNP	1970	0.9	2.9	0.9		2.6		3.1	2.1
	1978	2.2	7.2	0.8		2.4		3.9	1.1
Exports of goods and services	1970	13.5	9.7	20.9		7.9		19.4	8.2
	1978	28.4	23.0	9.4		8.3		10.5	7.4

Table 14 Flow of external capital

	Year	Brazil	Costa Rica	India	Ireland	Kenya	Korea, N.,	Korea, S.	Tanzania
Public and publicly guaranteed medium- and long-term loans (millions of dollars) Gross inflow	1970	1063	30	890		30		440	50
	1978	10055	396	1150		234		3919	171
Repayment of principal	1970	333	21	307		15		198	10
	1978	2406	174	595		69		1142	20
Net inflow	1970	730	9	583		15		242	40
	1978	7649	222	555		165		2777	151
Net direct private investment (millions of dollars)	1970	407	26	6	32	14	..	66	..
	1978	1886	66	..	250	67	..	61	..

Table 15 External public debt and international reserves

	Year	Brazil	Costa Rica	India	Ireland	Kenya	Korea, N.	Korea, S.	Tanzania
External public debt outstanding and disbursed									
Millions of dollars	1970	3589	134	7936		313		1797	248
	1978	28821	963	15326		953		11992	1095
As percentage of GNP	1970	8.0	13.8	14.8		20.3		20.9	19.4
	1978	15.6	29.3	13.1		17.9		26.1	25.1
Gross international reserves									
Millions of dollars	1970	1190	16	1023	698	220	..	610	65
	1978	12191	212	8316	2770	369	..	2828	96
In months of import coverage	1978	6.7	1.8	10.2	4.4	2.1	..	1.8	0.9

Table 16 Population growth, past and projected, and hypothetical stationary population[a]

	Year	Brazil	Costa Rica	India	Ireland	Kenya	Korea, N.	Korea, S.	Tanzania
Average annual growth of population (per cent)	1960–70	2.9	3.4	2.5	0.4	3.4	2.8	2.4	2.7
	1970–78	2.8	2.5	2.0	1.2	3.3	2.6	1.9	3.0
Projected population (millions)	1980	126	2	672	3	16	18	38	18
	2000	201	3	974	4	32	27	50	32
Hypthetical size of stationary population (millions)		345	5	1645	5	109	43	66	92
Assumed year of reaching net production rate of 1		2015	2005	2020	2005	2045	2010	2005	2045
Year of reaching stationary population		2075	2065	2150	2065	2140	2070	2070	2145

[a]For assumptions used in the projections see: IBRD, World Development Report 1980; Technical notes, pp. 162–3.

Table 17 Demographic and fertility-related indicators

	Year	Brazil	Costa Rica	India	Ireland	Kenya	Korea, N.	Korea, S.	Tanzania
Crude death rate per thousand population	1960	40	47	43	21	51	41	41	47
	1978	36	28	35	21	51	33	21	48
Crude birth rate per thousand population	1960	11	10	21	12	19	13	13	22
	1978	9	5	14	11	14	8	8	16
Percentage change in:									
Crude birth rate	1960–1978	−10.0	−40.4	−18.6	0.0	0.0	−19.5	−48.8	2.1
Crude death rate	1960–78	−18.2	−50.0	−33.3	−8.3	−26.3	−38.5	−38.5	−27.3
Total fertility rate	1978	4.9	3.6	5.0	3.5	7.8	4.5	2.8	6.5
Percentage of women in reproductive age group (Aged 15–44)	1978	43	46	44	39	39	44	47	40
Percentage of married women using contraceptives	1970	2	..	12	..	2[a]	..	32	..
	1977	..	67	17	..	4[a]	..	44	..

[a]Figures refer to years other than those specified but not more than two years distant from those specified.

Table 18 Labour force

	Year	Brazil	Costa Rica	India	Ireland	Kenya	Korea, N.	Korea, S.	Tanzania
Percentage of population of working age (15–64 years)	1960	54	50	57	58	50	53	54	54
	1978	55	57	56	58	48	56	60	51
Percentage of labour force in:									
Agriculture	1960	52	51	74	36	86	62	66	89
	1978	41	29	74	20	79	49	41	83
Industry	1960	15	19	11	25	5	23	9	4
	1978	22	23	11	37	8	32	37	6
Services	1960	33	30	15	39	9	15	25	7
	1978	37	48	15	43	13	19	22	11
Average annual growth of labour force (per cent)									
	1960–70	2.7	3.4	1.5	(.)	2.9	2.3	2.9	2.1
	1970–80	2.8	3.6	1.7	1.0	2.8	2.9	2.8	2.3
	1980–2000	2.9	2.7	2.0	1.6	3.3	2.7	2.0	2.7

Table 19 Urbanization

	Year	Brazil	Costa Rica	India	Ireland	Kenya	Korea, N.	Korea, S.	Tanzania
Urban population									
As percentage of total population	1960	46	37	18	46	7	40	28	5
	1980	65	43	22	58	14	60	55	12
Average annual growth rate (per cent)	1960–70	4.8	4.2	3.3	1.6	6.6	5.0	6.2	6.3
	1970–80	4.3	3.4	3.3	2.2	6.8	4.3	4.8	8.3
Percentage of urban population									
In largest city	1960	14	67	7	51	40	15	35	34
	1980	16	64	6	48	57	12	41	50
In cities over 500,000 persons	1960	35	0	26	51	0	15	61	0
	1980	52	64	47	48	57	19	77	50
Number of cities of over 500,000 persons	1960	6	0	11	1	0	1	3	0
	1980	14	1	36	1	1	2	7	1

Table 20 Indicators related to life expectancy

	Year	Brazil	Costa Rica	India	Ireland	Kenya	Korea, N.	Korea, S.	Tanzania
Life expectancy at birth (years)	1960	57	62	43	69	47	54	54	42
	1978	62	70	51	73	53	63	63	51
Infant mortality rate (aged 0–1)	1960	128	80	..	29	126	..	62	..
	1978	92[a]	28[a]	..	16[a]	..	..	37	185[a]
Child death rate (aged 1–4)	1960	13	10	28	1[a]	25	13	13	32
	1978	9	3	18	1	14	5	5	20

[a]Figures refer to years other than those specified but generally not more than two years distant from those specified.

Table 21. Health related indicators

	Year	Brazil	Costa Rica	India	Ireland	Kenya	Korea, N.	Korea, S.	Tanzania
Population per:									
Physician	1960	3600[a]	2600	5800[a]	950[a]	10560[a]	..	3000[a]	21020
	1977	1700	1390	3620[a]	830	11950[a]	..	1960	15450
Nursing person	1960	..	1700	9630[a]	180[a]	2230[a]	..	..	10440
	1977	..	450	5680[a]	200	1120[a]	..	510	2760
Percentage of population with access to safe water	1975	77	77	33	..	17	..	62	39
Daily calorie supply per capita									
Total	1977	2562	2550	2021	3541	2032	2837	2785	2063
As percentage of requirement	1977	107	114	91	141	88	121	119	89

[a]Figure refers to years other than specified; but generally within two years of those specified.

Table 22 Education

	Year	Brazil	Costa Rica	India	Ireland	Kenya	Korea, N.,	Korea, S.	Tanzania
Number enrolled in primary school as percentage of age group									66[a]
Total	1960	95	96	61	110	47	..	94	25
	1977	90[a]	111	80	109[a]	104	113[a]	111[a]	70[a]
Male	1960	97	97	80	107	64	..	99	33
	1977	89[a]	111	95	110[a]	110	115[a]	111[a]	79[a]
Female	1960	93	95	40	112	30	..	89	18
	1977	90[a]	110	64	109[a]	98	112[a]	111[a]	60[a]
Number enrolled in secondary school as percentage of age group	1960	11	21	20	35	2	..	27	2
	1977	24[a]	44	28[a]	92	17	..	88[a]	3[a]
Number enrolled in higher education as percentage of population aged 20–24	1960	2	5	3	9	(.)	..	5	..
	1976	12[a]	18	6	18[a]	1[a]	..	11[a]	(.)
Adult literacy rate (per cent)	1960	61	..	28[a]	..	20[a]	..	71	10[a]
	1975	76[a]	90	36	98[a]	40[a]	..	66[a]	93

[a] Figures refer to years other than those specified by generally not more than two years divergence.

Table 23 Income Distribution

Year	Brazil 1972	Costa Rica 1971	India 1964–65	Ireland	Kenya	Korea, N.	Korea, S. 1976	Tanzania
Percentage share of household income, by percentage groups of households[a]								..
Lowest 20 per cent	2.0	3.3	6.7	..	..	..	5.7	..
Second quintile	5.0	8.7	10.5	..	..	..	11.2	..
Third quintile	9.4	13.3	14.3	..	..	..	15.4	..
Fourth quintile	17.0	19.9	19.6	..	..	..	22.4	..
Highest 20 per cent	66.6	54.8	48.9	..	..	..	45.3	..
Highest 10 per cent	50.6	39.5	35.2	..	..	..	27.5	..

[a] These figures should be treated with extreme caution.

Index